Jennifer Thackaberry
November 1995

Watershed Research Traditions in Human Communication Theory

❦

SUNY Series, Human Communication Processes

Donald P. Cushman and Ted J. Smith III, Editors

WATERSHED RESEARCH TRADITIONS IN HUMAN COMMUNICATION THEORY

❧⌘❧

EDITED BY
DONALD P. CUSHMAN
AND BRANISLAV KOVAČIĆ

State University of New York Press

Published by
State University of New York Press

© 1995 State University of New York

For information, address State University of New York Press,
State University Plaza, Albany, N.Y. 12246

Production by M. R. Mulholland
Marketing by Dana E. Yanulavich

Library of Congress Cataloging-in-Publication Data

Watershed research traditions in human communication theory, edited
by Donald P. Cushman and Branislav Kovačić.
     p.   cm. — (SUNY series, human communication processes)
     Includes bibliographical references (p.   ) and index.
     ISBN 0-7914-2597-5 (alk. paper). — ISBN 0-7914-2598-3 (pbk.
alk paper)
     1. Communication—Social aspects. 2. Interpersonal communication.
I. Cushman, Donald P.   II. Kovačić, Branislav. 1957-   .
III. Series: SUNY series in human communication processes.
HM258.W38   1995
302.2—dc20   94-37655
                                                               CIP

10 9 8 7 6 5 4 3 2 1

Each of us is dedicating this book
to the most important person in his life—
SARAH S. KING AND GORDANA RABRENOVIĆ

They have taught us how to share pleasures and pains through
communication, and to appreciate Hugh Prather's advice:
*"To have this kind of sharing I cannot enter a conversation
clutching myself. I must give myself to the relationship,
and be willing to be what grows out of it."*

☙❧

CONTENTS

PREFACE

At a time of increased politicalization and radicalization of the intellectual processes involved in theoretic inquiry, there is a need to stand back from that process and locate a few theoretic benchmarks that can help us mark our progress toward understanding the human communication process. Such benchmarks are of course human preferences and therefore subject to discussion and debate.

Politicalization and radicalization can lead to a relativism and a focus upon extremes. Relativism has always used the tools of critique to diminish the significance of all theoretic claims and methodological procedures in an attempt to cast doubt upon the validity of inquiry itself. A focus upon extreme claims and procedures seeks to undermine what is common and central to theoretic inquiry and elevate the extreme and bizaar to a controlling position.

Intellectual benchmarks are one way of tempering these trends. They attempt to separate the plurality of better paths from the relativity of all paths being more or less equal. Similarly, they attempt to separate out what is central to our understanding of human communication processes and what is not.

This then is our task, our assumptions regarding the task, and our intellectual markers for staying the course of theoretic inquiry into human communication processes.

Donald P. Cushman
Branislav Kovačić

1

HUMAN COMMUNICATION THEORY: ITS NATURE, FUNCTION, AND SCOPE

DONALD P. CUSHMAN

The primary purpose of human communication is to share symbolic information to establish, maintain, and terminate relationships among people and human institutions. Occasionally, very occasionally, a research scholar will pose a question or raise an issue regarding this foundational communication process that, when an answer is provided, will attract the attention and focus the energy of a group of scholars over an extended period of time. Frequently, that collective effort will put to rest the question or issue raised by providing an answer that is suggestive but temporary, insightful but not sustainable. Less frequently, but perhaps more significantly, a question is posed, an issue raised, and an answer provided by a group of scholars employing diverse methodologies that must be considered controlling in its insightfulness and enduring in its suggestiveness and thus is foundational to the study of human theory.

When such questions are posed and answers given, they normally attract sufficient attention to inspire a broad range of research that inquires into the question raised at philosophic, theoretic, and practical levels of analysis; then it may be termed *a watershed research tradition in human communication theory.* This book is a sampling of such contributions to our understanding of human communication processes.

This book represents a series of case studies of groups of researchers whose works are considered foundational to our understanding of human communication processes. This collection of intellectual efforts can never be comprehensive nor complete. The limits on space in a single book preclude comprehensiveness and dictate sampling from the available pool. In addition, completeness is equally impossible because all of these theories and research traditions are examples of ongoing arguments that seek to raise new issues, make new claims, and provide new proof for these claims. Such inquiries are, in a sense, a journey rather than a destination.

This book attempts to capture the excitement of several such journeys and shed insight into the skills and passions involved in pursuing such an inquiry with intellectual excellence. It also seeks to manifest how human communication theory is developed, defended, and extended at the philosophic, theoretic, and practical levels of inquiry from a plurality of research perspectives. In short, this book attempts to illustrate and inspire theoretic inquiry.

A research program normally arises when someone asks a question or raises an issue so central to the phenomena under analysis that an answer to that question or resolution of that issue can focus the productive inquiry of a group of scholars over an extended period of time. The human communication theorists in this book ask such questions and raise such issues as

- How are the meanings shared in human interaction formed?
- How does a speaker adapt to an audience?
- What motivates human communication?
- What role does the sequence of information play in communication coherence?
- What communication processes govern and guide the formation of interpersonal relationships?
- When does human communication become a controlling concern in organizations?
- How should communication function within an organization?
- What effects do mass media have?
- What are the central communication processes within a culture?

This book explores some of the more enduring answers to these questions and their implications for human communication theory. Whereas the questions and issues that are to serve as the beginning points for intellectual inquiry have multiple sources, as already indicated, the answers to those questions or the resolution of those issues that are to count as theories all take a common form. Each one takes the form of an argument supported by evidence. For an answer to count as a theory rather than a hypothesis, it must contain both an argument and a body of evidence in support of that argument; thus, we can draw a distinction between a well-formed or -grounded theory and a speculative hypothesis. When over time a given theory attracts a number of researchers employing a variety of examinable methodologies, we have a watershed research program.

Theories or arguments provided by a number of scholars employing a variety of diverse methodologies can seek to answer a question or resolve an issue at one or more of three levels of abstraction: (1) a philosophic level, (2) a theoretic level, or (3) a practical level.

A *philosophic perspective* seeks to provide an argument and evidence to resolve a question or issue by asking an audience to make certain assumptions about the nature of communication. Then it seeks to demonstrate the unique insights into human interaction processes that come from investigating communication from within those assumptions. In this book, philosophic theories are developed that invite the reader to explore human interaction processes from within

- Structural rules
- Constructivist theory
- Self-monitoring
- Sequential interaction
- Functional rules
- Critical theory
- High-speed management
- Media effects
- Ethnographic sets of assumptions

In each case, the evidence and arguments presented seek to provide a unique and suggestive vantage point within which to explore human communication processes.

A *theoretic perspective* seeks to provide an argument and evidence in response to a question or issue that specifies a precisely verifiable set of relationships between a web of concepts and to demonstrate a unique and suggestive set of insights that comes from doing so. We sometimes forget how powerful a precisely specified web of relationships can be. In this book, arguments and evidence are provided for such a precise web of relationships between

- Hierarchy and meanings
- Cognitive complexity and meanings
- Uncertainty reduction, anxiety, and communication
- Sequential interaction and coherence
- Self-concept and different types of interpersonal relationships
- Speed to market and organizational success
- Democracy and organizational communication
- Environmental scanning, value chain, and continuous improvement communication
- Personal identity, social relations, and conduct in cultural communication

In each case, the evidence and argument presented seek to provide a unique and suggestive insight into human interaction processes.

A *practical perspective* seeks to provide an argument and evidence in response to a question or issue that outlines a strategy to be taken or a tool to be employed in consciously selecting a means to some end, a way of practically obtaining a goal. We sometimes call these *message strategies* or *means of persuasion*. A practical perspective seeks to demonstrate the unique and suggestive insights that come from the appropriate use of such message strategies or tools of persuasion. In this book, practical theories are provided of

- Unwanted repetitive episodes
- Inculturation
- Coordination
- Message comprehensives
- Message adaptation
- Persuasion
- Establishing interpersonal relationships
- Maintaining interpersonal relationships
- Terminating interpersonal relationships
- Corporate colonization
- Alternatives to corporate colonization
- Communication in Teamsterville
- Communication in America
- Communication in Israel
- America's value system

In each case, one or more message strategies is provided for practically reaching some goal that provides unique and suggestive insight into human communication processes.

A watershed research program normally resolves questions or issues at each of these levels of analysis and, in so doing, provides an in-depth treatment of the phenomena under analysis.

This, then, is our book, our inquiry into the nature, function, and scope of watershed research programs in human communication theory. Enjoy the journey, profit from the insights and suggestiveness of the evidence and argument provided. The challenge for you is to begin a new or extend an existing watershed research program in human communication theory.

PART I

☙⊰⊱❧

THEORIES OF THE HUMAN COMMUNICATION PROCESS

BRANISLAV KOVAČIĆ

The first set of theories contained in this book seeks to illuminate the general processes involved in human interaction. They do so by exploring the role of hierarchy, cognitive complexity, uncertainty reduction and anxiety, and interactional sequences in the human communication process. Let me summarize the questions asked and answers presented at the philosophic, theoretic, and practical levels of inquiry.

Chapter 2: The Coordinated Management of Meaning Theory

At the philosophic level, the coordinated management of meaning theory formulated by Pearce, Cronen, and associates views communication as the primary social process rather than a tool. Through communication collective process resources are expressed and (re)constructed in practices. Resources are rules—in the form of the stories, images, symbols, concepts, perceptions, memories, and institutions—that contain a logic of meaning and action. Practices are actions. Communication as the process not only links rules and practices but also creates meaning itself. Such assumptions provide the unique insight into the structure of individual communicative rules, how individuals apply such rules in interaction, and the interactive consequences of meshing of individual-specific communicative rules. Such assumptions imply that inter-subjective realities are not stable. Rather, they are tentative and interaction specific.

At the theoretic level, Pearce, Cronen, and associates claim that from an individual's viewpoint rules cluster into the frames of reference or contexts for interpreting acts or actions. Such frames of reference are nested but usually unstable hierarchies of four elements: (1) archetypes or images of general truth, (2) self-concepts, (3) episodes or events as predictable sequences of acts, and

(4) relationships or mutual expectations. Rules, in addition, define four different types of obligation or exert four different types of logical force on communicators' interpretations of acts or actions: (1) a prefigurative-causal force or an antecedent-to-act linkage, (2) practical force or an act-to-consequence linkage, (3) contextual force or taken for granted frames of reference, and (4) implicative force or a pressure to transform or change taken for granted frames of reference. Not only may each individual have a differently structured frame of reference and a different content of categories, but each individual also may invoke different logical force to account for the same act or action. Interactions, therefore, often have unintended consequences. It is possible, for example, that people in an interaction achieve coordination without understanding one another or the converse. An example of the latter are unwanted, repetitive patterns (URPs)—a cluster of particular relationships and specific topics—that entrap interactants.

Pearce, Cronen, and associates refuse to specify beforehand relationships between individual frames of reference—individual hierarchies of rules and meanings—and interactional consequences. Because consequences are interaction specific, they can be accounted for after the occurrence, but not necessarily predicted and controlled in advance.

At the practical level, if meanings are constructed through individual interpretations of acts or actions, researchers can describe and understand them only through careful observations, interviews, and analysis of discursive sequences. Facts cannot be taken for granted; rather, they are "negotiated" by researchers and the researched interactants. The main practical contribution of researchers is to make interactants aware of the logic of their past interactions and relationships. Individuals, then, can use these insights to address problems in interpersonal coordination such as unwanted repetitive episodes. Such insights do not necessarily eliminate interpersonal or small-group conflict. However, they do make participants more rational and enlightened in that interactants become aware of unique logics of interaction. Insights provided by research can be used in therapy and consulting.

Chapter 3: Constructivism

At the philosophic level, the constructivism of Delia, Clark, and associates argues that reality is socially constructed and individually interpreted. Communication is a series of ongoing processes of interpretation through which individuals cocreate social realities and experience their life worlds. Through socialization, language structures are integrated into individual cognitive structures. This forms the basis for intersubjective understanding. However, communication itself is viewed as the fulfillment of a need for expression of internal or psychological states rather than accomplishment of interpersonal and social tasks. Such assumptions provide the unique insights into the links between individual cognitive maps of varying degrees of complexity—general interpretive schemes or social rules for interaction and specific interpretive schemes or rules coordinating particular kinds of acts—and the consequences of the implicit negotiation of schemes for interaction.

At the theoretic level, like the theory of coordinated management of meaning, constructivism contends that individual cognitive structures—or personal constructs—constitute a link between interpretation and behavior, and it stresses that individual differences in personal constructs account for different individual strategies used in communication. Unlike the coordinated management of meaning theory, constructivism posits that, with age and social experience, individual cognitive structures develop in a definite direction. They become increasingly complex. Individual cognitive complexity is a combination of cognitive differentiation—an ever larger number of constructs and their hierarchical integration—and the ever more abstract content of constructs. Delia, Clark, and associates posit that individuals with more complex cognitive structures (1) coordinate interactions better (2) more accurately form impressions about others, (3) select more appropriate message strategies, (4) use a more persuasive, person-oriented communication, and (5) understand multiple perspectives better and, consequently, better predict the success of their courses of action. When compared to the theory of coordinated management of meaning, constructivism relates invisible cognitive complexity with observable message production in a much more straightforward, linear fashion. However, constructivism, like the theory of coordinated management of meaning, posits that meanings are constructed through individual interpretations.

At the practical level, the constructivism of Delia, Clark, and associates espouses "reflective empiricism" as a research process aimed at understanding and interpreting the links between invisible individual cognitive maps, their observable message production, and the interactive consequences of individual persuasive strategies. These researchers call for triangulated research, which combines standard psychometric instruments, experiments, role playing, interviews, interaction analysis, naturalistic observation, and ethnographic analysis with free response data collection techniques. Such a complex combination of research techniques is intended to provide indisputable evidence on the relationships between individuals' cognitive processes of interpretation and communicative behaviors.

At the practical level, examples of successful messages, message adaptations, and message comprehension can be identified, analyzed, and taught to people. In such a process, individuals not only learn new and effective persuasive message strategies, but also increase their own cognitive complexity and, in the long run, become more rational and effective communicators. In this view, then, individual cognitive complexity is used not only to account for the varying degrees of effectiveness of the past interactions, but also to predict and control the future selection and application of message strategies or means of persuasion.

Chapter 4: The Uncertainty Reduction and Anxiety-Uncertainty Management Theories

The anxiety-uncertainty centered theories of Berger, Gudykunst, and associates claims, at the philosophic level, that individuals use artificial names, concepts, and labels to create their "subjective" realities. Shared intersubjective realities are assumed to be sufficiently stable that individuals usually consider this shared portion as an "objective" reality. The basic process of communication, which is assumed to be the same across cultures, consists of individual communicative behaviors ranging from habitual, scripted, taken for granted patterns of interaction to mindful, conscious choices made in the face of obviously unsuccessful and unproductive habits. Individuals' interpretations of their own communication and researchers' observations of individuals' communication provide useful, mostly unproblematic, data for generating and testing theories. Such assumptions provide the unique insights into the processes of self-monitoring that account for the reasons individuals communicate. Berger, Gudykunst, and associates contend that people communicate not only to reduce, but also to manage, uncertainty and anxiety.

At the theoretic level, uncertainty in initial interactions with strangers compels us to communicate. Communicators can be uncertain about other individuals and groups to which others belong. Communicators must deal with five types of uncertainty: (1) predictive, when they are unsure about the future interactions; (2) explanatory, when they try to account for the past interactions; (3) cognitive, when they possess insufficient knowledge about others; (4) behavioral, when they are unsure as to how to behave in a predictable way in interactions with others; and (5) relationship specific, when they cannot take the nature of their relationships with others for granted. People therefore communicate—by using passive, active, and interactive strategies for information gathering—to reduce initial uncertainly in interactions with strangers. A variant of this view is that people communicate not only to reduce and manage uncertainty in initial interactions with other individuals, but also to reduce and manage anxiety—the affective equivalent of uncertainty—in intergroup relationships.

As a theoretic perspective, the original uncertainty reduction theory consists of seven axioms—seven variables linked to reducing uncertainty—and twenty-one theorems generated from these axioms. Its variant, the anxiety-uncertainty management theory provides forty-seven additional axioms (theorems still have to be developed) by incorporating (1) intergroup factors such as social identity; (2) maximum and minimum thresholds for uncertainty and anxiety; (3) positive and negative expectations; (4) mindfulness or conscious choosing in the face of the blatantly inadequate habitual, scripted behavior; and (5) intercultural adaptation as the desired outcome of effective interpersonal and intergroup communication. Stated schematically, indirect causes such as culture and group membership and structural, situational, and environmental factors influence uncertainty and anxiety, which, in turn, directly influence effectiveness of communication and intercultural adaptation. Such mostly linear relationships between a web of concepts are claimed to be culture free or universal. They are tested by sophisticated statistical methods of causal modeling.

The unique contribution of this watershed research tradition is provided by its formidable amount and quality of evidence supporting the theoretical claim of the linear relationships between uncertainty, anxiety, and communication not only in initial interactions with strangers, but also in romantic and other types of developed relationships across cultures, in intercultural encounters, and in different contexts. At the practical level, once the fundamental relationships between uncertainty, anxiety, and communication are specified, tested, and supported, individuals and groups can use these insights to explain, predict, and control their communicative practices in multiple contexts.

Chapter 5: The Sequential Inferential Theories

Sanders argues, at the philosophical level, that the sequential-inferential paradigm stakes out its position between the "rhetorical" approach and the "ecological" approach to communication. Whereas the rhetorical approach focuses on the strategic series of single communicative acts used by the actors to change the beliefs, values, and behaviors of their "audience," the ecological approach diminishes the importance of the actors by postulating that their communicative actions have complex and indeterminate consequences from the vantage point of larger cultural and symbolic configurations. In contrast, the sequential-inferential paradigm stresses the sequence of acts that individuals interactively produce with others as the principal influence over what happens between communicators. Although each interactant contributes to such sequences, none of them controls these ordered wholes of the component acts. Consequently, contends Sanders, the sequential-inferential paradigm is relevant to (1) interpersonal and group communication, (2) public campaigns and movements, and (3) mass media effects more broadly. The sequential-inferential paradigm claims that unique insights into communication processes and practices consist of establishing not whether particular communicative acts change what an audience thinks or does, but whether and how the timing-based relevance of communicative acts to particular points in the sequence contributes to making progress toward one of its possible resolutions.

At the theoretical level, Sanders discusses mainly two general theories of interactions: (1) his own theory of the formal-cognitive basis for the strategic and coherent, future-oriented course of interaction, and (2) Gottman's theory of marital interaction as the basis for successful and unsuccessful personal relationships. All theories of interactions have to account for mechanisms for weaving particular interactional sequences. Usually referred to as *restrictions* or *constraints*, such mechanisms may take the form of either (1) a discourse "grammar" that organizes interactional sequences like language structures larger than the sentence or (2) adjacency pairs of a communicative "demand" and its "resolution."

Sanders develops an alternative conceptualization of restrictions on interactional sequences. He implies that members of a given culture share the same set of, relatively stable and homogeneous, formal-cognitive rules for participating coherently in interactions. Given some initial act, the rules specify all possible alternative sequences that can follow that initial act. Consequently, each observed sequence in the chain of interactions is only one option among alternative possibilities. According to Sanders, in naturally occurring interactions, both the participants and the observers or researchers rely ideally on the same set of the formal-cognitive rules to compare the acts that occur with possible alternatives. In other words; such comparisons are the basis for making inferences and attributions from interactional sequences about (1) the course of an interaction, (2) others' dispositions and capabilities, and (3) the mutual compatibility of the persons interacting. It follows that the task of the theorist is to specify the formal-cognitive rules of interaction, and then provide empirical evidence that actors really use such rules of inference to coordinate the business at hand.

Sanders also analyzes Gottman's theory and research on marital interaction and the marital trajectory in the form of dissolution and stability. Gottman focuses on how sequences of acts in interaction distinguish between "successful" and "unsuccessful" marital relationships. In general, Gottman has found that distressed couples coproduce a significantly narrower set of "rigidified" and predictable interactional patterns than nondistressed couples. More specifically, Gottman traced two particular types of interactional sequences and their effect on the stability of marriage. First, a *process cascade*—a criticism-contempt-defensiveness-stonewall chain—is most strongly predictive of marital dissolution. Second, Gottman also isolated an *emotional cascade* and labeled it the *distance and isolation cascade*. Such a chain starts with a "flooding" or complaint that is interpreted by the partner as "unexpected," discontinuous emotions. Partners then work out problems individually, start living parallel and not interactive lives, and eventually experience severe loneliness in the marriage.

At the practical level, Sanders implies that the explicit knowledge and awareness of the formal-cognitive rules, postulated by his theory, would enhance our skills in the strategic comanagement of interactions. On his part, Gottman has engaged in clinical intervention, based on his theory, for distressed couples by teaching them "social skills." Although such skills involved learning new ways of producing specific acts and responses, they ultimately transform larger sequences of interactions between marital partners.

2

THE COORDINATED MANAGEMENT OF MEANING THEORY OF PEARCE, CRONEN, AND ASSOCIATES

GERRY PHILIPSEN

In the late 1970s and early 1980s W. Barnett Pearce and Vernon E. Cronen proposed an important new theory of communication, one that they call the *coordinated managment of meaning* (Pearce and Cronen, 1980). The coordinated management of meaning, abbreviated CMM by Pearce and Cronen, is an important theory of human communication for two reasons. First, it treats *an important social process*, that is, the ways in which individuals achieve, in their social interactions with each other, some degree of mutual understanding and acting together toward mutually desirable ends. Mutual understanding between persons and the effective meshing of interpersonal actions are, we can assume, important basic accomplishments in human life. Second, the work pursuant to the theory has a record of *notable successes in research and practical application*. CMM is not only a theory but also a research enterprise that encompasses original concepts and propositions, a diverse array of empirical studies, and many examples of successful applications of the approach to important human problems. CMM not only deals with something of fundamental importance to human beings, but also has a demonstrated record of intellectual and practical success.

In this chapter I survey, selectively, some of the key assumptions, concepts, questions, and exemplar studies that, taken together, constitute at least in part, the enterprise Pearce and Cronen established. This review is limited in two ways necessitated by the nature of CMM writings and by the scope of the theoretic program. First, anyone who reads a sample of the large body of writings in the coordinated management of meaning tradition will be struck by inconsistencies across writings in the use of terms and the basic claims made. This makes it difficult to pin down the authors on many key points. For example, the nature of coordination, one of the core terms of the theory and program's name, is treated on different occasions as both process and effect. In defense of Pearce and Cronen, they believe that meanings are not fixed, unchanging points of reference but rather are communicative resources and accomplishments, which are to be negotiated in interaction. Although there is an openness to Pearce and Cronen's use of language across time, for a review essay of these authors' works it helps to fix what they say, and here I have presented my own interpretation of where they come to rest, as it were, in relation to certain key concepts in their theory.

A second difficulty in reviewing CMM work is that the program is very ambitious. Pearce and Cronen have endeavored to integrate a great range of scholarly and empirical materials. Their work includes a sweeping review of the history of social inquiry, with implications for their own theorizing; they have integrated cultural and personal perspectives on and a variety of causal and noncausal approaches to human communication; and their methods of inquiry range from the formalized study of simulattd conversations to a distinctive version of the interpretive strudy of cases. I do not pretend to have synthesized or even to have surveyed the whole of CMM. Rather, I present a selective and illustrative exposition of key ideas, findings, and approaches of this research tradition. In focusing on certain key themes, some important materials have, no doubt, been neglected.

I have suggested that CMM work is characterized by changing meanings and the sometimes chaotic integration of diverse perspectives. Pearce and Cronen would insist that these qualities of their work are quintessential features of any array of communicative acts, whether that array be the published items in a research program, such as that of CMM, or the complex configuration of interactions that constitute, for example, a family or a task-oriented organization. They use just such a fluid, diverse, and problematic image to characterize human communication. Specifically, it is the idea of "the unscripted drama" with which Pearce and Cronen introduce their "new idea of communication" (Pearce and Cronen, 1980). In the unscripted drama people mill about a stage on which there is no director and without benefit of a script. The players on such a stage produce "a cacophonous bedlam with isolated points of coherence" (Pearce and Cronen 1980; p. 121). Pearce and Cronen invented the phrase *the coordinated management of meaning* to describe their interest in the image suggested by the unscripted drama metaphor. They are concerned with the myriad ways that participants in the unscripted drama of life act toward, with, and against each other, with a particular concern with "the means [by which] and the extent to which they are coordinating their meaning" (Pearce and Cronen, 1980, p. 231).

They state (modified slightly here), "the means by which and the extent to which the players in an unscripted drama are coordinating their meaning" to help locate precisely the concern and the program Pearce and Cronen address. The metaphor of the undirected play suggests richly the idea of disordered, incoherent interaction and helps to suggest vividly the question of how interactors somehow manage to achieve, on particular occasions, some sense of order in their dealings with others on life's interpersonal stage.

Pearce and Cronen think of themselves as authors and scientists who are themselves actors in a particular social drama. They present their work as a radical departure from the mainstream assumptions and methods of inquiry of the social scientists to whom they address their work. Although I believe their perceived points of radical difference can each be shown to have been occupied by some predecessor, it is useful to consider some of the positions which Pearce and Cronen have self-consciously occupied and from which they have launched their unique story line.

A CMM Worldview

One of the seminal ideas informing communication theory in the second half of the twentieth century is the importance of interactional patterns, as distinct from the significance of the single act. Such authors as Bateson (1972) and Watzlavick, Beavin, and Jackson (1967) have proposed that, if human interaction is considered in terms of the complex patterns of interaction that can be observed between and among people, then a powerful vantage point of observation has been secured that yields understandings of human interaction not otherwise available. A very simple, hypothetical illustration of this is a family group studied as an interaction system. A focus on single acts, and the effects of these acts on the members of the family, might lead an observer to notice some particular remark and how other members of the family responded to it or a pattern of remarks exhibited by a family member, a pattern that could lead to the inference that the member is troubled, supportive, or whatever. The interactional view shifts the focus of observation to the ways in which the family members' several reactions relate to each other, as kinds of actions, such that the various members' actions constitute an observable system. It might be, for example, that every time the youngest child speaks in a family discussion, one particular parent makes a negative statement; such an observed pattern is treated as part of a complex system of interaction, the system constituting the unique experiential world of that particular family. Such interactional patterns, it has been proposed, are meaningful to those who produce them, even if their producers could not necessarily formulate the patterns themselves; and these patterns have important consequences for the functioning of the dyad, family, or other interactional system of which they are a part. Pearce and Cronen explicitly ally themselves with an interactional approach, in their *concern with the properties of interpersonal systems rather than with the effects of isolated acts.*

A second important idea that informs contemporary communication theory is that, through their capacity as interpreters and initiators of action, individuals construct a sense of meaning and order. Such authors as Delia (1975) and Garfinkel (1967) have written about the inventive capacity of humans to attribute meaning to objects and events, including acts of themselves and other. Where some students of communication might write as if the responding human is a kind of automaton who responds to stimuli in precisely predictable ways, various constructionists emphasize the importance of the individual's inventive capacities in constructing and interpreting lines of action. Pearce and Cronen ally themselves with those scholars who emphasize *the human proclivity for constructing and acting upon their interpretations of experience.*

A third important idea in contemporary communication theory follows from the two ideas just stated. If individuals are capable of interpreting and inventing lines of action in social life, and if those individual lines of action, juxtaposed to each other, constitute complex interactional patterns, then it follows that there is *a relationship of interdependence between individual actions and the interactional systems of which they are one constituent.* Such scholars as Gumperz and Hymes (1972) have proposed models of human action that emphasize, at once, the importance both of (1) a preexisting social structure, such as a speech community or shared code, in shaping the performance and interpretations of individuals actions and of (2) individual actions, in turn, not only reproducing existing social structures but influencing them as well (see also Philipsen, 1987). Pearce and Cronen are centrally concerned with this dialectic of individual and society, a concern they express in their proposal that communication and culture have a reciprocal causal relationship (Pearce and Cronen, 1980; Chapter 2).

A fourth important principle of contemporary communication theory is a methodological consequence of the first three. If communication consists, at least in part and at least from one view of it, as something artfully produced by inventive social actors, if there is meaning at the level of interactional patterns, and if individual actions and collective patterns have a mutual influence on each other, then it follows that an important methodological approach in the study of communication is to develop ways to study and learn from individual cases of communicative conduct. The unscripted human drama is best understood, Pearce and Cronen propose, by examining strips of human dramatic activity, examining the resources actors deployed in those strips, and *from (these) concrete particulars generalizing about the many ways in which interlocutors can construct meaning in social interaction.* Such a position can be opposed to one that emphasizes an exclusive reliance on universal propositions of human behavior, which take the form "if x, then y," as a way to predict and explain conduct.

The deemphasis on universal propositions, such as causal relationships among communicative phenomena, does not mean that CMM is atheoretical. Rather, CMM is concerned, radically, with particularity and, systematically, with ways to describe, interpret, and alter particularities. For example, some researchers have been concerned to discover and formulate universal propositions about the causes of interpersonal violence. Straus, for example, reports an extensive body of research that supports the propositions that verbal aggression tends to promote interpersonal violence and that civility (a calm, problem-focused kind of speech) tends to lessen the likelihood that two people will come to blows with each other (Straus 1974). Straus's findings are cast in the form of universal propositions which have the form if x, then y. CMM takes a different approach. It supplies a vocabulary and a system of investigative tools that permit a researcher to examine a particular pair (or larger group) of people, say a husband and a wife, and describe their communicative system in such a way as to help explain why it is they act violently toward each other or why it is they do not. In such a research program, *a fundamental concern with theory is the formulation of a general scheme that facilitates the apprehension of communicative particulars in a particular case.* Generalization in such a theoretical errterprise is directed toward a (general) theory of how to discover the dynamics of any given case, rather than toward propositions about universal causes of human behavior. In this regard, CMM is like the ethnography of speaking (Hymes, 1962), an enterprise in which theoretical advances are measured substantially by developments in the capacity to discover and describe particular cultural systems.

Finally, CMM is a critical and interventionist perspective on communication. It is critical in that its practitioners understand their investigations as designed to lead to some kind of diagnosis of a given interactional system, a diagnosis that locates problems or difficulties that can be traced to the communicative practices of the system. In this regard, (at least some) CMM practitioners start with a singular ideal for human life, the ideal of personal "liberation" (Cronen, Chen, and Pearce, 1988), liberation presumably from the oppressiveness of a communication system in which a person is enmeshed. CMM is interventionist in its enthusiasm for using the results of critical diagnosis to suggest communicative strategies that would alter or reconstitute the communication system as its participants experience it. *Communication, in the view of CMM, is both a site in which human oppression of other human beings can be located and a resource through which liberation can be effected.*

The Core Vocabulary of CMM

There are four key concepts (and related terms) in CMM. In this section, I present and discuss each of these concepts: coordination, social reality, order of social reality, and communication.

Coordination

Coordination is the chief object of explanation in CMM. In the course of acting together or toward each other, people either do or do not achieve coordination or achieve it in some measured degree. This is a central concern of the theory. *Coordination* refers to *the degree to which persons perceive that their actions have fitted together into some mutually intelligible sequence or pattern of actions.* For example, two people who are talking in the same room, at the same time, who afterward each say "I had a conversation" is an instance of coordination. To this bare description of a social situation, illustrative details can be added. Some examples drawn from the CMM literature are the inter-actions of spouses, over time and over a range of settings; the members of an organizational department, who interact with each other in the course of doing their work; and two political figures, from opposing camps, who find themselves engaged in some kind of sustained, mutual interaction, either at a distance or face to face. In each of these situations, all of the parties can ask, about an immediately preceding conversation or about a whole series of interactions, How predictable was my partner in this interaction? Presumably, if each party answers that his or her interlocutor was highly predictable, this suggests that, to some degree, the interlocutors were making sense to each other, were acting in mutually sensible ways, and were achieving some kind of harmonious pattern in their dealings with each other. Of course, this is the simplest version of coordination and its presumed harmony, and Pearce and Cronen complicate the matter in useful ways; for now, it is instructive to consider this simpler version, which is at the heart of most of the CMM researches.

The particular shape and degree of coordination varies across inter-personal events and interpersonal systems. Pearce and Cronen use a variety of concrete markers to assess degree of coordination between or among interacting people. One approach is to ask interlocutors whether their inter-actional partner's past conduct was predictable. Consider two people who have interacted with each other, who have played some kind of (scripted or unscripted) social scene together. Having enacted (or constructed) the scene, suppose they were asked to respond, agreeing or disagreeing on a nine-point scale, to the following statement: "In the just completed scene my partner's choices of actions were very predictable to me." One operational marker of coordination, in Pearce and Cronen's scheme, is the degree to which the participants in the scene agree with such a statement. The mutual perception of predictability presumably is a marker that the interlocutors' communicative actions meshed together smoothly.

CMM research also uses other, more behavioral indicators of coordina-tion. For example, it assesses whether two interacting people actually did fit their lines of action together in a harmonious way, at the level of observed behavior. One concrete example is a study in which it was observed whether two people successfully completed a game that required them to predict each others' actions and required them to be willing to cooperate with each other so that each person could contribute to a successful outcome (Pearce, Cronen, Johnson, Jones, and Raymond, 1980; Johnson 1979). In any case, what counts as coordination is the real or perceived fitting together of individuils' actions into an intelligible pattern.

Not all of social life is perfectly coordinated, and Pearce and Cronen argue that humanly important, and morally defensible, patterns of interaction can be observed in which coordination is only partially achieved. A group of colleagues, for example, might together accomplish important work even though the separate actions of the members are, in important ways, at cross purposes. That the separate actions of the members mesh in some ways or on some occasions, but not in other ways or on other occasions is, in Pearce and Cronen's view, a human circumstance every bit as important, practically and theoretically, as is the (idealized?) circumstance of perfect interpersonal coordination. Although many researchers before them were interested in interacting systems in which perfect coordination was not achieved, past researchers tended to treat such systems as dysfunctional. Pearce and Cronen are equally interested in interactions in which the parties meshed smoothly their separate acts and in interactions in which the fit between the parties' separate lines of action did not conform to some ideal of either the researcher or the participants. Many human interactions are more messy than clean and more awkward than elegant, and Pearce and Cronen are as concerned with examining the messy and the awkward as they are with examining the clean and the elegant.

Coordination is not necessarily the meshing of perfectly shared meanings. It is the perceived meshing of actions. Although the producers of those actions, and outside observers of them as well, might perceive them to mesh smoothly, this does not necessarily mean that the producers of those actions agree as to the meaning of the actions. An example drawn from Harris, Cronen, and McNamee (1979) is a case in which two people who lived together coordinated their actions perfectly in an important discussion with each other, but each perceived their actions differently from the way the other person perceived them. Specifically, Jan and Dave discussed Jan's getting a job. In the discussion, which Jan and Dave reported retrospectively to be quite predictable and satisfying, Dave gave explicit instructions as to what Jan should do ("Well, you're getting up at eight o'clock and we're leaving the house at nine" [to look for a job for Jan]). Although the statement apparently had an effect that consummated nicely the discussion and preceded Jan's successful effort to find a job the next day, Dave's utterance meant something very different to Jan and to Dave. Jan interpreted the utterance as an ultimatum, an assertion of control over Jan, which is what she wanted from him To Dave, the utterance counted as "backing down," an act by which he moved out of a dominating position vis-à-vis Jan. In this case, and in a second interaction studied by the researchers, Jan and Dave produced perfect coordination without mutual understanding; that is each had a different understanding of what had happened, but each judged what had happened to be perfectly fitted together.

Social Reality

The second key term in the theory is *social reality*. The concern with specifying an outcome of interaction, that is, coordination, and with explaining the occurrences of such an outcome in various cases is a starting point for the theory. The next concern is with identifying phenomena that might relate to such an outcome as coordination. The concern is not only with what interlocutors create in discourse, but also with *what interlocutors bring to the interaction process*. Height, weight, and gender are, for example, things interlocutors bring to an encounter. Pearce and Cronen are not concerned with such variables as these. They are concerned with something else which the interlocutors bring to the interaction—what they call *social reality*.

Social reality in Pearce and Cronen's scheme refers to *an individual's beliefs about meanings and action in the sphere of interpersonal conduct*. These beliefs can be expressed as rules. Pearce and Cronen identify two types of rules, constitutive and regulative. A constitutive rule is like an individual's definition of some social object, for example, if, for an individual, to utter the statement "you are beautiful" *counts as* the speech act of compliment, then that is, for that individual, a constitutive rule. A regulative rule specifies a sequence of action which the individual feels some pressure to perform under specified circumstances, for example, if an individual feels it is *socially obligatory* for her to pay a compliment to someone, on some given occasion, then that is, for that individual, a regulative rule.

An important feature of CMM is that constitutive and regulative rules are tied, and tied quite delicately, to given contexts or circumstances. To say that a rule is *tied to a context* suggests that, for an individual, always *under some particular circumstance* a behavioral performance counts as a particular kind of action or kind of action is felt to be socially obligatory. To say that rules in CMM are tied *delicately* to a context is to suggest that an individual's social reality is not fixed. There are myriad ways in which the individual's constitutive and regulative perceptions are invoked, adapted, influenced, and negotiated in social interaction. What remains constant is the human tendency to interpret and guide conduct with reference to some (albeit fluid) sense of what counts as what and what kinds of actions are appropriate, in particular occasions of interpersonal action.

CMM research provides a variety of ways to discover a picture of the social reality of an individual. These include participant observation, discourse transcription and analysis, the administration of questionnaires, and intensive interviewing of individuals. Typically, in a CMM study, rules are discovered and formulated by asking parties to some interaction what they believe their rule to be about some matter. A research subject is interviewed and, in the course of the interview process, is asked questions that reveal his or her constitutive or regulative rules; alternatively, after an initial period of fieldwork, subjects are given questionnaires to which they respond about their perceptions and beliefs pertaining to social interaction.

In any case, discovering an individual's rules requires some preliminary inquiry to determine prospective candidates for rules. The preliminary inquiry is necessary, according to CMM, because of the uniqueness of individuals and relationships. That is, it is always necessary to find out, for the particular individual or interpersonal system, what the possibilities are in terms of constitutive and regulative rules. In this regard, CMM researchers have a strong kinship with ethnographic students of communication. Having identified some possibilities, then the CMM researcher asks the research subject whether she or he agrees with the rule as formulated. Thus, the CMM strategy is an interplay between exploration and verification, with regard to the discovery of possible rules for an individual or an interpersonal system.

An example of discovering rules using the CMM procedure is the steps taken in a study of people who had experienced violence in some interpersonal relationship. Initially, the women who were studied were interviewed so as to elicit narrative accounts of their experiences. Having elicited a person's story of a violent experience, the researcher culled out various types of speech act that the person reported performing or observing her interlocutor perform. These speech acts were then put into an elicitation frame, as in the following: "Doing speech act———closely reflected who I am and what a person like me must do." The researcher inserted a particular act, drawn from the researcher's study of the interview protocol, for example, "show of anger," in the blank space in this question-item. The resulting statement, "Doing speech act 'show of anger' closely reflected who I am and that a person like me must do" was then put in the moment-by-moment context of the story the individual had earlier reported. Then, the researcher asked the individual to rate the resultant statement on a scale of "0" (strongly disagree) to "7" (strongly agree). Thereby the investigator obtained an estimate of the degree to which the individual felt a sense of pressure to perform an act in a particular context, that is, at a specified moment in a specified conversation with a specified person. In this way, the investigator discovered a regulative rule for the person being studied. Not all CMM research is this fine grained with regard to discovering and formulating rules, but this gives an example of one systematic way of proceeding that has been used in the research program.

Typically, a CMM research study focuses on an array of an individual's constitutive and regulative rules, yielding in particular cases something like an idiosyncratic vocabulary (constitutive rules) and grammar (regulative rules) of interpersonal action. The descriptive framework that has grown up around CMM consists of a series of models for describing and reporting individuals' rule systems. These include a variety of ways of formulating contexts of action, with "context" referring to all those features of a situation that make a difference to an individual in deciding among alternative courses of action or alternative interpretations; simple examples of such features are setting, the other people present, the nature of preceding utterances in the event, and so forth.

CMM authors have endeavored to construct a useful picture ot context. If, as defined previously, *context* refers to all those features of a situation that make a difference to an individual in deciding among alternative courses of action or alternative interpretations, then a model or picture of context would identify and organize all of those features, or at least it would organize some of the major features that have an influence on communication and coordination. There is a long tradition in the social sciences of answering the question, What are all the features of a situation that constitute the contextual backdrop against which communicative acts are produced and interpreted? The efforts of Gumperz and Hymes, in anthropology, are notable in this regard (see Gumperz and Hymes, 1972), following a long tradition in social anthropology and the ethnography of speaking.

The portion of the CMM descriptive framework that pertains to context has been described differently in different presentations, but a representative version of it includes the following five features. These features are several levels of interpretation at which individuals think about and interpret the actions of themselves and other.

Level 1 is *content*, specifically the content of a person's categories or percepts. These are the specific mental items or categories a person uses to intepret or perceive experience. The categories *intelligent* and *kind* are percepts: minimal categories of interpretation a person might use to make sense of "raw" experience. Such categories are among the resources for construing the meaning interlocutors bring to the planning and interpretation of particular acts.

Level 2 is *speech acts*, which equates to an individual's percepts or categories for intepreting human behaviors as one kind of spoken action or another. For example, an individual possesses a working scheme of categories pertaining to the kinds of actions people perform when they speak; such categories could include such notions as "threat," "promise," "inform," and "advise," as the kinds of things people do when they make spoken utterances. These are, presumably, the kinds of categories interlocutors bring to the planning and interpretation of particular acts as particular types of communictive acts.

Level 3 is *contracts*, which are a system of rules two or more individuals have jointly constructed that pertain to the relationship they have to each other. Contracts are relationship specific, that is they obtain for two or a few people who have, implicitly or explicitly, forged a system of agreements between or among themselves. When some people talk about their "relationships" (intro-duced as an American folk term by Katriel and Philipsen, 1981), they are talking about what Pearce and Cronen have labeled a *contract*.

Level 4 is *episodes*, which are communicative routines people view as distinct wholes. Each episode consists of a describable sequence of speech acts. An example, taken from Saville-Troike (1982, p. 146), is a characterization of an episode type that is part of the Japanese door-to-door sales encounter, which has two participants, the salesperson, P1, and the housewife, P2. The opening sequence episode includes six sequential speech acts: (1) P1: greeting, (2) P2: acknowledgment, (3) P1: identification, (4) P2: question about purpose, (5) P1: information about purpose, and (6) P2: expression of disinterest or interest.

Level 5 is *life scripts*, which refers to "that repertoire of episodes that a person perceives as identified with him/herself, the array of interactive situations that are consistent with a recognition of 'this is me' or 'this is something I would do' " (Pearce and Cronen, 1980, p. 136).

Each of these five levels of context refers to a kind of feature of a social situation from the standpoint of one individual who is a part of that situation. These are the kinds of situational elements with which, presumably, from the standpoint of the individual, one can make sense of—interpret—raw behaviors so as to endow them with meaning. Thus, if someone shouts someone's name, one brings to bear a system of resources for hearing—interpreting—that shout as having some kind of significance. The features of the social situation, as specified, are (among) the kinds of resources an individual uses to make such interpretations.

The reader will notice that these features of a context are presented here, as they are presented in CMM writings, in a hierarchical framework. That is, some features are higher—more important—than others. This expresses the CMM assumption that an individual's social reality is organized such that, for example, the individual's life scripts are more powerful interpretive resources than the individual's percepts.

The descriptive framework also includes a complex scheme for characterizing the force of rules in an individual's life. Broadly speaking, rules can have *prefigurative force* and *practical force* for an individual. Each of these terms refers to *the sense of oughtness an individual experiences regarding the performance of a particular act. Prefigurative force* refers, in particular, to *an individual's sense that one's action was controlled or determined by forces around one*, such as the expectations of one's social group; it is captured by whether a person can say "I did that because of (some social expectation that I act that way)." *Practical force* refers to *the sense an individual has that one's action serves one's own purpose in some social situation*; it is captured by whether a person can say "I did that in order to (accomplish some purpose I had)."

For any individual, there is an identifiable and reportable configuration of constitutive and regulative rules. To represent these for a given individual would require an intricate array of rules. The array would include constitutive and regulative rules, which implies a series of context-linked proposals. It would, furthermore, carry the qualification that all these rules are susceptible to revision, given the nature of persons as inventors of meanings and actions and given the nature of social interaction as fluid and dynamic. Nonetheless, it is possible, according to CMM, at any give time to fix systems of rules that for those individuals form social reality—a structured, identifiable, but complicated and dynamic thing.

Order in Social Reality

Social reality is something located within the individual. It is a complex, changing view of the world that an individual brings to social interaction. And although CMM is concerned with the social reality of individuals, it is fundamentally committed to a relational unit of observation. This means that one individual's beliefs about others are not as important, for purposes of understanding what does or does not get accomplished between them, as is *the configuration of two (or more) interactors' social realities*. For this idea, Pearce and Cronen (1980) use the expression *order in social reality*. Order in social reality is a relational phenomenon; it refers to the systemic configuration of two or more social realities. Whether you say "tomayto" or "tomahto" is not important in relational thinking; what is important is the relationship between what you say and what I say. Whether we "call the whole thing off," as the song says, is determined not by what you or I say, but by the relationship between what you and I say, for example, whether what we say is compatible, complementary, harmonious, and so on.

Order in social reality refers, roughly, to the match or mismatch of the interlocutors' beliefs about meanings and actions in the conduct of interpersonal life. Pearce and Cronen are concerned with ascertaining, for any given interpersonal system, how much agreement there is, across persons, in social reality and with what is the nature of the agreements and disagreements. A fundamental commitment of CMM is to explore what happens to social interaction, in terms of its process and its products, under various conditions of order in social reality.

A concrete example of order in social reality is presented in Harris, Cronen, and McNamee (1979). The two people studied were Dave and Jan, who were, at the time of the study, living together. Dave's and Jan's constitutive and regulative rules, for their interpersonal relationship with each other, were formulated on the basis of interviews, questionnaires, and observations of interaction. Dave described himself in such a way as to suggest that, for him, it is a regulative rule in his relationship with Jan, not to play a dominant or controlling role. Dave also desired to effect in Jan assertive behavior on her part, including assertive behavior toward him and toward efforts at finding a job. Jan, on the other hand, desired that Dave assert himself toward her, by making an effort to dominate her. Jan initiated episodes in which she tried to force Dave into a dominant role. Dave's and Jan's desires were at cross-purposes, Dave wishing Jan to be assertive in the face of his passivity, Jan wishing Dave to be assertive in controlling her. These are two seemingly different "interpersonal logics" at the level of regulative rules.

There are two dimensions of *order of social reality*. One of these is *similarity versus difference*. The case of Dave and Jan illustrates the dimension of difference—Jan and Dave differed in their social reality, at least that portion of their respective social realities which pertained to their relationship with each other. One gross judgment that can be made for any communicative system is the degree of similarity in social reality across the participants. A second dimension is *content*. An order of social reality can be described in terms of constitutive rules, regulative rules, or as is typical, both. Descriptions of content provide a qualitative assessment of a communication system, in that they specify the particular rules that, juxtaposed, show the participants in the system to be in conflict or disagreement. It could be that two people disagree only on one or two rules, but these could be extremely important rules to them. Thus, order in social reality is something characterized uniquely for each communication system studied, with attention both to the degree of agreement and the configuration of similarities and differences of the persons who constitute the system. For any communicative system it is, at least in principle, possible to ascertain a complex configuration of similarity and difference with regard to the rules subscribed to by the various participants in the system. A fundamental concern of CMM is to be able to provide such characterizations of order in social reality.

Communication

The fourth key concept in the CMM scheme is *communication*, which Pearce and Cronen treat as the process or activity by which social reality is created, deployed, and managed. Coordination pertains to a state achieved in interaction, social reality or order of social reality is what the individual or social system brings to interaction, and communication is what the participants do in social interaction.

Findings

Some programs of research advance by generating and testing a body of empirically supported theories, as in the case of uncertainty reduction theory (see Gudykunst, Chapter 4 of this book). CMM is a different kind of theoretical enterprise from such programs. It proceeds not so much by the development of a system of lawlike propositions as it does by the application of its descriptive-interpretive apparatus to a series of themes and contexts, with the aim of refining the stance it takes toward the social world. Although CMM research has in practice relied extensively on hypothesis testing of a sort that would look quite familiar to the lawlike theorists, it is probably fair to say that when CMM researchers write in this way it is a kind of maneuver by which they aim to arrive eventually, somewhere other than at a lawlike generalization. In what follows, I describe four important CMM studies that illustrate this methodological strategy. In the process I hope not only to illustrate how CMM researchers have pursued their particular goal, but also to show some of the particular findings they have generated.

Coherent Conversation and Indirect Responses

Pearce and Conklin (1979) report what appears to be the first empirical study in the CMM program. It reveals several key features of the program, including its emphasis on interactors' interpretations of messages and the use interactors make of context in making their interpretations. Pearce and Conklin (1979) build on Nofsinger's (1976) influential study of how people make use of subtle rules (or interpretive principles) to interpret a message as one kind of message or another. Nofsinger and other researchers had observed that people often do not answer questions directly but rather make a remark that, on the surface, is not an answer to a question but that the speaker and hearer of the utterance take to be an answer. For example, the utterances "yes" and "does a rabbit like another rabbit?" can each be heard by a listener as the speaker's "yes" answer to a question. Listeners do this, Nofsinger argues, by using certain rules of interpretation for hearing "does a rabbit like another rabbit?" as a "yes" answer.

Obviously, the kind of insight Nofsinger produced was important to CMM theorizing, because it apparently showed that interactors make use of what Pearce and Cronen eventually would label *constitutive rules*, principles that specify what a particular behavior is to count as. If interlocutors use rules to constitute as answers behaviors that on the surface appear not to be answers, then one of the key assumptions of CMM was given some empirical backing. But CMM proposes something more than that interlocutors use rules to constitute behaviors as particular actions; it specifies further that interlocutors bring to bear an elaborate working model of interpretation that is hierarchical. That is, interlocutors consult several levels of context in producing their communicative acts. Nofsinger's study suggests one concrete phenomenon, answering questions indirectly, which could be used to illustrate and test CMM's position.

The conversational segments used by Pearce and Conklin (1979) are as follows:

1.) Jim: Did you do well on the exam?
   Bill: (*Direct response*) No, I didn't.
             (*Indirect response*) Does the Pope have a mother-in-law?

Jim: Sorry to hear it. Better luck next time.

2.) Pat: Would you like to go to the concert with me tonight?
    Mike: (*Direct response*) Yes, I would.
            (*Indirect response*) If the sun still rises in the east.
    Pat: I'll be over about nine.

3.) Tom: Hot enough for you today?
    Harry: (*Direct response*) It sure is.
            (*Indirect response*) I always sweat like this when I'm cold.
    Tom: This heat's got to break sometime.

Note that there are two versions of each episode, one in which a direct response is given and one in which an indirect response is given. These two versions permit a researcher to investigate patterns of response to "answers" that are direct versus indirect.

In episodes 1 and 2 respondents overwhelmingly interpreted indirect responses as answers, but in the "hot enough" episode only 44 percent of the respondents said that the indirect response counts, for them, as an answer. The entire pattern of interpretations of indirect answers as answers suggests that the respondents were doing quite a bit of contextualizing or interpreting, and this is consistent with the CMM view of people as active constructors of meaning. For episode 3, the division among respondents provided an opportunity for some theoretical speculation by Pearce and Conklin, and the speculation is revealing as to the nature of the CMM approach. That approach would suggest that respondents would interpret the behavior of answering indirectly as a particular kind of act in such a way as to reveal the use of a higher level of context than the act level. The statement, "I always sweat like this when I'm cold," is a small piece of behavior sampled from a stream of behavior. As such it can be interpreted as a particular kind of speech act, the speech act being one level in the hierarchy of contextual levels. If the hearer brought to bear his or her understanding of various kinds of speech acts (level 2), the hearer could conceivably construct this statement as one kind of act or another, and 44 percent of the respondents in Pearce and Conklin (1979) reported that for them it counted as an answer. But CMM proposes that if the hearer brings to bear an understanding from a higher level in the hierarchy, say from the episode (level 4) or life script (level 5) level, then the meanings from the higher level would take precedence over the meanings from the lower level. In this case, presumably if the hearers conceptualized the utterance as part of a particular kind of episode (level 4) they would hear it as a particular kind, of act.

Pearce and Conklin's (1979) interpretation of the "hot enough" response pattern provides an illuminating insight into the logic of CMM. In the experiment all subjects were asked not only to determine whether the indirect answer counted for them as an answer, but also to judge the *episode* as "good communication" or "poor communication" and to rate the *speech act* itself in terms of whether they judged it to be "appropriate," "respectful," and "friendly." Pearce and Cronen later wrote about this,

Our reasoning was the interpretation of the message as good or poor communication would depend on whether a satisfactory frame could be imposed, and the ability to locate a satisfactory frame would depend on the interpretation of the appropriateness of the metacommunicational message. The data indicated that virtually all of the subjects who described the message as poor communication also described the indirect response as inappropriate, disrespectful, and unfriendly.... This finding suggests that persons have a complex network of relations among meanings within and among various hierarchical levels, and implies that a theory of persons as processors of information must describe several levels of meaning and the organization within and among levels. (Pearce and Cronen, 1980; pp. 129–130)

In short, the Pearce and Conklin (1979) "hot enough" data provide evidence to support the claim that the people studied used resources from the *episode* level to construct the meaning, for them, of a behavior as a particular kind of speech act.

In terms of the discussion as I have presented it here, Pearce and Cronen's (1980) discussion reveals two central tenets in the logic of CMM: (1) people actively construct meanings of behaviors by invoking various aspects of context that determine for the person, what that behavior counts as, in that context, and (2) the aspects of context that people draw from in constituting meanings are hierarchically ordered—that is, some levels are higher or more important than other levels.

Although the early theorizing (Pearce 1976) and the early experimental data (Pearce and Conklin 1979) argue for a strong version of the hierarchical ordering of various contextual features (e.g., life scripts are more important than basic percepts in influencing an individual's interpretations and intentions), by the time Pearce and Cronen's (1980) book was published a much less ambitious view of context was set forth. Pearce and Cronen (1980) wrote about the hierarchical model of context: "our purpose is to model the way persons process information, not to describe a true ordering. We expect persons to differ in the number of levels of abstraction they use, in the sequence of levels, and in the extent to which meanings at various levels are consistent with those on other levels.... The levels of meaning in the hierarchy model... serve as a heuristic device..." (p. 130). With this statement, and subsequent others, Pearce and Cronen take away much of the confidence of the early model and replace it with a general affirmation of the importance of context as a way to characterize and organize the resources interlocutors bring to interaction. They have never abandoned the model, but they have qualified it substantially and they have moved on to other matters. Nonetheless, the early data on indirect answers provide some minimal empirical validation of the usefulness of the CMM approach.

Coordination in Simulated Conversation

One way to capture the use of contextual resources, that is, rules specifying what counts as what and what kind of action should be performed in a given situation, is to elicit or observe the judgments people make about various communicative acts. That was the strategy used in Pearce and Conklin (1979). The strategy yielded some evidence that humans are rule-using creatures when they judge the sense and appropriateness of messages. Another way to observe the use of rules is to create an artificial situation in which the rules are imposed on interactants. If one could specify the rule system one person uses (that is, that person's social reality), then specify a rule system for another person (that is, the second person's social reality), then assign them a task the performance of which requires some communicative interaction, one would be in a position to observe the effects, as it were, of rule systems on the coordinative outcome achieved. It was just such a strategy that Cronen, Kaczka, Pearce, and Pawlik (1978), Johnson (1979), and Pearce, Cronen, Johnson, Jones, and Raymond (1980) developed and implemented. The strategy is revealed in the game Coordination.

Coordination is a two-person game played in a manner simulating conversation. An artificial language was developed such that users of it were provided a limited number of resources with which to construct messages. These resources consisted of a "vocabulary" of four colored shapes, here represented by R (red), B (black), G (green), and Y (yellow). Having constructed a vocabulary, consisting of a limited number of items and the symbols that count as their expression, it was possible, further, to specify regulative rules of the sort "if one's partner displays red, then one should display black in return." Then, two interactants could be given a task, such as "in a total of four turns between you, together display the jointly constructed sequence RGBY" (this is my interpretation of the game, GP).

As simple as this scheme might appear at first glance, a little speculation about the possible combinations reveals that it is possible to create a variety of interesting orders of social reality. Each person can be supplied with similar or different constitutive rules, that is, rules of definition, and with similar or different regulative rules, that is, rules specifing which actions one should take under which circumstances. The game permits a researcher to create various orders of social reality and then to observe the coordinative results of people interacting under these various conditions of order of social reality. The simplest condition obtainable is that each interlocutor is supplied the same constitutive and regulative rules; other conditions provide for varying degrees of difference between the two interlocutors' rule systems. Observing various people under various conditions these researhers were able to ascertain some of the effects of different orders of social reality on the coordinative success of two persons playing Coordination. As might be expected, there was a strong relationship between the match of interactors' rule systems and their actual coordinative success. Of further importance in these studies, it was found that subjects' sex, role-taking ability, and perceived freedom to choose among optional actions were only very weakly related to coordinative success. This is important in its implications for CMM thinking because it suggests the importance of social reality, and more precisely of order of social reality, in affecting the outcomes of interaction, an importance that cuts across and is not undercut by social (sex) and cognitive (role-taking ability) factors.

Studies using the game Coordination yielded a complex set of empirical observations. The most fundamental conclusion derived from these results is that the degree of isomorphism between individuals' rules affects their ability to coordinate, at least in the early stages of conversation. The results of studies of how people interpret indirect messages provided a rough measure of support for the utility of the principle that people use some kind of contextual model in message interpretation; that was an important finding for the CMM program. But as useful at that finding was, its usefulness was limited for the development of the CMM perspective because it focused on the isolated communicator. The Coordination game constitutes an important advance in the CMM studies because it focuses directly not simply on one person's rule system but on the juxtaposition of two rule systems and the effect of this juxtaposition on coordinative outcomes.

Unwanted Repetitive Patterns

The studies of coherent conversation and indirect responses and of coordination in simulated conversation represent the early style of CMM research, in their use of relatively artificial and concocted methods of research. The first used hypothetical messages and responses in natural language, and the second used real messages and responses, in an artificial language. These simple but reductive experiments were extremely useful in the development of CMM thinking, and they are useful today because they help to show with operational clarity how CMM concepts have been measured and used. Later research in the CMM program built upon these early studies and approaches, but it turned quite sharply toward more anecdotal and naturalistic kinds of studies. In one of these turns, Cronen, Pearce, and Snavely (1979) introduced some of the key elements of CMM thinking and research style as they have been applied to case studies of events and relationships which were found and not created for research purposes.

The events that prompted the study by Cronen, Pearce, and Snavely (1979) concerned an ongoing, troubled relationship between two work colleagues. These individuals were obligated to discuss a variety of matters pertaining to their work life in a common unit. Although each professed in private a desire to work amicably with the other person, "their discussions quickly turned into extended, hostile, and ego-scarring duels ('quips, at twenty paces')" (Pearce and Crones, 1980, p. 246). This seemed, to the investigators, precisely the kind of phenomenon that CMM might be pressed to explain. They called this phenomenon *unwanted repetitive patterns*, or URPs. A URP is a sequence of jointly produced actions by two or more people that recurs over time, is stable across topics, that is perceived by all parties as conflictive, and that is considered by all parties to be unwanted.

Having established the existence of URPs, as exemplified in the case of the colleagues and in a variety of other cases of social life, the investigators were concerned to explain such phenomena. CMM yielded the explanation that "persons' intrapersonal rule systems could be modeled in such a way that the juxtaposition of them would create strong logical force obligating the precise patterns of speech acts observed in the verbal fights" (Pearce and Cronen, 1980, p. 247). Clearly, URPs presented a situation in which interlocuters' actions were fitting together predictably but unharmoniously. Could the explanatory apparatus of CMM be used to account for such a coordinative pattern? Thus was set the stage for using that apparatus, and this study provided the occasion for a further articulation and the implementation of that apparatus.

The idea of rule is at the core of CMM explanation. Individuals' actions can be interpreted and explained, as CMM would have it, in terms of rules for action that the actors themselves can report, or at least imply, retrospec-tively—that is, after their actions. Cronen, Pearce, and Snavely (1979) provided an occasion to delineate some of the particular ways that rules are used by actors themselves and observers to explain observed communicative conduct.

For the explanation cf URPs, the authors introduced a measurement model for specifying rules and their force in interpersonal action. Here I present enough of this model to suggest the flavor of it, with the qualification that it is much reduced from the original. At the heart of the model are the concepts of linkage and enmeshment. *Linkage* refers to the perceived relationship between two phenomena, with the further sense that somehow the two phenomena are inseparably connected. With regard to human action, the figure "action chain" is fitting, with the implication that various parts of the chain are linked, inseparably together; in terms of human action, it suggests that actions are inseperably linked—or chained—to something else. CMM, of course is concerned with rules and actions and, thus, with the link between rules and actions. *Enmeshment* has a similar sense but it seems to focus on the strength rather than the shape of the relationship. In terms of CMM, the concern is with how strongly an individual feels a linkage is to herself or himself.

Cronen, Pearce, and Snavely (1979) show how linkage and enmeshment have been operationalized. They were interested in the logical force rules have for two people who find themselves enmeshed in a URP. Their answer is *prefigurative force*, which is, it will be remembered, an individual's sense that one's actions are determined by forces around one. *Practical force* refers to the sense an individual has that one's action serves one's own purpose in some social situation. CMM is concerned with the interplay of prefigurative and practical force, with how the individual's rule system—applied to the act, episode, or relationship—influences actions that person performs and how those actions serve the individual's purposes.

To measure prefigurative force the researchers asked thirty subjects to reconstruct orally in a research interview a recent enactment of a URP and assess his or her own speech acts in a recent enactment of that pattern. Three components of prefigurative force were identified and examined.

For the first of these components, *functional autonomy*, the subject was asked, about a particular act, whether

1.) his or her own act "was what I wanted to say and what the other person would do next would not change my need to do it."

The individual rated the degree to which she or he agreed with these statements, in relation to a particular act. The individual's response to 1 suggests one key component of prefigurative force, the degree to which the individual has a sense of *autonomy*, that is, that one can do what one wants to do, in the particular circumstance. From the standpoint of CMM theory, this is an important part of prefigurative force for that individual, as it pertains to that act in that situation.

For the second of these components, *antecedent-to-act linkages*, the individual was asked, about a particular act, whether

2.) the speech act the other performed "seemed to require me to respond with [the] act [I performed]";

3.) the "episode" we were engaged in "seemed to require me to respond with [the act I performed]";

4.) "It was very important to us—to my sense of who we are—that I perform this act";

5.) "Doing [the particular] speech act. . .closely reflected who I am and what a person like me must do."

Notice that in 2, 3, 4, and 5 the individual is asked to characterize his or her own act in terms drawn from the hierarchical model of context and in terms of some sense of perceived linkage. Item 2 links the *speech act* the other performed to the individual's sense of what the individual felt his or her response should be; item 3 links the *episode* to what his or her response should be; item 4 links the *master contract* between the two people in the episode to what the individual's response should be; and item 5 links the individual's sense of *life script* to what the response should be. Each of these items, that is, is thought of as a potential force exerting pressure on the individual to act, with each pressure being linked to some feature of the context—speech act, episode, master contract, and life script all being levels of the CMM hierarchical model.

For the third of these components, the *range of alternative speech acts*, the individual was asked to comment on the act in terms of the following

6.) "What other speech acts could you have performed that would be legitimate in the situation?" (Responses could be "none" or any other item volunteered by the individual.)

The response to this item suggested the degree to which the individual perceived that one had any alternatives to what one had done in the episode at that particular juncture.

The investigators (Cronen, Pearce, and Snavely, 1979) label these components F for functional autonomy, item 1; A for antecedent act, items 2 through 5; and R for range of alternative speech acts, item 6. When the scores for F, A, and R are multiplied it produces a complex estimate of prefigurative force. Thus, they proposed the formula $A \times F \times R$, with A, F, and R assuming values from 0.0 to 1.0, the product of which is an estimate of the refigurative force an individual experiences with regard to particular speech acts in a particular situation. This formula, and the items used to generate the values it integrates, provides an estimate of the degree to which an individual feels one must act in a particular way in an episode.

Having elicited from an individual those responses that enabled him or her to estimate that individual's sense of pressure to perform a URP, Cronen, Pearce, and Snavely (1979) then asked the individual a series of other questions. One of these, question 14, pertains to the variable the investigators call *enmeshment*. Enmeshment is the degree to which a person feels he or she must repeat the episode and cannot control one's participation in it. This is estimated by asking the individual about a particular episode that exemplifies, for him or her, a URP, whether "doing this episode over and over again seems out of my control, it just seems to happen."

Thus, the interview procedure facilitated the gathering of data that would enable the investigators to determine, for an individual in relation to a URP, two estimates—*prefigurative force* and *enmeshment*. CMM would predict that the higher is the prefigurative force, the higher is the enmeshment. The results of the statistical analysis showed that each of the three components of prefigurative force was positively related to enmeshment and that, taken together, the three-component estimate of prefigurative force, accounted for over 50 percent of the variance in enmeshment. In short, prefigurative force, as estimated by interpreting the answers the subject gave to questions 1 through 6, was a reliable predictor of enmeshment, as estimsted by the answers the subject gave to question 14. The statistically significant and strongly positive relationship between the two variables, prefigurative force and enmeshment, provides strong support for one of CMM's basic principles that "the characteristics of an episode are functions of the rule structures that conversants employ" (Pearce and Cronen, 1979, p. 250).

A series of other CMM studies provides additional support for the reasoning first tested in Cronen, Pearce, and Snavely (1979) including Harris (1980), Harris, Cronen, and McNamee (1979), and Harris and Cronen (1979). Thus CMM theory, with support from multiple independent research studies, provides a generalized strategy for explaining URPs. All of these studies provide support for the principle that a particular structure of regulative rules is the origin of a logic that creates URPs with a strong sense of perceived enmeshment.

Contextual Reconstructions

A fundamental assumption of CMM is that of the reciprocal causal influence of persons' actions and context. Context can refer either to an individual's social reality or to a social reality that transcends individuals, for example, shared and institutionalized social realities. CMM is concerned to treat context as something that is a force in individual perceptions and decisions, but as something also amenable to change, or reconstruction, in and through individual acts. Using the language both of "acts" and of "texts," Branham and Pearce (1985) wrote that: "Every communicative act is a text that derives meaning from the context of expectations and constraints in which it is experienced. At the same time contexts are defined, invoked and altered by texts. Particular communictive acts simultaneously depend upon and reconstruct existing contexts" (p. 19).

Branham and Pearce (1985) borrow from Gregory Bateson the images of text and context constituting "a dance of interacting parts" and a "zigzag ladder of dialectic between form and process" (p. 21). The images of one partner leading, the other following, or of the neat symmetry of a zipper, are not what Branham and Pearce focus on in these images. Rather, their attention is focused on the give and take, the interplay and interdependence, of action and context.

In drawing attention to the indeterminacy of context in shaping human thoughts and actions, CMM practitioners make both an intellectual and a moral commitment. The moral commitment is to take seriously the fact that much communicative action does not fit the social, cultural, or political expectations of some context and that such acts are as humanly important, or valuable, as acts that are neatly designed to adjust to a context or designed to deviate only so far as is necessary to take an individual stance while nonetheless speaking from within a previously constructed system of understandings and proprieties. The long and widely held view that individual action that seeks to influence social realities should take due cognizance of the prevailing mood is directly challenged in CMM writing, which deliberately and explicitly makes a place for acts that are incoherent within a prevailing—or privileged—system. As with the moral commitment, so too, there is in CMM an intellectual commitment to examining the ways in which acts—or texts—relate to contexts, and some CMM research is devoted explicitly to this agenda.

Two essays by Branham and Pearce (1985 and 1987) exemplify CMM's concern with the innovative aspects of communicative acts. The first, "Between Text and Context: Toward a Rhetoric of Textual Reconstruction" (Branham and Pearce, 1985), announces its general themes in its title: the nexus of text and context, a rhetoric or principle of change, and the reconstructing of extant social constructions. In the essay they give pride of place to something they propose other communication scholars have neglected; that is, "texts that do not 'fit' the context which elicited them" (Branham and Pearce, 1985, p. 22).

Branham and Pearce (1985) draw upon a framework articulated earlier by Cronen, Johnson, and Lannaman (1982), who identified three general text-context relationships: charmed loops, subversive loops, and strange loops. In a charmed loop, the text is conventional and the context is stable. The text loops back onto the context in a mutually compatible way. In such loops, persuasive appeals are grounded in shared, historically sanctioned premises, which provide a background against which to experience some acts as deviant or infelicitous. In this realm, as Branham and Pearce quote Roland Barthes, "Once uttered, speech enters the service of power" (Branham and Pearce, 1985, p. 23). The case of the rhetor appealing to the common values of an audience fits neatly within the frame of a charmed loop.

In a subversive loop, the relation between text and context is irreparably breached. When, for example, someone says, "I just can't tell you," in answer to a question about what they feel or why they acted as they did, the appeal to ineffability implies that the context of shared assumptions is a resource that is inadequate for the expression of the individual's feelings or motives. As such, the appeal to ineffability subverts the context—it renders it practically inadequate to the task at hand.

In a strange loop, the act profanes and imperils the context through the performance of an unspeakable act. This is the site of the outrageous act, one that is outrageous not simply because it is improper but because in its impropriety it threatens the perceived coherence and legitimacy of the code it violates. Like charmed loops, subversive and strange loops thematize the relationship of the act to the context. That is, each focuses on the reflexive quality of the act in relationship to the context. The act in a charmed loop reinforces the coherence and legitimacy of the context; in a subversive loop the act reveals the impotency of the context; and in the strange loop the act constitutes a direct challenge to the legitimacy of the context.

Building upon the three-part scheme of Cronen, Johnson, and Lannaman (1982), Branham and Pearce (1985) formulate a fourth text-context relationship: contextual reconstruction. "Contextual reconstruction occurs," they write, "when a text occurs in but alters the expectations in which it is understood and evaluated" (Branham and Pearce, 1985, p. 29). They identify for each text-context relationship a quintessential means of coping with the apparent conflict between text and context. For charmed loops, it is conformity, for subversive loops, it is nonparticipation; for strange loops, it is desecration; and for the new relationship they identify, it is contextual reconstruction. *Contextual reconstruction* refers to a process wherein "a text occurs in but alters the expectations in which it is understood and evaluated" (Branham and Pearce, 1985, p. 29).

Although Pearce and Branbram (1985) mention several concrete ways contextual reconstruction is accomplished, communicatively, their special focus is self-reference in public address. They examine two historically prominent public addresses, Senator Edward Kennedy's "Television Satement to the People of Massachusetts" and President Abraham Lincoln's "Gettysburg Address." In each of these addresses, Pearce and Branham point out, the rhetor faced a difficult rhetorical situation, in that for him the situation was personally problematic. And in each the speaker used a kind of contextual reconstruction as the strategic means for acting effectively in the situation.

Kennedy faced a situation in which his listeners had been supplied information sufficient to judge him to be a person of bad character. At issue was Kennedy's actions in connection with the death by drowning of a young woman who was a passenger in a car Kennedy drove off a bridge. As a United States senator with presidential ambition, Kennedy's culpalility in the situation provided substantial evidence of a weakness in his character that would render him unfit for public office, at least in the minds of many citizens.

Pearce and Branham show how, through a series of linguistic maneuvers focused on those of his own acts that had led his character to become the subject of public criticism, Kennedy was able to reconstruct the definition of the context in which his acts were accountable. These maneuvers formed a rhetorical configuration of confession, self-labeling, contextual definitions, and retrospective moral posturing. In and through these acts, Branham and Pearce propose, Kennedy successfully (1) distanced his present persona from the one that performed the objectionable acts, (2) cast himself in the role of judge of his own objectionable actions, thus preempting that role for the listener and casting himself in the role of moralist, and (3) linguistically constructed a situation in which the listeners were invited to play the role of the forgiving person of the rhetor now addressing them. The context, a situation in which upright and courageous action were called for and in which a man of little virtue acted irresponsibly, had been redefined by Kennedy's text, or so Branham and Pearce propose, and it had been done through an artful use of self-referring tactics.

The principal contribution of the study is to suggest and explore the idea of contextual reconstruction and to set that process within the framework of the larger CMM framework of text-context relations. The study shows how Kennedy performed the art of contextual reconstruction. The study itself is not a detailed examination of the text or the context. It does not exemplify and illustrate the use of a generic system of categories for describing the rhetorical process of contextual reconstruction. But it does illustrate an important feature of the CMM program: the application and development of a framework of text-context relations, including (1) generating a new type of text-context relationship, that is, contextual reconstruction; (2) arraying a series of communicative strategies that are quintessentially linked with the various text-context relationships previously formulated; and (3) exploring the diagnostic and critical applications of the framework to cases.

A great deal of the CMM work that has been reviewed here, in this section and others, is descriptive in that the researchers have been concerned with examining the way things are in various human situations. From its outset, the CMM program has been concerned to develop a kind of activist style of research in which not only descriptions but diagnoses of and prescriptions for communicative conduct could be made. Once the basic tools for description and interpretation had been developed and applied, CMM researchers began to adopt an interventionist approach to their practice, particularly in the therapeutic context (see Cronen, Pearce, and Tomm, 1985; McNamee 1983, 1985; Tomm 1985). The text-context framework, and such uses of it as the study of contextual reconstruction, are wholly consistent with this interventionist, critique-oriented direction. The Kennedy study, for example, illustrates the inclination to ask not only what happened but how the resources of communicative action can be used to construct or reconfigure new social realities and new patterns of coordination. This direction has also been taken in a series of studies concerned with communication in situations characterized by incompatability and incommensurability across persons and groups (Branham and Pearce, 1987, is an example; see also Cronen, Chen, and Pearce, 1988).

Conclusions

In the preceding pages I have introduced CMM, identified some of its key assumptions, defined its key vocabulary, and reviewed a sample of representative research studies carried out in its name. As stated at the outset, this is a selective and partial view of a very broad and complex field of intellectual and practical action. Although much of the CMM program has not been essayed here, I believe the core of CMM has been encompassed. This leaves the task of assessment: How successful has this program been?

First, CMM researchers have succeeded in proposing a robust and powerful theory that enables them to explain observed patterns of coordination. It is robust in that their mode of explanation has been applied across a wide array of human situations, including intimate discussions, interactions in task-oriented organizations, intercultural contact and accomodation, and public discourse. It is powerful in that they have identfied precise conditions that are associated with various states of coordination. Specifically, they have shown that an individual's social reality is a powerful force in shaping the individual's acts and that an interperson order of social reality is a powerful force in shaping the ways the acts of interlocutors do or do not fit together in various coordination patterns.

The argument for the explanatory power of CMM rests on two things. One, CMM theorists have located and formulated precisely a generative mechanism for coordination: individual social realities placed in contact with each other, or what CMM calls the *order of social reality*. Two, CMM researchers have produced multiple experiments and case studies in which they have shown a strong empirical relationship between ccordination and either social reality or the order of social reality.

At the level of explanation there are limitations to the CMM record. The studies provide evidence that from approximately 30 to approximately 50 percent of the statistical variation in coordination or enmeshment is explained by the order in social reality or social reality. Cronen, Pearce, and Snavely (1979), is a case in point. It presents a ground-breaking application of rules theory to a strategy for explaining conversational structure. Specifically, it suggests that conversational structure, at least URPs, is determined by a complex product of forces ($A \times R \times F$), and the data in the study constitute strong statistical evidence for this relationship. But it is clearly an exploratory study, by the authors' own statement. Although approximately 50 percent of the variance in *enmeshment* is explained by *prefigurative force* variables, one would expect that prefigurative force would account for more than 50 percent because prefigurative force, as operationally defined in the study, is almost the same thing as enmeshment, as operationally defined in the study. Thus, although those of us enamored with a rules-based approach to explanation are forced to sit up and take notice of such results, the evidence as presented is not yet in a strong enough form to convince readers who do not share the basic premises of the CMM program that its approach provides the basis for explaining unwanted repetitive patterns or other patterns of social interaction. It might be that psychological, sociological, or cultural variables could produce just as strong a result independent of prefigurative force or other CMM variables—these other variables could add to the variance explained if they were incorporated into the measurement model. This is a state of affairs that runs throughout the program—it reads like a series of quick and exploratory studies that yield an enticing but not repeatedly and rigorously tested set of claims. This leaves one wondering, Is there evidence to support any of the generalizations proffered by CMM?

Second, CMM researchers have succeeded in developing an array of descriptive-diagnostic concepts that facilitate the examination of cases of communication, social reality, and coordination. They have produced and tested the utility of an original framework for characterizing various social realities, a framework of configurations or orders, of social reality, and a framework for characterizing various states of coordination. The evidence for their success is that they have drawn their initial frameworks from previously published frameworks and have then evaluated and extended these frameworks in and through the construction of case studies. Thus, in terms of each of the three parts of their overarching framework—social reality, order in social reality, and coordination—they have produced empirically based extensions of their descriptive framework. Of course, no part of the descriptive framework has been developed to any point of completion. In part, this is in the nature of an exploratory, ground breaking enterprise.

Although the basic concepts of coordination, social reality, and order in social reality are, for the most part, defined and developed in and through the program of research, the "communication" part is not well developed. In short, no theory or framework of discourse informs and guides the program. As a result, the reader is left asking whether the forms, contents, and styles of *communication* are very important in this theory. I take it for granted that they are. Certainly, the CMM researchers must also believe that is true. For one thing, the term *communication* runs throughout the writings of CMM. And in most CMM studies there is at least an implicit or a weakly developed framework for communicative action. In Branham and Pearce (1985), for example, there is discussion of how various rhetorical devices were used, but not much attention is given to the devices themselves and only in passing. Certainly, there is no implicit or explicit framework of rhetorical or communicative acts, such as is found in a variety of frameworks for describing the details of communicative conduct (for an example of what I mean by a systematic framework for categorizing communicative acts, see Stiles 1992). An early formulation of CMM (Pearce 1976) included a preliminary formulation for characterizing communicative acts as types of acts, but later and recent formulations do not address this theme (Cronen, Chen, and Pearse 1988, for example, is a recent summary statement of the program, and it makes no mention of a taxonomy or category scheme for communicative acts).

It is well and good to say, about a descriptive framework for communicative acts, that these should be elicited from the interlocutors being studied, and that, of course, is at the heart of the ethnographic study of communication. But for CMM it seems that a theory of discourse acts and strategies is crucial. This becomes particularly obvious when CMM researchers try to explain change in social realities or orders in social reality and when they propose to offer critical, liberating approaches to social life. It would seem that in such studies, that is, in explanations of change and in interventionist studies, it would be crucial to have a preformulated framework of discursive acts and strategies, because the communication part of the framework would supply the resources through which a process of change would be effected. At this time, the CMM framework provides no such formulation.

Third, over time the CMM theorists and researchers have modified their moral stance, in terms of what they believe to be the ideal end of human interaction. In an early CMM essay (Pearce, 1976) there is a clear endorsement of coordination as the fitting together of divergent actions into a pattern of harmonious interaction. I believe the CMM researchers would now say that this is a naive and limited perspective, one that ignores the injustice and cruelty that can be subsumed under the ideal of simply fitting lines of action together into an intelligible pattern (there is, for example, a harmony of sorts to some versions of slavery). The early view of "coordination" ignores, or at least slights, diversity, conflict, and difference. In the middle writings (Pearce and Cronen, 1980) there is a shift to an openness to embracing a variety of patterns of human interaction. In these middle writings, there is, in my view, a maturing of the teleological stance—an explicit acknowledgment that "coordination" may be a code word for repression and that many patterns of human interaction that do not fit neatly under some version of coordination should be acknowledged as morally legitimate and practically defensible. And the writings of the middle period emphasize an openness to the various configurations of social reality that might produce coordination. This is an advance over the simplistic notion that commensurate social realities is a moral and practical ideal.

In the later writings however, there is a shift to a clear and singular emphasis on "liberation" as the activity that "makes us distinctively human" and the ideal of human existence (Cronen, Chen, and Pearce, 1990, p. 77). This constitutes a shift from an essentially liberal, open, and pluralistic ideal, in the middle period, to one that celebrates "liberation" as the highest end of human life. The celebration of "liberation" seems, to me, to provide one, culture-bound ideological notion as the rationale for a theoretical program that, at one time, raised the possibility of a more open and exploratory stance. The middle stance left open the possibility that "coordination," "coherence," "tradition," and "preservation" can be argued to be among the goods of human social life (see Philipsen, 1992, Chapter 7, for a discussion of this issue), where in the later stance there is only "liberation." The question "Liberation from what?" is not answered, and I am left feeling that the "liberation" formulation is just as restrictive as the earlier, simplistic endorsement of "coordination."

In summary, although many of the principles, propositions, or generalizations of CMM research have yielded only modest results, in terms of the variance explained in particular studies, this has really not been the aim of CMM. These studies have been successful because they showed the possibility of certain kinds of investigation, description, explanation, and interpretation. One fundamental aim of CMM, from the start, has been to provide a working vocabulary for a new style of study in human communication and in the process to open up topics that had previously been left relatively closed or at least unattended. This has been accomplished, and impressively so. CMM has produced a series of theoretical treatises that essay human communication as an activity substantially driven by the social realities of those who engage in it, has provided a language for characterizing that process in general and for describing its operation in particular cases, has generated a series of empirical strudies that illustrate the application of the language and suggest the fruitfulness of its application, and has opened up the study of the variety of forms in which humans coordinate their interpersonal activity and the variety of ways that social realities impinge on human interaction. This is a remarkable achievement, and it is one of the reasons why CMM has attracted so many followers. Furthermore, it is one of the reasons why CMM should continue to provide the basis for a great deal of further research into the dynamics of human communication.

References

Bateson, G. (1972). *Steps to an ecology of mind*. New York: Ballantine Books.

Branham, R., and Pearce, W. B. (1985). "Between text and context: Toward a rhetoric of textual reconstruction." *Quarterly Journal of Speech* 71: 19–36.

——— (1987). "A contract for civility: Edward Kennedy's Lynchburg address." *The Quarterly Journal of Speech* 73:424–443.

Cronen, V., Chen, V., and Pearce, W. B. (1988). "Coordinated management of meaning: A critical theory." *International and Intercultural Communication Annual* 12: 66–98.

Cronen, V., Johnson, K., and Lannaman, J. (1982). "Paradoxes, double binds, and reflexive loops: An alternative theoretical perspective." *Family Process* 20: 91–112.

Cronen, V., Kaczka, E., Pearce, W. B., and Pawlik, M. (1978). "The structure of interpersonal rules for meaning and action." *Proceedings of the winter conference on simulation*. Washington, D.C.: National Bureau of Standards.

Cronen, V., Pearce, W. B., and Snavely, L. (1979). "A theory of rules structure and episode types, and a study of perceived enmeshment in unwanted repetitive patterns." In D. Nimmo (Ed.), *Communication yearbook III*. New Brunswick, N.J.: Transaction Books.

Cronen, V., Pearce, W. B., and Tomm, K. (1985). "A dialectical view of personal change." In K. Gergen and K. Kavis (Eds.), *The social construction of the person*, pp. 203–244. New York: Springer Verlag.

Delia, J. (1975). "The dependency of interpersonal evaluations on content-relevant beliefs about the other." *Communication Monographs* 42: 10–19.

Garfinkel, H. (1967). *Studies in ethnomethodology*. Englewood Cliffs, N. J.: Prentice-Hall.

Gumperz, J., and Hymes, D. (Eds.). (1972). *Directions in sociolinguistics: The ethnography of communication*. New York: Holt, Rinehart and Winston.

Harris, L. (1980). "The maintenance of a social reality: A family case study." *Family Process* 19: 19–33.

———— and Cronen, V. (1979). "A rules-based model for the analysis and evaluation of organizational communication." *Communication Quarterly* 27: 12–28.

———— Cronen, V., and McNamee, S. !1979). "An empirical case study of communication episodes." Paper presented to the National Council on Family Relations, Boston.

Hymes, D. (1962). "The ethnography of speaking." In T. Gladwin and W. C. Sturtevant (Eds.), *Anthropology and human behavior*, pp. 13–53. Washington, D.C.: Anthropological Society of Washington.

Johnson, K. (1979). "The effects of the structure of communication rules on persons' simulated conversations." Paper presented to the International Communication Association. Philadelphia.

Katriel, T., and Philipsen, G. (1981). " 'What we need is communication': 'Communication' as a cultural category in some American speech." *Communication Monographs* 48: 302–317.

McNamee, S. (1983). "Therapeutic change in family systems: A communication approach to the study of convoluted ineractive patterns." Unpublished doctoral dissertation, University of Massachusetts, Amherst.

———— (1985). "Theory and practice integration: Social change as research, clinical practice, and daily interaction." Paper presented to the Eastern Communication Association, Providence, R. I.

Nofsinger, R. (1976). "On answering questions indirectly: Some rules on the grammar of doing conversation." *Human Communication Research* 2: 172–181.

Pearce W. B. (1976). "The coordinated management of meaning: A rules-based, theory of interpersonal communication." In G. Miller (Ed.), *Explorations in interpersonal communication*, pp. 17–36. Beverly Hills, Calif.: Sage Publications.

———— and Conklin, F (1979). "A model of hierarchical meanings in coherent conversation and a study of 'indirect responses'." *Communication Monographs* 46: 75–87.

———— and Cronen, V. (1980). *Communication, action and meaning: The creation of social realities*. New York: Prager Publishing.

———— Cronen, V., Johnson, K., Jones, G., and Raymond, R. (1980). "The structure of communication rules and the form of conversation: An experimental simulation." *Western Journal of Speech Communication* 44: 20–34.

Philipsen, G. (1987). "The prospect for cultural communication." In D. Kincaid (Ed.), *Communication theory from Eastern and Western perspectives*, pp. 245–254. New York: Academic Press.

———— (1992). *Speaking culturally: Explorations in social communication*. Albany: State University of New York Press.

Saville-Troike, M. (1982). *The ethnography of communication: An introduction*. Oxford, England: Basil Blackwell.

Stiles, W. (1992). *Describing talk: A taxonomy of verbal response modes*. Newbury Park, Calif.: Sage Publications.

Straus, M. (1974). "Leveling, civility, and violence in the family." *Journal of Marriage and the Family* 36: 13–30.

Tomm, K. (1985). "Circular interviewing: A multifaceted clinical tools." In D. Campbell and R. Draper (Eds.), *Applications of systemic family therapy: The Milan method*, pp. 33–46. London: Academic Press.

Watzlawick, P., Beavin, K., and Jackson, D. (1967). *Pragmatics of human communication*. New York: W.W. Norton.

3

THE CONSTRUCTIVIST THEORY OF
DELIA, CLARK, AND ASSOCIATES

ANNE MAYDAN NICOTERA

Introduction

Constructivism is a theory of human communication, rooted in a particular perspective of human sensemaking and interpretive processes. Many scholars have developed the theory and applied it to research. Most notable among these scholars is Delia (1972, 1974, 1975, 1976a, 1976b, 1977a, 1977b, 1980). Others of note are the works of B. O'Keefe (1982), D. O'Keefe (1980), Applegate (1978), Kline (1978), Burleson (1980), Sypher (Sypher, Nightingale, Vielhaber, Sypher, 1981), Hale (1980), Clark (Clark and Delia, 1977), Jackson and Jacobs (1980), and Swanson (1982).

Constructivism is included in this book as an important theory of human communication because of its holistic approach. The theory is well-grounded in a set of philosophic assumptions, sets forth clearly organized theoretic claims, and has a rich tradition in research applications. Furthermore, these assumptions, claims, and applications of constructivism have important implications for research methodology. The theoretic tradition of constructivism aims at the development of a comprehensive theory of human communication.

The theory of constructivism rests on a specific set of epistemologic and metaphysical assumptions—assumptions about the nature of knowledge and the nature of reality, respectively. Within the parameters of these assumptions lies the substantive theory, composed of a set of theoretic claims about human interpretation, human action, human interaction, and human communication. These theoretic claims have been applied in a variety of research areas, many of which overlap considerably. The areas include listener-adapted communication, development, cognitive complexity, the organization of interaction, impression formation, message production, persuasion, and perspective taking. Moreover, constructivist research is guided by particular methodological choices relevant to the philosophy and substantive theory. This chapter shall discuss each of these things in turn, concluding with a summary and basic critique of the theory's arguments.

Arguments of Constructivism

The Philosophic Level: Constructivist Assumptions

The architects of constructivism have briefly laid out the philosophic assumptions that underlie and guide the substantive theory. At the philosophic level, Delia, O'Keefe, and O'Keefe (1982) make a distinction between a philosophy of science—assumptions about the nature of inquiry—and "philosophical anthropology"—assumptions about the nature of humans. In this argument (also articulated in Delia, 1977b; Delia and Grossberg, 1977; D. O'Keefe, 1975), the philosophy of science follows Suppe's (1971) *Weltanschauungen*. According to Polkinghorne (1983), the *Weltanschauungen* (or world outlooks) analysis is a skeptical response and a challenge to logical positivism. Logical positivism (also called *positivism, logical empiricism, empircism*, or the *received view*) is the view of all science (including human or social science) as a deductive, empirical, and objective process that will ultimately uncover covering laws and timeless truths about the phenomenon under study (for a detailed explanation of positivism, see D. O'Keefe, 1975). Unlike logical positivism, a *Weltanschauungen* perspective posits that "all knowledge is relative to one's perspective; there is no absolute point of view outside of one's historical and cultural situation" (Polkinghorne, 1983, p. 103). The *Weltanschauungen* position offers the insight that science is a human activity taking place in various historical contexts (Polkinghorne, 1983). To the constructivist, science is *not* a process of formal logic attaining timeless truths as logical positivist philosophy would argue, but rather a human activity of understanding and interpretation. Science is seen to make cognitive progress toward more accurate descriptions of reality (Polkinghorne, 1983). Epistemologically, then, constructivists must assume that knowledge is subjective and personal. Knowledge—including scientific knowledge—is a sense making process. Such knowledge is *socially created and maintained* and thus can be apprehended only by delving into the reality of individual human beings.

The constructivists' "philosophical anthropology"—their view of the nature of humans—also embraces an interpretive orientation. Humans are seen as engaging in active and ongoing processes of interpretation to cocreate social realities. Metaphysically, then, reality is equivalent to the experienced lifeworld. "Human experience involves a continuous lived relationship in which there is a unity of person and world, of knower and known. There are no 'pure facts' existing outside this lived experience" (Delia and Grossberg, 1977, p. 32). Thus, for the constructivist, there is no objective reality—in contrast to the positivist.

The positivist believes that reality is "out there," separate from the observer. The constructivist believes that the ground of objectivity is embedded in "historically developed standards of rationality operating within particular communities. . . . Fact, value, and meaning coexist within a complex, dense texture which is always occurring within an ongoing process of unabstracted interpretive understanding" (Delia and Grossberg, 1977, p. 33). This means that the constructivist assumes that reality is socially constructed and individually interpreted. According to constructivist philosophy, reality cannot be "out there"; reality *cannot exist* separate from human cognition. "All our knowledge of the world, in common-sense as well as in scientific thinking, involves constructs. . . . Strictly speaking, there are no such things as facts" (Delia and Grossberg, 1977, p. 33, quoting Schutz, 1971). Further, constructivists assume that humans act based on context-relevant interpretations and that humans are foremost interpretive beings. Reality is socially constructed in a creative and emergent interplay between the individual's interpretive process and the historically constituted contexts and processes of the community. Thus, the individual is confronted with a world that is already meaningful by virtue of the existing community's creation of reality. In the process of socialization the individual incorporates the community's universe of shared meaning, engages in an ongoing interpretation process, and accommodates to the social reality of the lifeworld (Delia and Grossberg, 1977).

The Theoretic Level: Constructivist Claims

Theoretical Bases. In addition to its philosophic underpinnings, constructivism is based upon several theoretical traditions, most notably Kelly's cognitive psychology, Werner's organismic-developmental orientation, and Blumer's sociocultural-interactionist perspective (Clark and Delia, 1979). Kelly (1955) provides a theoretic structure—the personal construct—that allows for a connection between interpretation and behavior. Personal constructs are the individual's mode of sensemaking. Individuals give their world structure and meaning by grouping events on the basis of their similarities and differences. Constructs are bipolar contrasts (e.g., tall-short) used for such grouping of events. Constructs are seen by constructivists as the most basic units of cognitive organization (Delia, O'Keefe, and O'Keefe, 1982).

Following the developmental theory of Werner (1948, 1957), the individual's system of constructs is seen as changing and developing with age and social experience (Delia, Kline, and Burleson, 1979). As this development occurs, constructs become more differentiated and hierarchically integrated (Delia, Clark, and Switzer, 1974; Delia, Kline, and Burleson, 1979; D. O'Keefe and Sypher, 1981). Constructs also shift from concrete (e.g., tall-short) to abstract (e.g., friendly-unfriendly), reflecting a corresponding shift in the individual's perception from physical appearances to more intangible general characteristics (Delia, Kline, and Burleson, 1979).

Blumer (1969) provides the sociocultural theoretic structure to which constructivists attach the developmental cognitive processes of individuals. To understand human communication from the constructivist view, "cognitive developments must not be divorced from the study of sociocultural understanding framing events of communication" (Clark and Delia, 1979, p. 189). The organization of interaction and communication is facilitated by both individual cognitive development and socioculturally shaped cognitive orientations. Such integration is intended to provide an understanding of how language structures (a subsystem of cultural structures) are integrated into cognitive structures (Clark and Delia, 1979). Again, through socialization the individual incorporates the community's universe of shared meaning, but at the same time she or he engages in an ongoing interpretation process (Delia and Grossberg, 1977). A constructivist approach is particularly interested in this interrelationship between culture and cognition (Clark and Delia, 1979).

These theoretical bases lead constructivists to a central concept—cognitive complexity. Before moving on to a discussion of the specific theoretical claims of constructivism, it is important to address this concept and its centrality to the constructivist approach. Construct systems vary in complexity; development entails increasing levels of complexity; and the interrelation of culture and cognition further contributes to complexity. Following Kelly, Crockett (1965) posits that a system of personal constructs governs each individual's perceptions. Further, an individual's system of interpersonal constructs constitutes a "cognitive template" that guides analysis and interpretation of others' actions. Following Werner's developmental view, the system of interpersonal constructs develops through interaction with others and the acquisition of socially shared interpretations of others' behavior. And so, according to Crockett, construct systems develop along a dimension of simplicity-complexity (Delia, Clark, and Switzer, 1974). "A cognitive system is 'considered relatively complex in structure when (a) it contains a relatively large number of elements [constructs] and (b) the elements are integrated hierarchically by relatively extensive bonds of relationship' " (Delia, Clark, and Switzer, 1974, p. 300, quoting Crockett, 1965, p. 49).

Theoretical Claims. From its philosophic and theoretic base, the substantive theory of constructivism is committed to several central theoretical claims. Delia, O'Keefe, and O'Keefe (1982), in their summary of the constructivist approach, classify these claims into four domains: claims about interpretive processes, claims about human action, claims about human interaction, and claims about human communication. For our purposes in summarizing the basic theoretical claims of constructivism, this same classification will be used. The summary of constructivism written by Delia,

O'Keefe, and O'Keefe (1982) is paraphrased heavily throughout the next section of this chapter.

First, in regard to *interpretive processes*, Delia and his associates view human beings as simultaneously biological and social entities (Delia, O'Keefe, and O'Keefe, 1982). Each individual's personal construct system guides his or her cognitive organization of experience; at the same time these cognitive orientations are socioculturally shaped (Delia and Grossberg, 1977). The operation of personal construct systems represents natural (biological) activity. "Through the application of cognitive schemes, experience is segmented into meaningful units and interpreted, beliefs about the world are created and integrated, and behavior is structured and controlled" (Delia, O'Keefe, and O'Keefe, 1982, p. 151).

Although constructs are seen as the most basic unit of cognitive organization, the most general units are termed *interpretive schemes*. Interpretive schemes, most generally, are any classification device used to make sense of the world.

> Classification of an object, persons, or event involves not only identification or recognition of same but also placement of the objects, person, or event in relation to kindred objects, persons, and events. Hence, every interpretive scheme simultaneously serves the functions of identification and placement. To take an object to *be* something is to simultaneously place it in regard to its functions, its routine occurrence, its expected operation or behavior, and its routine surroundings. (Delia, O'Keefe and O'Keefe, 1982, p. 151)

The example given is Sacks's (1972) illustration: "The baby cried. The mommy picked it up." These two sentences make up a coherent story because of the categorization-interpretation of the words *baby* and *mommy*. Both *baby* and *mommy* are interpreted with their routine surroundings and expected behaviors. Hence, the "story" makes sense within the interrelations of the interpretive schemes for babies and mommies.

Thus, according to Delia and his associates, an interpretive scheme provides more than mere categorization: an interpretive scheme places the event in a larger context of meaning and expectation. As construct systems become more abstract, interpretive schemes arise. Following Werner, the constructivist approach views interpretive processes as structural and developmental. Cognitive organization is a biological human process that organizes experience and guides activity. Constructivists further claim that the processes of interpretation and sense-making are nonconscious. Although individuals experience the world through cognitive representation, the cognitive processes of representation are beneath the individual's level of awareness (Delia and O'Keefe, 1977).

As argued by Delia and Grossberg (1977), humans are also social entities. When an individual enters a sociocultural community, whether by birth or otherwise, others in the community already share their own socially constructed interpretations. Individual perceivers interact in the social world to develop interpretive processes. From a constructivist viewpoint, then, culture is a historical process of sensemaking that provides preconstituted meaning and transcends individuals. Individual construct systems are integrated with socio-cultural meaning systems. In departure from Kelly, constructivists claim that individuals create their interpretive schemes mainly through "communication with and accommodation to the meaningful, pervasive, and enduring social world into which they are born" (Delia, O'Keefe, and O'Keefe, 1982, p. 155).

Interpretive schemes are then seen to produce context-relevant intentions and beliefs that guide *human action*, entering us into the second domain of theoretical commitment. By making situations meaningful, interpretive schemes also produce alternative lines of action through which intentions can be achieved. An actor chooses from among these alternative lines of action, applying one and making it concrete. This is termed a strategy, and multiple goals may require the enactment of multiple strategies. The term *strategy* does not imply cons-cious planning, but merely implies the tacitly employed methods for directing one's own behavior (Delia, O'Keefe, and O'Keefe, 1982).

The major implication of this view is that human action is always situated in a context and driven by context-relevant intentions and beliefs. Actions are emergent, because the unfolding situation is filtered through interpretive schemes and is reflected in the context-relevant beliefs that result from the application of interpretive schemes. Because intentions are future oriented, choice of strategy is dependent on the individual's predictions for the future, which are based on past experience—made meaningful through interpretive schemes. Human action functions as a test of those predictions and thus as a validation of interpretive schemes. "Present action permits validation or modification of interpretive schemes; future choices will reflect the success or failure of the present choice. In this way, every act collapses past, present, and future; and thus, every act emerges from a new past into a new future" (Delia, O'Keefe, and O'Keefe, 1982, p. 156).

This view of human action provides the base for the third domain of theoretic commitment—*human interaction*. "We see interaction as a process in which persons *coordinate* their respective lines of action through the application of shared schemes for the organization and interpretation of action" (Delia, O'Keefe, and O'Keefe, 1982, p. 156, emphasis added). For coordination of action, interpretive schemes are then classified into general and specific categories. The general category includes assumptions about social rules for interaction. These are assumptions that allow the individual to link general social rules to the particular unfolding interaction (e.g., appropriate turn-taking behavior in conversation).

The specific category includes interpretive schemes relevant for coordinating particular kinds of acts. Schemes in the specific category are referred to as *organizing schemes*; they allow coordination for a variety of interactional types, such as speech events (e.g., a staff meeting), adjacency pairs (e.g., question-answer), routine procedures for accomplishing tasks (e.g., family morning routines), and institutional behavior (e.g., ordering a meal in a restaurant). Organizing schemes operate within and depend upon on the more general interpretive schemes for social rules. Organizing schemes are beneath the level of full awareness, are necessarily social, and classify acts in relation to other acts. They are *coordination devices*. They allow each person to produce acts that have clear implications for the other's behavior, and they allow each to respond appropriately and coherently. Organizing schemes allow individuals to interpret the behavior of others and design their own actions. Finally, coordination of action is possible because individuals in a community share these general and specific interpretive schemes (Delia, O'Keefe, and O'Keefe, 1982).

The process is, however, much more complex than the simple application of rules because individuals do not possess precisely identical interpretive schemes. Individuals must coordinate their actions through the implicit negotiation of orderly schemes for interaction. This is a very important concept; social reality and social structure are created through this implicit negotiation and demonstration of compliance to an orderly scheme. Thus, the social definition of reality is ongoing. Individuals bring to social interaction their definitions of reality. Through the implicit negotiation of orderly schemes for interaction, shared social reality is created and extended. "This ongoing process of defining reality and creating social order is the life of a sociocultural community. . . . the continuing and historically emergent processes of human group life unfold through. . .everyday actions and interactions" (Delia, O'Keefe, and O'Keefe, 1982, pp. 158–159).

To summarize thus far, we have seen that humans interpret the world through the development and applications of personal constructs. These personal constructs are cognitively developed in the context of socialization into a preexisting set of meanings and interpretations. As constructs become more sophisticated, they merge to produce interpretive schemes. Interpretive schemes allow coordination of actions by providing general rules for social interaction and specific guidelines for particular situations (organizing schemes). To bridge differences in individual interpretive schemes, as individuals interact they coordinate their actions through implicit negotiation of orderly schemes. Such negotiation and its outcomes constitute the ongoing and emergent nature of social reality and social organization.

We shall now turn to the fourth domain of theoretical commitments, claims about *human communication*. Human communication is a specific category of human interaction. Delia and his associates define human communication as an interaction process in which communicative intentions are the focus of coordination. For their purposes, communicative intentions are the origin of communication; communicative intentions involve simply the expression of private states. In communication, then, the strategies of each individual are guided by one's own and others' expressions of internal states. Communication among persons is characterized by the intention of each to express, the recognition of such intentions, and the organization of action and interaction around these reciprocal intentions. Communication is not seen as synonymous with interpretation, action, or interaction. Rather, as a subset of interaction, communication is grounded in interpretation, involves coordination of action, and displays the processes of organized interaction. The fulfillment of a need for expression of internal states characterizes communication.

The Practical Level: Constructivist Research

Research Applications. Constructivist theory has been applied to a variety of research areas. These areas overlap considerably, and another list of constructivist research topics might use different categorizations. For example, Delia, O'Keefe, and O'Keefe (1982) list three very broad categories: interpersonal impressions, communicative strategies, and "other." Within these categories, they list several specific topics. All of the research topics addressed here could be subsumed under a basic approach investigating the role of social-cognitive processes in communication (Delia, O'Keefe, and O'Keefe, 1982) with particular emphasis on listener-adapted communication (D. O'Keefe, 1978). The purpose of this section is to acquaint the reader with a sampling of topics in which constructivist research has been conducted. This discussion is not intended as exhaustive or comprehensive literature review; the reader should not expect to find such treatment of constructivist research here. Rather, various topics to which constructivist theory has been applied will be generally discussed with an eye to characterizing the way each has been approached rather than describing the research efforts in full detail. The topics discussed here are communicative development, organization of interaction, impression formation, message production, persuasion, and perspective taking. Although this is by no means an exhaustive list, it represents the research topics most commonly studied by constructivists.

Constructivist research holds at its core the assumption that persons make sense of the world through systems of personal constructs. These construct systems are the basis for each individual's perceptions. As described earlier, actions are based on these perceptions. Thus, it can easily be seen that personal construct systems allow the organization of interaction, the formation of impressions about others, the production of messages, the strategic choices made in attempts to persuade, and the ability to develop and process multiple perspectives.

In constructivist research, the area of *communicative development* is the most fundamental and therefore might be considered the most important. As their construct systems develop, individuals become more cognitively complex. As already discussed, a basic tenet of the constructivist perspective is that each individual's system of constructs changes and develops with age and social experience (Delia, Kline, and Burleson, 1979). Understanding the operation and development of construct systems is thus intertwined with understanding the process of communicative development. The framework utilized in constructivist research on communicative development is discussed in full by Delia and O'Keefe (1979). Basically, constructivist research in this area has emphasized the centrality of cognitive development to communicative development (Applegate and Delia, 1980; Clark and Delia, 1979; Delia and Clark, 1977; Delia, Kline, and Burleson, 1979; Delia and O' Keefe, 1979).

The constructivist approach to development differs from stage theories of development (e.g., Piaget). In stage theories, behavior is seen simply as a reflection of the general stage of development. In the constructivist approach, behavior influences—and is influenced by—ongoing and situation-specific interpretations. The mode of interpretation is, of course, the personal construct system. As such, behavior involves the "progressive hierarchic integration of control over communication at the nonverbal, linguistic, sociocultural, and tactical/strategic levels" (Clark and Delia, 1979, p. 191). Development of the ability to integrate control over communication reflects construct development. As they develop, construct systems become more differentiated, hierarchically integrated, and abstract (Delia, Clark, and Switzer, 1974; Delia, Kline, and Burleson, 1979; D. O'Keefe and Sypher, 1981).

A constructivist approach to communicative development also involves a cultural view (Clark and Delia, 1979; Delia and B. O'Keefe, 1979). Simultaneous to the differentiation, integration, and abstraction of their construct systems, individuals acquire constructs from their socialization into the speech community. Cultural knowledge, or shared knowledge, is seen as a culturally shared system of constructs or dimensions for defining persons, situations, and events. Thus, "just as individuals develop systems of personal constructs that channel their behavior by providing expectations concerning particular events and situations, so individuals socialized within the same culture acquire similar constructs for organizing commonly recurring situations and classes of events" (Clark and Delia, 1979, p. 191).

Finally, a constructivist approach to communicative development entails an interactive view. As described previously, human interaction involves the coordination of actions between individuals. Interaction is thus governed by situationally emergent understandings (Clark and Delia, 1979; Delia and B. O'Keefe, 1979). These understandings reciprocally influence development of cognitive structures. The negotiation of order in interaction is a developmental process, and social reality is continually constructed and reconstructed through interaction.

Constructivist researchers have developed a theoretic framework specifically for application in investigations of such negotiation of order. This framework for the study of the *organization of interaction* is discussed in detail by B. O'Keefe, Delia, and D. O'Keefe (1980). This framework is intended as a reaction against traditional approaches to interaction analysis that examine sequences of acts mathematically by coding discrete acts and analyzing transition probabilities. The constructivist framework for interaction analysis is based on the constructivist interpretivist philosophy and on the tenet that organizing schemes allow the coordination of behavior.

This constructivist framework posits that the organization of interaction has five central characteristics (summarized here from B. O'Keefe, Delia, and D. O'Keefe, 1980). First, organization of interaction is schematic. Whereas traditional approaches to the organization of interaction examine simple sequential connections between acts, a constructivist view rests on the premise that acts are connected by their reference to preexisting organizing schemes. Organizing schemes are the abstract structures through which acts are interpreted as being connected.

Second, organization of interaction is local. No scheme universally connects one type of act to another. Rather, behavior is organized and interpreted according to the schemes that are specifically relevant to participants' understanding of the specific interaction event. Acts are organized by schemes relevant to the "local feature of the interaction, not in terms of some general relations among types of acts" (B. O'Keefe, Delia, and D. O'Keefe, 1980, p. 28). This local aspect of organization is understood in terms of the third characteristic, that organization of interaction is hierarchic. The schemes that organize a specific interactional segment are embedded within larger and more general schemes, which in turn are embedded in even more general schemes, and so on.

Fourth, organization of interaction is emergent. The process of coordinating action is not given in organizing schemes. Rather, organizing schemes merely provide procedures for interpreting and producing behavior. The coordination of that behavior is realized only through the actual process interaction. Hence, the fifth characteristic: that organization of interaction is an interactional achievement. As individuals successively fit together their lines of action within organizing schemes, they achieve an orderliness in their interaction. "Such orderliness is created through the active involvement of individuals in the coordination of behavior, in the interpretation of another's act through reference to some scheme, and through management of one's own conduct in reference to such schemes" (B. O'Keefe, Delia, and O'Keefe, 1980, p. 29).

The constructivist view of the organization of interaction is based on the basic interpretive philosophy and the constructivist focus on cognitive processes. Organization of interaction is based in part on interpretation of another's acts. Such interpretation is based not only on a set of organizing schemes, but also on each individual's perception of the other. Just as individuals base their general perceptions on construct systems, they base their perceptions of others on personal construct systems. In other words, other person perception is a specific case of an individual's perception of the world. Constructivist research has paid considerable attention to this process of *impression formation*—how individuals make sense of other persons (Delia, 1972, 1975; Delia, Clark, and Switzer, 1974; Delia, Crockett, Press, and O'Keefe, 1975; Delia, Gonyea, and Crockett, 1971; B. O'Keefe, Delia, and D. O'Keefe, 1977; see also Delia, O'Keefe, and O'Keefe, 1982, for a comprehensive list of research citations in this area of study).

The personal construct system is composed of interpretative subsystems. One type of subsystem is the interpersonal construct system, which is composed of constructs specifying the behavioral, interpersonal, and psychological characteristics of other persons—roles, personalities, habits, attitudes, values, intentions, beliefs, and emotions. In the constructivist view of impression formation, individuals construe the behavior of another as representing stable qualities of that other and infer links between constructs to produce impressions more elaborate than the information immediately available from the observed behavior. Impressions are thus reflective of the individual perceiver's interpersonal construct system (Delia, O'Keefe, and O'Keefe, 1982).

The interpersonal construct system is also seen as the mechanism that directs communicative choices. Hence, a great deal of constructivist research has investigated the processes of *message production* (Applegate, 1978, 1980a; Applegate and Delia, 1980; Burleson, 1980; Clark and Delia, 1979; Delia and B. O'Keefe, 1979; Hale, 1980; B. O'Keefe and Delia, 1982; D. O'Keefe and Sypher, 1987). In this vein of research, interpersonal construct systems are treated as the basis upon which persons develop repertoires of strategies from which they adapt their actions to fit their impressions of others. When situations are person oriented, interpersonal construct systems guide choices of action. Messages (strategies) are not produced merely by construct systems, however. Strategies are courses of action intended to fulfill particular goals (situated intentions); also, a repertoire of strategies builds as the individual perceives differences among persons and intentions. In the construction of this repertoire, the individual must assess likely responses to predict the likelihood of success of alternative courses of action. "Thus, the individual must represent the communications relevant differences and work out courses of action that will work predictably" (Delia, O'Keefe, and O'Keefe, 1982, p. 163). Moreover, cognitively complex individuals who perceive other persons and social situations multi-dimensionally, will design courses of action that simultaneously address multiple goals (D. O'Keefe and Sypher, 1987).

Constructivism has been widely applied in two overlapping areas of research that can be seen as subsets of message production research; these are *persuasion* (Clark and Delia, 1977; B. O'Keefe and Delia, 1979) and *perspective taking* (Clark and Delia, 1977; Hale and Delia, 1976). Persuasion is an instance of person-oriented communication, and perspective taking is part of the cognitive process individuals go through in predicting the success of their courses of action. Social perspective taking is the ability of the individual to represent the perspectives of others,

> to recognize and sustain the other's perspective on the situation in order to see how the other defines the situation (and thus, what code is appropriate), to see how the other expects the conversation to progress (and thus, what utterances and topics are appropriate), and to see how the other sees himself (and thus, what title or name is appropriate). . . . Not surprisingly considerable evidence has shown that the level of one's perspective-taking capacity directly mediates the developmental progression from egocentric to listener-adapted speech. (Hale and Delia, 1976, p. 196, parenthetical phrases in original)

Therefore, both persuasion and perspective taking are seen as developmental. "Developmental change in the interpersonal construct system is accompanied by an increased number and increasing sophistication of arguments and appeals in persuasive messages" (Delia, O'Keefe, and O'Keefe, 1982, p. 163). Also, cognitive complexity and construct quality (the abstractness and comprehensiveness of construct systems) are related to the level of perspective taking in persuasive message strategies of children, adolescents, and adults (Clark and Delia, 1977; Delia and Clark, 1977; Delia, Kline, and Burleson, 1979; B. O'Keefe and Delia, 1979). Construct quality, cognitive complexity, and perspective-taking ability are positively related to strategic adaptation of persuasive messages—a key factor in persuasive skill (Clark and Delia, 1977; B. O'Keefe and Delia, 1979).

Research Methodology. Constructivist philosophy has important implications for methodological choices. The philosophic assumptions lead to a particular definition of the research process and to particular aims and attitudes of researchers. The Weltanschauungen philosophy of science posits that research is a human activity taking place in various historical contexts. "All knowledge is [seen as] relative to one's perspective" (Polkinghorne, 1983, p. 103). This viewpoint has two important implications. First, "research [must] be accompanied by reflective analysis of the implicit assumptions and ordering principles underlying research questions and methods" (Delia, B. O'Keefe, and D. O'Keefe, 1982, p. 167). Constructivist philosophy posits that an empirical world does exist and can be learned about, but that the process of learning about it cannot be independent of the interpretive framework employed. Because the research process is so highly dependent on the theoretical perspective, the perspective (assumptions and ordering principles) must be continually reflected upon. Delia, O'Keefe, and O'Keefe (1982) call this process *reflective empiricism*. *Research* is defined as a process aimed at understanding and interpretation.

Second, research must be well-grounded in a carefully constructed theoretic framework. Constructivists pay considerable attention to building frameworks that specify their general theoretic claims to the particular phenomenon of interest. Research is then conducted within these frameworks. For example, constructivist researchers have carefully laid out frameworks for the study of communicative development (Delia and O'Keefe, 1979) and the organization of interaction (B. O'Keefe, Delia, and D. O'Keefe, 1980). These frameworks are intended to guide research that can, in turn, extend the scope and precision of the theoretical framework. The very aim of constructivist research is to systematically extend, elaborate, and defend a theoretical framework (D. O'Keefe, 1975). The *Weltanschauungen* philosophy defines *research* as a process of continual progression toward more accurate *descriptions of reality.* "The task of the social scientist is that of providing progressively broader and more precise accounts of the social world" (Delia, O'Keefe, and O'Keefe, 1982, p. 168). Constructivist research must be programmatic because "theory must be systematically challenged through empirical research, for it is in the confrontation with the empirical world that a theory's ability to illuminate communication can be most directly assessed" (Delia, O'Keefe, and O'Keefe, 1982, p. 170).

The constructivist call for programmatic research conducted within a well-developed theoretic framework is specifically intended as a criticism of the tradition of variable analytic research. Variable analytic research is not necessarily atheoretic. However, constructivists criticize such research as fragmented because it does not begin with a unified set of assumptions. "Different theoretic frames typically serve to generate the conceptualization and measurement of each variable, while still other considerations lead to their hypothesized interrelations" (Delia, 1977b, p. 74). In addition, still other theoretic frames are often employed in the interpretation of results (Delia, 1977b; Delia, O'Keefe, and O'Keefe, 1982).

Another constructivist criticism of the variable analytic tradition is that, even when researchers accomplish one investigation within a unified framework, they jump to another framework with each successive research effort. Their philosophy leads constructivists to the following claim: "Only a full-fledged commitment to a particular theory is likely to produce research that shows both the limitations and the generality of a given framework. . . .One will never be sure of the genuine limitations of any particular theory [if] no effort [is] made to push the theory as far as it will go" (Delia, O'Keefe, and O'Keefe, 1982, p. 169). For the same reason, constructivists claim that even when single investigations adhere to internally consistent frameworks, variable analytic research cannot possibly result in a comprehensive account of communication offering insight into a broad range of communication phenomena. Constructivist research has at least the potential for doing so. If it is at all possible to achieve such a goal, constructivists claim convincingly that their approach to theory and research can achieve it.

Constructivist researchers are also philosophically obligated in their choices of techniques for measurement, data collection, and data analysis. First, measurement choices must be made with particular attention to their appropriateness for the nature of the research question and the phenomenon under study. Constructivists object to overreliance on standard psychometric instruments (Delia, O'Keefe, and O'Keefe, 1982). Constructivist research has used this type of measurement only when it is appropriate to the research question and phenomenon (e.g., Delia, Crockett, Press, and O'Keefe, 1975). Constructivist research has also used traditional experimental manipulation (e.g., Delia and Crockett, 1973; Press, Crockett, and Rosencrantz, 1969), as well as role playing, interviews, and interaction analysis (e.g., Delia, Clark, and Switzer, 1979). Other research has used more interpretive methods, such as naturalistic observation (e.g., Clark, 1980; Taylor, 1977) and ethnographlc analysis (Applegate, 1980b).

Second, constructivists call for the employment of free response data collection techniques. Any technique of data collection necessarily introduces a structure to the data. "Thus, the issue is not whether to introduce structure, but how much to introduce, when to introduce it," and the reasons for its introduction (Delia, O'Keefe, and O'Keefe, 1982, p. 172). The primary concern of constructivist research is to discover and understand persons' natural cognitive structures. Therefore, the choice is often to introduce structure to the data after it is collected, to introduce only as much as is necessary to answer the relevant research question, and to introduce it for the express purpose of abstracting the naturally occurring structure of the phenomenon of interest. The emphasis is upon data collection techniques, specifically free response, that "facilitate an understanding of the pregiven natural structure of the social world" (p. 172). Free response data (such as a list of attributes of a peer) are then subjected to theoretic analysis to uncover the subject's cognitive processes. For example, a respondent might be asked to list everything he or she knows about a peer; this list is then subjected to analysis that reveals the respondent's interpersonal construct system. Codes can then be assigned for cognitive complexity and construct quality. Respondents are not asked to be reflective or theoretically analyze their own construct systems. Such questions would be inappropriate because the personal construct system is assumed to exist at the nonconscious level. However, because the personal construct system is assumed to produce communicative behaviors, free response techniques are assumed to reveal these nonconscious processes (Delia, O'Keefe, and O'Keefe, 1982).

Such reliance on free response data necessitates sophisticated theoretically based schemes for data analysis. Analysis of free response data presents the challenge of conducting analyses that are theoretically rich and able to illuminate important features of human communication. Often, analysis of free response data concentrates too much on surface level features, overlooking the potential for analysis that can provide deeper understanding and explanation of underlying processes of human communicative behavior. Delia, O'Keefe, and O'Keefe (1982) discuss this method and its implications in great detail.

Finally, constructivists call for triangulated research. This means that phenomena should be studied under diverse conditions and with a variety of methodologies. Any research methodology necessarily makes some processes inaccessible, even as it illuminates others. The application of a variety of methodologies, therefore, allows a more well-rounded view of a phenomenon. When such practice is accompanied by a consistent philosophic and theoretic frame, such as constructivism, the potential for a rich understanding and explanation of a broad range of communicative phenomena can be maximized.

Conclusion and Some Criticism

The constructivist perspective is philosophically and theoretically well-grounded. Research stemming from the general theoretic frame has generally been methodologically rigorous and programmatically sound. Still, constructivism has been criticized from many directions. To provide an appropriate frame for understanding this criticism, the basic limits of the theory must be reiterated. Central to constructivist assumptions is a *cognitively based* view of meaning. Other theories reviewed in this collection have distinctly different views of meaning. For Phillipsen, meaning is *behaviorally based*; whereas for Cushman, meaning is *interactively based*. Each view has distinct strengths and weaknesses. A *behavioral* view of meaning has the advantage of positing a direct relationship between what individuals say and what they do; yet from such a view we cannot be sure how individual interpretations are linked to behaviors. A major strength of an *interactive* view of meaning is that shared meanings are central to the interpretation of messages. However, such a view offers no insight into individual meanings. The constructivist approach to meaning as a *cognitive* and individually based phenomenon does offer understanding of individual interpretations and how they develop. Like the other approaches, however, this individually based view has its weakness. Research shows that individuals do not consistently act based on their individual meanings. The constructivist view, therefore, cannot reliably link individual interpretations to behavior.

Constructivism's theoretical purview is limited to a focus on the cognitive interpretation of individuals. It is important to note this boundary when considering the criticisms that have been leveled against the theory. Every viewpoint illuminates some aspects of a phenomenon in a unique way but is unavoidably unable to see other things about the phenomenon. The benefits of a consistent philosophic and theoretic frame far outweigh this limitation. The confines of the theoretic purview are clearly spelled out in Delia's explanations of constructivism's philosophic and theoretic assumptions. The limits on constructivism's focus must be kept in mind when considering the criticisms that follow.

One of the most common criticisms is that the assumption of the existence of cognitive structures is neither verifiable nor falsifiable. A commonly used analogy is the claim that a creature lives in the refrigerator who runs to turn out the light when the door is closed. The catch is that this creature appears only when no one can see it. One can neither prove that the creature exists nor that it does not exist. The observation of another mechanism that turns out the light does not preclude the theory that when you cannot see it, the creature turns out the light.

Constructivist theory posits that personal constructs drive our perceptions, actions, interactions, and communication. Yet personal constructs are not observable. They are not even observable to the individual himself or herself, because they are assumed to operate at the nonconscious level. Constructivist theory rests on the assumption that external behaviors, from interaction with others to paper and pencil responses, are systematically reflective of internal processes. Critics who reject this assumption must necessarily reject the theoretic whole. The criticism, therefore, is generally not a criticism of the theory itself, but rather of the explicit assumption that highly structured cognitive processes exist and the implicit assumption that they are manifested in behavior.

Another criticism is aimed at an inconsistency in constructivist writings. In a discussion of constructivist research, an explicit assumption that such cognitive processes exist is clearly stated: *"There is an empirical world to be learned about,* even though what is learned is never wholly independent of the interpretive frameworks employed" (Delia, O'Keefe, and O'Keefe, 1982, p. 167, emphasis added). This is in direct contradiction to the set of constructivist philosophic claims articulated by Delia and Grossberg (1977) and elsewhere (Delia, 1977a, 1977b; and even in the first pages of Delia, O'Keefe, and O'Keefe, 1982). The following quotes are from Delia and Grossberg (1977), and all emphasis is added. "The *ground of objectivity is shifted from* questions concerning the correspondence of descriptions and *reality*...to questions of historically developed standards of rationality" (p. 33). "There *are no 'pure facts'* existing outside...lived experience" (p. 32). *"Fact*, value, and meaning coexist within a complex, dense texture which is always occurring within an ongoing process of *unabstracted interpretive understanding"* (p. 33). "All our knowledge of the world, in common-sense as *well as in scientific thinking*, involves constructs. ...Strictly speaking, *there are no such things as facts*" (p. 33, quoting Schutz, 1971). "All science, including the study of communication, is rooted in the life-world" (p. 34). Delia and Grossberg (1977) go on to explain how evidence for scientific abstractions for the life world must stem from the meaningfulness of the phenomenon for the actors in the life world.

Criticism of these assumptions stems from two directions. First, the ground for evidence of this set of assumptions (Delia and Grossberg, 1977) is rooted in the assumptions themselves, making the argument tautological. Second, it is difficult to reconcile the set of assumptions articulated by Delia and Grossberg (1977) and elsewhere (e.g., Delia, 1977a, 1977b; and even in Delia, O'Keefe, and O'Keefe, 1982) with Delia, O'Keefe and O'Keefe's (1982) claim that an empirical reality exists, even though as scientists we can never know it independent of our interpretations. Constructivist research has been criticized because of this internal contradiction. Research has operated under a methodological assumption that reality exists separate from interpretation, even though it cannot be apprehended without interpretation. However, at the philosophic level, constructivists have clearly stated the assumption that reality is *not separate from* interpretation. As such, "pure fact" is distinguished from "interpreted fact," and the inconsistency can be explained.

Another criticism of internal inconsistency points to the type of reasoning utilized at different levels of abstraction. Although the philosophy underlying the theory is interpretive suggesting an inductive viewpoint, the substantive theoretic claims are highly linear and deterministic. An inductive philosophy is paired with a deductive theory; this combination is then followed by research that advocates that methods be chosen from either way of thinking, provided the method is appropriate to the specific research question and phenomenon of interest.

Criticism of this practice stems from a traditional view of social science research. Indeed, the arguments of constructivism represent one of the first bodies of argument against strict positivistic thinking. Constructivism implicitly recognizes that social science research need not be a purely positivistic enterprise to be rigorous. At the time that constructivism was first articulated, the field of communication was locked in a fierce debate over philosophic and methodologic choices. Postpositivist arguments held that deductivism and the search for generalizable covering laws be rejected entirely. Inductive research aimed at building specific theory was advocated instead. As the field matured, however, the recognition was reached that either approach was acceptable, provided that it was appropriate to the research question and phenomenon under study.

Constructivist writers may have been the first to take this one step further—to argue that either approach is acceptable, *even within a single research program*. Daniels and Frandsen (1984) later articulated this approach as a neo-positivistic philosophy, which claims that nomothetic-inductivism is a valid approach to social science research. Nomothetic-inductivism advocates a combination of inductive and deductive approaches, such that research is conducted inductively to build theory that might then evolve into generalizable set of principles.

Positivism begins with hypotheses deduced from covering laws and seeks to validate the hypotheses and thus the theory. Postpositivism begins with theory-free observation aimed at building theory specific to and not generalized beyond the particular event observed. Neopositivism begins with theoretically guided observation, seeking to inductively derive a theory that builds to a general explanation of the phenomenon represented by the specific events observed. The constructivist perspective seems to represent this latter approach. The philosophy guides the substantive theory, which guides the construction of a specific theoretic framework for a particular phenomenon, which in turn guides the research effort to understand that phenomenon. The research process then is intended to extend the scope and precision of the theoretical framework. Research is thus conducted with the simultaneous purposes of defending and refining the theory (D. O'Keefe, 1975). The philosophy, theory, and methodological recommendations of constructivism are well-suited to such an attempt. The judgment as to whether constructivist research has accomplished its aims must be the subject of intense analysis of its literature.

References

Applegate, J. L. (1978). "Four investigations of the relationship between social cognitive development and person-centered regulative and interpersonal communication." Doctoral dissertation, Universtty of Illinois at Urbana-Champaign.

———— (1980a). "Adaptive communication in educational contexts: A study of teachers' communicative strategies." *Communication Education* 29: 158–170.

———— (1980b). "Person- and position-centered communication in a day care center." In N. K. Denzin (Ed.), *Studies in symbolic interaction*, vol. 3. Greenwich, Conn.: JAI Press.

———— and Delia, J. G. (1980). "Person-centered speech, psychological development, and the contexts of language usage." In R. St. Clair and H. Giles (Eds.), *The social and psychological contexts of language.* Hillsdale, N. J.: Lawrence Erlbaum and Associates.

Blumer, H. (1969). *Symbolic interactionism: Perspective and method.* Englewood Cliffs, N. J.: Prentice-Hall.

Burleson, B. R. (1980). "Develonmental and individual differences in comfort intended message strategies: Four empirical investigations." Doctoral dissertation, University of Illinois at Urbana-Champaign.

Clark, R. A. (1980). "Single word usage: Two stages?" *Central States Speech Journal* 31: 75–84.

———— and Delia, J. G. (1977). "Cognitive complexity, social perspective-taking, and functional persuasive skills in second- to ninth-grade children." *Human Communication Research* 3: 128–134.

———— and Delia, J. G. (1979). *Topoi and rhetorical competence. Quarterly Journal of Speech* 65: 187–206.

Crockett, W. H. (1965). "Cognitive complexity and impression formation. In B. A. Maher (Ed.), *Progress in experimental personality research, II.* New York: Academic Press.

Daniels, T. D., and Frandsen, K. D. (1984). "Conventional social science inquiry in human communication: Theory and practice." *Quarterly Journal of Speech* 70: 223–240.

Delia, J. G. (1972). "Dialects and the effects of stereotypes on interpersonal attraction and cognitive processes in impression formation." *Quarterly Journal of Speech* 58: 285–297.

———— (1974). "Attitude toward the disclosure of self-attributions and the complexity of interpersonal constructs." *Quarterly Journal of Speech* 41: 119–126.

———— (1975). "Regional dialect, message acceptance, and perceptions of the speaker." *Central States Speech Journal* 26: 188–194.

———— (1976a). "A constructivist analysis of the concept of credibility." *Quarterly Journal of Speech* 62: 361–375.

———— (1976b). "Change of meaning processes in impression formation." *Communication Monographs* 43: 142–157.

———— (1977a). "Alternative perspectives for the study of human communication: Critique and response." *Communication Quarterly* 25: 46–62.

———— (1977b). "Constructivism and the study of human communication." *Quarterly Journal of Speech* 63: 66–83.

—— (1980). "Some tentative thoughts concerning the study of interpersonal relationships and their development." *Western Journal of Speech Communication* 44: 97–103.

—— and Clark, R. A. (1977). "Cognitive complexity, social perception and the development of listener-adapted communication in six-, eight-, and twelve-year-old boys." *Communication Monographs* 44: 326–345.

—— Clark, R. A., and Switzer, D. E. (1974). "Cognitive complexity and impression formation in informal social interaction." *Speech Monographs* 41: 299–308.

—— Clark, R. A., and Switzer, D. E. (1979). "The content of informal conversation as a function of interactants' interpersonal cognitive complexity." *Communication Monographs* 46: 274–281.

—— and Crockett, W. H. (1973). "Social schemas, cognitive complexity, and the learning of social structures." *Journal of Personality* 41: 413–429.

—— Crockett, W. H., Press, A. N., and O'Keefe, D. J. (1975). "The dependency of interpersonal evaluation on context-relevant beliefs about the other." *Speech Monographs* 42: 10–19.

—— Gonyea, A. H., and Crockett, W. H. (1971). "The effects of subject-generated and normative constructs upon the formation of impressions." *British Journal of Social and Clinical Psychology* 10: 301–305.

—— and Grossberg, L. (1977). "Interpretation and evidence." *Western Journal of Speech Communication* 41: 32–42.

—— Kline, S. L., and Burleson, B. R. (1979). "The development of persuasive communication strategies in kindergartners through twelfth-graders." *Communication Monographs* 46: 242–256.

—— and O'Keefe, B. J. (1979). "Constructivism: The development of communication in children." In E. Wartella (Ed.), *Children Communicating*. Beverly Hills, Calif.: Sage Publications.

—— O'Keefe, B. J., and O'Keefe, D. J. (1982). "The constructivist approach to communication." In F. E. X. Dance (Ed.), *Human Communication Theory*, pp. 147–191. New York: Harper and Row.

—— and O'Keefe, D. J. (1977). "The relation of theory and analysis in explanations of belief salience: Conditioning, displacement, and constructivist accounts." *Communication Monographs* 44: 166–169.

Hale, C. L. (1980). "Cognitive complexity-simplicity as a determinant of communication effectiveness." *Communication Monographs* 47: 304–311.

—— and Delia, J. G. (1976). "Cognitive complexity and social perspective-taking." *Communication Monographs* 43: 195–203.

Jackson, S. A., and Jacobs, C. S. (1980). "The organization of argument in conversation: Pragmatic bases for the enthymeme." *Quarterly Journal of Speech* 66: 251–265.

Kelly, G. A. (1955). *The psychology of personal constructs*, 2d ed. New York: W. W. Norton.

Kline, S. L. (1978). "The effect of construct system development upon the situational variability of construct repertory grid ratings." Doctoral dissertation, University of Illinois at Urbana-Champaign.

O'Keefe, B. J. (1982). "Language and symbol in human life." In W. D. Brooks and D. L. Swanson (Eds.), *Speech communication: Selected readings*. Dubuque, Iowa: Wm. C. Brown.

——— and Delia, J. G. (1979). "Construct comprehensiveness and cognitive complexity as predictors of the number and strategic adaptation of arguments and appeals in a persuasive message." *Communication Monographs* 46: 231–240.

——— and Delia, J. G. (1982). "Impression formation and message production." In M. E. Roloff and C. R. Berger (Eds.), *Social cognition and communication*, pp. 33–72. Beverly Hills. Calif.: Sage Publications.

——— Delia, J. G., and O'Keefe, D. J. (1977). "Construct individuality, cognitive complexity, and the formation and remembering of interpersonal impressions." *Social Behavior and Personality* 5: 229–240.

——— Delia, J. G., and O'Keefe, D. J. (1980). "Interaction analysis and the analysis of interactional organization." In N. K. Denzin (Ed.), *Studies in symbolic interaction: A research annual*, vol. 3, pp. 25–71. Greenwich, Conn.: JAI Press.

O'Keefe, D. J. (1975). "Logical empiricism and the study of human communication." *Speech Monographs* 42: 169–183.

——— (1978). "Constructivism and its philosophical foundations." Paper presented at the annual meeting of the Speech Communication Association, Minneapolis.

——— (1980). "The relationship of attitudes and behavior: A constructivist analysis." In D. P. Cushman and D. McPhee (Eds.), *The message-attitude-behavior relationship: Theory, methodology, and application*. New York: Academic Press.

——— and Sypher, H. E. (1987). "Cognitive complexity measures and the relationship of cognition to communication." *Human Communication Research* 8: 72–92.

Polkinghorne, D. (1983). *Methodology for the human sciences: Systems of inquiry*. Albany: State University of New York Press.

Press, A. N., Crockett, W. H., and Rosencrantz, P. S. (1969). "Cognitive complexity and the learning of balanced and unbalanced social structures." *Journal of Personality* 37: 541–553.

Sacks, H. (1972). "On the analyzability of stories by children." In J. J. Gumperz and D. Hymes (Eds.), *Directions in sociolinguistics*. New York: Holt, Rinehart and Winston.

Schutz, A. (1971). *Collected papers*, Volume 1: *The problems of social reality*, ed. M. Natanson. The Hague: Martinus Nijhoff.

Suppe, F. (1977). "The search for philosophic understanding of scientific theories." In F. Suppe (Ed.), *The structure of scientific theories*. Urbana: University of Illinois Press.

Swanson, D. L. (1982). "A constructivist approach to political communication." In D. Nimmo and K. R. Sanders (Eds.), *Handbook of political communication*. Beverly Hill, Calif.: Sage Publlications.

Sypher, H. E., Nightingale, J., Vielhaber, M., and Sypher, B. D. (1981). "The interpersonal constructs of Machiavellians: A preliminary report." *British Journal of Social Psychology* 20: 155–156.

Taylor, S. A. (1977). "The acquisition of the roles of conversation: A structural-developmental perspective and methodological comparison." Doctoral dissertation, University Illinois at Urbana-Champagne.

Werner, H. (1948). *Comparative psychology of mental development*, rev. ed. New York: Follett Books.

———— (1957). "The concept of development from a comparative and organismic point of view." In D. B. Harris (Ed.), *The concept of development*. Minneapolis: University of Minnesota Press.

4

THE UNCERTAINTY REDUCTION AND ANXIETY-UNCERTAINTY REDUCTION THEORIES OF BERGER, GUDYKUNST, AND ASSOCIATES

WILLIAM GUDYKUNST

Uncertainty reduction theory (URT) was developed originally by Charles Berger and his colleagues to explain communication in initial interactions (Berger and Calabrese, 1975). It has been expanded systematically to romantic relationships (Parks and Adelman, 1983) and other developed relationships (e.g., acquaintances and friendships; Gudykunst, Yang, and Nishida, 1985).[1] URT is one of the few theories to have been tested across cultures (e.g., Gudykunst and Nishida, 1986; Gudykunst et al., 1985). It also has been extended from relationships between members of the same culture and ethnic group to include relationships between people from different cultures and ethnic groups (e.g., Gudykunst, 1985). URT is used by a wide variety of scholars[2] and to explain communication across different contexts.[3]

In extending URT to explain interpersonal and intergroup relationships, modifications are necessary. To illustrate, one of the major factors influencing intergroup communication in the United States is the amount of anxiety that individuals experience. Anxiety, however, also is present to some degree when people from the same group communicate. Gudykunst (1988, 1993, in press), therefore, incorporates anxiety as the affective equivalent of cognitive uncertainty in his extension of URT. Gudykunst's theory is referred to as *anxiety-uncertainty management* (AUM) theory.[4]

My goal in this chapter is to outline URT and AUM. It is impossible to present all of the nuances of both theories in a chapter like this. I, therefore, focus on the major trends in the development of the two theories. The way that I present the two theories is slightly different. This is due, in part, to the state of development of the theories (e.g., URT is more fully developed than AUM) and, in part, to the goals of the two theories (e.g., AUM is designed to help individuals improve the quality of their communication, URT is not). Because URT provides the foundation for AUM, I begin with URT.

Uncertainty Reduction Theory

My purpose in this section is to outline the current status of URT. I begin by outlining the original version of the theory. Next, I look at major extensions of the theory. I conclude the discussion of URT by looking at the major criticisms of the theory.

Original Theory

Berger and Calabrese (1975) assume that the primary concern anytime individuals meet someone new is uncertainty reduction. In response to critics who argued that individuals do not always try to reduce uncertainty, Berger (1979) modifies this position, arguing that individuals try to reduce uncertainty when strangers will be encountered in the future, provide rewards, or behave in a deviant fashion. It is important to recognize, however, that individuals may not be conscious of their attempts to reduce uncertainty. To explain URT, I begin by looking at how uncertainty is defined, then I present the axioms and theorems in the theory. Following this, I briefly summarize tests of the theory.

Defining Uncertainty. Berger and Calabrese (1975) isolate two distinct types of uncertainty present in initial interactions with strangers.[5] First, predictive uncertainty is the uncertainty individuals have about predicting others' attitudes, feelings, beliefs, values, and behavior.[6] Individuals need to be able, for example, to predict which of several alternative behavior patterns strangers will choose to employ. The second type of uncertainty is explanatory uncertainty, the uncertainty individuals have about explanations of others' attitudes, feelings, thoughts, and behavior.[7] Whenever individuals try to figure out why others behave the way they do, the individuals are engaging in explanatory uncertainty reduction. The problem being addressed is one of reducing the number of possible explanations for the others' behavior. This is necessary if individuals are to understand others' behavior and, thus, be able to increase the ability to predict their behavior in the future.

Berger (1979) also differentiates between cognitive uncertainty and behavioral uncertainty. Cognitive uncertainty involves individuals' knowledge about others, whereas behavioral uncertainty involves the degree to which individuals are relatively certain that others will behave in a predictable way. The differences between the two types of uncertainty are illustrated in initial interactions with strangers. In interacting with strangers, individuals have cognitive uncertainty about strangers but they may possess sufficient behavioral certainty to interact effectively because of the scripts that guide initial interactions with strangers.

Scripts are "a coherent sequence of events expected by the individual involving him [or her] either as a participant or observer" (Abelson, 1976, p. 33).

Baxter and Wilmot (1984) and Duck and Miell (1986) argue that individuals not only experience uncertainty regarding others as individuals, they also experience uncertainty about their relationships with others. Relationship uncertainty involves uncertainty about the nature of the relationships individuals have with others. Duck and Miell, for example, point out that "the development of friendships is rather an uncertain, nonlinear (fluctuating), speculative business rather than the automatic, linear, and straightforward process. . . . For this reason, subjects appear to give considerable thought to strategic control of relationships and strive to correct the feelings that they do not know where they are going" (p. 141).

Gudykunst and Nishida (1986) contend that the nature of uncertainty with which individuals are concerned varies across cultures. To illustrate these differences is necessary to look at how cultures differ. Cultures differ in terms of the emphasis placed on individualism or collectivism (see Triandis, 1988, for a review). In individualistic cultures, individuals' goals take precedence over group goals, and individuals develop relationships with others by gathering information about them as individuals. Individuals tend to communicate in a direct fashion in individualistic cultures. In collectivistic cultures, group goals take precedence over individual goals, and individuals get to know others initially by understanding their group memberships. Individuals tend to communicate in an indirect fashion in collectivistic cultures to maintain harmony in the in-group.

Gudykunst and Nishida (1986) point out that individuals use direct communication to reduce uncertainty in individualistic cultures like the United States. This reguires gathering information about others' attitudes, values, beliefs, and behavior. The type of information used to reduce uncertainty, therefore, is person based. In collectivistic cultures (e.g., Japan where the study was conducted) individuals use indirect communication to gather information to reduce uncertainty. To reduce uncertainty in collectivistic cultures, individuals need to know whether others are members of their in-groups and whether others are of the same status or higher or lower in status than they. The type of information used to reduce uncertainty, therefore, is group based. Gudykunst and Nishida (1986) argue that both types of uncertainty exist in all cultures, but one predominates.

Axioms and Theorems. Berger and Calabrese (1975) argue that individuals try to reduce uncertainty about others in initial interactions. They isolate seven variables linked to reducing uncertainty. First, the greater is the amount of verbal communication, the more uncertainty can be reduced (Axiom 1; the formal axioms are presented in Table 4.1). Second, the greater is the nonverbal expression

TABLE 4.1

Summary of Berger and Calabrese's (1975) URT

Axioms

1. Given the high level of uncertainty present at the onset of the entry phase, as the amount of verbal communication between strangers increases, the level of uncertainty for each interactant in the relationship will decrease. As uncertainty is further reduced, the amount of verbal communication will increase.

2. As nonverbal affiliative expressiveness increases, uncertainty levels will decrease in initial interaction situations. In addition, decreases in uncertainty level will cause increases in nonverbal affiliative expressiveness.

3. High levels of uncertainty cause increases in information seeking. As uncertainty levels decline, information seeking decreases.

4. High levels of uncertainty in a relationship cause decreases in the intimacy level of communication content. Low levels of uncertainty produce high levels of intimacy.

5. High levels of uncertainty produce high rates of reciprocity. Low levels of uncertainty produce low reciprocity rates.

6. Similarities between persons reduce uncertainty, whereas dissimilarities produce increases in uncertainty.

7. Increases in uncertainty produce decreases in liking; decreases in uncertainty produce increases in liking.

Theorems

1. The amounts of verbal communication and nonverbal affiliative erpressiveness are positively related.

2. The amount of communication and the intimacy level of communication are positively related.

3. The amount of communication and information seeking are inversely related.

4. The amount of communication and the reciprocity rate are inversely related.

5. The amount of communication and liking are positively related.

6. The amount of communication and similarity are positively related.

7. Nonverbal affiliative expressiveness and the intimacy level of communication content are positively related.

8. Nonverbal affiliative expressiveness and information seeking are inversely related.

continued

TABLE 4.1 *continued*

---

9. Nonverbal affiliative expressiveness and the reciprocity rate are inversely related.

10. Nonverbal affiliative expressiveness and liking are positively related.

11. Nonverbal affiliative expressiveness and similarity are positively related.

12. The intimacy level of communication content and information seeking are inversely related.

13. The intimacy level of communication content and the reciprocity rate are inversely related.

14. The intimacy level of communication content and liking are positively related.

15. The intimacy level of communication content and similarity are positively related.

16. Information seeking and the reciprocity rate are poitively related.

17. Information seeking and liking are negatively related.

18. Information seeking and similarity are negatively related.

19. The reciprocity rate and liking are negatively related.

20. The reciprocity rate and similarity are negatively related.

21. Similarity and liking are positively related.

---

that individuals use that indicates they have positive feelings for the other person, the more uncertainty will be reduced (Axiom 2). Third, the more uncertainty there is, the more individuals seek out information about the other person (Axiom 3). Fourth, the more uncertainty individuals have about others, the less intimate their communication will be (Axiom 4). Fifth, the more uncertainty there is, the greater is the reciprocity between the communicators (Axiom 5). Sixth, the more similarities the communicators observe, the more they can reduce their uncertainty (Axiom 6). Seventh, the more uncertainty there is, the less communicators like each other (Axiom 7).

The theorems in the original theory are generated using a transitivity rule: if A affects B and B affects C, then A affects C. To illustrate, consider Axioms 6 and 7. Axiom 6 states that "similarities between persons reduce uncertainty," and Axiom 7 states that "increases in uncertainty produce decreases in liking." If similarities and liking are both related to uncertainty, then similarity and liking are related to each other. The nature of the relationship (positive versus negative) is derived by the relationships between the variables in the axioms. In this case, similarity is related negatively to uncertainty, and liking is related negatively to uncertainty. Because both variables are related to uncertainty in the same way, they are related to each other positively. The theorem, therefore, becomes "similarity and liking are positively related" (Theorem 21). This theorem is consistent with the "similarity-attraction hypothesis" (e.g., Byrne, 1971). The twenty-one theorems generated by this procedure are presented in Table 4.1.

    Tests of Theory. There have been numerous tests of different aspects of URT. My focus here is on those tests that question the axioms or assumptions of the theory. More general criticisms of the theory are discussed.

    Kellermann's (1986) research focuses on Berger's (1979) assumption that anticipating future interaction with strangers leads individuals to try to reduce uncertainty. Her study indicates that anticipating interaction has little effect on individuals' desire to reduce uncertainty or their actual attempts to reduce uncertainty. Kellermann argues that "the failure of anticipation of future interaction to create differences in uncertainty is a serious problem for the theory. . . much of the analysis of why anticipation of future interaction should elevate uncertainty deals with the potential reward [another assumption of URT) of a pleasant future relationship or encounter. . . . Although high uncertainty may occur, on occasion, the typical initial interaction may not be characterized by high uncertainty about the conversational partner" (p. 66). Kellermann goes on to admit, however, that her study might not have created a sufficient level of anticipation of future interaction to create a difference in the information that individuals tried to obtain about each other.[8]

    Kellermann and Reynolds's (1990) research supports Berger's (1979) assumptions that individuals try to reduce uncertainty when others behave in a deviant fashion and when others have incentive (reward) value (the tests of these assumptions were used to extend URT; the extensions are discussed later). They also argue, however, that Axiom 3 of Berger and Calabrese's (1975) original theory needs to be dropped from the theory. They contend that information seeking is not linked directly to uncertainty. Rather, Kellermann and Reynolds's research suggests that a low tolerance for uncertainty leads to information seeking. Tolerance for uncertainty involves individuals' thresholds for certainty. Kellermann and Reynolds suggest that tolerance for uncertainty is related to information seeking, but not to the amount of uncertainty.

    Berger and Calabrese's (1975) original version of URT (which is designed to explain communication in initial interactions) appears to generalize across cultures. Gudykunst, Yang, and Nishida (1985), for example, demonstrate that URT extends to acquaintance relationships, close friendships, and dating relationships in Japan, Korea, and the United States. With the exception of Axiom 3, it appears that all axioms of URT (Berger and Calabrese, 1975) generalize to initial interactions and developed relationships in other cultures (see Berger and Gudykunst, 1991, for a review of the research). The patterns of support and lack of support for the theorems in Berger and Calabrese's theory, however, are not as clear. This is due, at least in part, to all possible theorems being generated using a transitivity rule. Any of the relationships posited, therefore, may be mediated by other variables (e.g., some theorems may be due to the "fallacy of the excluded middle").

Extensions of the Theory

There have been several formal and informal extensions of URT. Communication networks (Parke and Adelman, 1983) and deviance and incentive values (Kellermann and Reynolds, 1990) have been incorporated into the theory. URT also has been extended to intergroup relationships (this extension is dicussed under AUM). Other extensions also have been made (e.g., the ways individuals use plans to reach their goals).

Communication Networks. Parks and Adelman (1983) extend URT in two ways: (1) they incorporate the concept of communication networks, and (2) they extend URT from initial interactions to romantic relationships. They point out that the relationships of individuals "do not spring from a social void. They are embedded in the ongoing social context created by [romantic] partners' communication networks" (p. 56). Parks and Adelman go on to argue that communication with partner's communication networks (i.e., the partner's family and friends) is important because the networks provide third-party information about the partner. Network "members may comment on the partner's past actions and behavioral tendencies. They may supply ready-made explanations for the partner's behavior or serve as sounding boards for the individual's own explanations" (p. 57). Parks and Adelman's research indicates that the more individuals communicate with their partners' communication network, the less uncertainty they experience and the less likely they are to break up with their partners.

Parks and Adelman's research suggests one additional axiom and seven additional theorems for URT. These theoretical statements are summarized in Table 4.2.

Deviant Behavior and Incentive Value. Kellermann and Reynolds's (1990) research examines individuals' motivation to reduce uncertainty. As indicated earlier, this study tested two of Berger's (1979) assumptions: that individuals will try to reduce uncertainty when others act in a deviant fashion and when others provide rewards. When Berger (1979) outlines the three conditions under which individuals try to reduce uncertainty, he is responding to critics who

TABLE 4.2

Summary of Parks and Adelman's (1983) Extension of URT

Axiom

    8. Shared communication networks reduce uncertainty, whereas lack of shared networks increases uncertainty.

Theorems

    22. Shared communication networks and the amount of verbal communication are related positively.

    23. Shared communication networks and nonverbal affiliative expressiveness are related positively.

    24. Shared coomunication networks and information seeking are related inversely.

    25. The shared communication level and the intimacy level of coomunication are related positively.

    26. Shared communication networks and reciprocity rates are related inversely.

    27. Shared communication networks and similarities are related positively.

    28. Shared communication networks and liking are related positively.

Note: The theorems were generated by the same procedure used by Berger and Calabrese (1975). This table was first presented in Berger and Gudykunst (1991).

argue that individuals do not always try to reduce uncertainty about strangers as Berger and Calabrese (1975) claim. He does not, however, integrate the three antecedent conditions with the other variables in the theory.

    Kellermann and Reynolds (1990) studied the three antecedent conditions in relationships to information seeking, liking, and tolerance for uncertainty (discussed earlier). Their research reveals that others' deviant behavior increases uncertainty and others' incentive value reduces uncrtainty. They define incentive value as "the belief that other persons can satisfy certain needs that one has or serve as potential sources of support" (p. 15). When these findings are put in axiomatic form, the statements in Table 4.3 emerge.

    Plans. Berger's work in recent years has focused on how individuals use plans to reduce uncertainty in their interactions with others (e.g., Berger, 1987b, 1988, in press; Berger and Bell, 1988; Berger, Karol, and Jordon, 1989).[9] Berger (1988), for example, proposes that communication is a major way individuals try to accomplish their goals. This involves generating plans for communication. "A plan specifies the actions that are necessary for the attainment of a goal or several goals. Plans vary in their levels of abstraction. Highly abstract

TABLE 4.3

Summary of Kellermann and Reynolds's (1990) Extension of URT

Axioms

9. As the target's behavior becomes more deviant, the level of uncertainty increases.

10. The greater is the incentive value of the target, the lower is a person's level of uncertainty.

Theorems

29. Deviance and liking are associated negatively.

30. Incentive value and liking are associate positively.

31. Deviance and intimacy are associated negatively.

32. Deviance and perceived similarity are associated negatively.

33. Deviance and amount of verbal communication are associated negatively.

34. Incentive value and intimacy are associated positively.

35. Incentive value and perceived similarity are associated positively.

36. Incentive value and amount of cnmmunication are asociated positively.

Note: I have continued numbering axioms and theorems from Table 4.2. Only variables included in Kellermann and Reynolds's study are used in generating theorems.

plans can spawn more detailed plans. Plans can contain alternative paths for goal attainment from which the social actor [or actress] can choose" (Berger, 1988, p. 96).

Berger (1988) points out that individuals are not necessarily aware of their plans, but they become conscious of planning their communication behaviors when their plans fail. Individuals may have multiple goals in a particular situation. Individuals' plans also vary in their complexity. Berger and Bell (1988), for example, demonstrate that individuals who develop complex plans perform better in social interactions than individuals who do not develop complex plans. The ability to develop complex plans, however, appears to be situation specific, rather than a general trait individuals have (Berger and Bell, 1988).

The work on plans is designed to better understand uncertainty reduction processes. Berger and Gudykunst, for example, argue that

distinguishing among goal, plan, and tactical uncertainty has distinct theoretical advantages. Although any one of these kinds of uncertainty is likely to prove to be debilitating to communicative performances, understanding the precise source of uncertainty enables one to sharpen predictions about the relationships between cognition and human action. Uncertainty with reference to goals, for example, does not imply that an individual lacks optimal plans for reaching particular goals once the decision is made to pursue them. Poorly articulated plans may or may not be associated with uncertainties at the tactical level. Furthermore, uncertainties of various kinds may have different influences on how action sequences are enacted. (Berger and Gudykunst, 1991, p. 29)

Reducing uncertainty is critical for individuals to achieve their social goals.

Other Extensions. Several other extensions to URT have been proposed in recent years. As noted earlier, Kellermann and Reynolds (1990) suggest that individuals' tolerance for uncertainty be incorporated in future work on URT. This idea is similar to Douglas's (1991) notion of global uncertainty. Douglas argues that "strangers" uncertainty is not simply a consequence of mutual unfamiliarity but a product of their past initial interaction performances and their recollection of those performances" (p. 356). He goes on to point out that individuals are more or less uncertain about how they and any other person will communicate during an initial interaction. Douglas contends that individuals low in global uncertainty are better able to reduce uncertainty about strangers than individuals high in global uncertainty. He, therefore, proposes that global uncertainty must be taken into consideration when studying uncertainty reduction processes.

Honeycutt (1993) argues that individuals enter into interactions with others with expectancies about how those others will respond. One way expectancies are created is by imagined interactions. "Imagined interactions are internal dialogues that individuals have with real-life significant others using verbal and visual imagery" (Honeycutt, 1993, p. 471). Imagined interactions involve "cognitive representations of conversations" (Honeycutt, Edwards, and Zagacki, 1989–1990, p. 17). The rehearsal function of imagined interactions reduces uncertainty prior to interaction (Honeycutt, Zagacki, and Edwards, 1989). Many of the findings discussed earlier can be linked to expectancies (e.g., Douglas's, 1991, study of global uncertainty; Kellermann & Reynolds's 1990, test of the assumptions; it also is incorporated in AUM discussed later). Expectancies clearly influence uncertainty reduction processes and future work is needed to explain how. Expectancies also are related closely to the development of plans, but these linkages have not be outlined to date.

Criticisms of the Theory

As indicated earlier, the assumptions Berger (1979) outlines have been called into question and tested (e.g., Kellermann and Reynolds, 1990). Two other major criticisms of the theory need to be explicated as well: uncertainty does not always decrease and uncertainty is not the primary concern in initial interactions.

Increases in Uncertainty. One area where research has been conducted is on the reduction of uncertainty over time. Douglas's (1990) study, for example, suggests that uncertainty decreases in the course of six minutes of initial conversations with strangers. Van Lear and Trujillo's (1986) research indicates that uncertainty decreases from the first week to the second week of a new relationship. Not all research, however, demonstrates a clear trend for uncertainty to decrease over time. In fact, one of the major criticism of URT has been that uncertainty does not always decrease in relationships.

Several studies (e.g., Baxter and Bullis, 1986; Planalp and Honeycutt, 1985; Planalp, Rutherford, and Honeycutt, 1988; Sodetani and Gudykunst, 1987) clearly support the contention that uncertainty does not always decrease. Planalp and Honeycutt, for example, point out that the information individuals gather about others can increase uncertainty when it is inconsistent with prior knowledge of the other person or when it undermines prior knowledge of the other person. Their research suggests that most people remember events that increase uncertainty in their relationships with others. Planalp and Honeycutt isolate six types of events that increase uncertainty: obtaining information about competing relationships, unexplained loss of contact or closeness, learning about unexpected sexual behavior, detecting deception, changes in other person's personality or values, and the other person betraying a confidence. This research indicates that the majority of events that increase uncertainty in relationships lead to relationships being terminated or becoming less close, but some events do bring relational partners closer. Planalp, Rutherford, and Honeycutt's (1988) study, however, demonstrates that events that increase uncertainty do not necessarily have a negative effect on relationships. Sodetani and Gudykunst's (1987) study supports Planalp and Honeycutt's findings in interethnic relationships.

Baxter and Bullis (1986) point out that some turning points in conversations increase uncertainty in relationships, whereas others decrease uncertainty. Baxter (1988) extends this line of reasoning, arguing that uncertainty is a dialectic in most relationships. Individuals need predictability in their relationships, but too much predictability leads to relationships becoming boring. Individuals, therefore, also have a need for novelty. The amount of predictability and novelty in relationships varies over time. Baxter contends that predictability-novelty is one of the major dialectical tensions with which individuals must deal in their relationships.

Uncertainty Is Not the Main Concern in Initial Interactions. Sunnafrank (1986) argues that uncertainty is *not* the primary concern in initial interactions with others. Rather, he believes that the primary concern is maximization of relational outcomes. Sunnafrank, therefore, proposes a predicted outcome value (POV) theory. He contends that the impressions individuals form of others "are employed to forecast outcomes likely to be obtained in the future. . . individuals should employ these predictions in making decisions about whether to restrict, or seek further relational contact, as well as how to proceed with the interaction given these predictions. The primary consideration in such decisions should be the individual's desire to maximize future outcomes" (p. 10). The more positive individuals' predicted outcomes are for future interactions, the more likely they would continue with the relationship. Given this argument, Sunnafrank (1986) restates Berger and Calabrese's (1975) axioms. His reformulated axioms are presented in Table 4.4.

Berger (1986) argues that POV is a factor that influences the desire to reduce uncertainty in initial interactions (it is very close to Berger's, 1979, reward value). Several studies have attempted to test the veracity of Berger and Calabrese's (1975) and Sunnafrank's (1986) predictions. The results, however, are equivocal. Sunnafrank's (1988, 1990) research, for example, supports his POV perspective using self-reports and regression designs that cannot isolate the time sequencing of the influence of uncertainty and POV. Similarly, Grove and Werban's (1991) research ostensibly supports POV, but they studied only information seeking (Axiom 3 in original URT). Unfortunately, this is the one aspect of URT consistently questioned by other researchers (e.g., Kellermann and Reynolds, 1990). Jones's (1989) research supports Sunnafrank's positive POV predictions, but not his negative POV predictions. Her study, however, also supports the original version of URT. Similarly, Barnes's (1988) research provides support for both theories.

Honeycutt (1993) attempts to reconcile the roles of uncertainty and POV in initial interactions. He argues that "uncertainty reduction and affiliation [POV] can occur simultaneously, although uncertainty reduction often precedes affiliation. . . . People are concerned about reducing uncertainty about others' affiliative tendencies toward them. . . . predicted outcome values are a result of the uncertainty reduction function of interactions" (p. 462).

Although I cannot resolve the debate regarding the importance of uncertainty or POV here, it is important to recognize that individuals all have a need for others' behavior to be minimally predictable. J. H. Turner (1988), for example, contends that individuals "need to 'trust' others in the sense that, for the purposes of a given interaction, others are 'reliable' and their responses 'predictable' " (p. 56). When others' behavior is predictable, individuals feel that there is a rhythm to their interactions with others. When others' behavior is not predictable, there is no rhythm to interaction, and individuals experience diffuse anxiety (Turner, 1988). Given that predictability is a fundamental human need (Tuner, 1988), it appears that predictability is the primary issue, when POV is of concern. Lack of predictability could easily lead to individuals developing negative POV expectations for their interactions with others.

TABLE 4.4

Summary of Sunnafrank's (1986) Reformulation of URT

Propositions

1. During the beginning stage of initial interactions, the amount of both verbal communication and uncertainty increase. Further increases in the amount of verbal communication occur when the uncertainty reduction results in positive predicted outcome values, whereas decreases in the amount of verbal communication follow from negative predicted outcome values.

2. During the beginning stage of initial interactions, increases in listeners' nonverbal affiliative expressiveness produce reduction in their uncertainty levels. When this uncertainty results in positive predicted outcome values, further increases in nonverbal affiliative expressiveness occur. Uncertainty reduction associated with negative predicted outcome values produces decreases in nonverbal affiliative expressiveness.

3. High levels of uncertainty produce increased information seeking in beginning initial interactions. Decreased uncertainty, when associated with positive outcome values, produces increased information seeking. When associated with negative outcome values, reduced uncertainty produces decreased information seeking.

4. Given high uncertainty levels at the onset of initial interactions, communication content is low in intimacy. When subsequent uncertainty reduction is associated with positive predicted outcome values, the intimacy level of communication content increases. When uncertainty reduction is associated with negative predicted outcome values, the intimacy level is maintained or decreases to low levels.

5. During the beginning stage of initial interactions, high uncertainty levels are associated with high rates of reciprocity. When uncertainty reduction is associated with positive predicted outcome values, reciprocity rate declines. When uncertainty reduction is associated with negative predictod outcome values, greater decreases in reciprocity rate occur.

6. Both similarities and dissimilarities between persons reduce uncertainty. Greater uncertainty reduction will result from similarities when dissimilarities reflect groupings that are not highly familiar to individuals.

7. When decreased uncertainty is associated with positive predicted outcome values, liking increases. When associated with negative predicted outcome values, liking decreases.

Anxiety-Uncertainty Management Theory

AUM emerges out of an attempt to integrate URT with work on intergroup relations (e.g., Giles and Johnson, 1987; Tajfel, 1978; Stephan and Stephan, 1985). The theory has been developed in several stages. Initially, a theory of intergroup adaptation (Gudykunst and Hammer, 1988b) was developed. This theory was simplified to a more general theory of adaptation and effective communication in interpersonal and intergroup settings (Gudykunst, 1988). Then the theory was modified so that it could be used by individuals to improve their communication (Gudykunst, 1993, in press). To put the current theory in context, I begin with the general theory adapted from Gudykunst's (1985) extension of URT.

Original Theory

Gudykunst (1985) extends URT to explain the reduction of uncertainty in interpersonal and intergroup encounters. Gudykunst (1988) adapts this model to explain the reduction of uncertainty and anxiety in interpersonal and intergroup encounters, and Gudykunst and Hammer (1988b) present a special version of the theory designed to explain intercultural adaptation.[10] In extending URT, Gudykunst (1988) attempts to address several of the major criticisms of the theory.

Inclusion of Intergroup Factors. A complete theory of communication must incorporate explanations from all levels of analysis. To illustrate, Doise (1986) isolates four levels of analysis: intrapersonal, interpersonal, intergroup, and cultural. The intrapersonal level focus is on what is going on *within* individuals when they are communicating. The interpersonal level deals with what is going on *between* individuals when they communicate (e.g., what often is referred to as the *relational* or *dyadic level*). The intergroup level involves the group networks in which individuals are embedded and the relations between these groups in society. The cultural level deals with the ideological factors that influence our communication.

Most theorizing in communication, including URT, focuses only on the intrapersonal or interpersonal levels. One way that intergroup factors can be incorporated into theories is by incorporating self-concepts. Self-concepts consist of three general types of identity: human, social, and personal (J. C. Turner, 1987).[11] Individuals' human identities involve those views of themselves that they share with all other humans. Individuals' social identities involve those views of themselves that they assume they share with other members of their in-groups. In-groups are important to individuals. Social identities may be based on the roles individuals play (e.g., student, professor, parent), demographic categories (e.g., nationality, ethnicity, gender, age), membership in formal or informal organizations (e.g., political party, organization, social clubs), avocations or vocations (e.g., scientist, artist, gardener), or stigmatized groups (homeless person, person with AIDS). The degree to which individuals identify with these various groups varies from situation to situation. Individuals' personal identities involve those views of themselves that differentiate them from other members of their in-groups—those characteristics that define them as unique individuals.

Communication behavior can be based on personal, social, or human identity. In a particular situation, individuals may choose (either consciously or unconsciously) to define themselves communicatively as unique persons or as members of groups. When individuals' communication behavior is based mostly on their personal identities, interpersonal communication takes place. When individuals define themselves mostly in terms of their social identities (including their cultural and ethnic identities), in contrast, intergroup communication occurs. Gudykunst and Hammer's (1988a) research demonstrates that social identity is important in explaining uncertainty reduction processes between people from different ethnic groups. Individuals' personal and social identities influence all of their communication behavior, even though one may predominate in a particular situation. Because both identities are involved in all interactions, theories of communication must address both interpersonal *and* intergroup factors (Gudykunst, 1988).

Addition of Anxiety. Anxiety refers to the feeling of being uneasy, tense, worried, or apprehensive about what might happen (Stephan and Stephan, 1985). It is an affective (i.e., emotional) response, not a cognitive or behavioral response like uncertainty. J. H. Turner (1988) believes that the amount of diffuse anxiety individuals experience influences their motivation to communicate with others. If diffuse anxiety is too high, individuals are not motivated to communicate. Many writers (e.g., Lazarus, 1991; May, 1977) also argue that anxiety is the fundamental problem with which all humans must cope.

When individuals communicate with members of other groups they have a high level of anxiety. The anxiety individuals experience when communicating with members of other groups usually is based on negative expectations. Actual or anticipated interaction with members of different ethnic groups, therefore, leads to anxiety. Stephan and Stephan (1985) argue that individuals fear four types of negative consequences when interacting with members of other groups: (1) negative consequences for self-concepts (e.g., feeling incompetent), (2) negative behavioral consequences (e.g., performing poorly), (3) negative evaluations by strangers (e.g., being ridiculed, rejected), and (4) negative evaluations by members of in-groups (e.g., in-group members will disapprove of interaction with members of other groups). Anxiety is present, however, anytime individuals communicate. It tends to be higher in initial interactions with members of other ethnic groups or cultures than in initial interactions between people from the same ethnic groups or cultures. To understand either interpersonal or intergroup encounters, anxiety must be incorporated.

Including Expectations. As indicated in the discussion of extensions to URT, expectations clearly have a influence on communication. Expectations involve looking forward or anticipating something (positive or negative) in the future.[12] Expectations are a function of individuals' knowledge, beliefs, attitudes, stereotypes, self-conceptions, roles, prior interaction, and characteristics of the communicators. Individuals' stereotypes and attitudes (e.g., prejudice, sexism), for example, create expectations.[13] Stereotypes and attitudes, however, create expectations in encounters between members of different groups *and* encounters between members of the same group. The general argument Gudykunst (1988) presents is that positive expectations reduce uncertainty and anxiety, whereas negative expectations increase uncertainty and anxiety. This argument is supported by Gudykunst and Shapiro's (1994) research.

Specifying Outcomes. Although uncertainty reduction itself can be considered an outcome of communication, it also is a process. The focus on other outcomes in AUM emerges from the initial version of the theory (Gudykunst and Hammer, 1988b) being designed to explain intercultural adaptation. Also, Gudykunst (1988, 1993, in press) believes that theories should be able to be used to improve the effectiveness of communication. Effective communication is defined as minimizing misunderstandings within the theoretical framework (see Gudykunst and Kim, 1992, for rationale).

Axioms in the Theory. Lieberson (1985) suggests that theorists need to isolate the "basic causes" of the phenomenon under investigation. In generating the axioms for the theories, Gudykunst (1988, 1993, in press) assumes that uncertainty and anxiety are basic causes influencing effective communication and adaptation. Other variables (e.g., identity, positive expectations, similarity), therefore, are treated as "superficial causes" of effective communication and adaptation (i.e., they influence uncertainty and anxiety but are not directly related to the outcomes). The influence of these superficial causes on effective communication and adaptation is mediated through uncertainty and anxiety. Gao and Gudykunst's (1990) research supports this assumption in studying adaptation processes.

The 1988 version of AUM (Gudykunst, 1988) contains thirteen axioms. The first nine axioms link the superficial causes to uncertainty and anxiety. Axioms 10 and 11 link the basic causes, uncertainty and anxiety, to the outcomes, adaptation and effective communication. Axioms 12 and 13 are included to *illustrate* how culture influences the variables included in the theory.[15]

Criticisms of the Theory. Ting-Toomey (1989) and Sunnafrank (1989) responded to Gudykunst's (1989) summary of research on uncertainty reduction in intercultural relationships. Ting-Toomey isolated five conceptual issues that need to be addressed in future work. First, she argues that the motivational bases for reducing uncertainty need to be clarified. She supports Kellermann's (1986) position and also indicates that there is a need to understand how dispositional factors (e.g., tolerance for ambiguity) influence uncertainty reduction processes. Second, Ting-Toomey contends that the dialectical aspects of uncertainty need to be incorporated to explain the subtle relational changes that take place in intercultural relationships. Third, she points out that the interactive dynamics involved in negotiating relationships between people from different cultures and ethnic groups need to be addressed. Fourth, she suggests that the influence of the larger social context in which intercultural relationships are formed need to be incorporated into the theory (e.g., situational and network influences). Fifth, Ting-Toomey believes that issues of the Western bias toward intimacy need to be addressed; that is, people in non-Western cultures do not value intimacy to the same extent as people in Western cultures. Many of these issues are addressed in the extensions to Gudykunst's (1988) theory discussed in the next section.

Sunnafrank (1989) reinterprets much of the research on uncertainty reduction across cultures and in intercultural relationships in terms of his POV model. He argues that the research summarized in Gudykunst's (1989) review generally supports a POV interpretation. Although the results Gudykunst summarized can be interpreted within a POV framework, they also clearly support Berger's (1979) and Kellermann and Reynolds's (1990) contention that individuals try to reduce uncertainty when others provide incentive value.

Extensions to Theory

In discussing the theory, Gudykunst (1988) points out that several issues needed to be addressed in the future. First, issues of increases and decreases in uncertainty and anxiety needed to be incorporated. These issues are addressed by Gudykunst and Kim (1992). Another issue that needs to be addressed in developing the theory is more completely specifying how uncertainty and anxiety influence effective communication. Gudykunst (1991) argues that mindfulness is the moderating process affecting the influence of uncertainty and anxiety reduction on effective communication.

Thresholds for Uncertainty. Some degree of uncertainty exists in all relationships. Individuals can never totally predict or explain another person's behavior. Everyone has a maximum and minimum thresholds for uncertainty.[15] If uncertainty is above individuals' maximum thresholds, they do not have enough information to predict or explain others' behavior comfortably. When their uncertainty is below their maximum thresholds, individuals have sufficient information to make some predictions and explanations. Individuals may not be highly confident of their predictions and their predictions may not be highly accurate, but they have sufficient information to be able to interact with the other person with some degree of comfort. If uncertainty is below individuals' minimum threshold, they see the other person's behavior as highly predictable.

When this occurs, there may not be sufficient novelty in the relationship for individuals to sustain interest in interacting with the other person. Individuals may also think that they can predict others' behavior, but their predictions may be inaccurate. When individuals see others' behavior as highly predictable they, therefore, are likely to misinterpret their messages because they do not consider the possibility that their interpretations are wrong.

Generally, as individuals get to know others their uncertainty regarding their behavior tends to decrease. Uncertainty, however, does not always decrease as relationships change over time. It also can increase (e.g., Planalp et al., 1988). Depending on the nature of the event and how individuals handle the uncertainty, increases in uncertainty can have positive or negative consequences for relationships with others. Uncertainty can be viewed as a dialectic with individuals trying to balance predictability and novelty in their relationships with others at any given point in the relationship.

Thresholds for Anxiety. Everyone has maximum and minimum thresholds for anxiety. If anxiety is above individuals' maximum thresholds, they are so uneasy that they do not want to communicate with others and they are not capable of gathering accurate information about others. If anxiety is below individuals' minimum thresholds, not enough adrenaline is running through their systems to motivate them to communicate with others. To be motivated to communicate with others, individuals' anxiety has to be below their maximum thresholds and above their minimum thresholds. The role of anxiety in interpersonal communication is similar to its role in our performance on tests. If individuals are too anxious, they do not perform well on tests. Similarly, if individuals are not at all anxious, they do not perform well. Csikszentmihalyi (1990) believes that there is an optimal level of anxiety that facilitates our having "flow" experiences (e.g., optimal experiences).

Generally, as individuals get to know others, the anxiety they experience in interacting with them tends to decrease. This does *not* imply, however, that anxiety continually decreases. Although there is a general trend for anxiety to decrease the more individuals get to know others, their anxiety can increase or decrease at any particular point in a relationship, depending on what is going on in the relationship and how they interpret what is happening. Individuals must balance the anxiety dialectic that involves tension between fear and trust at any given point in their relationship with others.[16] Trust involves the "confidence that one will find what is desired from another, rather than what is feared" (Deutsch, 1973, p. 149).

Mindfulness. Much of individuals' communication behavior is habitual. When individuals are communicating habitually, they are following scripts. When individuals first encounter a new situation, they consciously seek cues to guide their behavior (Langer, 1978). As individuals have repeated experiences with the same event, they have less need to consciously think about their behavior. "The more often we engage in the activity, the more likely it is that we rely on scripts for the completion of the activity and the less likely there will be any correspondence between our actions and those thoughts of ours that occur simultaneously" (Langer, 1978, p. 39).

When individuals are engaging in habitual or scripted behavior, they are not highly aware of what they are doing or saying. To borrow an analogy from flying a plane, they are on automatic pilot. In Langer's (1978) terminology, individuals are "mindless" (Bellah et al., 1991; Csikszentmihalyi, 1990, use paying attention when discussing what Langer calls *mindfulness*).

To communicate effectively in nonscripted situations, individuals must become "mindful" of their thought processes. Langer (1989) isolates three qualities of mindfulness: "(1) creation of new categories; (2) openness to new information; and (3) awareness of more than one perspective" (p. 62). She points out that "categorizing is a fundamental and natural human activity. It is the way we come to know the world. Any attempt to eliminate bias by attempting to eliminate the perception of differences is doomed to failure" (p. 154).

Langer (1989) argues that mindfulness involves making more, not fewer, distinctions. To illustrate, Langer uses an example of people who are in the category "cripple." If individuals see all people in this category as the same, they start treating the category in which they place a person as his or her identity. If individuals draw additional distinctions within this category (e.g., create new categories), on the other hand, it stops them from treating the person as a category. If individuals see a person with a "lame leg," they do not necessarily treat her or him as a "cripple."

Openness to new information and awareness of more than one perspective are related to focusing on the process, rather than the outcome. Langer believes that focusing on the process (e.g., how we do something) forces individuals to be mindful of their behavior and pay attention to the situations in which they find themselves.

Anxiety, Uncertainty, Mindfulness, and Effective Communication. If uncertainty and anxiety are above individuals' maximum thresholds, as they often are when first interacting with members of other groups, individuals are too anxious and uncertain to communicate effectively. In most initial interactions with members of the same group, however, there are sufficiently clear norms and rules for communication that uncertainty and anxiety are reduced below individuals' maximum thresholds. Even if uncertainty and anxiety are below the maximum threshold, either or both may still be too high for individuals to communicate effectively. To communicate effectively anxiety needs to be sufficiently low that individuals can accurately interpret and predict others' behavior. When anxiety is too high individuals communicate on automatic pilot and interpret others' behavior using their own cultural frame of reference.

If uncertainty and anxiety are low, individuals may not be motivated to communicate. If both uncertainty and anxiety are consistently below individuals' minimum thresholds in a particular relationship, for example, the relationship will become boring. Kruglanski (1989) points out that individuals all have a need to avoid closure on topics or people to allow for "mystery" to be maintained. To communicate effectively, our uncertainty and anxiety both must be above our minimum threshold.

Uncertainty and anxiety do not necessarily increase and decrease at the same time. Individuals may reduce their uncertainty and be highly anxious. To communicate effectively, individuals' anxiety must be sufficiently low (well below maximum threshold, but above minimum) that they can reduce their explanatory uncertainty. If anxiety is high, individuals must cognitively "manage" their anxiety (i.e., become mindful) if they are to communicate effectively and adapt to other cultural environments. If individuals are not mindful when they communicate with members of other groups, uncertainty reduction may not lead to effective communication because the predictions and explanations they make will be based on their cultural frame of reference. When individuals are mindful, they can search for alternative interpretations of others' behavior and select the interpretation they believe to have the greatest accuracy.

Current Version

The 1993 and current versions of AUM (Gudykunst, 1993, in press) are presented for two reasons.[17] First, numerous extensions to the original theory had been made and these changes involved modifications to the theory. Second, the 1988 version of the theory is highly abstract and its application is not straightforward. The 1993 and current versions are designed to be applied to improving the effectiveness of interpersonal and intergroup communication.

Axioms. In updating AUM theory, Gudykunst (in press) rewrote all of the axioms of the 1993 version to make them clearer. He also emphasizes the accuracy of our predictions of strangers' behavior because this is critical to effective communication. Axioms involving cross-cultural variability in all superfical and basic causes of effective communication also are included in the current version of AUM (see Table 2 in Gudykunst, in press). These axioms, however, are omitted here to conserve space.

Gudykunst (in press) includes new axioms involving ability to complexly process information, rigidity of attitudes, openness to new information, awareness of alternative perspectives, gathering appropriate information, categorizing strangers in the same categories they use, being mindful when negative expectations are activated, activation of independent or interdependent self-construals, quality and quantity of prior contact, the percentage of in-group members present during interactions with strangers, interdependence with strangers, intimacy of relationships with strangers, moral inclusiveness, and respect for strangers.

Gudykunst (1993, in press) presents the theory in a form so that it has direct application to improving the effectiveness of communication.[18] This requires that the theoretical statements be written at a more concrete level than in the 1988 version of the theory. Reynolds (1971) points out that "in dealing with logical systems that are completely abstract. . .a common criteria is to select the smallest number of axioms from which all other statements can be derived, reflecting a preference for simplicity and elegance. There is reason to think that this is inappropriate for a substantive theory, particularly when it makes it more difficult to understand the theory" (p. 95). In addition to making the axioms as concrete as possible, Gudykunst also states the axioms informally to make applications easier.[19]

Table 4.5 contains the axioms in the current version of AUM theory. The axioms are organized under seven headings: self and self-concept; motivation; reactions to strangers; social categorization; situational processes; connections with strangers; and anxiety, uncertainty, mindfulness, and effective communication.

Theorems. Theorems can be generated from the axioms in Table 4.5 by logically combining the axioms. To illustrate, if Axioms 1 and 2 are combined, Theorem 1 can be generated: there is a positive association between our need for group inclusion and sustaining our self-conceptions. This theorem is consistent with J. H. Turner's (1988) theory of motivation. Some theorems generated will be consistent with previous research and some will form hypotheses for future research. To illustrate, combination of Axioms 21 and 23 yields the similarity-attraction hypothesis that has received extensive empirical support (e.g., Byrne, 1971). Combination of Axioms 6 and 11 yields the theorem that the rigidity of our attitudes is related negatively to our ability to process information complexly.

Not all axioms should be combined to form theorems. Some combinations of axioms will involve the fallacy of the excluded middle and should not be generated. To illustrate, if A→C and B→C, then it can be deduced that A and B are related. The fallacy of the excluded middle involves not recognizing that there may be another variable mediating the relationships between the two variables (e.g., A→D→B).

General Comments on AUM. AUM is an initial attempt to formally state a general theory of effective interpersonal and intergroup communication. Gudykunst (in press) states that it should be considered a preliminary working version that is in the process of being reformulated to increase parsimony and clarity. AUM incorporates constructs at all levels of analysis. Motivation (e.g., needs), uncertainty orientation, need for closure, category width, tolerance for ambiguity, and empathy, for example, are individual level phenomenon.

TABLE 4.5

Summary of Current Verion of AUM

Self and Self-Concept

1. An increase in the degree to which our social identities influence our interaction with strangers will produce an increase in our ability to manage our anxiety and an increase in our confidence in predicting their behavior. Boundary Condition: This axiom only holds if strangers are perceived to be members of another group and they are perceived to be typical group members.

2. An increase in the degree to which our personal identities influence our interactions with strangers will produce an increase in our ability to manage our anxiety and an increase in our ability to accurately predict their behavior. Boundary Condition: This axiom holds only in individualistic cultures.

3. An increase in our use of our independent self-construals to guide our interactions with strangers will produce a reliance on person-based information to reduce uncertainty about their behavior; an increase in our use of our interdependent self-construals to guide our interactions with strangers will produce a reliance on group-based information to reduce uncertainty about their behavior.

4. An increase in our dependence on our in-qroups for our self-esteem when interacting with strangers will produce an increase in our anxiety end a decrease in our ability to accurately predict their behavior.

5. An increase in our self-esteem (pride) when we interact with strangers will produce an increase in our ability to manage our anxiety.

6. An increase in our shame when we interact with strangers will produce a decrease in our ability to manage our anxiety and a decrease in our ability to accurately predict their behavior.

Motivation

7. An increase in our need for a sense of group inclusion when we interact with strangers will produce an increase in our anxiety.

8. An increase in our need to sustain our self-conceptions when we interact with strangers will produce an increase in our anxiety.

9. An increase in the degree to which strangers confirm our self-conceptions when we interact with them will produce a decrease in our anxiety.

10. An increase in the predictability of strangers' behavior will produce a decrease in our anxiety. Boundary Condition: This axiom applies only to increases in predictability that bring uncertainty below our maximum thresholds.

continued

TABLE 4.5 *continued*

11. An increase in our sense of security in our personal and social identities when we interact with strangers will produce a decrease in our anxiety and an increase in our confidence in predicting their beavior.

Reactions To Strangers

12. An increase in our ability to complexly process information about strangers will produce an increase in our ability to accurately predict their bhavior.

13. An increase in the rigidity of our attitudes toward strangers will produce an increase in our anxiety and a decrease in our ability to accurately predict their behavior.

14. An increase in our self-monitoring when we intract with strangers will produce an increase in our ability to manage our anxiety and an increase in our confidence in predicting their behavior.

15. An increase in our ability to tolerate ambiguity when we interact with strangers will produce an increase in our ability to manage our anxiety.

16. An increase in our ability to empathize with strangers will produce an increase in our ability to accurately predict their behavior.

17. An increase in the degree to which strangers accommodate to our behavior will produce a decrease in our anxiety and an increase in our confidence in predicting their behavior.

18. An increase in our ability to adapt our communication to strangers will produce an increase in our ability to manage our anxiety and an increase in our confidence in predicting their behavior.

Social Categorization

19. An increase in our understanding of similarities and differences between our groups and strangers' groups will produce an increase in our ability to manage our anxiety and our ability to accurately predict their behavior.

20. An increase in the personal similarities we perceive between ourselves and strangers will produec an increase in our ability to manage our anxiety and our ability to accurately predict their behavior.

21. An increase in our ability to categorize strangers in the same categories they categorize themselves will produce an increase in our ability to accurately predict their behavior.

22. An increase in the degree to which we attribute strangers' behaviors to their group memberships will produce a decrease in our ability to manage our anxiety and a decrease in our ability to accurately predict their behavior.

continued

TABLE 4.5 *continued*

23. An increase in the variability we perceive in strangers' groups will produce an increase in our ability to manage our anxiety and an increase in our ability to accurately predict their behavior.

24. An increase in our positive expectations regarding strangers' behavior will produce a decrease in our anxiety and an increase in our confidence in predicting their behavior.

25. An increase in our awareness of strangers' violations of our positive expectations or their confirming our negative expectations will produce an increase in our anxiety and a decrease in our confidence in predicting their behavior.

Situational Processes

26. An increase in the complexity of our scripts for communicating with strangers will produce a decrease in our anxiety and an increase in our confidence in predicting their behavior.

27. An increase in the informality of the situation in which we are communicating with strangers will produce a decrease in our anxiety and an increase in our confidence in predicting their behavior.

28. An increase in the cooperative structure of the goals on which we work with strangers will produce a decrease in our anxiety and an increase in our confidence in predicting their behavior.

29. An increase in the normative and institutional support for communicating with strangers will produce a decrease in our anxiety and an increase in our confidence in predicting their behavior.

30. An increase in the percentage of our in-group members present in a situation when we interact with strangers will produce a decrease in our anxiety.

Connection with Strangers

31. An increase in our attraction to strangers will produce a decrease in our anxiety and an increase in our confidence in predicting their behavior.

32. An increase in our moral inclusiveness toward strangers will produce an increase in our ability to manage our anxiety.

33. An increase in our respect for strangers will produce an increase in our ability to manage our anxiety and an increase in our ability to accurately predict their behavior.

34. An increase in the quantity and quality of our contact with strangers and members of their groups will produce a decrease in our anxiety and an increase in our ability to accurately predict their behavior.

continued

TABLE 4.5 *continued*

35. An increase in our interdependence with strangers will produce a decrease in our anxiety and an increase in our confidence in predicting their behavior.

36. An increase in the intimacy of our relationships with strangers will produce a decrease in our anxiety and an increase in our confidence predicting their behavior. Boundary Condition: This axiom applies only to broad trends across stages of relationship development. Within any stage of relationship development or within specific conversations anxiety and uncertainty will fluctuate (i.e., act as dialectics).

37. An increase in the networks we share with strangers will produce a decrease in our anxiety and an increase in our confidence in predicting their behavior.

Anxiety, Uncertainty, Mindfulness, and Effective Communication

38. An increase in our ability to gather appropriate information about strangers will produce an increase in our ability to accurately predict their behavior.

39. An increase in our ability to decrease strangers' behavior will produce an increase in our ability to accurately predict their behavior. Boundary Condition: This is possible only if we are mindful of the process of communication and our anxiety and uncertainty are between our minimum and maximum thresholds.

40. An increase in our understanding the stocks of knowledge of the groups of which strangers are members will produce an increase in our ability to manage our anxiety and our ability to accurately predict their behavior. Boundary Condition: This axion holds only when we are mindful.

41. An increase in our knowledge of strangers' language (dialect, jargon, slang) will produce an increase in our ability to manage our anxiety and an increase in our ability to accurately predict their behavior.

42. An increase in our openness to new information about strangers and our interactions with them will produce an increase in our ability to accurately predict their behavior. Boundary Condition: This axiom holds only when our anxiety and uncertainty are between our minimum and maximum thresholds.

43. An increase in our ability to place strangers in new categories (or recognize how strangers are different from other members of their groups) will produce an increase in our ability to accurately predict their behavior. Boundary Condition: This axiom holds only when our anxiety and uncertainty are between our minimum and maximum thresholds.

44. An increase in our awareness of the perspectives strangers use to interpret our messages (and the perspectives strangers use to transmit their messages to us) will produce an increase in our ability to accurately predict their behavior. Boundary Condition: This axiom holds only when our anxiety and uncertainty are between our minimum and maximum thresholds.

continued

TABLE 4.5 *continued*

---

45. An increase in our anxiety above our maximum thresholds or a decrease below our minimum thresholds when we interact with strangers will produce a decrease in our ability to accurately predict their behavior.

46. An increase in our ability to be mindful when our negative expectations (e.g., stereotypes) for strangers' behavior are activated will produce an increase in our ability to manage our anxiety and an increase in our ability to accurately predict their behavior.

47. An increase in our ability to manage our anxiety about interacting with strangers *and* an increase in the accuracy of our predictions and explanations regarding their behavior will produce an increase in the effectiveness of our communication. Boundary Condition: This axiom holds only when we are mindful. Anxiety and uncertainty below our minimum thresholds will not produce increases in our effectiveness; anxiety and uncertainty above our maximum threshold will produce decreases in effectiveness.

Note: The axioms presented are drawn from Gudykunst (in press). The axioms were not finalized when this chapter went to press, but these axioms present a more accurate picture of AUM than the 1993 axioms.

Interpersonal constructs include, but are not limited to, self-conceptions, attraction, attunement, social bonds, and accommodation. Social identities, stereotypes, intergroup expectations, and social networks are examples of the intergroup phenomenon included in the theory. The dimensions of cultural variability (e. g., individualism-collectivism) are the cultural level phenomenon. These constructs are linked directly to managing anxiety or reducing uncertainty in the theory.

It is important to point out that the general processes included in the AUM should generalize across cultures. There will be differences, however, in what constitutes uncertainty and anxiety across cultures. As indicated earlier, Gudykunst and Nishida (1986) found that uncertainty is more person based in individualistic cultures than in collectivistic cultures and more group based in collectivistic cultures than in individualistic cultures. This position is compatible with Hamill's (1990) argument that humans are endowed with innate logical structures, but cultures create unique meanings out of the innate knowledge. Although AUM is complex and involves a large number of theoretical statements, most, but not all, statements are empirically testable. As with any theory, however, AUM includes some statements that are not testable.

Future Refinements Needed

Because AUM is designed to be a preliminary working theory, refinements are necessary. One area where refinements are needed is in incorporating the dialectical aspects of uncertainty and antiety into the theory. As indicated earlier, the uncertainty dialectic involves predictability-novelty (similar to Baxter's, 1988, dialectic). The anxiety dialectic involves fear-trust. This requires developing a way to write theoretical statements that include causal relationships and dialectical relationships.

A second area where additional specification is needed is in the relationship between the management of anxiety and uncertainty and effective communication. What, for example, are the optimal levels of uncertainty and anxiety that increase the effectiveness of communication? Similarly, the role of mindfulness in moderating this process needs to be more fully explicated. One issue that needs to be addressed to increase the applicability of the theory is isolating the cues individuals can use to trigger their mindfulness when misunderstanding is occurring.[20]

Notes

I want to thank Stella Ting-Toomey for her comments on an earlier version of this chapter.

1. See Berger (1987a), Berger and Bradac (1982), and Berger and Gudykunst (1991) for reviews of URT.

2. URT is used by many scholars who have no "family" connection to Chuck Berger. By family connection I mean his students or students of his students.

3. URT has been used in organizational communication (e.g., Lester, 1983; Schlueter, Barge, and Case, 1987; Wilson, 1986) and mass communication (e.g., Perse, 1986) to name only a few of the applications. My focus in this chapter is on its use in interpersonal and intergroup communication.

4. A name may seem like a small thing when it comes to theory, but this is not the case. Until I named the theory, many people assumed that it was still totally consistent with URT and referred to the theory as URT. Although AUM is derived from URT, it is clearly a different theory.

5. This distinction originally was made by Berger (1975).

6. Most research on URT has focused on predictive uncertainty using measures derived from Clatterbuck (1979). This measure assesses attributional confidence—the opposite of predictive uncertainty. When attributional confidence is zero, for example, uncertainty is 100 percent. When attributional confidence is 100 percent, uncertainty is zero.

7. Predictions and explanations in URT and AUM always refer to others' thoughts, feelings, attitudes, beliefs, behavior, and so forth. Because this becomes tedious

to write and read I will often focus on behavior. Please keep in mind, however, that the other factors are also involved.

8. See Douglas (1985, 1988) for two other tests of the effect of anticipated interaction. These tests, however, do not supply a definitive test of the assumption.

9. A separate chapter could easily be written on the work on plans. Because the research on plans has not yielded new axioma for URT, I will provide only a brief overview of this line of research.

10. The specific and general theories were developed almost simultaneously. The specific theory was published about six months before the general theory. The general theory also was designed to simplify the specific theory.

11. When identity is incorporated into theories in the United States, generally only personal identity is addressed.

12. Sunnafrank's POV can be subsumed under the more general construct of expectations.

13. See Hamilton, Sherman, and Ruvolo (1990) for a review.

14. Axioms could be written linking culture to all variables in the theory.

15. This idea was hinted at in earlier writing, but the first place I actually stated it was in Gudykunst and Kim (1992).

16. This notion is presented in Gudykunst (in press).

17. The theory was first labeled AUM in Gudykunst (1993). Prior to this it often was referred to as URT.

18. The theory has been used to design and implement general cultural awareness training programs, cultural adjustment training programs, and training programs designed to help participants manage conflict between members of different groups.

19. One reason people do not see theories as "practical" (to use Kurt Lewin's term) is that the theoretical statements are highly abstract with no connection to everyday life. I have stated the theorems at a lower level to make them easier to apply. This, however, necessitates an increase in the number of statements needed.

20. Some of these issues are addressed in Gudykunst (1994).

References

Abelson, R. (1976). "Script processing in attitude formation and decision making." In J. Carroll and J. Payne (Eds.), *Cognition and social behavior*. Hillsdale, N.J.: Lawrence Erlbaum and Associates.

Barnes, K. (1988). "An exploration into the relative utility of uncertainty reduction theory and predicted outcome value theory." Paper presented at the Speech Communication Association Convention.

Baxter, L. A. (1988). "A dialectical perspective on communicative strategies in relationship development." In S. Duck (Ed.), *A handbook of personal relationships*. London: John Wiley & Sons.

———— and Bullis, C. (1986). "Turning points in developing romantic relationships." *Human Communication Research* 12: 469–494.

———— and Wilmot, W. (1984). " 'Secret tests': Social strategies for acquiring information about the state of a relationship." *Human Communication Research* 11: 171–201.

Bellah, R., Madsen, R., Sullivan, W., Swidler, A., and Tipton, S. (1991). *The Good society*. New York: Basic Books.

Berger, C. R. (1975). "Proactive and retroactive attribution processes in interpersonal communication." *Human Communication Research* 2: 33–50.

———— (1979). "Beyond initial interaction." In H. Giles and R. St. Clair (Eds.). *Language and social psychology*. Oxford: Basil Blackwell.

———— (1986) "Uncertain outcome values in predicted relationships." *Human Communication Research* 13: 34–38.

———— (1987a) "Communicating under uncertainty." In G. Miller and M. Roloff (Eds.), *Interpersonal processes*. Newoury Park, Calif.: Sage Publications.

———— (1987b). "Planning and scheming." In R. Burnett, P. McPhee, and D. Clarke (Eds.), *Accounting for relationships*. London: Meuthen.

———— (1988). "Planning, affect, and social action generation." In L. Donohew, H. Sypher, and E. Higgins (Eds.), *Communication, social cognition, and affect*. Hillsdale, N.J.: Lawrence Erlbaum and Associates.

———— (1993). "Uncertainty and social interaction." In S. Deetz (Ed.), *Communication yearbook 16*. Newbury Park, Calif.: Sage Publications.

———— (In press). "A plan-based approach to strategic communication." In D. Hewes (Ed.), *Cognitive bases for internersonal communication*. Hillsdale, N.J.: Lawrence Erlbaum and Associates.

———— and Bell, R. (1988). "Plans and the initiation of social relationships." *Human Communication Research* 15: 217–235.

———— and Bradac, J. (1982). *Language and social knowledge*. London: Edward Arnold.

———— and Calabrese, R. (1975). "Some explorations in initial interactions and beyond: Toward a developmental theory of interpersonal communication." *Human Communication Research* 1: 99–112.

—— and Gudykunst, W. B. (1991). "Uncertainty and communication." In B. Dervin and M. Voigt (Eds.), *Progress in communication sciences*, vol. 10. Norwood, N.J.: Ablex.

—— Karol, S. H., and Jordon, J. M. (1989). "When a lot of knowledge is a dangerous thing: The debilitating effects of plan complexity." *Human Communication Research* 16: 91–119.

—— and Kellermann, K. (1994). "Social information seeking." In J. Wieman, and J. Daly (Eds.), *Communicating strategically*. Hillsdale, N.J.: Lawrence Erlbaum and Associates.

Byrne, D. (1971). *The attraction paradigm*. New York: Academic Press.

Clatterbuck, G. (1979). "Attributional confidence and uncertainty." *Human Communication Research* 5: 147–157.

Csikszentmihalyi, M. (1990). *Flow: The psychology of optimal experience*. New York: Harper and Row.

Deutsch, M. (1973). *The resolution of conflict*. New Haven, Conn.: Yale University Press.

Doise, W. (1986). *Levels of explanation in social psychology*. Cambridge: Cambridge University Press.

Douglas, W. (1985). "Anticipated interaction and information seeking." *Human Communication Research* 12: 243–258.

—— (1998). "Question-asking in same- and opposite-sex initial interactions: The effects of anticipated future interactions." *Human Communication Research* 14: 230–245.

—— (1990). "Uncertainty, information-seeking, and liking during initial interactions." *Western Journal of Speech Communication* 54: 66–81.

—— (1991). "Expectations about initial interactions: An examination of the effects of glocal uncertainty." *Human Communication Research* 17: 355–384.

Duck, S. W., and Miell, D. (1986). "Changing the development of personal relationships." In R. Gilmour and S. W. Duck (Eds.), *The emerging field of personal relationships*. Hillsdale, N.J.: Lawrence Erlbaum and Associates.

Gao, G., and Gudykunst, W. B. (1990). "Uncertainty, anxiety, and adaptation communication." *International Journal of Intercultural Relations* 14: 301–317.

Giles, H., and Johnson, P. (1981). "The role of language in intergroup relations." In J. Turner and H. Giles (Eds.), *Intergroup behavior*. Chicago: University of Chicago Press.

—— (1987). "Ethnolinguistic identity theory." *International Journal of the Sociology of Language* 68: 69–90.

Gouldner, A. (1960). "The norm of reciprocity." *American Sociological Review* 25: 161–179.

Grove, T., and Werkman, D. (1991). "Conversations with able-bodied and visibly disabled strangers." *Human Communication Research* 17: 507–534.

Gudykunst, W. B. (1985). "A model of uncertainty reduction in intercultural encounters." *Journal of Language and Social Psychology* 4: 79–98.

————— (1988). "Uncertainty and anxiety." In Y. Y. Kim and W. B. Gudykunst (Eds.), *Theories in intercultural communication*. Newbury Park, Calif.: Sage Publications.

————— (1989). "Culture and the development of interpersonal relationships." In J. Anderson (Ed.), *Communication yearbook 12*. Newbury Park, Calif.: Sage Publications.

————— (1991). *Bridging differences: Effective intergroup communication*. Newbury Park, Calif.: Sage Publications.

————— (1993). "Toward a theory of effective interpersonal and intergroup communication: An anxiety/uncertainty management perspective." In R. Wiseman and J. Koester (Eds.), *Intercultural communication competence*. Newbury Park, Calif.: Sage Publications.

————— (1994). *Bridging differences: Effective intergroup communication*, 2d ed. Newbury Park, Calif.: Sage Publications.

————— (In press). "Anxiety/uncertainty management theory: Development and current status." In R. Wiseman (Ed.), *Intercultural communication theory* (tentative). Newbury Park, Calif.: Sage Publications.

————— and Hammer, M. R. (1988a). "The influence of social identity and intimacy of interethnic relationships on uncertainty reduction processes." *Human Communication Research* 14: 569–601.

————— and Hammer, M. R. (1988b). "Strangers and hosts." In Y. Kim and W. Gudykunst (Eds.), *Cross-cultural adaptation*. Newbury Park, Calif.: Sage Publications.

—————and Kim, Y. Y. (1992). *Communicating with strangers*, 2d ed. New York: McGraw-Hill.

————— and Nishida, T. (1986). "Attributional confidence in low- and high-context cultures." *Human Communication Research* 12: 525–549.

————— and Nishida, T. (1989). "Perspectives for studying intercultural communication." In M. Asante and W. B. Gudykunst (Eds.), *Handoook of international and intercultural communication*. Newbury Park, Calif.: Sage Publications.

————— and Shapiro, R. (1994) "Communication in everyday interpersonal and intergroup encounters." Paper presented at the Speech Communication Association Convention, New Orleans.

—— and Ting-Toomey, S., with Chua, E. (1988). *Culture and interpersonal communication*. Newbury Park, Calif.: Sage Publications.

—— Yang, S. M., and Nishida, T. (1985). "A cross-cultural test of uncertainty reduction theory: Comparison of acquaintances, friends, and dating relationships in Japan, Korea, and the United States." *Human Communication Research* 11: 407–454.

Hamill, J. (1990). *Ethno-logic: The anthropology of human reasoning*. Urbana: University of Illinois Press.

Hamilton, D., Sherman, S., and Ruvolo, C. (1990). "Stereotyped-based expectancies." *Journal of Social Issues* 46, no. 2: 35–60.

Hofstede, G. (1980). *Culture's consequences*. Beverly Hills, Calif.: Sage Publications.

Honeycutt, J. M. (1993). "Components and functions of communication during initial interactions, with extrapolations to beyond." In S. Deetz (Ed.), *Communication yearbook 16*. Newbury Park, Calif.: Sage Publications.

—— Edwards, R. and Zagacki, K. (1989–1990). "Using imagined interaction features to predict measures of self-awareness." *Imagination, Cognition, and Personality* 9: 17–31.

—— Zagacki, K., and Edwards, R. (1989). "Intrapersonal communication and imagined interactions." In C. Roberts and K. Watson (Eds.), *Readings in intrapersonal communication*. Scottsdale, Ariz.: Gorsuch Scarisbrick.

Jones, E. (1989) "Predicted outcome value and uncertainty reduction." Paper presented at the Western States Communication Association Convention, Spokane.

Kellermann, K. (1986). "Anticipation of future interaction and information exchange in initial interactions." *Human Communication Research* 13: 41–75.

—— (1993). "Extrapolating beyond: Processes of uncertainty reduction." In S. Deetz (Ed.), *Communication yearbook 16*. Newbury Park, Calif.: Sage Publications.

—— and Reynolds, R. (1990). "When ignorance is bliss: The role of motivation to reduce uncertainty in uncertainty reduction theory." *Human Communication Research* 17: 50–75.

Kruglanski, A. (1989). *Lay epistemics and human knowledge*. New York: Plenum Press.

Langer, E. (1978). "Rethinking the role of thought in social interaction." In J. Harvey, W. Ickes, and R. Kidd (Eds.), *New directions in attribution research*, vol. 2. Hillsdale, N.J.: Lawrence Erlbaum and Associates.

Langer, E. (1989). *Mindfulness*. Reading, Mass.: Addison-Wesley.

Lazarus, R. S. (1991). *Emotion and adaptation*. New York: Oxford University Press.

Lester, R. (1983). "Organizational culture, uncertainty reduction, and the socialization of new organizational members." In S. Thomas (Ed.), *Studies in communication*, vol. 3. Norwood, N.J.: Ablex.

Lieberson, S. (1985). *Making it count: The improvement of social research and theory.* Berkeley: University of California Press.

May, R. (1977). *The meaning of anxiety.* New York: Ronald.

Parks, M. and Adelman, M. (1983). "Communication networks and the development of romantic relationships: An expansion of uncertainty reduction theory." *Human Communication Research* 10: 55–80.

Perse, E. (1986). "Attributional confidence, cognitive complexity, and parasocial interaction in soap opera viewing." Paper presented at the International Communication Association Convention, Chicago.

Planalp, S., and Honeycutt, J. (1985). "Events that increase uncertainty in personal relationships." *Human Communication Research* 11: 593–604.

——— Rutherford, D., and Honeycutt, J. (1988). "Events that increase uncertainty in personal relationships II." *Human Communication Research* 14: 516–547.

Reynolds, P. (1971). *A primer in theory construction.* Indianapolis: Bobbs-Merrill.

Schlueter, D., Barge, J., and Case, K. (1987). "Uncertainty reduction in the employee selection process." Paper presented at the International Communication Association Convention, Montreal.

Sodetani, L. L., and Gudykunst, W. B. (1987). "The effects of surprising events on intercultural relationships." *Communication Research Reports* 4, no. 2: 1–6.

Stephan, W., and Stephan, C. (1985). "Intergroup anxiety." *Journal of Social Issues* 41: 157–166.

Sunnafrank, M. (1986). "Predicted outcome value during initial interactions." *Human Communication Research* 13: 3–33.

——— (1988). "Predicted outcome value in initial conversations." *Communication Research Reports* 5: 169–172.

——— (1989). "Uncertainty in interpersonal relationships." In J. Anderson (Ed.), *Communication yearbook 12.* Newbury Park, Calif.: Sage Publications.

——— (1990). "Predicted outcome value and uncertainty reduction theories." *Human Communication Research* 17: 76–103.

Tajfel, H. (1978). "Social categorization, social identity, and social comparisons." In H. Tajfel (Ed.), *Differentiation between groups.* London: Academic Press.

Ting-Toomey, S. (1989). "Culture and interpersonal relationship development." In J. Anderson (Ed.), *Communication yearbook 12*. Newbury Park, Calif.: Sage Publications.

Triandis, H. C. (1988). "Collectivism vs. individualism." In G. Verma and C. Bagley (Eds.), *Cross-cultural studies of personality, attitudes, and cognition*. London: Macmillan.

Turner, J. C. (1987). *Rediscovering the social group*. London: Basil Blackwell.

Turner, J. H. (1988). *A theory of social interaction*. Palo Alto, Calif.: Stanford University Press.

Van Lear, A., and Trujillo, N. (1986). "On becoming acquainted." *Journal of Personal and Social Relationships* 3: 375–392.

Wilson, C. (1986). "Organizational socialization, uncertainty reduction, and commnication networks." Paper presented at the Speech Communication Association Convention, Chicago.

5

THE SEQUENTIAL INFERENTIAL THEORIES
OF SANDERS AND GOTTMAN

ROBERT SANDERS

That communicative acts are not self-standing has received attention in a scattering of both qualitative and quantitative studies of interpersonal and group interactions. Such acts occur as parts of *sequences* of acts that generally are interactively produced. But there is no unity among these studies about exactly why sequence matters or what difference it makes. For the most part, in fact, studies that take sequencing into account have retained a concern with the occurrence of individual acts and attended to sequence as either an ordered chain of "causes" and "effects" of component acts, or a complex initial condition for the occurrence of certain acts of interest, or a "context" that influences the interpretation of component acts. Interactional sequences have also been examined as a temporal series of incremental changes from one state of an interpersonal relationship to another or as evidence of the practical contingencies that make the performance of each act in a sequence dependent on the completion of a prior one.

These diverse reasons for an interest in sequence have obscured ways in which the findings of some studies cohere and whether studies that employ the term *sequence* are referring to the same thing or not. The purpose of this chapter is to show that there is a unitary notion of *sequence* that involves a distinctive approach to theory and research about communicative phenomena and that coheres a number of these studies: in this approach *sequences* of acts, ordered wholes and not the component acts individually, are the principal influence over what happens between people—not just on the level of interpersonal and group communication where much of the research has been done, but arguably on the level of public campaigns and movements and in mass media effects more broadly.

The bulk of this chapter provides an overview of this sequence-centered approach in terms of two distinct strands of research: Gottman's research on marital interaction, and my own work on interaction strategy. However, to anyone familiar with both Gottman's work and mine, it may strain credulity for our work to be paired at all, let alone as having jointly contributed to the development of a single paradigm. Gottman is concerned with the communicative-inter-actional basis for successful and unsuccessful personal relationships; my concern is the formal-cognitive basis for participating coherently and strategically in interactions. Gottman tends to view what happens between people as determinate from the patterns of their interaction; I tend to view patterns of interaction as self-determined and jointly achieved. Gottman gives primary emphasis to statistical regularities in sequences of interaction between relational partners; I give primary emphasis to the "novel," nonroutine interactional sequences in which people get involved at least occasionally, more probably with strangers and acquaintances than relational partners.

However, there is a shared interest underlying Gottman's work and mine, and a unique approach, that makes the conjunction of our work sensible. Like many others, we are both concerned with the potential in social interactions for interpersonal influence—regarding the trajectory of the relationship between the persons involved (Gottman) or coordination of the business at hand (Sanders). But the distinguishing element that our work has in common is that we both consider that the primary influence on persons engaged with each other is *the course of the interaction(s) between them*, not the other person's acts alone.

This connection between Gottman's work and mine is of central, paradigmatic importance: in different but complementary ways, our work positions the *sequences* communicative acts that persons *interactively* produce as being the central influence over what happens between them, and thus the basis for explaining it—again, referring to influence regarding either or both (1) the business at hand in specific interactions, and (2) the quality and trajectory of the interpersonal tie between the persons involved. And although an examination of interactional sequences is not unique, it is principally Gottman and I who position the sequencing itself as central to what happens between persons and jointly indicate theoretically why this should be so.

The term *sequence* is clarified in the next section of this chapter. For now, the term applies when there is interest in the "whole" or "pattern" formed by a sequence or in the interconnections among components on which sequential order is based. This can include what Gottman refers to in much of his work: sequences in the narrow, technical sense of statistically regular contingencies between the occurrence of one act and the acts that follow, found by applying a "lag sequence analysis" to observed interactions. A broader sense of *sequence* is intended here, however, one that includes as psychologically real not only sequences that observably progress from some initial act, but also possible alternative sequences that could have followed that initial act, based on under-lying principles that specify the coherent possible ways of sequencing communicative acts. From this perspective, observed sequences are functionally one option among alternative possibilities, and statistically regular sequences are not necessarily more coherent than nonstandard ones. Participants in interaction and observers or analysts alike must therefore consider, and make inferences accordingly, that the observed sequence of acts has not occurred for the sake of coherence alone but was preferred because of the formative situation and resulting "pattern" or trajectory of the interaction, as well as the dispositions, capabilities and compatibility of the persons involved.

As will be discussed, these principles and the broader sense of *sequence* involved are central to my work and are needed as well to support recent developments in Gottman's thinking. (How this applies to research other than Gottman's and mine is discussed in the concluding portions of this chapter.) The focus of much of my work is that persons evidently fashion communicative acts anticipatorily and proactively to increase the probability of achieving a desired resolution of the current interaction or of avoiding an undesired one. Gottman recently advanced a theoretical account of the relation between marital interactions and the trajectory of the relationship that centers on discontinuous jumps in participants' affect states that are evident when persons respond to specific acts in a way more oriented to the trajectory of the interaction than to the act. While Gottman focuses on the psychological processes that would explain such "jumps" during a marital interaction and the consequences of them, their occurrence exhibits first of all the same anticipatory and proactive orientation to the future course of the interaction that is apparent in my data also. Such anticipatory and proactive conduct seems necessarily dependent on the psychological reality of principles for coherently sequencing acts: "knowing" such principles would make it possible for people to infer the "pattern" or "whole" being produced during an interaction, and project what they can do to alter it or conclude that it cannot be altered.

Within what I will call the *sequential-inferential paradigm*, then, to say that the *sequence* of acts that persons interactively produce influences what happens between them is to say that the progression of component acts of an interaction forms an *inferred* "whole" or "pattern" that gives rise to certain psychological states and processes (Gottman) or interactional constraints (Sanders) that, in a progressively self-fulfilling way, delimit how individuals will seek (or expect) to have their interaction(s) conclude or what they seek (or expect) their interaction(s) to include. This obviously stands in sharp contrast to most paradigms, which posit that factors altogether independent of interaction are central influences over what happens between people. Within the sequential-inferential paradigm, such factors are at most influences secondary to and mediated by the interactional sequences people produce, including (1) the behavioral force of each person's psychological dispositions or wants, personal history, values, group memberships, gender, race, or ethnicity, or (2) the interdependence established between persons by their institutional rights and responsibilities (including relative power), the practical requirements of the task they are engaged in, or the configuration of relational costs and benefits each person creates for the other, or even (3) the effect of the occurrence of particular communicative acts produced by one or more of the persons involved that have a certain substance or qualities.

The following exposition about the sequential-inferential paradigm has three major sections: (1) a discussion of *sequence* as it applies to interactions and the basis provided by an interactional sequence for *inferences* about the "pattern" or "whole" the interaction is forming; (2) an overview of the research topics and data Gottman and I have each worked on, in relation to the sequential-inferential paradigm, and relevant work by others; and (3) a summary of the theoretical issues that emerge from Gottman's work and from mine respectively, and their interconnection.

Sequence and Inference in Interactions

Because there has been attention to "sequence" in several different lines of research, for different purposes, it is important to first clarify what the term means here and then to position this sense of the term in relation to other research concerns that employ it. Accordingly, I will first formulate what *sequence* involves in the broader sense referred to previouslly, based on my own work, and provide a rationale for that sense of the term and its centrality. I will then outline the basis such sequences provide for inferences about the course of the present interaction, and the motives of the other person(s) involved. I will reserve for later sections how these formulations apply to Gottman's work and mine.

In general, research concerned with interactional sequences is divided as to whether it is of concern only to describe and characterize ones that are standardized, or instead or in addition, to identify any principles of syntactic ordering involved in them (i.e., in terms of combinatorial rules, principles by which acts follow each other coherently or the like). The broad sense of *sequence* intended here arises from the latter, a concern with restrictions on the sequential order of acts in interactions.

Retrictions on Interactional Sequences

A concern with restrictions on the sequencing of acts in a discourse or inter-action is warranted insofar as it seems that not every sequence of acts is equally coherent and that some possible act sequences are incoherent or "anomalous." (The condition of "anomaly" or incoherence of an interactional sequence is on the surface a matter of intuition or judgment more than of objective properties of the sequence, as is also true of judgments of "ungrammaticality" in the case of sentences.) The question of interest here is whether those judgments have a systematic, impersonal basis, and if so, what it is. Although the former question is an empirical one, it seems almost certain that there are general, impersonal restrictions on the sequencing of acts if there are restrictions at all: people must have a shared basis for forming sequences to communicate interactively at all and do not generally produce incoherent sequences of acts.

Evidence that there are restrictions on sequence is that it appears to be a standing presumption that acts in sequence will be topically, semantically relevant to each other (e.g., Grice, 1975). Although Grice's work (and everyday experience) suggests that relevance of some kind can be found between most pairs of utterances if one presumes each next utterance was intended to be relevant to the prior one, in cases when relevance cannot be found readily, the sequence of acts seems incoherent or anomalous:

(1) A: I like the styling of the new cars this year.

?   B: My grandmother's sister was deported from Russia in 1905.

In addition to having to "be" relevant, if acts in a sequence do not evidently contribute to the "progress" of the sequence toward some kind of resolution, the sequence also seems anomalous or incoherent. This is a presumption in Edmondson's (1981) analysis of act sequences, where an utterance's contribution to the "progress" of a sequence toward a resolution is the basis for its interpretation as a speech act. In addition, following Grice (1975), Atlas and Levinson (1981) posited an "informativeness" maxim, a presumption that a response contributes information for which prior utterances create a "demand." More specifically, Schank (1977) argued that it is anomalous for an utterance to be followed with a redundant response, such as a response that asserts what the prior utterance presupposed:

(2) A: I'd like another cup of coffee.

?   B: Your cup is empty.

And Tracy (1982, 1983) found that when persons respond to an utterance, they are judged less competent if their response is to a subordinate component (an "event") in the prior utterance, instead of the "issue" that the prior utterance addressed:

(3) A: It would be fun if you'll come shopping with me at the new mall.

?   B: A lot of people go shopping just for the fun of it these days.

Restrictions on Sequence by a Discourse "Grammar." If there are restrictions on sequencing component units or acts in discourse and interaction, the obvious precedent for capturing those restrictions is the work in linguistics on formalizing them as "grammars." Such an approach was taken in linguistically based discourse studies (Sinclair and Coulthard, 1975; Rumelhant, 1975; van Dijk, 1972) that sought to provide an analytic basis for formulating "grammars" for language structures larger than the sentence. However, Levinson (1981) made a strong case in principle against the only obvious way of formulating such grammars, which would be to treat the basic units of these larger structures as speech acts, treating them as the discourse analog of parts of speech. The central problem with such an approach is that, unlike the fixed relationship at the sentence level between words and the grammatical categories (parts of speech) they belong to, there is a contingent and relatively uncertain relationship between specific utterances and the speech act(s) they count as.

Restrictions on Sequence by Adjacency Pairs. A quite different solution to the problem of capturing restrictions on interactional sequences would be to parse them into adjacency pairs (Sacks and Schegloff, 1973). However, the concept of adjacency pairs did not arise as a way to capture restrictions on interactional sequences, and for the reasons that follow they cannot do so, but enough work has been done that leads in this direction to warrant attention to it. Adjacency pairs are structural subunits of interaction that consist of two acts, where the first act of the pair creates a "demand" and the second act of the pair resolves it (e.g., question-answer pairs, compliment-acknowledgment pairs, complaint-redress pairs, or directive-compliance/refusal pairs). Further, adjacency pairs can be expanded by embedded matter between the first and second parts to encompass indefinitely large portions of an interaction (e.g., Jefferson, 1972; Edmondson, 1981, pp. 86–100; Schegloff, 1980). However, the adjacency pair itself does not create any restrictions on the sequencing of embedded matter between the first and second parts, unless that matter consists of other adjacency pairs.

Parsing interactions into adjacency pairs to capture restrictions on interactional sequences has two fatal limitations. The first is that communicative acts occur to which the concept of adjacency pairs does not apply. These acts neither make "demands" that would be satisfied by certain succeeding acts in particular nor satisfy such "demands" by prior acts, for example as is often true of reports, observations, comments and the like (assertives in Searle's, 1976, typology)—yet such acts are not uncommon and can even consume the majority of an interaction. This would not be a problem if sequencing restrictions did not apply to such acts, but they do, as in example 1, where a statement about the styling of new cars is followed by a statement about the speaker's grandmother's sister.

A second limitation in using adjacency pairs to capture restrictions on interactional sequences is that doing so analytically reduces interactions to unstructured collections of act pairs (regardless of whether each such pair is expanded by embedded matter). The problem is not so much that this counter-intuitively rules out that there are larger interactional structures and wholes, as indicated by the labels we have for them (as when interactions are said to constitute, e.g., an "argument," "teaching," an "interview," "bargaining," "seduction," and the like). Rather, the more serious problem is that if interactions are unstructured collections of act pairs, there is no basis for restrictions on sequencing from one such pair to the next, only within pairs. Yet sequences from one pair to the next are odd or anomalous if they fail to preserve relevance, as in 4, which follows, or fail to achieve progress toward a resolution of the whole (insofar as we admit that larger interactional wholes are analytically real), as in 5:

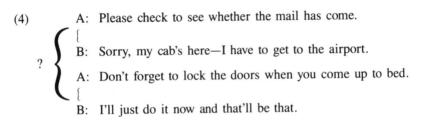

(4)   A: Please check to see whether the mail has come.

           B: Sorry, my cab's here—I have to get to the airport.
    ?
           A: Don't forget to lock the doors when you come up to bed.

           B: I'll just do it now and that'll be that.

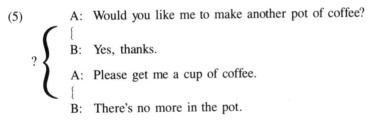

(5)   A: Would you like me to make another pot of coffee?

           B: Yes, thanks.
    ?
           A: Please get me a cup of coffee.

           B: There's no more in the pot.

One way around this problem would be to assign acts "double duty" as both the second part of one pair (by satisfying a "demand") and the first part of the next pair (by creating a "demand"). However, except at high levels of abstraction (e.g., coding all acts as "one-up," "one-across," or "one-down" moves per Rogers and Farace, 1975), attributing such dual functionality to acts would be strained and cumbersome in some cases and not feasible at all in others. For example, in 4, B's initial utterance ("Sorry, my cab's here—I have to get to the airport") may arguably create a vague or weak "demand" that A's next utterance does not meet, but in 5 it would be difficult to plausibly identify any "demand" that B's initial utterance creates ("Yes, thanks").

Restrictions on Sequence by Principle to Ensure Relevance and Progress.
The solution I have proposed (Sanders, 1980, 1987) is to formulate principles
that directly express restrictions on sequencing in interactions to preserve
relevance and ensure progress toward resolution of the interaction (or current
substructure). The resulting principles apply in such a way that, for any given
act in an actual sequence, an array of subsequent acts is specified that each
follow relevantly or make progress toward a resolution of the whole, and from
each of those alternative possible "next" acts, a further set of acts is specified
that each follow relevantly or make progress toward a resolution of the whole,
and so on. The result of applying these principles to an initial or base act,
A_1, is a branching network of communicative acts, as in Figure 5.1. Each pathway

FIGURE 5.1

Possible Interaction Sequences Following Act A_1 as a
Branching Network of Act Relevancies

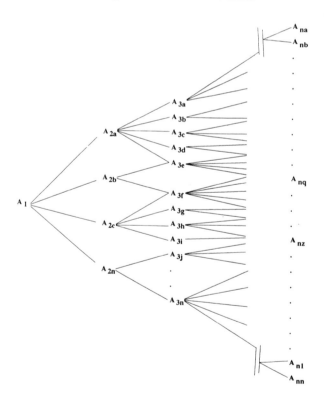

through such a network represents a possible sequence that follows from A_1 and has as possible resolutions members of the set of acts $\{A_n\}$, where successive members are each relevant to what preceded it in a pathway or contributes to progress along a pathway toward some resolution of the whole. Actual sequences thus are one pathway from among the alternatives in such a branching network, where each person's acts are a functional selection from among alternative possible acts at each node.

The most straightforward of the principles involved in this approach are ones that state what is required for an utterance or nonverbal display to be relevant to what has preceded or follows it. Even these are more involved than what is suggested by most conceptions of relevance: concepts of relevance among utterances have generally focused on their informational (semantic) relationships (e.g., Sperber and Wilson, 1986), overlooking the relevance of utterances in terms or their illocutionary force or their conversational implicature(s); and efforts to conceptualize the relevance of nonverbal displays to each other or to utterances have been in terms of their informational aspects (Sperber and Wilson, 1986) or their functioning to embellish or disambiguate concurrent utterance meaning (McNeill, 1985; Bavelas, 1994), but not as functional components of interactional sequences.

The principles of relevance I have formulated (Sanders, 1987) consider that utterances and nonverbal displays, respectively, are analyzable as having one or more distinct types of meaning, each of which has component features and presuppositions (e.g., propositional content, illocutionary force, or conversational implicature in the case of utterances; or for nonverbal displays per Ekman and Friesen, 1969, emblems, illustrators, regulators, adapters, and affect displays). Two communicative acts are then considered relevant to each other if they have in common a component feature or presupposition of at least one of their possible meanings (for details, see Sanders, 1987, pp. 79–100, 129–152). Thus, for example, B's utterance in 6, which follows, is relevant to A's on the basis of common elements in the semantics of each; in 7, B's utterance is relevant to A's on the basis of common elements in the semantics of B's utterance and the felicity conditions of the illocutionary act that A's utterance counts as; in 8, B's utterance is relevant to A's on the basis of common elements in the felicity conditions of the act each counts as:

(6) A: I'd like to see a movie tonight.

     B: Any particular one?

(7) A: Be careful driving home, it's icy.

     B: Relax, I'm not blind or suicidal.

(8) A: You've been late to work every day this week.

     B: I haven't been taking lunch.

(9) A: I thought was a great concert.

     B: (makes facial grimace)

Similarly, in 9, B's display of a facial grimace would be relevant to A's prior utterance insofar as A's utterance is a proposition about the speaker's positive affective response to the concert and the facial grimace displays the respondent's negative affective response (though it is ambiguous whether the response is to the concert or to the other's assessment). On the surface the relevance between the two is based on the common feature of expressing an affective response, but a more general basis for their relevance is that A's stated assessment or reference to the concert can be regarded as a proximate and sufficient cause of the affective state displayed by B's facial grimace.

The more complicated matter involves formulating the requirements for making progress toward resolution of the whole. The problem is to identify a basis (for observers or analysts and participants alike) for defining *the whole* and its possible ways of being resolved before the interaction has occurred or even in its initial stages. A partial solution is to appropriate Edmondson's (1981) idea that every interaction or its substructures is organized around "proffers" (acts that introduce an agenda or formulate the business at hand) and "satisfiers" (resolutions), where a given proffer implies a relatively small set of possible satisfiers. For example, a proffer might introduce the agenda of arranging a time and place to meet for lunch, with possible satisfiers being to agree on a time and place or agree that they cannot do so, and if the latter, then to either postpone planning or abandon the effort.

With reference to the set of possible satisfiers following a proffer, then, it can be specified whether a communicative act contributes to progress toward one or another satisfier. Progress toward a satisfier is then formalized as a reduction in the minimum number of communicative acts needed to progress coherently (relevantly) from the current act to a possible resolution (Sanders, 1987 pp. 94–97).

Of course, this reliance on a proffer-satisfier structure to account for restrictions on sequencing to ensure progress toward a resolution returns us to something resembling an analysis in terms of adjacency pairs: every proffer creates a structural "demand" for a small range of possible satisfiers, and many proffer-satisfy sequences can comprise just two acts or be expanded by intermediate matter. But, unlike an analysis of restrictions on sequencing in terms of adjacency pairs, the principles here for preserving relevance and ensuring progress toward a resolution capture restrictions on sequencing of embedded matter between a "proffer" and its resolution and when pertinent across a sequence of proffer-satisfier pairs. A less important difference in addition is that proffers encompass a much broader range of acts than adjacency pairs do (e.g., the initiating act of an effort to schedule a lunch may not be the first part of an adjacency pair such as a question or directive, but may simply be a statement, for example, within a conversation about a business problem, that a lunch meeting would be a convenient venue for working out details on the matter at hand).

Admittedly, not all interactions originate with the establishment of a clear agenda, or even have agendas that are introduced later, as when telephone callers introduce the "reason for call" after some preliminary small talk (e.g., Button and Casey, 1988–1989). However, interactions that do not comprise defined agendas are not evidence against this approach to capturing restrictions on sequencing; just the contrary. Note that such interactions are marked (e.g., there are labels for them, such as *small talk, chitchat, idle conversation*), and what distinguishes them is that they "wander" across a variety of topics or exhibit considerable repetitiousness, giving an impression of being "undirected" or "unfocused." This is precisely the quality one would expect an interaction to have when the only restrictions on sequencing are to preserve relevance, with no restrictions (in absence of a defined agenda) regarding progress toward a resolution of the whole.

Inferences and Attributions from Interactional Sequences

Within the sequential-inferential paradigm, the utility of this latter approach to capturing restrictions on interactional sequences is that it accounts for inferences that participants evidently make about the course the present interaction is taking—what it will include or how it will conclude—and the steps they take to facilitate or compensate for it. It also accounts for attributions or inferences that persons in interactions make about each other regarding their respective dispositions and capabilities and their mutual compatibility.

Principles that restrict interactional sequences are applicable to explaining such attributions and inferences in the following way. Inferences and attributions about the "causes" of social events or the qualities of other persons or the meanings of acts cannot be made solely on the basis of what observably occurs. Rather, *inferences and attributions about "causes," qualities, or meanings are based on contrasting what observably occurs with what could equally well have occurred under the same circumstances.* For example, if a person walking on a city street passes a stranger without being greeted, little can be inferred about that stranger's dispositions or capabilities, inasmuch as social convention indicates that no alternative (i.e., being greeted) could equally well have occurred. But if the same person in the same circumstance passes a friend without being greeted, then some inference about the friend would have been warranted because an alternative (being greeted) could equally well have occurred. The inferential process involved might be to array possible reasons why the friend did not offer a greeting (unable to do so or not disposed to do so, and if not disposed, then either because the occasion for greeting was not recognized or because the friend has stopped being friendly), and then to seek additional information that would verify one possible reason or rule out all but one.

Given that inferences and attributions are based on comparing what occurs with alternative possibilities, it is noteworthy that the previous principles for restricting interactional sequences provide a basis for participants and observers alike to compare any observed sequence and any component act with possible alternatives (i.e., the branching network of pathways in Figure 5.1 from which observed sequences are functional selections).

Inferences About the Course of an Interaction. The principles that capture restrictions on sequencing enable participants (and observers or analysts) to compare the acts that occur with possible alternatives. This provides a general basis for participants and observers alike to make inferences about the pattern or whole the interaction is forming, the course it is taking, as follows. If the acts that occur have certain qualities in common that have been functionally preferred, in companson with the alternatives, then it can be inferred that the interaction will continue in a course that results from a continued preference for acts with those qualities. If, on the other hand, an act occurs to the contrary and alters the inferred course of the interaction because it is a functional selection from among alternatives whose qualities were previously dispreferred, that act may be sufficient in itself for an entirely different inference about the course of the interaction.

Such inferences are greatly facilitated, however, when the interaction is (construed as being) organized around an agenda of some kind (as many if not most interactions are)—when it is analyzed as proceeding from some initial point or formative purpose that delimits possible resolutions. In that case, at each node of the underlying branching network of acts where certain options would move the interaction toward certain resolutions and away from others, a refined inference about its course or trajectory can be made. This makes it likely that there will be a point in an interaction when the occurrence of a single act is sufficient to foster certainty about the inferred trajectory and resolution of the interaction, even in the absence of any explicit indication of this or "official" pronouncements by participants.

It is important in this regard that these sequences of acts are *interactively* produced. Inferences a participant makes about the course being taken by an interaction can be "tested" by producing a communicative act that the participant projects would be responded to only in a certain way, among possible alternatives, if the participant's inference were correct. An example of this occurs in a marital interaction examined later, in the discussion of Gottman's research.

Inferences About Others' Dispositions and Capabilities. The same comparison of the qualities of acts functionally selected with the qualities of alternative possible acts can support inferences about the dispositions and capabilities of persons in an interaction. In the case of inferences about a participant's dispositions, it would be a matter of construing a set of values and intentions that would be necessary and sufficient for a participant to "select" acts with the qualities of the ones that occurred as opposed to possible alternatives or to "select" acts that move the interaction toward certain possible resolutions and away from others. Inferences about a person's capabilities would most readily occur in interactions organized around an explicit agenda and arise from assessing (1) whether the person's acts are fashioned to consistently move the interaction in the direction of a particular resolution or are inconsistent or equivocal about the resolution toward which they move the interaction; and (2) whether the person's acts make it relevant to continue efficiently (with minimum redundancy or digression) in the direction of the resolution toward which the interaction had been progressing.

Inferences About the Mutual Compatibility of Persons Interacting. Finally, whether persons are mutually compatible can be inferred from assessing, first, whether their acts combine "cooperatively" to move the interaction uniformly along a pathway toward the same resolution, and second, if there are any "conflicts" over the resolution toward which their respective acts move the interaction, whether they are able to resolve them or instead evince coordination problems and even a breakdown of interaction. An analysis of interactions between three supervisor-subordinate pairs (Sanders, 1995) revealed a contrast in their compatibility along these lines (arranged here from most to least compatible). The first pair engaged in consultation on a work problem brought to the supervisor by the subordinate, and both made reciprocal contributions of "problem definition" (subordinate) and "problem resolution" (supervisor). The second pair also engaged in consultation on a work problem, but each sought to move the interaction toward a different resolution; their difference was reconciled through a tacit role reversal, where the subordinate took control of the course of the interaction and the supervisor eventually reversed himself and acted to contribute to progress toward the same resolution as the subordinate. The third supervisor-subordinate pair were engaged in discussion of what action to take in response to current disruptions by "clients" of their agency, and throughout the interaction each acted to move the interaction toward a different resolution from the other; moreover, the subordinate at least twice changed the resolution toward which his acts moved the interaction, independent of what resolution the supervisor's acts were concurrently moving toward.

Overview of Research Topics and Findings

The overviews of Gottman's research and mine are not comprehensive, but the goal is not to provide a detailed summary of what we have each found out on the topics our research addresses. The focus here is on the application and development in our work of the sequential-inferential paradigm.

Gottman's Research on Interaction

Gottman's research addresses matters of substantive and methodological concern in family studies, broadly conceived. But rather than examine child-parent interactions, and family dynamics inclusively, he has separately examined interactions between marital partners and interactions between children at play. In both cases, his interest has been in identifying the differences in communication between "successful" and "unsuccessful" relational partners for the sake of devising clinical interventions regarding the communication of persons experiencing relational failure. Such relational failure results in marital dissolution for the adults, on the one hand, and social isolation and a potential for dysfunctional acts on the children's part.

The common element in his research on marital couples and on children is that Gottman went beyond the identification of differences in the communicative acts produced by "successful" and "unsuccessful" relational partners to reveal and identify *sequences* of acts in interaction (in the narrow sense of statistical regularities in contingencies of occurrence) that distinguish between them. In the case of his research on marital partners, however, his findings—and particularly his recent theorizing about them—tacitly indicate the centrality of the broad sense of "sequence" discussed ealier as influencing what happens between the persons involved. This will be discussed here.

Sequence in the broad sense does not apply readily to Gottman's data about children's interactions because no statistically regular sequences more extensive than specific act pairs were found (Gottman, Gonso, and Rasmussen, 1975; Gottman, 1983). This may have been because of the play "task" in which the children were engaged, or because the children were strangers without an established relationship and corresponding patterns of interaction, or because of the level of the children's communicative development. Regardless, the data of these studies are not applicable to the issues being addressed here and not included for that reason in the following discussion of Gottman's research.

Gottman's Research on Marital Interaction. Gottman's research on marital interaction had an explicit interest in going beyond other research that had focused only on the types of communicative acts produced by distressed versus nondistressed couples. Gottman (e.g., 1979, p. 29) conceived of married couples as "systems" whose communication could be fruitfully examined from a cybernetic perspective, citing Shannon and Weaver's (1949) work as the basis. From this perspective, Gottman's research investigated the possibility that it was a matter of the interconnections among communicative acts rather than or in addition to the acts themselves that differentiated distressed versus nondistressed couples.

In addition to considerable attention to the statistical and methodological aspects of analyzing sequences, Gottman's research in the 1970s (Gottman, 1976; Gottman et al., 1976b; Gottman, Markman, and Notarious, 1977) shows that there are notable differences between distressed and nondistressed couples in the interconnections (statistical regularities in the sequencing) of communicative acts in their interactions. This work was integrated and elaborated in a book (Gottman, 1979) that analyzed marital interactions in each of three distinct stages of problem-solving discussion the couples were asked to have. A number of differences in this regard were evident, ones moreover that could be addressed in clinical interventions to alter patterns of interaction correlated with marital distress (Gottman, 1979, pp. 105–168). For example, among distressed couples initial statements of feeling about the problem led to potentially extended sequences of reciprocal statements of feeling that Gottman described as "cross-complaining;" in contrast, among nondistressed couples similar initial statements led to short sequences involving either agreement or corroborating statements of feeling that Gottman described as "validation."

One contrast among the statistically regular sequences produced by distressed versus nondistressed couples is of particular interest here in relation to underlying principles for sequencing acts coherently. Given that actual sequences are one possible pathway among alternative possible pathways through a branching network of acts, Gottman's data indicate that there are fewer "branching" interconnections among acts for distressed than nondistressed couples: distressed couples thus tend to be more "rigidified" and predictable in the pathway their interactions follow than nondistressed couples are. This probably involves "unwanted repetitive palterns" (Cronen, Pearce, and Snavely, 1979). But beyond that it indicates that, for distressed couples, the acts they produce tend to make less difference to what happens next than among nondistressed couples. This is particularly striking (but not unique) for "sequences of contracting and counterproposal" (Gottman, 1979, p. 165). For distressed couples, initial statements of problem-solutions or information may be responded to by either agreement or a reciprocal statement, but regardless of the response, the subsequent interaction tends to be a reciprocating series of problem, solutions and information. For nondistressed couples, an initial problem solving or informational statement leads to a series of branchings where a reciprocal statement or an agreement is possible at each node (excepting two nodes following from husband's initial statement where wife tends to respond with a problem solving or informational statement regardless of whether husband previously produced one himself or produces agreement).

This quality of the sequences characteristically produced by distressed versus nondistressed couples has a potential negative affect. The "rigidity" of sequences produced by distressed couples could produce a sense of futility and inferences about the dispositions, capabilities, and mutual compatibility of the partners. Gottman's findings that distressed couples express more negative affect (but no less positive affect) may be an indication of their orientations to the reoccurrence of the emerging "pattern" of the interaction more than an expression of feelings about the substance of their respective acts or about their partner.

In this context, Gottman's approach to clinical intervention for distressed couples is noteworthy (Gottman et al., 1976a; Gottman, 1979, pp. 267–288). The approach was to teach distressed couples five "social skills" that each countered the apparent basis or quality of communicative acts and responses characteristically produced by distressed couples. In general these are not oriented to larger sequences but to learning new ways of producing specific acts. For example, the first three of these focus on the production of specific acts and responses, in terms of including acknowledgment of the others' point of view, particularizing attributions and characterizations, and self-consciously editing acts to include specific "polite-positive" components. However, what such skills combat is not only negative communicative acts, but conceivably the larger sequences typically engaged in and responded to by distressed couples, in this sense. First, each "skill" induces couples to attend to specific acts and stop responding to the larger sequences as they arguably had been doing. Second, these skills induce changes in the way specific acts are formulated that make relevant different, more positive, responses than had been typical of distressed couples and thereby make it possible to coherently progress toward other resolutions of the interaction than had been typical.

Gottman's Theory of Marital Dissolution and Stability. Recently, Gottman (1993) confronted the theoretical question, specifically in regard to marital dissolution and stability, of why there is a relationship between sequences of interaction characteristic of marital partners and the stability of their marriage. That theoretical account leaves moot all the issues about sequences themselves that are of interest here—but it nonetheless presupposes and depends on them.

Gottman (1993) worked from two key findings from his earlier research. One is that stable versus "unhappy" couples were statistically distinguished by whether they exhibited progressively positive, and net positive, act sequences, based on a scoring system that assigned "positive" and "negative" scores to acts based on their relational valence (e.g., agreement is positive, disagreement is negative). Second, a "process cascade" of negative acts was found to be most strongly predictive of dissolution (e.g., criticism leads to contempt, which leads to defensiveness, which leads to a stonewall). A particular "emotional" cascade was also identified that predicts moves toward partners' moves toward withdrawal, the "distance and isolation cascade," that Gottman (1993) speculated begins with "flooding": "the subject [claims] that the partner's negative emotions are unexpected ('seem to come out of nowhere'), unprovoked, intense, overwhelming, and disorganizing and that the partner will do anything to terminate the interaction" (p. 64). Flooding tends to initiate a "distance and isolation" cascade (perceiving marital problems as severe, moving to work out problems singly and not jointly, creating parallel and not interactive lives, and experiencing loneliness in the marriage).

Gottman's (1993) theoretical formulation, which he rooted in work on systems and thermodynamics in physics, borrows from "catastrophe theory" (a theory of discontinuous jumps in an otherwise continuous process). He proposed that flooding reflects such a discontinuity: when the process cascade in the interaction takes a negative direction with a downward slope that exceeds a certain threshold, there is a discontinuous affective "jump" from perceptions of well-being to the reverse, and that produces flooding and the "distance and isolation" cascade.

Of particular interest here, but not addressed by Gottman, is on what persons in interactions base these perceptions of the trajectory or "slope" of an interaction. What does it mean for a person to say that the partner suddenly exhibits emotions "that seem to come out of nowhere," and yet at the same time Gottman attributed such emotions to the person's perception of the trajectory of the interaction? Gottman (1993) provided an illustrative transcript that, together with the overview of "sequence" in the first section of this chapter suggests the answers.

In the sample interaction, husband and wife (H and W) are discussing what provokes W's feelings of jealousy. H first offers an actual case for discussion (H plans to ride with a woman to a business meeting), but W does not consider it problematic. H then presents as a hypothetical case, if he were to meet with a former, premarital, lover to see how she is ("just for a hypothetical, that, say, I wanted to see Jeannie again, just, say, for lunch"). W engages in discussion of this hypothetical and explains that she feels this would be a special case, and she would be opposed, because of the past relationship. However, several turns later W nonverbally manifests negative affect and then in her next turn abruptly says (indicative of flooding): "Wait a minute! Do you want to see her? Is that what you are saying?" And when H answers affirmatively, W asserts "Then I think we have a serious problem"—perhaps the onset of the distance and isolation cascade.

The question is, On what does W base her inference that the issue of Jeannie is not just a hypothetical case? The further question is, What does it mean *with reference to the interaction itself* to say that such an interactional moment fosters a perception of a negative trajectory in the interaction that crosses a threshold sufficient to produce flooding?

First, W's inference that the topic of seeing Jeannie again is not just hypothetical, that H actually wants to see her, has a clear basis in the course of the interaction:

(10) (Gottman, 1993, p. 70)

1. W: No, that's. Jeannie is a different story. You were lovers.
2.   (There is a bit of alarm in her voice, but slight.)
3. H: But that was way before I met you. And you know that I have
4.   made a commitment to our family. It's just not an issue.
5.   It's like seeing an old chum.
6. W: It doesn't matter. That's a very different kind of relationship.
7.   She simply has no place in our lives. It's not
8.   like a chum. She's a woman.
9. H: See, that's where I think you're wrong. She's a person that I
10.   once liked a lot, and it's a shame to lose touch with her.
11.   As a friend. As an acquaintance.
12. W: Why should she come into our lives, into our home? Why
13.   should my children know her? (There is sudden clear alarm
14.   in her voice and on her face.)
15. H: She's very interesting, you know. You both went to the same
16.   college. You'd have a lot in common.
17. W: Wait a minute. Do you want to see her? Is that what you
18.   are saying?

This segment of the interaction began with H's introduction of "Jeannie" as a hypothetical case to discuss the basis of W's feelings of jealousy. In terms of principles that restrict sequences to ensure relevance and progress toward a resolution, the interaction through line 8 proceeds relevantly toward resolution of this hypothetical (H proposes that seeing Jeannie is like seeing an old chum, W objects and disagrees that the two are comparable). The most directly relevant response for H that would pursue the same course (toward resolution of on what W's feelings of jealousy are based) would be to ask about or object to W's insistence that Jeannie is a special case because "she's a woman." But H's response is relevant in a way that does not move the interaction toward resolution of the issue of his meeting with a person *like* Jeannie, it is relevant in a way that moves it toward resolution of the issue of meeting with *that* person in particular (lines 9–11: "She's a person that I once liked a lot, and it's a shame to lose touch with her. As a friend. As an acquaintance"). Note that it is at just that point that W exhibits nonverbal indications of distress, but instead of challenging H she responds with a question that it would be possible for H to answer either in terms of the original hypothetical issue or the newly evident concrete issue (perhaps seeking confirmation of the inference deliberately). H's reply pursues the concrete issue, offering qualities of *that* person which make her someone in particular W could find "interesting." Only then does W issue an explicit challenge about what issue H is pursuing.

It is clear, then, that W has a basis from the course the interaction was taking for her inference that H was leading up to a proposal to actually meet with Jeannie. One can surmise that this also provided W with a basis for perceiving a sufficiently negative trajectory for the remaining interaction that she could assert that "we have a serious problem." Her basis for this anticipatory and proactive assertion (and potentially for "flooding") was conceivably that (1) H had deceptively introduced the topic of Jeannie in the first place to gain assent to meeting with her so the "agenda" was premeditated; (2) H had pursued that agenda despite W's objections to the hypothetical and objections to the particular (lines 12–13: "Why should she come into our lives, into our home? Why should my children know her?"). Based on what had already occurred and what relevantly followed and the possible resolutions the remaining interaction could have, W could project that a positive resolution was not possible: H's professed desire to see Jeannie would remain unchanged, and there would be a risk of something more damaging being said, whether she ended up giving in to his wishes to have such a meeting or H gave in to her objections.

Gottman's work comulatively provides a substantial corpus of empirical data that indicate that the principal influence over what happens between people is the course of the interactions between them. While this work tends to take for granted the cognitive processing on which this depends and thus disregards underlying principles for cohering sequences of communicative acts, it is consonant with my work on these matters and in fact is enriched by reference to them. My own work in contrast strikes the opposite balance from Gottman's between data gathering and theoriding and gives primary emphasis to those principles underlying interactions for ensuring relevance and progress toward a resolution. But our respective emphases, especially our theoretical work, combine to form a stronger whole—the sequential-inferential paradigm—than either of our contributions separately. This is developed in the section on theory.

Sanders's Analysis of Interaction

(Despite the artifice involved, I have opted to refer to myself in the third person in the following overview of my work. This distinguishes the person who authored the work being discussed from the person discussing it in this chapter.)

Sanders's Theoretical Work on Interpersonal Influence. Unlike Gottman, Sanders was not concerned originally with a particular social problem or practice in which interpersonal influence is a central factor. Rather, his concern was the lack of an adequate theoretical basis for core assumptions on which the notion of persuasion itself rests. The first of these was the assumption that what persons do and say is subject to being influenced by the discourse of others, not just by direct experience. It was not obvious why this should be so or how to account for the influence of discourse with sensitivity to the empirical fact that its influence is contingent, not necessary. The second assumption of interest was that individuals can and do fashion their discourse systematically to have a specific, intended influence on their audience, and that there is a quasi-rational basis for this either naturally or that can be devised.

Sanders considered as inherently deficient the available psychological explanations for why discourse is influential. The principal defect of these accounts was that they attribute the influence of discourse on an audience's public conduct to its prior influence on their beliefs and attitudes about the matter at hand. But this overlooks that what persons do and say may not express their own beliefs and attitudes, may even contradict them, not only to make jokes or lie, but just to comply with the social demands of the immediate situation (Sanders, 1989). Further, psychological accounts were typically stated in terms of mechanistic, causal relationships that are generically insensitive to the contingent rather than necessary influence that discourse exerts. Third (although some important advances have been made sine then, especially by Petty and Caccioppo, 1986), such explanations are insensitive to how and why the influence of a discourse depends on specifics of the way it is fashioned, such as its style, its organization, the medium of delivery, the timing, even whether key propositions are elaborated or simply stated.

The final shortcoming of psychological explanations was that they shed no light on what systematic basis individuals have for proactively fashioning their discourse to influence others. At best, they imply that fashioning discourse which is influential depends on having an accurate psychological profile of the person(s) one is addressing; but this leaves unsettled and ad hoc of what such "profiles" would consist or how they apply to the details of composition and cannot explain the commonplace occurrence that, in the absence of any specific knowledge about the persons they are addressing, individuals still proactively fashion discourse to influence others, often successfully (e.g., in courtrooms, automobile showrooms, doctor's offices).

During the 1970s these concerns surfaced fragmentarily and somewhat indirectly in Sanders's work, along two principal dimensions that became the basis for the theoretical solution he develped. One was a shift away from an information-centered to a social perspective on the influence of discourse (Larson and Sanders, 1975), consonant with the thinking of Burke (1945), indirectly Goffman (1959, 1967), and the majority of compliance-gaining "strategies" within Marwell and Schmitt's (1967) schema. A second theoretical strand that Sanders pursued was the development of a rules-based approach to communication that analyzed the production of acts with reference to their placement in sequential wholes, in contrast to other rule-based approaches that centered on the production of acts as self-contained events. In this approach, the basis for producing acts that are meaningful and functional, and being able to do so in "novel" as well as routine circumstances, was the principled inter-connections acts have with each other in forming coherent texts or interactions (Sanders, 1973, 1978; Sanders and Martin, 1975).

These two strands combined in Sanders's work in the 1980s to produce a theoretical solution to the questions about persuasion he had started with. Sanders (1987) integrated and fully developed this work in a book whose point of departure was that individuals sometimes find it problematic to uphold the first social-communicative imperative, to fashion their acts (utterances and behaviors) so they will be understood as they intend, or at least so they will *not* be understood in an unwanted way. Sanders posited that "controlling" understanding in this way is problematic because any utterance or behavior has a number of possible meanings and yet it receives a specific interpretation in any instance that may or may not be the "intended" one. Sanders theorized and developed supporting experimental evidence that an utterance's specific interpretation is the one among the possible meanings that makes the utterance relevant in the unfolding text or interaction. Applied as well to behavior, this proposition entails that people are constrained in what they can meaningfully do or say as a text or interaction progresses by what would be relevant to what has previously been done or said and further constrained by what would thereby receive a desired interpretation. Accordingly, Sanders postulated that, because of the way an individual's discourse constrains the coherence and the specific interpretation of what others might do or say in response, that discourse is influential. Note that, on this foundation, the influence of discourse can only be contingent, not necessary (i.e., discourse constrains—alters the relative probabilities of—what can be added to the unfolding sequence, rather than exerting "forces" on thought or conduct). It also provides grounds for explaining why details of the way a discourse is fashioned bear on its influence (i.e., the constraints by discourse on the progression of acts in an unfolding text or interaction may be changed by details of style, internal organization, the medium of transmission, and the timing of production). This theoretical foundation also applies to the other concern Sanders originally had, about explaining the ability of individuals to systematically fashion their discourse to have a specific influence on others. Consider that "knowledge" of principles of relevance is essential for being able to participate coherently in producing texts and interactions, and therefore such "knowledge" must be universal. This "knowledge" provides a basis for individuals to project how different possible ways of fashioning their discourse would constrain what can follow in an unfolding text or interaction and thus project what specific influence they would exert by fashioning their discourse in one way or another. Note that this basis for fashioning discourse anticipatorily to influence others explains the ability of individuals to do this with strangers whom they engage in interaction, not just persons whose psychological profiles are known.

Sanders's Analysis of Naturally Occurring Interactions. Sanders's (1991, 1992, 1995) recent work applies the theoretical foundation he developed to the analysis of more narrowly defined phenomena. This work has two primary thrusts, which have in common that they deemphasize the role of "power" his earlier work implied individuals have in bringing about the resolution of their interactions with other. Instead, these studies of particular cases indicate that the sequence of their communicative acts in itself can acquire a controlling influence over what each participant contributes and what the resolution is.

First, with reference to particular instances of naturally occurring interaction—when the participants are in conflict about the resolution of the business at hand or about the enactment of their respective role identities (Sanders, 1991, 1995)—the evidence shows that even when interacting individuals fashion their communicative acts to attain personal goals, the actual resolution of their interactions is jointly produced. It is possible moreover that the actual resolution may not be consonant with the preferences of any participant, and that when this happens it is arguably because of deficiencies or incompatibilities in the communicative competences of the participants (i.e., their competence to fashion communicative acts that both are responsive to the other person's acts and constrain future acts in a desirable way (cf. O'Keefe, 1991).

Second, Sanders (1992) applied his theoretical work to an analysis of events on a societal, actually a multinational, rather than interpersonal level. The central question was why a considerable number of separate governments in Eastern Europe, the Soviet Union, and the People's Republic of China experienced serious upheavals or full scale collapse all at the same time (in the second half of 1989). On the assumption that it was too great a coincidence for this to have happened on the basis of separate social, cultural, and economic forces within each nation, the only visible source of a concurrent and uniform influence over such a broad social landscape is the mass (especially electronic) media. However, there was no consistent or overt campaign through the mass media of those nations to influence people to overturn their governments. Instead, the only uniform matter communicated through the media was "news" about events within and across those countries. Sanders proposed that, as they do in the case of observing or taking part in interactions on an interpersonal level, consumers of mass media assume that component events within some frame are interconnected and form a progression from some initial point toward a resolution. If in this case the initial point was the election of Gorbachev in 1985 as chair of the Politburo, with his program of *Perestroika*, then the concern of the citizens of the Soviet Union and allied countries would have been where events would lead from there. It would be relatively straightforward to project what alternative possible events could relevantly follow and toward what alternative resolutions. Sanders proposed that if the unfolding of events between 1985 and 1989 had progressively ruled out alternative "scenarios" about what resolution they were headed for except just one, that being the collapse of the Communist party as a controlling force, then just when it became unequivocal that that was the resolution toward which events had been heading—and on this inferential basis it would have become unequivocal to everyone at the same time—people acted in a self-fulfilling way that made it be so.

What is noteworthy in that analysis, though Sanders did not elaborate on its significance, is that the components of that interactive progression of political and social events were not proactively fashioned as such by any person or group, that instead the progression of events took on its own coherence and direction for observers, and "ran out from under" the goals and purposes of those doing the communicating. In that case, the active communicative efforts of government and media figures to influence the course of events arguably were interpreted as "just other events" to be factored into observers' inferences about the coherence and eventual resolution of the whole.

Interactional Sequence in Other Research on Interpersonal Communication

As noted at the beginning of this chapter there has been attention to sequence in other lines of both qualitative and quantitative research, although the topics that have been addressed in this work are no less distinct from each other than Gottman's topics are from mine. Relevant studies generally have not gone as far as Gottman and I have in viewing the sequence itself as the central influence on what happens between people, but as indicated below, their findings tend to be cohered by the framework of the sequential-inferential paradigm presented ealier.

The subsections that follow briefly review three distinct lines of research in which a concern with sequences has been especially prominent. In two of these (conversation analysis, and Cappella's research on interactional behavior sequences), the data indicate that, at a level of micro detail much finer than either Gottman or I have considered, participants in interaction make anticipatory and proactive adjustments of their communicative acts, and perhaps even speech behaviors, as a result of inferences based on comparing the progress of the interaction with alternative possibilities. In the third area (coordinated management of meaning), there is some evidence that, when persons become enmeshed in circular patterns of interaction that are unwanted and dysfunctional, the therapeutic solution is to make them self-conscious about the sequence itself rather than the component acts.

Conversation Analysis. It is commonplace to view conversation analysis as uniformly emphasizing the sequential organization of talk in interaction, as with reference for example to adjacency pairs (Sacks and Schegloff, 1973), preference organization (Pomerantz, 1978, 1984; Sacks and Schegloff, 1979), side sequences (Jefferson, 1972), repair sequences (Schegloff, Jefferson, and Sacks, 1977), "presequences" (Schegloff, 1980), and a variety of other matters. The larger issue in conversation analysis is an application to the venue of conversation of the general concern in ethnomethodology with the basis people have for coordinating their participation in social processes and achieving social order. Standardized or regular sequential ordering in conversations is evidence of coordination, and the structural relations indicated by these regularities are presumably the basis for this.

Relevant studies have amassed considerable empirical evidence important to the sequential-inferential paradigm that people do make inferences about the course of the interaction or the dispositions of participants and adjust their participation accordingly, as evident when a "deviation" occurs from the standardized sequence (presumably based on inferences from a "comparison" between what occurred and what standardly would or could alternatively have occurred). Moreover, these "deviations" can occur and be detected even at the level of micro components of interaction, not just the analytically gross level of whole acts. For example, Davidson (1984) and Pomerantz (1984) each showed that pauses of fractions of a second that occur between a request or invitation, or assessment, and the response are oriented to as evidence of a disinclination to agree and adjustments made accordingly, because the "standard" sequence, or preference structure, favors an "agreement" reply that as such is unhesitating. Jefferson (1993), in an analysis of devices adopted by listeners to initiate a shift from recipientship to speakership, showed that the current speaker monitors the occurrence of such devices and may act to prevent the anticipated shift in speakership. For example, offering an assessment is one such device, and current speaker may "interrupt" the assessment to prevent the anticipated topic change by adding on to what was being said:

(11)   (Jefferson, 1993, p. 14)

A: . . . I did the same thing for he:r,h

B: *Oh*: well tha:t $\lceil$ was: thou $\rceil$ ght $\lceil$ ful hh

A: $\lfloor$ Uh:: $\rfloor$ $\lfloor$ the d*a*y before *yes*terday

Cappella's Research on Interactional Behavior Sequence. Cappella (1984) has examined interactional sequence as a primary indicator of behavioral coordination and interpersonal orientation between persons. However, this research does not examine interactions in terms of component acts and the social influence they combine to produce, but rather the emphasis is "mutual influence" on micro details of participants' speech behaviors over the course of an interaction, specifically "stylistic" behaviors and the (possible) social ramifications of such influence. Data consist of the temporal progression of details of "stylistic" speech behaviors of the interacting persons toward or away from congruity with each other or coordination (with reference for example to the temporal interplay between interacting persons' intervals of talk and silence, pause duration, laughter, gaze, manner of speech—rate, volume, and the like—and so forth). The term *sequence* thus is applied to statistically regular contingencies between the occurrences of particular "stylistic" behaviors, not acts.

Even though the behavioral-stylistic focus of this research gives it a tenuous relation to the sequential-inferential paradigm, it may not be wholly irrelevant. There is a possible tie to the concerns here because of the finding that there is (1) a high degree of coordination in progressions of behavior at a level too detailed and spontaneously produced to have been actively controlled, and yet (2) social dispositions must be involved in light of the tendency for each person's responses to "converge" with the other's manner of participation or "diverge" to display a positive or negative interpersonal orientation. This suggests that in some sense even details of speech behavior, stylistic behavior, are produced anticipatorily of the interpersonal alignment they display.

Cappella's preferred explanation for these phenomena is that if the other's behaviors in comparison with one's own "violate expectations"—referring to expectations about interactional behavior—this creates arousal, "energy" that participants direct to restoring equilibrium by making adjustments of their speech behavior to achieve convergence or divergence (Cappella and Greene, 1982). However, arousal alone does not explain why the behavioral adjustments made as a consequence will sometimes be reciprocal (convergence) or compensatory (divergence). The direction of these behavioral adjustments must depend on some kind of cognitive mediation.

Cappella (1985, pp. 423–424) reviewed alternative answers to this question, which differ as to whether these adjustments are considered proactive

(Patterson, 1982), which is consonant with the sequential-inferential paradigm, or reactive (Cappella and Greene, 1982). The proactive view is that behavioral violations of expectation foster inferences about the other or the situation that favor either reciprocal or compensatory behavioral adjustments. The reactive view is that behavioral expectations are formed (inferred?) from beliefs about the other or the situation, affecting the magnitude of any violations of expectation by the other's behaviors and thus the level of arousal they produce, with reciprocating behavioral adjustments said to result when arousal is below a threshold level and compensatory adjustments when it is above that level. What is common to both views is that inferences are made about the other or the situation, or about what behavioral expectations are warranted, on the basis of comparing sequentially ordered interactional behavior with alternative possibilities associated with the person and the situation. Moreover, these inferences apparently have a shaping influence on progressive adjustments during interaction in micro details of participants' behavior, though it is not clear whether these are proactive or reactive. Of course, this does not make the sequence itself the central influence on what persons say and do, as in Gottman's work and mine, but this is probably because stylistic speech behavior would exhibit more variability in relation to local stimuli and less to sequential wholes than communicative acts because of the way each is observed/identified.

   Coordinated Management of Meaning. Within Pearce and Cronen's work on CMM (cf. Philipsen, Chapter 2 in this book), special attention has been given to certain kinds of sequences, "unwanted repetitive patterns" (Cronen et al., 1979). These are sequences that have a "loop" built into them so that moving forward toward a resolution brings the interaction back to an initial point from which it proceeds all over again. For this to happen, participants in an interaction have to contextualize and interpret the same acts differently: each act in the sequence has an interpretation for one participant by which it is relevant and moves the interaction forward toward a certain resolution yet has an alternate interpretation for the other participant so that it is also relevant and moves the interaction forward toward a different resolution, and the progression of alternately interpreted acts that results is inherently circular and ends up back at its starting point.

   Cronen and his associates are concerned with the individualized interpretations and the underlying failure to coordinate meaning that gives rise to such sequences. However, what is noteworthy here is that persons who engage in such sequences must fail to detect the unresolved ambiguities on which they depend and thus must not have a basis for comparing the sequence with alternative possibilities that would enable them to make inferences about the course of these interactions, and adjust their acts accordingly. It is consistent with this that therapeutic "correction" of such unwanted repetitive patterns depends on getting the participants to become self-conscious about the pattern, the sequence itself and thus to alternative possibilities (Cronen, Pearce, and Tomm, 1985). Note that this therapeutic strategy is entirely the reverse of Gottman's (Gottman et al., 1976a), yet there is a rationale for each within the sequential-inferential paradigm. Gottman's strategy presupposes that marital couples have focused on the rigidified sequence that has formed, and he induces them to shift focus to the way specific messages are fashioned and thereby change the course of the sequences they produce. Cronen et al.'s, strategy, on the other hand, presupposes that marital couples have formed the rigidified sequences they have by focusing on the particular acts each produces, and they induce couples to attend to the sequence itself as preliminary to taking steps to alter it.

Formal and Psychological Components of Theory in the Sequential-Inferential Paradigm

Obviously, as pointed out in the introductory discussion, the specific research topics and issues that Gottman and I focus on are entirely different. The only common ground is that in our work we find the central influence over what happens between people is the sequences they interactively produce and the inferences they make from them. However, despite the marked differences in the theoretical accounts of interpersonal influence that Gottman and I favor, these turn out to involve complements. Both accounts are arguably incomplete in ways the other rectifies.

Gottman explains the influence that interactional sequences have on the interactional patterns of marital partners, and consequently on the trajectory of the marital relationship, in terms of the psychological states and processes they stimulate. But, in developing this account, Gottman left moot the question of the properties of those sequences and allied inferential processes that are the basis for the psychological effects he ascribes to them.

Conversely, with reference to the properties of those sequences and allied inferential processes—in terms of constraints they place on the coherence and meaning of participants' options—Sanders explained the influence that interactional sequences have on what resolution of the interaction participants act to attain and what resolution they actually attain. In developing this account, however, Sanders left moot the question of the psychological states and processes and the accompanying affect states that foster individual preferences for or aversions to certain resolutions.

Sanders' analytic work, together with Gottman's data (e.g., the illustrative interaction between husband and wife discussed previously) clearly indicate that what happens between people is influenced both by underlying principles that restrict the coherent possible ways of sequencing communicative acts and by psychological processes and accompanying affect states organized around (inferences regarding) the interactional sequence itself. The remaining theoretical problem neither of us has addressed is what is the relation between the two. There are three logical possibilities, and it seems that each can occur.

One possibility is that there is consonance, and possibly a bilateral influence, between constraints on acts by underlying sequencing principles and the wants and expectations of the participants about the course of the interaction. Such consonance would induce positive or at least neutral affect states of the participants toward each other and their interaction and be indicated by a cumulatively positive valence among the acts they produce. A second possibility, which can produce either of two results, is that there is dissonance between constraints on acts by underlying sequencing principles and the wants and expectations of the participants. One result of such a dissonant relationship would be for the wants and expectations of participants to be the dominant factor, thereby interfering with coherent participation in the interaction: this is arguably what was involved in the interaction between husband and wife that was examined and more generally what is involved in flooding and the distance and isolation cascade that Gottman (1993) described. The alternative possibility is that participants would "comply" with the constraints on what acts could be coherently produced in the interaction, at the expense of their wants and expectations, although this could result in negative affect states, most probably guilt or anger, that would be exhibited indirectly or in ways remote from the interaction(s) in question.

There is a further theoretical problem, based on the above, that neither Gottman nor I have addressed. When there is a dissonant relationship between the constraints of the interaction and the wants and expectations of participants, the question is why one or the other of these two results occurs. Whether persons give primacy to interactional constraints or to their wants and expectations is something that may lie in the personalities or other qualities of the persons involved or in the "cost-benefit" issues attendant on "complying" with the constraints of the interaction(s) or refusing to do so (e.g., Thibaut and Kelley, 1959).

The Sequential-Inferential Paradigm

This concluding section concerns the consequences of the sequential-inferential paradigm for communication practice, and correspondingly, research and theory on communication—not only interpersonal communication but public and mass communication as well. These are matters more implied than explicit in Gottman's work and mine, though they have been touched on by each of us.

The consequences of the sequential-inferential paradigm can be indicated most directly in terms of the practicalities of communication. Consider, then, that if sequence is the primary influence over what happens between people, not component acts, then from a practical standpoint:

1. The primary influence exerted by communicative acts is to warrant or exclude future acts, or resolutions, that can coherently be included in the present interaction, not to change what an audience thinks or does (or is disposed to do) about the external matters in question.
2. Communicative acts have to be fashioned to be relevant to what has already occurred in the current sequence and to make progress toward one of its possible resolutions, not simply to make known the producer's "message;" otherwise communicative acts will either be discounted or understood and responded to in unanticipated and possibly unwanted ways.
3. When a producer has some specific matter he or she wants to communicate, the communicative act has to be timed to occur at a point in the sequence when it is relevant and can have the intended influence over the progress of the sequence; otherwise it will be "too late" and (as in 2) either be discounted or understood and responded to in unanticipated and possibly unwanted ways.

These practicalities at the interpersonal level are equally binding on all participants, so that it is possible for strangers to coordinate their interaction and effectively fashion their acts to influence progress toward or away from certain resolutions in novel situations. Further, for persons who recurrently engage each other in interaction, these practicalities can lead to the standardization of certain sequences that inhibits their ability to alter the communicative acts they produce in interactions with the other or to exert much influence through specific communicative acts once such sequences become rigidified, unless a therapeutic intervention is employed of the kind Gottman et al. (1976a) or Cronen et al. (1985) devised.

At the level of campaigns and movements, and mass media effects more broadly, the practicalities are suggested by the case of the upheavals in Eastern Europe and the Soviet Union that seem to have been fostered through mass media (Sanders, 1992). If what influences mass publics is the sequence of communicative acts (i.e., separate broadcasts, news items, and the like), then persons or organizations seeking change may be impotent if they fashion acts that fail to foster a reconstruction of what course that perceived sequence is taking or that fail to effect a turn in the course of that sequence toward a different resolution. For example, during George Bush's presidency economic events seemed to form a progression toward erosion and decline of the status quo that government seemed helpless to prevent: Bush's efforts to counter public fears by denying that anything unusual was taking place or that there was a need for special government action cohered fully with the perceived sequence of decline and the government's helplessness, so that instead of allaying fears Bush probably intensified them. Arguably, the success of President Clinton's campaign in 1992 (and the political force exerted by Ross Perot) arose from openly acknowledging and responding to the sequence that events seemed to have formed and the resolution toward which they seemed headed and from proposing actions that could possibly alter the course of events toward a restoration of economic stability.

Probably in large measure the influence of the rhetorical tradition on our thinking about communication is responsible for the continued emphasis in much research and theory on the influence exerted by distinct communicative acts produced by individuals who fashion them to change the beliefs or values of their "audience" about the matter at hand. The matter is quite different, as the practicalities indicated earlier suggest, if the primary influence on what happens between people is the sequence to which acts contribute, not the component acts alone. This is a departure from the "rhetoncal" approach, in that it rules out that the influence exerted and "exertable" in any instance is at the discretion of any single producer or contingent on any acts in particular. The influence that is exertable depends on what possible resolutions can be achieved coherently at the point in the sequence when the question arises (e.g., when an influence attempt is considered). Further, it is a social construction what a given sequence in which certain acts occur encompasses (what its starting point and components are) and thus what its possible resolutions are. This is something not entirely the discretion of either the producer(s) of acts nor the consumer(s), but that is not arbitrary either: it is usually the case that there is an "official" or marked starting point (akin to the earlier notion of "proffers"), accepted as such by all the parties involved.

Some ramifications of this shift in perspective have already been anticipated in what I will call the "ecological" approach. In the context of research on interpersonal communication, this is reflected by the emergence of a concern with interactional *process* and an emphasis on the joint rather than individual achievement of interactional resolutions (as in ethnomethodology and conversation analysis, and recent work in communication, e.g., Sigman, 1995). In the context of public influence and mass communication, the "effects" of communicative acts have been said to involve more than the qualities of the acts alone, but in addition their visibility and congruence within larger information or symbolic "environments" of which they are a part (Becker, 1971; Nimmo and Combs, 1980). And the response to acts by audiences has been said to depend on more than the substance of the act and the dispositions of the audience; in addition, response depends on the audience's level of "expertise" and interest in the matter at hand (Petty and Caccioppo, 1986) and the limits of their discretion to act, considering that consumers are not independent agents, but interdependent with others (Janis, 1972; Fishbein and Ajzen, 1975).

However, the "ecological" approach as such probably underestimates the influence exerted by the person(s) communicating and the acts they produce, as much as the "rhetorical" approach overestimates it. The "ecological" approach implies that the influence exerted by communicative acts, fashioned in a certain way, is imponderable for both the person(s) communicating and the observer or analyst. Influence would be exerted by the larger information or "symbolic" environment to which specific acts would make an indeterminate contribution and depend on what responses were possible or not because of the social interdependencies among "consumers" (although Hall, 1982, would attribute such "symbolic" environments and the invisibility of those responsible for producing them to influence of economic elites for the purpose of maintaining the status quo).

The "rhetorical" and "ecological" approaches coalesce within the sequential-inferential paradigm, and a balanced view results of the role of the person(s) communicating and the influence exerted by acts, when the unit of analysis is the sequence and not the component acts. In that case, acts do not simply get absorbed in an unformed, unstructured "environment," but acquire an interconnection with other acts in ordered sequences. This provides a systematic basis on which producers can anticipate what influences can be exerted on the future progress of a sequence and fashion their act(s) accordingly and can assess the influence exerted by their acts in terms of changed understandings of the course of events, instead of changed beliefs and values about the substantive matters at issue in particular communicative acts.

Research and theory about what individuals do socially and what befalls them have generally cited either psychological factors or macro-level factors involving societal, macro cultural, economic, historical, political, or geographical forces on persons in the aggregate. The former attributes what befalls persons to their own qualities and capabilities as those interact with the circumstances of their environment. The latter attributes what befalls persons to their functional location in the structure and dynamics of systems of which they are members. In either case, what persons do is presumed to be a symptom of, not a contributing factor to, the forces that are determinate of what befalls them.

Only a relatively small body of work centered around the study of language and social interaction has pursued an intermediate course (given voice as a distinct mezzo approach by, for example, Mead, 1934; Goffman, 1959; Garfinkel, 1967; Sacks', 1992, lectures during the 1960s; Hymes, 1974; Harré, 1979; and Habermas, 1984). The common element in this work is that it addresses the components of a paradox, and sometimes the paradox itself, evident in the social lives of individuals: persons take an active part with other individuals in the social processes that affect them and have the discretion to cooperate with or obstruct others; but regardless, the part they play influences but is not determinate of what befalls them.

The sequential-inferential paradigm provides a coherent direction that research and mezzo theory can take in recognition of this paradox. The sequences of acts interactively produced by persons create constraints on their options and enable inferences about the possible resolution(s) of the interaction (Sanders), and those in turn stimulate psychological processes (Gottman) that motivate compensatory responses by each participant separately. The central influence over what befalls individuals is thereby the sequences of acts that they interactively produce with others—not the acts in themselves—where each person contributes but none controls the whole.

References

Atlas, J. D., and Levinson, S. C. (1981). "It-clefts, informativeness, and logical form: Radical pragmatics (revised standard version)." In P. Cole (Ed.), *Radical pragmatics*, pp. 1–61. New York: Academic Press.

Bavelas, J. B. (1994)."Gestures as part of speech: Methodological implications." *Research on Language and Social Interactions* 27: 201–221.

Becker, S. L. (1971). "Rhetorical studies for the contemporary world." In L. L. Bitzer and E. Black (Eds.), *The prospect of rhetoric*, pp. 21–43. Englewood Cliffs. N. J.: Prentice-Hall.

Burke, K. (1945). *A grammar of motives.* Berkeley: University of California Press, reprinted.

Button, G., and Casey, N. (1988–1989). "Topic initiation: Business-at-hand." *Research on Language and Social Interaction* 22: 61–92.

Cappella, J. N. (1984). "The relevance of the microstructure of interaction to relationship change." *Journal of Social and Personal Relationships* 1: 239–264.

——— (1985). "The management of conversations." In M. L. Knapp and G. R. Millers (Eds.), *Handbook of interpersonal communication*, pp. 393–438. Beverly Hills, Calif.: Sage Publications.

——— and Greene, J. O. (1982). "A discrepancy-arousal explanation of mutual influence in expressive behavior adult-adult and infant-adult interaction." *Communication Monographs* 49: 89–114.

Cronen, V., Pearce, W. B., and Snavely, L. (1979). "A theory of rule structure and types of episodes, and a study of perceived enmeshment in undesired repetitive patterns (URPs)." In B. Ruben (Ed.), *Communication yearbook III*, pp. 225–240. New Brunswick, N. J.: Transaction Press.

Cronen, V. E., Pearce, W. B., and Tomm, C. (1985). "The dialectic of personal change." In K. Gergen and K. Davis (Eds.), *Social construction of the person*, pp. 203–224. New York: Springer Verlag.

Cushman, D. P., and Whiting, G. (1972). "An approach to communication theory: Toward consensus on rules." *Journal of Communication* 22: 219–238.

Davidson, J. (1984). "Subsequent versions of invitations, offers, requests and proposals dealing with potential or actual rejection." In J. M. Atkinson and J. Heritage (Eds.), *Structures of social action*, pp. 102–128. Cambridge: Cambridge University Press.

Edmondson, W. (1981). *Spoken discourse: A model for analysis*. London: Longman.

Ekman, P., and Friesen, W. V. (1969). "The repertoire of nonverbal behavior: Categories, origins, usage, and coding." *Semiotica* 1:49–98.

Fishbein, M., and Ajzen, I. (1975). *Belief, attitude, intention and behavior: An introduction to theory and research*. Reading, Mass. Addison-Wesley.

Garfinkel, H. (1967). *Studies in ethnomethodology*. Englewood Cliffs, N. J.: Prentice-Hall.

Goffman, E. (1959). *The presentation of self in everday life*. Garden City, N. Y.: Doubleday Books.

——— (1967). *Interaction ritual: Essays on face-to-face behavior*. Garden City, N. Y.: Anchor Books (reprinted, New York: Pantheon Books).

Gottman, J. M. (1976). *Distressed marital interaction: Analysis and intervention*. Champaign, Ill.: Research Press.

——— (1979). *Marital interaction: Experimental investigations*. New York: Academic Press.

——— (1983). "How children become friends." *Monographs of the Society for Research in Child Development* 48, no. 3 (Serial no. 201). Chicago: University of Chicago Press.

——— (1993). "A theory of marital dissolution and stability." *Journal of Family Psychology* 7: 57–75.

——— Gonso, J., and Rasmussen, B. (1975). "Social interaction, social competence, and friendship in children." *Child Development* 46: 709–718.

——— Markman, H., and Notarius, C. (1977). "The topography of marital conflict: A study of verbal and nonverbal behavior." *Journal of Marriage and the Family* 39: 461–477.

——— Notarius, C., Gonso, J., and Markman, H. (1976a). *A couple's guide to communication*. Campaign, Ill.: Research Press.

————— Notarius, C., Markman, H., Bank, S., Yoppi, B., and Rubin, M. E. (1976b). "Behavior exchange theory and marital decision making." *Journal of Personality and Social Psychology* 34: 14–23.

Grice, H. P. (1975). "Logic and conversation." In P. Cole and J. L. Morgan (Eds.), *Syntax and semantics*. Vol. 3. *Speech acts*, pp. 41–58. New York: Academic Press.

Habermas, J. (1984). *The theory of communicative action*, trans. Thomas McCarthy. Boston: Beacon Press.

Harré, R. (1979). *Social being*. Oxford: Basil Blackwell.

Hall, S. (1982). "The rediscovery of 'ideology': Return of the repressed in media studies." In M. Gurevitch, T. Bennett, J. Curran, and J. Woollacoot (Eds.), *Culture, society and the media*, pp. 56–90. London: Methuen.

Hymes, D. (1974). *Foundations in sociolinguistics: An ethnographic approach*. Philadelphia: University of Pennsylvania Press.

Janis, I. (1972). *Victims of groupthink*. Boston: Houghton Mifflin.

Jefferson, G. (1972). "Side sequences." In D. Sudnow (Ed.), *Studies in social interaction*, pp. 294–338. New York: The Free Press.

————— (1993). "Caveat speaker: Preliminary notes on recipient topic-shift implicature." *Research on Language and Social Interaction* 26: 1–30. Originally appeared in 1983 as "Two papers on 'transitory recipientship'," *Tillburg Papers in Language and Literature* 30: 1–18.

Levinson, S. C. (1981). "Some pre-observations on the modeling of dialogue." *Discourse Processes* 4: 93–110.

Marwell, G, and Schmitt, D. (1967). "Dimensions of compliance-gaining behavior: An empirical analysis." *Sociometry* 30: 350–364.

McNeill, D. (1985). "So you think gestures are nonverbal?" *Psychological Review* 92: 350–371.

Mead, G. H. (1934). *Mind, self, and society from the standpoint of a social behaviorist*. Chicago: University of Chicago Press.

Nimmo, D., and Combs, J. E. (1980). *Subliminal politics: Myths and mythmakers in America*. Englewood Cliffs, N. J.: Prentice-Hall.

O'Keefe, B. J. (1991). "Message design logic and the management of multiple goals." In K. Tracy (Ed.), *Understanding face-to-face interaction: Issues linking goals and discourse*, pp. 131–150. Hillsdale, N. J.: Lawrence Erlbaum and Associates.

Patterson, M. L. (1982). "A sequential functional model of nonverbal exchange." *Psychological Review* 89: 231–249.

Petty, R. E., and Cacioppo, J. T. (1986). *Communication and persuasion: Central and peripheral routes to attitude change.* New York: Springer Verlag.

Pomerantz, A. (1978). "Compliment responses: Notes on the co-operation of multiple constraints." In J. Schenkein (Ed.), *Studies in the organization of conversational interaction*, pp. 79–112. New York: Academic Press.

———— (1984). "Agreeing and disagreeing with assessments: Some features of preferred/dispreferred turn shapes." In J. M. Atkinson and J. Heritage (Eds.), *Structures of social action*, pp. 57–101. Cambridge: Cambridge University Press.

Rogers, L. E., and Farace, R. V. (1975). "Analysis of relational communication in dyads: New measurement procedures." *Human Communication Research* 1: 222–239.

Rumelhart, D. (1975). "Notes on a schema for stories." In D. Bobrow and A. Collins (Eds.), *Representation and understanding: Studies in cognitive science*, pp. 211–236. New York: Academic Press.

Sacks, H. (1992). *Harvey Sacks: Lectures on conversation*, ed. G. Jefferson. Oxford: Basil Blackwell.

———— and Schegloff, E. A. (1979). "Two preferences in the organization of reference to persons in conversation and their interaction." In G. Psathas (Ed.), *Everyday language: Studies in ethnomethodology*, pp. 15–21. New York: Irvington.

Sanders, R. E. (1973). "The question of a paradigm for the study of speech-using behavior." *Quarterly Journal of Speech* 59: 1–10.

———— (1978). "Utterances, actions, and rhetorical inquiry." *Philosophy and Rhetoric* 11: 114–133.

———— (1980). "Principles of relevance: A theory of the relationship between language and communication." *Communication and Cognition* 13: 77–95.

———— (1987). *Cognitive foundations of calculated speech: Controlling understandings in conversation and persuasion.* Albany: State University of New York Press.

———— (1989). "Message effects via induced changes in the social meaning of a response." In J. Bradac (ed.), *Message effects in communication science*, pp. 165–194. Newbury park, CA: Sage Publications.

———— (1991). "The two-way relationship between talk in social interaction and actors' goals and plans." In K. Tracy (Ed.), *Understanding face-to-face interaction: Issues linking goals and discourse*, pp. 167–188. Hillsdale, N. J.: Lawrence Erlbaum and Associates.

———— (1992). "The role of mass communication processes in producing upheavals in the Soviet Union, Eastern Europe, and China." In S. S. King and D. P. Cushman (Eds.), *Political communication: Engineering visions of order in the socialist world*, pp. 143–162. Albany: State University of New York Press.

———— (1995). "The enactment of role-identities as interactive and rhetorical." In S. J. Sigman (Ed.), *The consequentiality of communication*, pp. 67–120. Hillsdale, N. J.: Lawrence Erlbaum and Associates.

———— and Martin, L. W. (1975). "Grammatical rules and explanations of behavior." *Inquiry* 18: 65–82.

Schank, R. (1977). "Rules and topics in conversation." *Cognitive Science* 1: 421–441.

Schegloff, E. A. (1980). "Preliminaries to preliminaries: 'Can I ask you a question?' " *Sociological Inquiry* 50: 104–152.

———— Jefferson, G., and Sacks, H. (1977). "The preference for self-correction in the organization of repair in conversation." *Language* 53: 361–382.

———— and Sacks, H. (1973). "Opening up closings." *Semiotica* 8: 289–327.

Searle, J. R. (1976). "A classification of illocutionary acts." *Language in Society* 5: 1–23.

Shannon, C. E., and Weaver, W. (1949). *The mathematical theory of communication*. Urbana: University of Illinois Press.

Sigman, S. J. (Ed.) (1995). *The consequentiality of communication*. Hillsdale, N. J.: Lawrence Erlbaum and Associates.

Sinclair, J. M., and Coulthard, R. M. (1975). *Towards an analysis of discourse*. London: Oxford University Press.

Sperber, D., and Wilson, D. (1986). *Relevance: Communication and cognition*. Oxford: Basil Blackwell.

Thibaut, J. W., and Kelley, H. H. (1959). *The social psychology of groups*. New York: John Wiley & Sons.

Tracy, K. (1982). "On getting the point: Distinguishing 'issues' from 'events,' an aspect of conversational coherence." In M. Burgoon (Ed.), *Communication yearbook 5*, pp. 279–301. New Brunswick, N. J.: Transaction Press.

———— (1983). "The issue-event distinction: A rule of conversation and its scope condition." *Human Communication Research* 9: 320–334.

van Dijk, T. A. (1972). *Some aspects of text grammars*. The Hague: Mouton.

PART II

⊚ഛ⊛

INTERPERSONAL THEORIES
OF COMMUNICATION

BRANISLAV KOVAČIĆ

Chapter 6: The Rules Theory of Interpersonal Relationships

As a philosophic perspective, "The Rules Theory of Communication in Interpersonal Relationships by Cushman, Nicotera, and Associates" views communication as intentional, choice oriented, and evaluative activities that require the cooperation of others. Individual self-concepts contain standardized or social communication rules actors use as before-the-fact explanations in interpersonal communication. According to this functional rules perspective, the content and sequence of interactions necessary for obtaining a given relational goal is guided by the standardized usage—the rules of reference previously established or standardized to obtain such a recurrent relational goal. Standardized usages or social communication rules may be of varying duration and coherence. A relational coordination task—a nonlinguistic task that generates the appropriate communication rules or the standardized usage—is the basic unit for analysis.

Because the standardized usage is a single pattern of conventions that are well monitored and enforced by all involved in a given situation, meanings are not constructed in interactions. Rather, they are publicly reproduced and applied in relational task-oriented interactions. This is a major departure from the theory of coordinated management of meaning and constructivism in that rule-governed patterns of behavior become obvious when some interactants publicly violate mutual expectations of what constitutes appropriate communication. To verify such standardized usage or social meanings, Cushman, Nicotera, and associates systematically observe empirical patterns of individual or group interpretation of symbols—the rules of social meanings—used to achieve a recurrent relational goal. They also suggest that researchers systematically observe (1) individual or group patterns of interaction or discourse patterns to detect the discourse rules governing and guiding the interaction, and (2) individual or group patterns of behavior that follow from symbolic interaction to obtain feedback on rule following and rule violating.

Such assumptions provide the unique insights into how functional communicative rules govern and guide the formation, maintenance, and termination of interpersonal relationships.

Because individual self-concepts are the locus of communication rules from an actor's point of view, individuals in interpersonal interaction communicate their preferred type of relationship to others. Such proposals are then accepted, negotiated, or rejected by others. At the theoretic level, proposing, negotiating, and accepting a certain type of relationship between interactants is called self-concept support. A rejection of the proposed relationship to others is accounted for by the lack of self-concept support. Although different types of interpersonal relationships—involving friends, mates, or colleagues—are rooted in different types of self-concept support, they all require increasing amounts of relationship-specific self-concept support to raise relational intimacy. A communication rules theory, then, locates and measures these types and levels of perceived self-concept support conveyed through interaction.

How, for example, are mate relationships established, maintained, and terminated? According to the theory, the establishment of such a relationship goes through a three-stage filtering process. Individuals (1) from a field of available others (which is constrained by social, demographic, cultural, and institutional factors) select according to entry rules (2) a field of approachable others (a subset of availables) to whom they signal interest in establishing mate relationship, and finally (3) if those others (a field of reciprocals or a subset of approachables) attempt to deepen the intimacy of the relationship by following intensity rules governing self-concept support, the relationship will develop fast. Although entry level or matching variables (one prefers as a mate another who is quite similar on those culture-specific variables) must be present to begin the relationship, they do not deepen the relationship through frequent communication. The culture-specific intensity variables when reciprocated, on the other hand, do increase the depth of intimacy the more often they are communicated. Perceived mate self-concept support can be communicated either directly or indirectly by talking about things one's mate is interested in. Once established, maintaining mate relationships over time depends on the manner in which mates handle conflict. In high-quality relationships conflict is addressed by a culture-specific rule-governed communication sequence that preserves and enhances intimacy by preserving and enhancing the number of topics the couple can talk about constructively in the future. In low-quality relationships the opposite is the case. Mate relationships are terminated by the lack of appropriate self-concept support and through inadequate handling of conflict. This phase is characterized by the interactants' use of culture-specific accounts such as excuses, justifications, concessions, and refusals in explaining the relational breakup to significant others.

The way this watershed research tradition in human communication theory specifies the relationship between functional communication rules—the standardized or social usage—and different types of interpersonal relationships has important practical consequences. Researchers in this tradition have collected systematic and consistent evidence, relying on different research methods and analytical techniques, in six different cultures on friendship and mate relationships. They have found that each culture has unique entry and intensity rules for establishing different interpersonal relationships, unique rules for productive handling of interpersonal and relational conflicts, and unique rules for appropriate termination of different interpersonal relationships. However, they also present evidence that the relationship between entry and intensity variables and establishment of a particular type of interpersonal relationship is culture free or universal. The unique insights provided by this watershed tradition describe and interpret standardized functional rules necessary to establish, maintain, and terminate interpersonal relationships in particular cultures. From the practical viewpoint, people can learn these rules, improve their communicative competence, and become more effective communicators in different relationships in different cultures.

6

THE RULES THEORY OF
INTERPERSONAL RELATIONSHIPS
BY CUSHMAN, NICOTERA, AND ASSOCIATES

ANDREW MOEMEKA AND BRANISLAV KOVAČIĆ

According to Cushman and his associates' rules theory of communication in interpersonal relationships, people communicate most effectively when using a limited number of the appropriate message contents and sequences of interactions governed by rules. Rules are the social normative devices actors use to coordinate their actions within heterogeneous social orders by relying on consensus concerning how to solve mutual problems.

Rules thus function as criteria for choice among alternatives (Cushman and Cahn, 1985, p. 10). When such alternatives are normatively rank ordered, then there is consensus regarding appropriate uses of talk for accomplishment of given goals.

The topic of this chapter is Cushman and his associates' rules theory of communication in mate and friend interpersonal relationships. There are five parts to this chapter. The first section outlines philosophical assumptions of the rules theory of communication. The second section presents and critically discusses the most relevant conceptual and operational definitions of constructs found in the original formulation of the rules theory of communication. The third section deals with theoretical propositions—specifications of the direction and strength of the relationships between constructs found in the original formulation of the rules theory of communication. This section also presents and critically evaluates empirical findings of the original investigations. The fourth section is concerned with theoretical extensions of the original theoretical formulations and empirical replications and extensions to the original empirical investigations. Finally, the chapter concludes with critiques of and future directions for the rules theory of communication in friend and mate interpersonal relationships.

Philosophic Assumptions

The work of Cushman and his associates constitutes the coordinative-functional rules perspective on communication—appropriate uses of talk—in accomplishing relevant goals in interpersonal relationships. Such a perspective depends on three metaphysical assumptions: motion-action, information processing-coordination, and creative-standardized usage.

The Motion-Action Assumption

Unlike *stimulus-response movements, actions are choice-oriented* and purposive. Actions are possible only if "persons have some degree of choice among alternatives, critique their performance, exercise self-monitoring capacities, and act in response to practical or normative forces" (Toulmin, 1969, p. 75; see also Von Wright, 1971; Fay and Moon, 1977). Action theory requires an explanation of individual human behavior in terms of the intentional link between an agent's perceptions, thoughts, and behavior so that the agent's perceptions and thoughts explain why the behavior occurred.

Explaining individual human behavior requires a *first-person practical syllogism*: "An individual A intends to bring about C; A considers that in order to bring about C he must do B; and therefore A sets himself to do B" (Cushman and Pearce, 1977; see also Von Wright, 1971). According to rules theorists, even if the actor's perceptions of what must be done are in error, the first-person practical syllogism is still a valid explanation of why the actor did what he or she did.

However, critics argue that the first-person practical syllogism has two serious weaknesses: it is nonproductive and nonverifiable. Because the practical syllogism can be constructed only after the occurrence of an event, its explanatory force is only ex post facto. In addition, the practical force that exists between premises and conclusion can be verified *only through the testimony of the actor.* Thus, there is no intersubjective source of verification.

The Information Processing-Coordination Assumption

Action theorists also assume that human actions are situations in which an agent's choice among alternative courses of conduct and efforts to achieve a goal do require the cooperation of others. In contrast to *information processing situations*, which regulate individual human perception and thought with regard to some goal, *coordination situations* regulate consensus among agents with regard to the cooperative achievement of a goal (Cushman and Whiting, 1972). Only within the domain of coordination situations does human action require the transfer of symbolic information or communication to facilitate goal-directed behavior. As summarized by Cushman and Whiting (1972) and noted by Cushman and Pearce (1977):

Communication rules theorists thus argue that: (1) there exists a class of human action which involves conjoint, combined, and associated behavior; (2) that the transfer of symbolic information facilitates such behavior; (3) that the transfer of symbolic information requires the interaction of sources, messages, and receivers guided and governed by communication rules; and (4) that the communication rules form general and specific patterns which provide the basis for the explanation, prediction, and control of communication behavior.

Several important implications regarding the nature of scientific inquiry into human communication processes follow from this second assumption. For example, when verbal episodes are sequenced in an appropriate way in the appropriate situation, they count as a marriage contract (Cushman, 1989). The *function* of human communication in such a context is to regulate the consensus needed to coordinate behavior; the *structure* of human communication is the content and procedural rules involved in regulating consensus; and the *process* of human communication entails the adaptation of the rules involved in regulating consensus to the task at hand (Cushman, Valentinsen, and Dietrich, 1982).

The Creative-Standardized Usage Assumption

Because in creative coordination situations interactants attempt through negotiation to generate the rules, such *creative situations* do not allow for the explanation, prediction, or control of human behavior in terms of antecedent conditions. In contrast, the rules already exist in *standardized situations* and thus such situations allow for the creation and verification of human communication theories within a traditional measurement model of antecedent conditions (Donohue, Cushman, and Nofsinger, 1980).

Standardized situations entail relatively enduring tasks that generate standardized usages. *Standardized usage* refers to the social rule structure that defines the set of alternative choices for a particular behavior (Cushman and Whiting, 1972; Cushman, Valentinsen, and Dietrich, 1972; Nicotera et al., 1993, Chapter 1). Action theorists seem to agree that standardized usage or a system of rule-governed, symbol-meaning associations has several important characteristics. First, such usage is organized and made meaningful for those who employ it by a shared class of intentions. When two or more interactants employ a standardized usage, they are indicating to each other their decision to participate in the class of intentional acts. Second, because such a standardized usage involves mutual cooperation in coordinated goal attainment, each participant holds the other or others to a common set of expectations and responsibilities regarding what their communicative actions mean. Deviations from these expectations require that the participants involved either provide a satisfactory account for their deviation (Scot and Lyman, 1968), adjust their behavior in conformity with the rule, or suffer the punishment invoked by the other or others involved in the coordination task (Pearce and Cushman, 1977). Third, standardized usage allows each individual involved to select sequences of communicative acts that reflect the individual's variable commitment to the class of intentions involved. Interactants thus reveal the variable strength of the practical force that compelled them to participate in the coordination task.

Cushman, Valentinsen, and Dietrich (1982) suggest standardized usage is necessary to overcome the problem of empirical tests of a rules theory; that is, empirically separating rule-governed from causally determined patterns of behavior. A pattern of behavior becomes empirically verifiable as rule governed when mutual expectations of what constitutes appropriate behavior—intersubjective interpersonal interpretations rather than the testimony of the single actor—serve as a standard to judge and evaluate conduct, which one now has the *right* to expect. Rules are evaluative of human behaviors and are thus monitored by those employing the rule.

Cushman and Pearce (1977) outline principles of empirical research within such a rules perspective. First, such research must locate tasks that require coordination because such tasks serve as the generative mechanism for communication rules that take the form of standardized usages. Next, a researcher must define and measure the generality and necessity of the standardized usage and its various episodic sequences. Finally, the generality and necessity of episodic sequences are modeled by three forms of the practical syllogism: the necessary and sufficient, the necessary but not sufficient, and the multiple sufficient.

Cushman and Pearce (1977) argue that each of these principles of empirical research is a necessary condition for rules research to have theoretic import. Collectively, they constitute the sufficient condition. All standardized coordination situations necessarily involve communication rules of differential stability that are carefully monitored to avoid deviations and thus intersubjectively verifiable. When researchers follow the aforementioned procedure in constructing and verifying rules theories of human communication processes, they correct the previously mentioned problems of ad hoc explanation and non-verifiability inherent in the first-person practical syllogism.

Cushman and his associates therefore have made three changes in the first-person practical syllogism to make the rules explanatory model predictive and verifiable. First, the major premise of the practical syllogism has been changed from an individual intention to a class of verifiable intentional situations—task coordination situations. Second, rule influence is conceptualized as the effect of a powerful rule-generating mechanism—coordination tasks—that exerts influence on minor premises—selection of standardized usages by the actors. Third, the categorical logic of practical necessity has been changed to the variable logic of practical force (Cushman, Valentinsen, and Dietrich, 1982; see also Adler, 1978). Such changes result in the *third-person syllogism*:

A = a class of actors;
C = a class of verifiable intentional situations (task coordination situations);
B = standardized usages (episodic sequences of talk).

* A intends to bring about C;
* A knows that without episodes B, C will not occur;
* A engages in episodes B.

Conceptual and Operational Definitions of Theoretical Constructs

Communication Rules are tacit understandings (generally unwritten and unspoken) about appropriate ways to interact (communicate) with others in given roles and situations; they are choices, not laws (though they constrain choice through normative, practical or logical force), and they allow interactors to interpret behavior in similar ways to share meaning).

(Schall, 1983)

Cushman and his associates' rules theory of communication in interpersonal relationships focuses on relational coordination tasks located in the dyad—relationship initiation and development, its maintenance and dissolution, and nourishment of its overall quality—and conventional or standard, symbolic patterns—standardized usages—that facilitate the completion of these non-linguistic tasks. We call such relational coordination tasks relationship trajectories. The decision to take a coordination task and its standardized usage as the basic unit for analysis thus requires:

1. The determination of recurrent tasks within a given society that recguire coordination;
2. Description of the episodic communication sequence that constitutes the standardized usage;
3. Locating the initial conditions that provoke communicators to employ the standardized usage.

In this view, interpersonal coordination tasks generate functional communication rules (standardized usages) that determine the content and sequential unfolding of the goal directed communication behavior required by such tasks. Because such functional rules are both general and necessary, they can be employed to develop theories (Cushman, King, and Smith, 1988).

This section of the chapter presents and critically discusses the most relevant conceptual and operational definitions of constructs found in the original formulation of the rules theory of communication in interpersonal relations. The relevant constructs are (1) self-concept, (2) interpersonal relationships, (3) characteristics of interpersonal relationships, (4) communication rules, and (5) communication as reciprocal self-concept support.

Self-Concept

Human actions that take place within a standardized situation require common intentions, an established set of rules for cooperative achievement of those intentions, and procedure for manifesting the variable practical force the actors feel for participating in the coordination task. But, to explain such actions, the researcher needs to determine the link between thoughts and behavior. The self-concept provides just such an empirically verifiable link (Cushman, 1990).

The Nature of the Self-Concept. Cushman and his associates identify two types of self-concept—ideal self and real self—each consisting of three classes of self-object relationships. The *ideal self* is the self one wants to be; the *real self* is the self one can sustain in interaction (Cushman and Cahn, 1985; Cushman, 1990; see also Mead, 1934). The degreee of overlap between the two types of self-concept vaires between individuals as well as during an individuals's life-cycle. The first dimension of the self-concept is the *identity self*, which designates relationships pertaining to what an individual *is*; for example, I am short, I am fat, I am intelligent. The identity self is concerned with naming or labeling the attributes of the individual in the context of his or her environment. The second dimension is the *evaluative self*, which describes how an individual *feels* about his or her relationship to objects: I am a good teacher; I am a reliable friend. The evaluative self is concerned with the individual's feelings about the quality of existing self-object relationships. The third dimension is the *behavioral self*, which prescribes *appropriate behavior* to be performed in regard to the self-object relationship: I am a good teacher and therefore I must not go to class unprepared. The behavioral self deals with expected behavior in the context of the relationship. "The behavioral self can be represented as a set of imperatives for action—rules governing an individual's behavior with respect to relevant objects in a situation" (Cushman, Valentinsen, and Dietrich, 1982).

Cushman (1989) asserts that a self-concept constitutes a ready-made format for processing experience and initiating action. The self-concept, as an organized set of self-object structures, provides the rationale for choice in the form of a culturally balanced repertory of alternative meanings, evaluations and plans of action.

The Self-Concept as a Cybernetic Control System. In the original formulation of the rules theory of communication in interpersonal relationships, the self-concept was operationalized as the individual's perception of his or her real and ideal selves (for a discussion see Nicotera et al., 1993, Chapter 13). The internal organization of the self-concept may remain stable or be modified by an individual's interaction with others and the environment. When Cushman and his associates restrict their domain of inquiry to communication behaviors involving human actions in coordination situations that are governed and guided by standardized rules, they are restricting the portions of the self-concept they seek to measure in three ways. First, they are attempting to measure a stable rather than a dynamic class of self-concept rules. Second, these rules are held in common by all those involved in the coordination task and thus are intersubjectively verifiable through measurement. Third, deviations from this stable set of rules are internally monitored and corrected by those involved in the coordination task. Thus, deviations from the rules are also intersubjectively verifiable.

The standardized rules that govern and guide social human action are thus manifest in the self-concept as scientifically measurable relationship between the individual and the objects in his or her experiential field. These measures can be made antecedent to action and employed to explain, predict, and control an individual's subsequent communication behavior, attitudinal change, and bebavioral change in a particular type of relationship (Cushman, 1990).

Interpersonal Relationships

In the original formulation of the rules theory of communication, *interpersonal relationships* were defined as a coordination system whose function is to develop and maintain consensus on individual self-concepts, whose structure is dyadic, and whose process entails the development, presentation, and validation of individual self-concepts (Cushman, Valentinsen, and Dietrich, 1982; Nicotera et al., 1993, Chapter 1).

Friend Relationship. Although friendships are crucial to one's sense of self, more than half of all those an individual wants to be friends with will not reciprocate (Booth, 1972). In America, friendships are interpersonal relationships based on trust, self-concept support, and helping behavior (La Gaipa, 1977; Crawford, 1977; and Gibbs, 1977). Cushman and Cahn (1985) define trust as a relationship based upon authenticity; self-concept support as communication of respect for another's social and psychological self; and helping behavior as reciprocal assistance in time of need. Friendships can grow in terms of increasing levels of intimacy, entail conflicts, or breakups. Cushman and Cahn (1985) identified two important roles friends play: confidant and companion. A confidant is one who provides evaluative self-concept support, whereas a companion is someone who provides behavioral self-concept support. The same friend may fill either one or both of these roles.

Mate Relationship. Cushman and his associates defined *mate* as any opposite sex relationship for which the individual clears the field of competitors. Such relationship, they assert, normally includes a major portion of individuals who are going steady, engaged, cohabiting, or married. Cushman and Cahn (1985) argue that mate relationships account for a great deal of the intense happiness, satisfaction, and meaning one finds in life and function as strong social integrating forces. Research indicates that in America mate relationships differ from friendships in the degree to which physical attraction and recipro- cated affection are necessary. The specific types of love and commitment involved in mate relationship are based on similar levels of mates' intelligence, physical attraction, sex appeal, and ideal "mateness" (Pam, Plutchik, and Conte, 1973).

Characteristics of Interpersonal Relationships

Having distinguished between friendships and mateships, Cushman and associates focus on several characteristics of interpersonal relationships in the original formulation of the rules theory of communication. They conceptualize four characteristics of such interpersonal relationships: (1) relational intimacy (or depth), (2) relationship attributes, (3) relationship trajectories or relational coordination tasks, and (4) relationship quality.

Relational intimacy (or *depth*) is defined in terms of stages of relationship development. It is often referred to as stable and significantly different semantic markers for increasing degrees of intimacy or distinct, discrete, and identifiable levels of relational intensity (Nicotera et al., 1993). Relationship intimacy is operationalized as perceived distances between the individual's real and ideal selves and stages of relationship development. These distances are expected to significantly decrease with each higher stage of the relationship intimacy. In America, the levels of increasing friendship intimacy are acquaintance, casual friend, good friend, and best friend (Valentinsen, Cushman, and Schroeder, 1981); the levels of increasing intimacy of the mate relationship are casual date, steady date, fiance, and spouse (Valentinsen, Cushman, and Schroeder, 1981; Cushman and Chan, 1993).

Relationship attributes are defined as elements that distinguish relationship types. Attributes that most sharply distinguish relationship types—for example, friendships and mateships—are labeled *entry variables.* Other attributes that account for growth and deeper levels of intimacy of a specific type of relationship, however, are labeled *intensity variables.* Entry variables are operationalized in terms of their perceived equidistance from all relationship levels. In America, entry attributes of the friendship seem to be trust and respect, whereas the entry attributes of the mateship are physical attractiveness, sexual appeal, and intelligence (Valentinsen, Cushman, and Schroeder, 1981). Intensity variables, on the other hand, are operationalized in terms of the perception that distances between such attributes and each higher stage of the relationship intimacy significantly decrease.

Relationship trajectories or relational coordination tasks are conceptualized as different paths of interpersonal relationships. Cushman and associates first formulate a three-step filtering process for *relationship development* (Cushman, Valentinsen, and Dietrich, 1982; Cushman and Cahn, 1985). From a field of availables, actors "select" a subset of individuals—the field of approachables—and with some of them initiate interpersonal relationships, either friendship or mateship, by relying on a set of entry communicative rules. If and when reciprocated, the relationship moves to the field of reciprocals. By relying on a set of intensity communicative rules, partners increase intensity or intimacy of their interpersonal relationship. *Relationship maintenance* refers loosely to partners' ability to negotiate differences on crucial relationship variables. *Relationship dissolution* refers to partners' grave and sustained violation of relationship-specific entry and intensity communicative rules, which destroys the relationship. In America, intensity attributes of the friendship seem to be psychological support and authenticity (Valentinsen, Cushman, and Schroeder, 1981), whereas intensity attributes of the mateship are respect, affection, and psychological support (Cushman and Cahn, 1993). Finally, *relationship quality* is defined in terms of relational intimacy, personal growth, and effective communication on the crucial relationship variables. In a sense, relationship quality, like relationship maintenance, is based on the partners' ability to negotiate differences on crucial relationship variables. Conversely, conflict over crucial relationship variables may threaten and, eventually, destroy the relationship.

Communication Rules

Communicative rules are defined as tacit understandings about (in)appropriate ways to interact in a particular type of relationship. In the original formulation of the rules theory of communication in interpersonal relationships, rules were viewed as prescriptive social conventions that could be violated by individuals or changed by groups, but usually they entailed social sanctions. Such a formulation implies that rules are subculture—or culture—specific. Communication rules in the form of standardized usage are, then, standardized normative guidelines for accomplishing interpersonal relational tasks or trajectories such as relationship initiation, development, maintenance, nourishment of its quality, or dissolution. In the original formulation of the theory, Cushman and associates articulated three dimensions of communicative rules: (1) rule homogeneity, (2) rule conventionality, and (3) rule stability. *Rule homogeneity* refers to the distribution of the rule structure in a given population; that is, how common the rule structure is and how many people know it. Rule homogeneity is operationalized by a sample variance of the rule distribution: the larger is the variance, the more heterogeneous is the rule. *Rule conventionality* is conceptualized as the level of agreement on the relationship attributes, both entry and intensity variables, observed within the samples. The more conventional the standardized usage is, the narrower is the choice of symbolic expressions— sequences of communicative acts—available to interactants. In other words, rule conventionality is inversely related to the number of appropriate communicative alternatives. Rule conventionality is operationalized as the percentage of the standard error of agreement in the relationship attributes. The smaller is the percentage of the standard error, the more conventional are the rules. *Rule stability* refers to the time period during which the standardized usage exerts a consistent and stable normative force.

Communication as Reciprocal Self-Concept Support

Cushman and his associates, early in their research endeavors, attempted to delimit the broad and recurrent interpersonal relational tasks within a given culture for which coordination and standardized communication rules are required (Cushman and Florence, 1974). Such tasks or relationship trajectories are, for example, initiation, development, maintenance, breakup, and nourishment of the overall quality of friendships and mate relationships. Such tasks require communication in which individuals describe, assert, and propose their preferred relationship to others; for example, I love you; I want to be your friend; I hate you but I can persuade you to go to the movies; You must let me know what your stand is. These descriptions, assertions, and proposals are then accepted, questioned, or denied by others in communication. This process of development, presentation, and validation of one's personal identity based on varying degrees of overlap between one's ideal and real selves—one's ideal and real identity, evaluative and behavioral self-concept—is what Cushman and Florence (1974) termed *interpersonal communication*. It is therefore postulated that communication in the form of *reciprocal self-concept support* serves as a necessary basis for any interpersonal relationship.

Cushman, Valentinsen, and Dietrich (1982) argue that self-concept support consists of one individual attempting to manifest, symbolically, support for another individual's specific relationships to objects. Such a support, they assert, is contingent upon a recognition of the unique scope, depth, and configuration of another's self-concept and the knowledge of the specific communication rules that govern and guide how one creates messages conveying such support. Messages expressing self-concept support, they point out, must endorse one or more of the three dimensions of self-object relationships—identity, evaluative, and behavioral—in attempting to make another individual perceive self-concept support. Such self-concept support accounts for varying degrees of overlap between one's real and ideal self-concepts.

Theoretical Propositions: Relationships Between Concepts

Establishment and development of interpersonal relationships is explored by Cushman and associates through a three-stage communication filtering process that involves (1) a field of availables, (2) a field of approachables, and (3) a field of reciprocals. Initiation of interpersonal relationships requires communication of self-concept support that is regulated by entry rules relevant to one's field of approachables. Deepening the intimacy of interpersonal relationships requires communication of self-concept support that is regulated by intensity rules relevant to one's field of reciprocals. Maintaining interpersonal relationships requires communication of self-concept support that is regulated by the relationship-specific quality rules. Finally, terminating interpersonal relationships is regulated by the relationship-specific rules for aligning problems in actions. A particular means of aligning actions takes the form of accounts such as excuses, justifications, concessions, and refusals.

The Direction and Strength of the Relationships Between Constructs

Friendships. Cushman and associates (Cushman and Cahn, 1985, p. 52; Cushman, Valentinsen, and Dietrich, 1982, pp. 107–108; see also Nicotera et al., 1993, Chapter 1) identify three normative variables—entry rules—that within the field of approachables govern and guide the friendship initiation process. The first two variables specify the individual perceptions that form the antecedent conditions for generating messages aimed at establishing a friendship. These antecedent perceptions are the information an individual obtains in initial interaction with others in the field of availables. The third variable specifies the type of message contents that, when presented, will be perceived by others as self-concept support or an attempt to establish a friend relationship.

1. The greater is an individual's perceived relationship between attributes of one's own self-concept and the perceivid attributes of another's real self-concept, the greater is the likelihood that communication will be initiated.
2. The greater is an individual's perceived likelihood that the other will accept an offer of friendship, the greater is the likelihood that communication will be initiated.
3. The more frequently an individual provides messages that support some positive identity, evaluative or behavioral self-object relationships of another's self-concept, the greater is the likelihood that the other individual will perceive those messages as an attempt to initiate a friend relationship.

Two normative variables—intensity rules—in the field of reciprocals guide the process of friendship growth from acquaintances to casual friends to good friends to best friends.

1. The greater is an individual's perceived accuracy with regard to the relationship between one's own and another's self-concept, the greater is the likelihood that a friend relationship will grow.
2. The greater is the reciprocated perceived self-concept support, the greater is the likelihood that a friend relationship will grow.

Mate Relationships. Formally, the same three-stage filtering process takes place in both friendship and mateship formation and development. However, to the extent that mateship and friendship are different types of relationships, communication rules are different. For example, in addition to the causal and normative forces that constrain the field of available friends, the availability of mates is further constrained by the marriage roles, the divorce rate, and number of individuals whose mates die (Hacker, 1979). Availability here means freedom from any or the previous mateship responsibility. Five normative variables—entry rules—govern and guide the initiation process within the field of approachables (Cushman and Cahn, 1985, pp. 57–58; Cushman, Valentinsen, and Dietrich, 1982, pp. 109–110; see also Nicotera et al., 1993, Chapter 1).

1. The greater is an individual's perception that a member of the opposite sex is as intelligent, physically attractive, and sexually appealing as one thinks one is, the greater is the likelihood of initiating commmication aimed at establishing a mate relationship.
2. The greater is an individual's perception that someone of the opposite sex has a real self-concept similar to one's ideal self for a mate, the greater is the likelihood of initiating communication aimed at establishing a mate relationship.
3. The greater a woman's perception that the man's real-ideal self-concept discrepancy is small, the greater is the likelihood of initiating communication aimed at establishing a mate relationship.
4. The greater is in individual's perception that an opposite-sex other is likely to accept one's offer of a relationship, the greater is the likelihood of initiating communication aimed at establishing mate relationship.
5. The more frequently an individual provides messages that (a) manifest self-concept support for an opposite-sex other's physical attractiveness, sex appeal, and intelligence; (b) characterize that other as relating to the individual's ideal mate; and (c) indicate a perceived lack of discrepancy between the man's real and ideal selves, the greater is the likelihood that

the other individual will perceive those messages as an attempt to initiate a mate relationship.

Two normative variables—intensity rules—in the field of reciprocals regulate communication of self-concept support necessary for the intimacy of mateship to increase from a casual date, to a steady date, to an engagement, to marriage (Cushman and Cahn, 1985, p. 58; Cushman, Valentinsen, and Dietrich, 1982, p. 111; see also Nicotera et al., 1993, Chapter 1).

1. The greater is a woman's perception of lack of discrepancy between her mate's real and ideal self-concepts, the greater is the likelihood the relationship will grow.
2. The greater is the perception that there is reciprocation of self-concept support in regard to the mate selection rules, the greater is the likelihood the relationship will grow.

The Original Empirical Investigations

A rules theory of the friend and mate formation processes, originally formulated by Cushman, Valentinsen, and Dietrich (1982), was initially tested by Valentinsen, Cushman, and Schroeder (1981). Their goal was first to develop valid and reliable dependent and independent measures of the key constructs, then to test theoretical propositions or the direction and strength of the relationships between the concepts, and finally, to make inferences about communication rules (for a discussion, see Nicotera et al., 1993, Chapter 3). The original empirical investigations relied on a particular measuring system— the multidimensional Galileo system that uses spatial analysis to model interrelationships in the form of distances among a set of concepts. Communication in friendship was examined in two samples, one consisting of twenty-nine, and the other of fifty-eight American undergraduate students. The role of communication in mateship was tested in a sample of thirty-one male and female American undergraduate students.

Validation of Concepts. Valentinsen, Cushman, and Schroeder (1981) reported two relevant findings concerning the validation of single concepts. First, they found that the subjects do not distinguish sharply between a companion and a confidant as two friendship roles. And second, the researchers found that the friendship levels—acquaintance, casual friend, good friend, and best friend—are arrayed ordinally from low to high when measured in terms of their significant mutual distances. (The mateship levels, however, were not explicitly tested. It was simply assumed that they are also arrayed ordinally from low to high.)

Tests of Theoretical Propositions. Valentinsen, Cushman, and Schroeder (1981) reported seven relevant findings—five on the friendship, and two on the mateship—regarding theoretical propositions or the direction and strength of the relationships between the concepts.

The researchers reported first that the levels of the friendship intensity or intimacy, when measured by the subjects' perceptions of their distances from their ideal selves, are ordered as hypothesized. However, there is virtually no perceived difference between acquaintance and casual friend from the ideal self. Second, the researchers found that, when measured in terms of the friendship levels' perceived distances from the real self, each higher level of the friendship intensity is closer to the real self. A third important finding was that a companion (behavioral self-concept support) seems to be equidistant from all friendship levels. Fourth, these levels get progressively closer to a confidant (support for the evaluative self). Finally, the researchers reported that the perceived distances between two friendship attributes—psychological support and authenticity—and levels of the friendship get progressively. smaller. However, for the attributes trust and respect, evidence for the trend is not as clear-cut. Consequently, psychological support and authenticity are the intensity variables, whereas trust and respect are the entry variables of the friendship. Trust and respect do not increase the level of the friendship intimacy, but without such attributes the friendship is impossible.

Valentinsen, Cushman, and Schroeder (1981) reported two significant findings regarding mateship. First, the perceived distances between the ideal mate and the different levels of mate relationship show a trend in the form of ascending order from the most intimate to the least intimate—spouse, fiance, steady date, and casual date respectively. And second, the mateship attributes—physical attractiveness, intelligence, and sexual appeal—do not vary with the different levels of mate relationship. These attributes seem to be equidistant from all levels of the mateship intensity. Consequently, physical attractiveness, intelligence, and sexual appeal are the entry variables of the mate relationship. Communication of such attributes does not increase the intimacy of the mateship but without such attributes the mate relationship cannot be initiated, developed, and sustained. (In another study, Cushman and Cahn, 1993, established that communication of respect, affection, and psychological support does increase the intimacy of the mate relationship. In other words, respect, affection, and psychological support are the intensity variables of the mate relationship in America.)

Inferences Regarding Communication Rules. The empirical evidence warrants a conclusion that perceived self-concept support with varying degrees of overlap between the ideal and real selves—and their dimensions, the identity, evaluative, and behavioral selves—is a necessary communicative mechanism for initiation and development of friendships and mateships. It also appears that support for the ideal self-concept is more important than support for the real self in the earlier stages of friendship. This was indicated by significantly smaller distances of two friendship levels—acquaintance and casual friend—from the ideal self than from the real self.

As far as the appropriate and necessary content of self-concept support, whose sources are the friendship and mateship attributes, is concerned, Valentinsen, Cushman, and Schroeder (1981) reported the following two findings. First, being a companion in friendships (providing behavioral or social support) seems to be an entry variable based on an either-or condition. This suggests that communicating social support—behavioral self-concept support—is equally necessary at all levels of the friendship. On the other hand, being a confidant (providing evaluative or psychological support) is a progressively more important role at every higher level of the friendship. This suggests that communicating psychological support—evaluative self-concept support—becomes more important as the friendship intimacy increases. Consequently, a confidant seems to be a quantitative or intensity variable. Overall, then, the role of companion is seen by the subjects as less intimate than the role of confidant in friendship initiation and development. In addition, although psychological support and authenticity seem to be intensity friendship attributes, trust and respect appear to be entry variables. Second, because the mateship attributes—physical attractiveness, intelligence, and sexual appeal—do not seem to vary with the different levels of the mate relationship, these attributes are of a matching (entry) guality. This suggests that in mateships, the appropriate self-concept support must contain messages on partners' physical attractiveness, intelligence, and sexual appeal if the mate relationship is to be initiated and, by implication, maintained. However, such messages will not deepen the intimacy of the relationship.

As far as the degree of conventionality of the rules guiding the formation of mateship and friendship is concerned, the researchers drew a cautious conclusion. In the light of all errors ranging from 5.70 to 49.88 percent, Valentinsen, Cushman, and Schroeder (1981) suggested that the conventionality of the communication rules is rather variable.

Significant Implications

The original empirical investigations of the rules theory of communication in friendships and mateships have three significant implications. First, they validated a general theoretical structure built by Cushman and associates. Second, they established variables that in later works are referred to as entry or intensity variables. Finally, they offered the standards for interpretation and the guidelines for the future research endeavors (for a discussion see Nicotera et al., 1993, Chapter 3).

Extensions of the Rules Theory of Communication
in Interpersonal Relationships

Cushman and associates have extended the rules theory of communication in interpersonal relationships by both refining a web of relationships between concepts and by diversifying empirical tests of the theory. Three theoretical extensions are important: (1) logical formalization of the theory in the form of the seven propositions (Korn and Nicotera, 1993, Chapter 2), (2) an interpersonal topic penetration profile that influences indirect self-concept support (Cushman, 1977, 1989; Nicotera, Cushman, and Lin, 1991; Bahk, 1993, Chapter 5; Korn, 1993, Chapter 4; Nicotera et al., 1993, Chapter 9; see also Cushman and Kovacic, 1994), and (3) conceptualization of different types of friendship. There are also three relevant empirical extensions:

1.)   In addition to mateship initiation and development, researchers have examined other coordination tasks such as maintenance and termination that are the subsequent "segments" of the mateship trajectory (Cahn, 1985; Cushman and Cahn, 1985, 1986; Cushman, 1989).

2.)   Friendships and mateships were studied with samples from different cultures (Bahk, 1993, Chapter 5; Korn, 1993, Chapter 4; Moemeka and Nicotera, 1993a, 1993b; Nicotera et al., 1993, Chapter 9; Ju, 1993, Chapter 12; see also Cushman and Kovacic, 1994).

3.)   These empirical studies went beyond a Galileo program by using *t*-tests, analysis of variance (ANOVA), factor analysis, and contingency tables as alternative methods of statistical analysis.

Let us briefly present each of these extensions in turn.

Theoretical Extensions

Formalization of the Theory. Korn and Nicotera (1993) formulated seven empirically confirmable propositions derived from the general conceptual theory (Cushman and Cahn, 1985; and Cushman, Valentinsen, and Dietrich, 1982) and other relevant literature.

1.)   Perceived self-concept support is the basis of interpersonal attraction.

2.)   Different types of perceived self-concept support are the basis for different types of interpersonal relationships.

3.)   Different types of self-concept support are the basis for entry into and increasing intensity of interpersonal relationships.

4.)   The type and form of self-concept support is homogeneous by culture.

5.)   Conflict that threatens self-concept support on crucial relationship variables—the lack of it or attacks on it—is the most potentially dangerous type of conflict in interpersonal relationships.

6.)   Negotiation of differences in perceptions of self-concept support on crucial relationship variables cements interpersonal relationships.

7.)   Quality interpersonal relationships consist of intimacy, personal growth, and effective communication on the crucial relationship variables.

Such logical formalization provides not only a template for cross-cultural investigations of interpersonal communication in friend and mate relationships but also a standard for evaluating a cumulative growth of the research program (for a similar argument see Rosengren, 1993).

Topic Penetration and Self-Concept Support. Cushman and associates treat the relationship attributes or dimensions construct as a culture-specific source of the appropriate content in interpersonal communication in friend and mate relationships. An interpersonal penetration analysis extends the conceptualization of the culturally appropriate content of communication in different types of interpersonal relationships. This concept is relevant because it allows for tracking what topics are most discussed between mates or friends in different cultures. Such topics form one type of the content of perceived *indirect* self-concept support—when partners take turns talking about the things that interest the other—in interpersonal relationships. In operationalizing and measuring interpersonal penetration, Cushman and associates drew on the work of Gudykunst (Gudykunst, 1985; Gudykunst and Nishida, 1983) and Taylor and Altman (1966).

Conceptualization of Different Types of Friendship. Bahk (1993, Chapter 5) extended the definition of friendship to explicitly include the gender and culture of partners. Consequently, one can investigate communication within the following types of friendship dyads: (1) same-sex friends (both are either male or female) from the same culture, (2) same-sex friends (both are either male or female) from different cultures, (3) opposite-sex friends (one male and one female) from the same culture, and (4) opposite-sex friends (one male and one female) from different cultures. Such conceptualization allows for the examination of a degree of variability of both communicative mechanisms in the form of self-concept support and the content of communication derived from the relationship attributes and interpersonal penetration across different types of friendship.

Empirical Extensions

Maintenance and Termination of Mate Relationships. Cushman (1989) argues that the maintenance of a mate relationship in America is tantamount to maintaining the quality of that relationship and that such quality depends mainly on the manner in which mates handle conflict. If, as Korn and Nicotera (1993, Chapter 2) contend, conflict threatens self-concept support on crucial relationship variables—that is, attributes—then the reciprocal communication of psychological support, affection, and respect engenders a quality mate relationship. These intensity variables determine what types of intensity self-concept support must be communicated for the intimacy of the mateship to increase (Cushman and Kovacic, 1994). Conversely, the reciprocal communication of negative affect, competition, and criticism brings about the lack of a high-quality relationship.

Some researchers suggest that only 20 percent of mate relationships are characterized by high-quality communication patterns (Copland, Bugaighis, and Schumm, 1983). Korn and Nicotera (1993, Chapter 2) also maintain that negotiation of differences, such as conflict resolution in mate relationships, in perceptions of self-concept support on crucial relationship variables (attributes) cements a mate relationship. Cushman (1989) identified two patterns or sequences of conflict resolution in mate relationships in America. A high mateship quality is generated by the following communication sequence: (1) a focused issue or problem is introduced with neutral affect, (2) the respondent then obtains agreement on a proportionate issue with neutral affect, (3) the couple draws out implications of the issue or problem to the relationship, (4) the couple explores potential solutions, and finally (5) the couple establishes a consensus on a solution and implements it. In contrast, a low-quality mateship is brought about by the following communication sequence: (1) a complaint is lodged with negative affect, (2) a mate then responds by confronting, defending, and cross-complaining, (3) a partner then communicates with neutral or negative affect, (4) the couple then reciprocates negative affect which, finally, leads to (5) withdrawal or escalation. The negative sequence becomes an enduring pattern that eventually destroys the relationship. Conversely, the high-quality communication pattern demonstrates psychological support, affection, and respect, and deepens intimacy.

Cahn (1987) studied how people productively assess their most intimate relationships—those between friends and mates—and how they preserve, repair, or leave such relationships when problems arise. Relational assessment takes place when partners experience inattention, boredom, breakdown, excitement, happiness and growth, or disintegration of the relationship. Such reassessment brings about four alternative outcomes: (1) continuation, (2) repair, (3) renegotiation, and (4) disengagement.

Cahn (1985) contends that individual and relational development are associated with feelings of self-worth and relational satisfaction, which are, in turn, the products of (1) perceived, mutual, positive self-concept support; (2) self-concept accuracy (the ability to perceive and interpret the other's behavior); and (3) interaction management or interpersonal communication skills such as accurate cueing, listening, interpretation, and negotiation.

Cahn (1985) found that when relational partners see themselves as having a common set of self-concept qualities that each (1) admires, (2) perceives as complementary to each other's self-concept, and (3) perceives as encouraging to the development of one's own self-concept, reassessment usually results in a decision to *continue* with the relationship. However, even the best of friends and the best of mates do fall out time and again. When this happens, reassessment (even of the mildest type) usually takes place either quietly by each individual or openly between them. Such open attempts, called *repair*, usually demand an account, which is a particular type of utterance that attempts to bridge the gap between one's unexpected behavior and another's expectations. Accounts take the form of (1) admitting fault without admitting responsibility (excuse), (2) acceptance of responsibility but denial of bad consequences (justifications), (3) admission of wrongdoing and willingness to make restitution (concessions), and (4) outright denial of wrongdoing and its effect (refusals) (for the typology of accounts see Schonback, 1980). A type of account used depends on the individual's self-concept. Conversely, the self-concept of the relational partner will determine the acceptance or rejection of the account. In general, when relational partners share as many or more positive self-concept qualities than there are qualities that cause friction, they will normally settle for *repair.*

On the other hand, relational partners may try to *renegotiate* or change the nature or type of a relationship. Such changes—for example, from very close friends to acquaintances, or from a fiance to a friend—require the careful use of one's interactional management skills, accounts, and negotiating skills. One partner may provide strong and accurate positive self-concept support for those qualities of the other's self-concept that will form the basis of the new relationship. One may carefully isolate self-concept qualities of the old relationship and explicitly or implicitly reject them. One may account for— justify—the rejection. Finally, one may express support for the feelings that underscore the new relationship. Renegotiation is an acceptable alternative to relational disintegration when reassessment shows more strong and positive mutual self-concept qualities than strong but negative qualities. Finally, times may arise when another person has become destructive to one's own self and all of one's relationships with others (Mathews and Clark, 1982). Such instances invite relational reassessment aimed at *relational disengagement* or *disintegration.* Such termination of a relationship may involve the following four strategies: (1) withdrawal or avoidance (a complete stoppage of all relational interactions), (2) positive tone (justification for or rationalization of the process), (3) Machiavellianism (manipulating one's partner into a position to either lose face or break off the relationship), and (4) openness (a very explicit and straightforward statement as to why the relationship cannot continue).

In a similar fashion, Cushman and Cahn (1986) have explored how fifteen American divorced couples used accounts in explaining the relational breakup to sixty-two of their children. They also examined whether parents and children perceived a type of account given in the same manner.

Cross-Cultural Studies of Friendships and Mateships. We will briefly summarize the findings of six cross-cultural studies of interpersonal communication, three of friendships and three of mate relationships. (A summary of the findings of seven earlier studies of the mate selection process in six cultures throughout the world can be found in Cushman and Kovacic, 1994).

Korn (1993, Chapter 4) and Bahk (1993, Chapter 5) conducted independent studies in which each compared interpersonal communication in friendships in one American and one Korean sample of undergraduate students. Moemeka and Nicotera (1993a) used a sample of civil servants and graduate students from different parts of Nigeria to examine communication in friendships in the Nigerian cultural environment. Let us briefly discuss the results of each of the three studies in turn (see Table 6.1).

Korn (1993, Chapter 4) reported that American subjects perceived acquaintances, casual friends, good friends, and best friends as the semantic markers that indicate increasing degrees or levels of friendship intimacy. He also found that the communication of psychological support (evaluative self-concept support), trust, respect, and authenticity—the friendship attributes—are intensity variables. Put differently, the increasing amount of self-concept support for the four friendship attributes deepens the intimacy of the friendship in the United States. In the Korean sample, Korn found that subjects perceived acquaintances, ordinary friends, close friends, and best friends as the semantic markers that represent increasing degrees or levels of friendship intimacy. He also reported that the communication of congeniality, sympathy, unselfishness, responsibility, honesty, generosity, and intelligence—the friendship attributes—are intensity variables. In other words, the higher is the frequency of self-concept support for the seven friendship attributes, the higher is the intimacy of the friendship in Korea.

As far as interpersonal penetration (levels of frequency and intimacy of topics discussed among friends) is concerned, Korn detected significant differences in topics discussed among close Korean and American friends. For example, American respondents discussed most frequently (the breadth) and intimately (the depth) the following topics: (1) sexual morality; (2) self-esteem derived from accomplishments in school, work, or society; (3) the extent of premarital sexual relations; (4) ideal sexual partner prior to marriage; (5) one's experiences; and (6) feelings or thoughts about one's outward appearance. Korean respondents listed the following topics discussed most frequently and intimately: (1) one's preferences for something new or unusual; (2) the importance of education; (3) self-esteem gained from school, work, or societal accomplishments; and (4) duty or responsibility.

Bahk (1993, Chapter 5) reported essentially the same results as Korn regarding the levels of the friendship intimacy. Both American and Korean

TABLE 6.1

Friend Selection Process

	USA	Korea	Nigeria
Entry Rules (start)			Humor Intelligence
Intensity Rules (develop)	Psychological support Trust Respect Authenticity	Congeniality Sympathy Unselfishness Responsibility Honesty Generosity Intelligence	Tolerance Caring Trustworthiness
Levels of Intimacy (low-high)	Acquaintance Casual friend Good friend Best friend	Acquaintance Ordinary friend Close friend Best friend	Casual level: acquaintance and ordinary friend Close level: close and best friend
Social Penetration (discussed most frequently and intimately with a close friend)	Sexual morality Self-esteem Premarital sex Ideal sexual partner prior to marriage Experiences Feelings about looks	Preferences for new and unusual Education Self-esteem Duty and responsibility	
Source of data	Korn, 1993, Chapter 4; Bahk, 1993, Chapter 5	Korn, 1993, Chapter 4; Bahk, 1993, Chapter 5	Moemeka and Nicotera, 1993a

respondents perceived acquaintances, ordinary friends, close friends, and best friends as the semantic markers that indicate increasing degrees of the friendship intimacy. However, for the first three levels of the friendship—acquaintance, ordinary friend, and close friend—perceived distances from oneself were significantly larger for the Korean than American respondents. Perceived distances between oneself and the most intimate friendship level—best friend— were virtually identical for both the American and Korean subjects. But when these results were decomposed in terms of culture (American vs. Korean), type of friendship (same sex vs. opposite sex), and the gender of respondents (male vs. female), the picture was more nuanced. Overall, the gender of respondents seems to play a more important role in Korea, whereas the type of friendship appears to be more strongly influencing perceptions of the number of the stages of the friendship intimacy in America.

In both samples, Bahk (1993, Chapter 5) operationalized self-concept support for best friends in terms of its five dimensions: (1) self-concept similarity (between best friends in terms of the seven friendship attributes—congeniality, sympathy, unselfishness, responsibility, honesty, generosity, and intelligence); (2) self-concept accuracy (in predicting the feelings, value judgments, thoughts, and behavior of one's best friend); (3) perceived understanding (belief that one's best friend might understand feelings and thoughts that one did not express by either words or behavior); (4) perceived liking (feeling confident that your best friend likes you); and (5) conversational penetration (the relative importance of conversational topic areas discussed among best friends).

He reported the following findings. First, American students, except for male same-sex friendships, show higher self-concept similarities than Korean students. Second, American students perceive more self-concept accuracy than their Korean counterparts. More specifically, students from both cultures are more confident in accurately perceiving their same-sex best friend's self-concept than their opposite-sex friend's self-concept. Third, American students claim a higher perceived understanding by their best friend than Korean students. However, students from both cultures report being better understood by same-sex best friends than by opposite-sex best friends. Fourth, Americans are more confident than Koreans that their best friends like them. Interestingly, subjects from both cultures feel more liked by same-sex best friends than by opposite-sex best friends. Finally, women from both cultures show a higher conversational penetration (discuss more topics more frequently and intimately) than men. Although Bahk examined eight clusters of conversational penetration topics, the three most relevant are (1) sexual relations, (2) interpersonal issues, and (3) emotional experiences. Bahk reported that, overall, American students converse more about sex with their best friends than Korean students. However, same-sex best friends, especially in Korea, talk more about sex than opposite-sex best friends. Interpersonal topics are discussed more frequently and intimately by American subjects, especially women, than by Korean subjects. However, Korean men and women discuss interpersonal issues with their best friends to the same extent. Finally, Korean men and women discuss emotional experiences with their best friends in the same fashion. Interestingly, Korean men talk more about emotional experiences than American men. In America, women talk more about emotions than men.

Moemeka and Nicotera (1993a) report that in Nigeria subjects distinguished sharply casual levels (acquaintances and ordinary friends) of the friendship from close levels (close and best friends). They also found that humor and intelligence are entry level attributes of friendship in Nigeria. Consequently, self-concept support for another's sense of humor and intelligence is equally important for all stages of the friendship intimacy. The more frequent self-concept support for these two attributes does not deepen the friendship intimacy, but without it the friendship is impossible. In addition, Moemeka and Nicotera present a tentative evidence that tolerance, caring, and trustworthiness are intensity attributes of the friendship in Nigeria. The higher frequency of self-concept support for another's tolerance, caring, and trustworthiness does deepen the intimacy of the friendship.

Nicotera et al. (1993, Chapter 9) researched comparatively interpersonal communication in mate relationships in two American samples and one Korean sample of undergraduate students. Moemeka and Nicotera (1993b) used a sample of civil servants and graduate students from different parts of Nigeria to examine communication in the mate relationship in the Nigerian cultural context. Finally, Ju (1993, Chapter 12) analyzed one Chinese, one Korean, and one Japanese sample to detect criteria for mate selection in these three sociocultural contexts. Let us briefly discuss the results of each of the three studies in turn (see Table 6.2).

Nicotera (1993, Chapter 9) reports that in her first American sample subjects distinguished only two levels of the mate relationship intimacy: a casual level (casual date), and close level (steady date, fiance, and spouse). In the second American sample, subjects also perceived only two levels of the mate relationship intimacy, but differently composed: a casual level (casual date and steady date) and close level (fiance and spouse). Nicotera speculates that, because of the institution of long-term cohabitation, a fiance may not be a relevant stage of the mate relationship intimacy for American undergraduates. In the Korean sample, subjects differentiated four levels of the nonarranged mate relationship intimacy: opposite-sex acquaintance, opposite-sex friend, engaged, and spouse. The Korean mate relationship attributes are less clear, however. It is not evident whether the eight attributes of the Korean mate relationship—intelligent, attractive, honest, easy to talk to, assertive, in sound health, understanding, and handles money well—are entry or intensity variables, or some combination thereof. Nicotera speculates that the eight attributes may be entry variables, those that distinguish the nonarranged Korean mate relationship from other types of Korean interpersonal relationships.

Nicotera also examined topics discussed (the interpersonal penetration) by mates in the two cultures. In the American sample, Nicotera, identified three dimensions of the interpersonal penetration: (1) what subjects have told their current dating partner, (2) what subjects have asked their current dating partner, and (3) what subjects' current dating partners have told them. She reported the following findings. First, American respondents have told their dates the

TABLE 6.2

Mate Selection Process

	USA	Korea	Nigeria
Entry Rules (start)	Intelligence Physical attractiveness Sexual appeal	Intelligence Attractiveness Honesty Ease in talking to Assertiveness Health Understanding Ability to handle money	Good looks Politeness Intelligence
Intensity Rules (develop)	Respect Affection Psychological support		Love or affection Honesty Caring
Levels of Intimacy (low-high)	Casual date Steady date Engagement Spouse	Opposite-sex acquaintance Opposite-sex friend Engagement Spouse	Casual level: casual date Close level: regular date and steady date, and spouse
Source	Cushman and Cahn, 1993, Chapter 8		
Social Penetration (with a current date)	Told most Frequently: Sexual morality Pressures of studies Asked most Frequently: Ambitions Goals Been told most Frequently: Ambitions Goals Career choice	Talked most Frequently: School and work Talked most Intimately: Personal attitudes, values, and judgments	
Sources	Nicoters et al., 1993, Chapter 9		Moemeka and Nicotera, 1993b

most about sexual morality and pressures of studies, and the least about long-range health worries, how parents ought to deal with children, and past illness. Second, respondents have asked their dates the most about ambitions and goals, and the least about long-range health worries and past illness. Finally, their dates have told American subjects the most about ambitions and goals and career choice, and the least about past illness. In the Korean sample, current dates talked most frequently about school and work and least frequently about money and property. The same respondents talked most intimately with their current date about personal attitudes, values, and judgments, and least intimately about money and property.

Moemeka and Nicotera (1993b) detected a gap between casual (casual date) and more serious mate relationships (regular date, steady date, and spouse) in Nigeria. The researchers suggest that in the Nigerian context regular dating indicates serious intent for marriage. In addition, Moemeka and Nicotera report that good looks, politeness, and intelligence—the attributes of the mate relationship—are entry variables that predict initiation of the mate relationship. Increased frequency of self-concept support for one's partner on these attributes does not deepen the intimacy of the mate relationship. However, without such self-concept support, the mate relationship in Nigeria is not possible. On the other hand, love or affection, honesty, and caring are the intensity attributes of the mate relationship in Nigeria. The more frequent is self-concept support for one's partner on these attributes, the deeper is the intimacy of the mate relationship.

Ju (1993, Chapter 12) presents the evidence for the contemporary Chinese, Japanese, and Korean criteria for mate selection. Chinese respondents listed the following three most important criteria for mate selection: (1) high moral standards (47.4 percent of the sample listed it as the most important criterion), (2) emotional compatibility (45.3 percent of the sample), and (3) common interests (39.9 percent of the sample). Japanese respondents listed the following criteria: (1) love (64.4 criteria of the sample listed it as the most important criterion), (2) emotional compatibility (53.8 percent of the sample), and (3) high moral standards (46.0 percent of the sample). Finally, Korean respondents listed the following criteria: (1) work ability (59.9 percent of the sample listed it as the most important criterion), (2) love (56.4 percent of the sample), and (3) looks (38.6 percent of the sample). Although the three cultural traditions share the Confucian root, argues Ju, their different rank ordering of the criteria for mate selection indicates that these three societies have been undergoing radical cultural transformations. Such changes have pushed one's family social position—traditionally the most important criterion for mate selection in all three cultures— into oblivion. Ju contends that in China this is due to the revolution and ideological campaigns, and in Japan and Korea to industrialization and modernization. Put succinctly, mate selection criteria change in response to larger cultural transformations.

Implications of the Cross-Cultural Studies of Communication in Friendships and Mate Relationships. We stress two implications of such studies. First, the abstract theoretic structure of Cushman and associates' rules theory of communication can be applied cross-culturally to yield powerful insights. The theory's constructs such as self-concept, communication as reciprocal self-concept support, and communication rules help us explain, predict, and control processes captured by another construct—relationship coordination tasks or trajectories of different types of interpersonal relationships. Such an abstract theoretical skeleton is rather stable or invariant and free of any specific content.

Second, Cushman and associates' theory is sensitive to "local" cultural variations. When used in research, Cushman and associates' theory gets filled with a specific, culturally relevant content. First, the self-concept content—ideal and real selves, and their identity, evaluation, and behavioral dimensions—is always culturally relevant. Second, levels of friendship or mateship intimacy are also culture specific. In other words, the number of such levels, their ranks, and particular labels (semantic markers) are specified by culturally relevant injunctions. Third, the relationship attributes—their number and the distinction between entry and intensity attributes—are specified by a particular culture. Consequently, communication rules of direct self-concept support are variable mainly across cultures. Fourth, conversational penetration, consisting of clusters of topics that are discussed with varying frequency and intimacy in a particular type of relationship, is also culture specific. As a consequence, communication rules of indirect self-concept support vary mainly across cultures. Finally, all relational coordination tasks or "segments" of relationship trajectories—its formation and growth (development), its maintenance and termination, and its overall quality—are shaped by direct self-concept support for relevant entry and intensity relationship attributes, conflict over and negotiation of differences on culturally relevant entry and intensity variables, conflict that threatens culturally relevant entry and intensity variables, and effective communication of both direct and indirect self-concept support, respectively (for a related discussion see Nicotera et al., 1993, Chapters 7 and 11).

Critique of and Future Directions for the Rules Watershed Research Tradition

Cushman and associates' rules theory of interpersonal communication in relationships is not only embedded in the tradition of theorizing about relationships, but it also integrates different theories of relationship development. It weaves in a single theoretical framework issues relevant to (1) theories of interpersonal attraction, (2) theories of relationship attributes, (3) theories of relationship stages (the discrete levels of deeper intimacy), and (4) theories of relationship growth (movements between those levels of intimacy) (see also Nicotera et al., 1993, Chapter 13).

Cushman and associates have grounded the entire theoretical edifice in the self-concept. It is crucial, however, to emphasize that the rules watershed research tradition differs fundamentally from the constructivist approach to the study of human communication (Chapter 3). The constructivist approach stresses individual cognitive processes in message construction and interpretation (the first-person practical syllogism). In contrast, the rules tradition focuses on situations in which an agent's choice among alternative courses of action is constrained by the already existing communication rules and whose efforts to achieve a goal require the cooperation of others (the third-person syllogism). What at first sight may be confusing is Cushman and associates' empirical research of intersubjective, interpersonal interpretations and choices of appropriate rules for different types and frequency of both direct and indirect self-concept support. They rely exclusively on individual self-concepts. To get at the intersubjectivity of communication processes, they chose a methodological route for establishing the conventionality and stability of communication rules. However, the Galileo multidimensional measurement system, on which they predominantly rely, is extremely sensitive even to minor variations. Consequently, if within small samples researchers find a strong agreement on the crucial relationship attributes, they may be reasonably confident that such an agreement represents a strong cultural norm (the conventionality of rules). Moreover, without exception operationalizations of concepts were not dyadic and longitudinal. This is why the further vitality of this research program hinges upon alternative operationalizations of both types of the self-concept—ideal self and real self—and their three dimensions: identity self, evaluative self, and behavioral self.

The further vitality of the rules watershed research tradition lies, in our opinion, not in the elaboration of its philosophical assumptions or even in the thicker and denser web of relationships between ever more constructs, but in its "bolder" empirical moves and their practical applications. First, empirical investigation of communication and relational coordination tasks or trajectories of intercultural relationships—mateships and friendships—between the partners from different cultures is long overdue. Second, relational coordination tasks or trajectories of male and female homosexual mate relationships deserve the attention of rules-oriented researchers. Third, with the exception of Cahn's (1985) examination of the renegotiation of relationships, the rules-oriented researchers have neglected communication that shapes transitions between different types of relationships, for example, from friendships to mateships and vice versa (see also Nicotera et al., 1993, Chapter 13).

Such an agenda is made more feasible by Korn and Nicotera's (1993) formalization of the theory in the form of the seven empirical propositions. The proposed research agenda has three benefits. First, it would address indirectly the issues of cultural transformations within and across cultures and their influence on communication rules for appropriate communication in relationships. Second, it would gather relevant information on new "mainstream" communication rules, as well as on rules for communicating in "alternative" types of relationships such as between intercultural and gay partners. Finally, the new research focus would enlarge our knowledge of the communication rules and thus enable us to improve the quality of our lives by nourishing our relationships that make us who we are.

References

Adler, K. (1978). "An evaluation of the practical syllogism as a model of man for human communication research." *Communication Quarterly* 26: 8–18.

Altman, I., and Taylor, D. (1973). *Social penetration: The development of interpersonal relationships*. New York: Holt, Rinehart and Winston.

Bahk, C. (1993). "Interpersonal perceptions of same-sex and opposite-sex friendships in the United States and Korea." In A. Nicotera et al., *Interpersonal Communication in Friend and Mate Relationships*, pp. 79–106. Albany: State University of New York Press.

Booth, A. (1972). "Sex and social participation." *American Sociological Review* 37: 183–192.

Cahn, D. (1985). "Relative importance of perceived understanding of initial interaction and development of interpersonal relationship." *Psychological Reports* 53: 923–929.

——— (1987). *Letting Go: A Practical Theory of Relationship Disengagement and Re-Engagement*. Albany: State University of New York Press.

Copland, J., Bugaighis, M., and Schumm, W. (1983). "Relationship characteristics of couples married thirty years or more: A four sample replication." *Life Styles: A Journal of Changing Patterns* 11: 248–257.

Crawford, M. (1977). "What is a friend?" *New Society*: 116–117.

Cushman, D. P. (1977). "The rules perspectives as a theoretical basis for the study of human communication." *Communication Quarterly* 25, no. 1 (Winter): 30–45.

——— (1989). "Communication in establishing, maintaining, and terminating interpersonal relationships: A study of mateship." in S. S. King (ed.), *Human communication as a field of study: Selected contemporary views*, pp. 87–104. Albany: State University of New York Press.

—— (1990). "The rules approach to communication theory: A philosophical and operational perspective." In A. Tsujimura and L. Kincaid (Eds.), *Communication theory: Eastern and Western Perspectives*, pp. 149–163. Japan, Nippon Ltd.

—— and Cahn, D. (1985). *Communication in interpersonal relationships*. Albany: State University of New York Press.

—— and Cahn, D. (1986). "A study of communication realignment between parents and children following the parents' decision to seek divorce." *Communication Research Reports* 3: 80–85.

—— and Cahn, D. (1993). "Mate relationship markers, intensity and communication variables: A preliminary study." In A. Nicotera et al., *Interpersonal Communication in Friend and Mate Relationships*, pp. 139–146. Albany: State University of New York Press.

—— and Florence, B. T. (1974). "The development of interpersonal communication theory." *Today's Speech* 22: 11–15.

—— King, S., and Smith, T. (1988). "The rules perspectives on organizational communication." In G. Goldhaber and G. Barnett (Eds.), *Handbook of organizational communication*, pp. 53–97. Norwood, N.J.: Ablex.

—— and Kovacic, B. (1994). " Human communication: A rules perspective." In F. L. Casmir (Ed.), *Building communication theories: A socio/cultural approach*, pp. 269–295. Hillsdale, N. J.: Lawrence Erlbaum and Associates, Publishers.

—— and Pearce, W. B. (1977). "Generality and necessity in three types of human communication theory—special attention to rules theory." In D. Ruben (Ed.), *Communication Yearbook 1*, pp. 173–183. New Brunswick, N. J.: Transaction Press.

—— Valentinsen, B., and Brenner, D. (1981). "An interpersonal communication theory of the friendship formation process." Paper presented to the International Communication convention.

—— Valentinsen, B., and Dietrich, D. (1982). "The rules theory of interpersonal relationships." In F. E. X. Dance (Ed.), *Human Communication Theory: Comparative essays*, pp. 90–119. New York: Harper and Row.

—— and Whiting, G. C. (1972). "An approach to communication theory: Toward consensus on rules." *Journal of Communication* 22 (September): 217–238.

Donohue, W. A., Cushman, D. P., and Nofsinger, J. R. (1980). "Creating and confronting social order: A comparison of rules perspectives." *Western Journal of Speech Communication* 44 (Winter): 5–19.

Fay, B. and Moon, J. D. (1977). "What would an adequate philosophy of social science look like?" *Philosophy of the Social Sciences* 7: 209–227.

Gibbs, S. (1977). "A comparative analysis of friendship functions in six age groups of men and women." Ph.D. dissertation, Wayne State University.

Gudykunst, W. B. (1985). "An exploratory comparison of close intracultural and intercultural friendships." *Communication Quarterly* 33: 270–283.

—— and Nishida, T. (1983). "Social penetration in Japanese and American close friendships." In R. N. Bostrom (Ed.), *Communication Yearbook 7*, pp. 592–610. Beverly Hills, Calif.: Sage Publications.

Hacker, A. (1979). "Divorce a la mode." *New York Review of Books* (May): 23–30.

Ju, Y. (1993). "Mate selection as culture choice: Reflections on findings in China, Japan, and Korea." In Nicotera et al., *Interpersonal Communication in Friend and Mate Relationships*, pp. 201–218. Albany: State University of New York Press.

Korn, C. J. (1993). "Friendship formation and development in two cultures: Universal constructs in the United States and Korea." In A. Nicotera et al., *Interpersonal Communication in Friend and Mate Relationships*, pp. 61–78. Albany: State University of New York Press.

—— and Nicotera, A. M. (1993). "Friend and mate relationship literature: Empirical propositions and methodology." In A. Nicotera et al., *Interpersonal Communication in Friend and Mate Relationships*, pp. 13–42. Albany: State University of New York Press.

La Gaipa, J. (1977). "Testing a multi-dimensional approach to friendship." In S. Duck (Ed.), *Theory and practice of interpersonal attraction*, pp. 249–271. New York: Academic Press.

Matthews, C., and Clark III, R. (1982). "Marital satisfaction: A validation approach." *Basic and Applied Social Psychology* 3: 169–186.

Mead, G. H. (1934). *Mind, self and society*, p. 243. Chicago: University of Chicago Press.

Moemeka, A. A., and Nicotera, A. M. (1993a). "The friendship formation process in Nigeria: A preliminary study of cultural impact, communication pattern, and relationship variables. In A. Nicotera et al., *Interpersonal Communication in Friend and Mate Relationships*, pp. 107–124. Albany: State University of New York Press.

—— (1993b). "The mate selection process in Nigeria: A preliminary study of cultural impact, communication pattern, and relationship variables." In A. Nicotera et al., *Interpersonal Communication in Friend and Mate Relationships*, pp. 169–186. Albany: State University of New York Press.

Nicotera, A., Cushman, D., and Lin, T. (1991). "Development of mate relationships in two cultures: Theoretical universals in the United States and Korea." In A. Nicotera et al., *Communication in Friend and Mate Relationships*. Albany: State University of New York Press.

Nicotera, A. et al., (1993). *Communication in friend and mate relationships*. Albany: State University of New York Press.

Pam, A., Plutchik, R., and Conte, H. (1973). "Love: A psychometric approach." In *Proceedings of the 81st Annual Convention of the American Psychological Association*, pp. 159–161.

Rosengren, K. E. (1993). "From field to frog ponds." *Journal of Communication* 43 (Summer): 6–17.

Schonback, P. (1980). "A category system for account phases." *European Journal of Social Psychology* 10: 195–200.

Scot, M., and Lyman, S. (1968). "Accounts." *American Sociological Review* 33: 46–62.

Taylor, D., and Altman, I. (1966). "Intimacy-scaled stimuli for use in studies of interpersonal relations." *Psychological Reports* 19: 729–730.

Toulmin, S. (1969). "Concepts and the explanation of human behavior." In T. Mischel (Ed.), *Human Action*, pp. 71–104. New York: Academic Press.

Valentinsen, B., Cushman, D. P., and Schroeder, L. E. (1981). "The friendship and mate formation processes." Paper presented at the Annual Convention of the International Communication Association, Minneapolis.

Von Wright, G. H. (1971). *Explanation and understanding*. Ithaca, N. Y.: Cornell University Press.

PART III

❦

ORGANIZATIONAL COMMUNICATION THEORIES

BRANISLAV KOVAČIĆ

Chapter 7: High-Speed Management and Organizational Communication

At the philosophic level, the high-speed management theory developed by Cushman, King, and associates argues that communication activities are at the core of organizational strategy, as the source of cross-organizational theoretic principles. Such an assumption provides unique insight into the reasons why human communication becomes a controlling concern in organizations. This happens when speed of response has become not only the primary source of competitive advantage, but also a crucial means for obtaining any kind of competitive advantage.

At the theoretic level, under current conditions, organizations' survival and success depend on a very rapid coordination of organizational internal and external interdependencies. Global competition requires successful corporations to provide ever better products and services at an increasingly faster pace. This is possible only if organizations use communication simultaneously for environmental scanning, value chain coordination, and continuous improvement to coalign their internal and external resources. Such a rapid coalignment entails a rapid negotiation—that is, communication—of interests, concerns, and contributions regarding organizational goals and means agreed upon by strategic alliances of "internal" and "external" organizational stakeholders organized in teams. A rapid negotiation of political and functional differences through organizational communication becomes a necessary, although not sufficient, condition of organizational survival and success. Organizational communication, so conceived, becomes a crucial additional resource organizational decision makers use to respond to severe time constraints. Relationships between environmental scanning, coalignment of value chain, continuous improvement, and organizational success cannot be specified beforehand in a simple fashion.

Rather, they depend upon organization-specific strategies based on the principles of high-speed management communication. By studying communication practices of the most successful corporations in the world, Cushman, King, and their associates provide the unique insights into the communication skills necessary for environmental scanning, value-chain configurations, and continuous improvement. In their detailed case studies they also provide a list of practically relevant communication skills necessary for the processes of organizational coordination, integration, and control.

Chapter 8: The Democracy and Organizational Communication

The critical theory approach to democracy in organizational communication, as developed by Deetz, Mumby, and their associates is rooted in the philosophic assumption that communication produces and reproduces social reality of arbitrary inequalities, injustices, and power differences. Very often, however, not only are we unaware of such social reality, we give it our support and legitimacy. Such assumptions provide the unique critical insights into the ways organizations, as the most significant site of social life and communication in modern capitalism, systematically but relatively invisibly undermine the present and the future of democracy. Such assumptions also provide the critical insights into the ways communication should function in organizations if a radically participative democracy is our most important moral commitment.

In this view, the theoretical claim is that organizational communication is characterized by the systematic violations of the ideal speech situation that take the form of discursive closure and privilege managers over all other organizational stakeholders such as stockholders, employees, partners, competitors, customers, and the representatives of the larger society. Discursive closure consists of "quiet, repetitive micro practices" such as disqualification, naturalization, neutralization, topical avoidance, subjectification of experience, meaning denial and plausible deniability, legitimation, and pacification. These processes are unveiled by critical analysis of organizational stories. The more these processes occur simultaneously or sequentially, the stronger and more pronounced are discursive closure and systematic distortions in organizations. Consequently, domination through consent rather than a radically participative democracy in organizations and society become our everyday experience. If a radically participative democracy is to take root, "quiet, repetitive micro practices" of discursive closure must be permanently counteracted or resisted by local practices anchored in the ideal speech situation as the preferred organizational design. Relationships between micro practices of discursive closure and a radically participative democracy are political rather than theoretical. They depend on the ever shifting configurations of power within and between specific organizations.

Although similar to the theory of coordinated management of meaning, and constructivism, Deetz, Mumby, and their associates set their position apart by a radical view of social construction of reality. In such a view, communication produces and maintains invisible power inequalities. Because they espouse the ideal of a radically participative democracy, at the practical level, even the research process—a critical ethnography—is to be based on the ideal speech situation. Facts are not only to be negotiated by researchers and the researched but to be negotiated in interactions of radical equality. In such interactions with organizational members they study, critical theorists as researchers, consultants, and teachers contrbute to practices of local resistance. Such practices keep going the ideal of and struggles for a radically participative democracy.

7

THE HIGH-SPEED MANAGEMENT AND ORGANIZATIONAL COMMUNICATION: CUSHMAN, KING, AND ASSOCIATES

SARAH SANDERSON KING AND DONALD P. CUSHMAN

High-speed management is a new organizational communication theory being used to obtain competitive advantage by some of the most successful organizations in the world: General Electric; Toyota; ASEA, Brown, and Boveri; Motorola; Intel; Matsushita. These firms make decisions faster, develop new products quicker, turn a customer's orders into deliveries sooner, and are more effective in adapting to consumer needs than their competitors. As a result they turn fast cycle time into financial savings, increased market shares, and higher profits.

For example, Gary Rogers, the head of GE's appliance operations, reduced the time between the receipt of an order and the delivery of its product from sixteen weeks to six days, saving GE more than $300 million per year (B. Feder, *New York Times*, January 3, 1992, p. C3). Similarly, it takes GM four to six years to bring a new car to market whereas Toyota can do it in two and a half years. That gives Toyota a $300 million reduction in product development costs (Hillkirk, 1989, p. 10B). Motorola introduced its land mobile radio to the European market eighteen months ahead of schedule. Every day it saved meant $100,000 in added sales (Hillkirk, 1989, p. 10B). Reduced cycle time creates, competitive advantage, better products, higher sales, and larger profits.

In these very successful companies fast cycle time or high-speed management translates into two important organizational capabilities. First, it creates a high level of performance that management can build into a firm's operating systems. More specifically, increases in effective communication are employed to eliminate bottlenecks, delays, and errors in production, cutting costs and improving quality. Second, high-speed management is an organizational strategy that improves continuously a firm's integration, coordination, and control systems. More specifically, it transforms all of a firm's communication activities such as leadership, corporate climate, teamwork, worker and unit interface, process mapping, and outside linking processes into a more responsive customer adaptation system (Bowers and Hout, 1988).

It is the purpose of this chapter to explicate this high-speed management organizational communication theory. In so doing we will (1) discuss the historical roots and survey the methodology employed by Cushman and King in developing the theory and their colleagues in extending it; (2) explicate the philosophic, theoretic, and practical principles of the theory; and (3) explore the internal critiques of this theory.

The Historical Roots and Methodology Employed

During the latter half of the 1970s three trends converged that gave rise to the emergence of high-speed management. First, several breakthroughs in information and communication technology dramatically altered the operating environments of organizations. The advent of computers along with global telecommunications networks made possible monitoring a firm's potential customers, capital requirements, labor and raw materials anywhere in the world. This in turn allowed firms to locate and coordinate their R&D, manufacturing, and marketing units wherever in the world it could to obtain a competitive advantage, thus creating a global marketplace.

Second, this information and communication revolution helped facilitate a dramatic increase in world trade. Between 1980 and 1994 world trade grew on average three times faster than the national gross domestic product. It also gave rise to the American free trade zone, the European Economic Community, and the Asian development zone. The result was that firms which wanted to grow rapidly and make large profits had to become multinational in focus.

Third, this rapid rise in world trade created a volatile business climate characterized by rapidly changing technology, quick market saturation, and unexpected competition, making success in business difficult. Technological breakthroughs led to many products becoming outdated and no longer marketable. Quick market saturation created increased pressure to develop more products more quickly. Unexpected competition led to the rise of world class quality and performance standards.

As early as 1984 Fraker began to locate the functional prerequisites a new management system must display to be successful in such a volatile and rapidly changing competitive climate.

1. *Companies must stay close to both their customers and their competitors.* Successful companies always know what the customer needs and attempt to provide it. When products and manufacturing processes change rapidly, it is crucial to keep up with the investment strategies and product costs of rival companies. To accomplish this, companies must develop and

maintain a rapid and accurate intelligence system capable of preventing surprises.

2. *Companies must think constantly about new products and then back that thinking with investment fast.* A good new product strategy requires a large, active, and focused research and development team with ready access to and the prudent use of large amounts of capital.

3. *Rapid and effective delivery requires close coordination between design, manufacturing, testing, marketing, delivery, and servicing systems.* The interdependence of these systems combined with the short lead time in product delivery makes certain that any error within or between systems will delay product delivery, endangering market penetration. Close cooperation between these systems requires strong, quick and responsive integration, coordination, and control systems.

4. *Product quality, user friendliness, ease of service, and competitive pricing are essential for market penetration.* In an environment where consumer and investor representatives compare, rate, and effectively communicate product differences, market penetration depends on quality, utility, and readily serviceable products. This in turn requires the active monitoring, testing, and checking the servicing of one's own and one's competitors products.

5. *Companies that introduce new products must consider the processes and costs required to cannibalize their own products and retrench the workers involved.* Companies faced with rapidly changing technology, quick market saturation, and unexpected competition must be prepared to change or withdraw their own products rather than let their reputation and market shares be eroded by a competitor. Corporate planning for new products must include contingencies for shifting, retraining, or retrenching large product sectors rapidly.

6. *A corporate culture must be developed that emphasizes change, allows for the assimilation of new units with alternative values, and encourages members to learn from mistakes without reprisal.* Corporate cultures that cannot change rapidly will impede market adaptation. Corporations faced with stiff competition will often acquire other corporations with alternative values that will have to be integrated without delay into their corporate culture. Finally, a certain number of new initiatives are doomed to failure for all the reasons previously cited. Talented members of an organization must learn quickly from their failures and press on to new projects. A corporate culture's responsiveness to these issues will require a strong integration of labor and management interests, group and individual needs, and the values of consumers, investors, and the corporation.

7. *A corporate strategy must be developed that scans the globe for potential acquisitions, joint ventures, coalitions, value added partnerships, and*

tailored trade agreements that can give a corporation a technological edge, market access, market control, or rapid response capabilities. Such a pooling of corporate resources is necessary for survival in a rapidly changing, highly competitive, international economic environment.

Each of these seven issues forms the basis for a new set of corporate assumptions and practices regarding how to effectively and successfully reorient an organization to a rapidly changing business climate.

Volatile environmental change creates organizational problems, but it also creates organizational opportunities. Anticipating the rise of a new organizational management paradigm to cope with these changes, Cushman and King began to conduct several case studies of firms across several product environments. Over fifty firms were examined beginning in 1988 in the auto, computer, electronics, drug, and conglomerate operating environments. Over the next ten years, with the help of students and colleagues, organizational audits, consultancies, interventions, case studies, and literature reviews, they developed a high-speed management theory. The researchers sought to discover the philosophies, theories, and practices operating in the world's most successful firms at adapting to these volatile changes.

High-Speed Management Philosophy, Theory, and Practice

High-speed management is a set of philosophic, theoretic and practical organizational communication principles for responding effectively to rapid and volatile environmental change. More specifically, high-speed management decreases the response time required to get a desired product or service to the customer ahead of one's competitors. It does so by employing three separate theories and sets of practices. First, it employs environmental scanning theory to locate the customer's need for new products or services and one's competitors' response to that need. Second, it employs value chain theory to identify areas within and across firms where the information and communication processes involved in an organization's integration, coordination, and control system can be improved. Third, it employs a unique continuous improvement theory to reengineer a firm's integration, coordination, control systems, or communication processes, thus increasing the speed to market of products, thereby creating competitive advantage. An organization's communication and management systems must have certain specifiable characteristics to respond to the opportunities created by successive, rapid, environmental change. It must be *innovative, adaptive, flexible, efficient, and rapid in response*—a high-speed management system.

Our examination of high-speed management will be divided into three sections. First, we shall answer a series of philosophic questions regarding the significance of high-speed management to the development of organizational communication theory. Second, we shall examine the three subtheories of high-speed management and demonstrate how they are responsive to the functional prerequisite for successfully doing business in a volatile and rapidly changing environment. Third, we shall explore the transformations in a firm's integration, coordination, and control processes or the major practical communication systems involved in high-speed management.

The Philosophic Perspective Underlying High-Speed Management

The first question to be asked as we begin our discussion of the philosophic perspective underlying high-speed management is, *Why should students, researchers, scholars, and practitioners in the field of communication be interested in high-speed management?* The search for theoretic principles capable of yielding significant organizational communication theories has been disappointing. The reason is simple. Up to this point in time, organizational strategy, the prime candidate for locating powerful cross organizational theoretic principles, has had at its core noncommunication activities. For example, consider an organization that pursues a strategy of competitive advantage based on product cost. The central organizational strategy or process operating must, by necessity, focus on lowering the cost of production or manufacturing activities. Or take an organization that concentrates its efforts on obtaining competitive advantage based on product differentiation. The central organizational strategy or process operating for success is product uniqueness or R&D activities.

True, human interaction or communication is involved in both organizational manufacuring and R&D activities, but the primary cross organizational theoretic activities are organizational manufacturing and technological innovations, not communication processes. Communication processes function as second-level support activities and are given their regularities based on the primary organizational activities of production and innovation.

However, when speed of response or time becomes the primary source of competitive advantage, this all changes. Effective communication becomes the primary organizational theoretic activity and other organizational processes such as R&D, manufacturing, sales, and servicing products become support activities to the primary process of speed and are adjusted accordingly (Stalk, 1988). For those who study the communication process, and in particular those in organizational communication, communication becomes the locus of control in obtaining competitive advantage.

The answer to the first question partially answered our second one: *Why should high-speed management be of value to an organization?* High-end pricing and larger market shares that erode slowly are the driving forces behind the acceptance and practice of a speed-to-market strategy.

Speed to market or time as a controlling strategy or source of competitive advantage has several unique features other sources of competitive advantage do not produce. To reduce the time it takes to get a product customers desire to market before a competitor, a firm must understand what a customer wants and then simplify and reengineer its value chain to rapidly respond to change. Such a strategy first creates a customer focus on pent-up and measurable demand in product design, production, and delivery to a well-defined market. Second, such a strategy places product quality within a time frame with a customer focus, creating affordable high quality. Third, speed to market seeks to increase productivity but within a time frame that will allow the market to absorb the product, quickly leading to marketable productivity motivating other firms to want to benchmark or buy the productivity system (Carnevale, 1992). Speed to market thus invokes a cluster of variables effecting a competitive advantage—a customer focus (what does the customer want), highest affordable quality (what is the customer willing to pay), and marketable productivity (how much can we sell)—while keeping these sources of competitive advantage within their most effective and efficient range, thus avoiding the problem of providing too little or too much of these qualities.

The Theoretic Perspective of High-Sneed Management

To understand the rationale and mechanisms for systematically employing a high-speed management system, we need a theoretic framework to guide the development and maintenance of such a world class information and communication rapid response capability. In decreasing the response time required to get a desired product or service to the customers ahead of one's competitors, high-speed management as a corporate strategy is based on three separate but interdependent theories and sets of practices. First, environmental scanning theory functions to locate the need for new products or services and to ascertain the response of competitors to that need. Second, value chain theory functions to identify areas across and within firms where the information and communication processes involved in an organization's integration, coordination, and control systems must be improved. Third, the unique information and communication continuous improvement theory functions to reengineer a firm's integration, coordination, and control processes, thus increasing the speed to market of products, thereby generating a competitive advantage.

Environmental Scanning Theory. Environments create both problems and opportunities for organizations. Organizations must cope with changes in the cost of capital, labor, raw materials, shifts in consumer taste, government regulations, political stability, and unexpected competition. Similarly organizations depend upon the environment for scarce and valued resources, market growth, and acquisitions, joint ventures, coalitions, value added partnerships, and tailored trade agreements. An organization's environment, perhaps more than any other factor, affects organizational strategy, structure, and performance. However, whether such changes in organizational strategy, structure, and performance lead to positive or negative consequences rests entirely on the speed, accuracy, and interpretation of the information and communication regarding the significance of the various environmental changes and the rapid reorientation of an organization's strategy, structure, and resources to take advantage of such changes. This process is termed *environmental scanning*.

Environmental scanning generates information regarding what it will take from customers, competitors, and suppliers for a firm to get to the market first. From customers, there is the need to know what the pent-up demand is for products in the area in which a firm is operating and the dimensions by which customers differentiate one's product from those of one's competitors. From competitors, there is the need to know the competitors' core capabilities, the products they intend to bring to market, and the cycle time for delivering those products to market. From suppliers, there is the need to know the amount of training, performance standards, and the price at which they can deliver materials to one's firm.

Environmental scanning thus locates a pent-up demand for a product, analyzes the qualities the customer wants in the product, determines how one's competitors intend to meet that demand, determines how the firm can beat its competitors to market, locates what can or might go wrong, and determines how to enhance one's core competencies to see that nothing does go wrong.

Value Chain Theory. Value chain theory allows one the opportunity to focus on the internal relationships that influence an organization's reorientation to external forces (See Figure 7.1).

Value chain theory involves the examination of an organization's functional units and process links and evaluates their current and desired levels of performance. At the functional business level the focus is internal, at the service, design, engineering, purchasing, manufacturing, distribution, and sales units, and external, at the suppliers and customers. At the business process level evaluation focuses on links between the functional units that make up product development, product delivery, service, and management processes (Rockart and Short, 1989; Porter, 1986). And, in each evaluation, applying high-speed management as a corporate strategy, one takes stock of the information and communication coalignment processes that cut across and are at the heart of the operation of each unit in the value chain.

Competitive advantage gained in one functional unit or business process can be added to or cancelled out by an organization's performance in other functional units or business processes. This is what is meant by value-added or value-diminishing chains of activities. When those various sources of

FIGURE 7.1

An Organization's Value Chain

Functional Business Unit Level

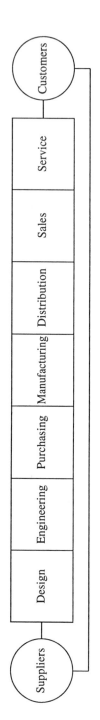

Business Process Level

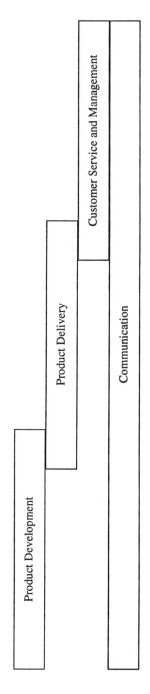

(Revised from J. Rockart and J. Short, "IT in the 1990's," *Sloan Management Review* 30 (1989): 12).

competitive advantage are cumulative in force, a firm's entire range of functional units and business processes must be linked and configured effectively through the appropriate use of information and communication systems or high-speed management.

In an organization utilizing high-speed management as a corporate strategy, environmental scanning data is compared with that of competitors to determine the timeline for getting the product to market first. One asks oneself: (1) What are the organization's and the competitors' core competencies? (2) What must be included in a campaign so customers will perceive one's core competencies as a controlling concern? (3) What changes in core capabilities must be made to provide the firm with the strongest lead time in getting the product to market before competitors? (4) What must be done, inhouse or outside to make the deadline or how quickly can the process change if such is necessary? (5) If the firm goes outside, with whom? In addition to answers to these questions, value chain theory tells why one must begin a change, how great a tension must be created to motivate employees to abandon old organizational practices for new ones, motivating constructive change; and what skills are involved.

Let us illustrate the use of environmental scanning and value chain theory within the automobile industry. The international auto market is a multibillion dollar industry. Ten firms account for approximately 78 percent of world sales. The top three firms—General Motors, Ford, and Toyota—account for over 38 percent of the world auto market. We shall, for reasons of space, limit our environmental scanning and value chain analysis to the international competition among these top three firms in the U.S. core market.

The central competitive dynamics operating in the global automobile industry, according to Harold Poling, CEO of Ford Motor Corporation, are "vehicle attributes, customer satisfaction and value for money" (Poling, 1989). *Vehicle attributes* refers to styling, power train performance, and road handling. *Customer satisfaction* refers to vehicle comfort, safety, quality, and ease of maintenance. *Value for money* refers to cost, standard features, gas mileage, and insurance costs. Figure 7.2 and Table 7.1 provide the relevant environmental scanning and value chain high-speed management data.

General Motors Corporation is the world's largest producer of automobiles. Its U.S. market shares have fallen from 45 percent in 1980 to 35 percent in 1993. A one percentage point drop amounts to 114,526 cars or a billion dollars. GM's market shares at the lower end auto price range have been eroded by Ford Escort and Toyota Tercel; at the middle price range by Ford, Taurus, and Tempo and the Toyota Corolla; and at the upper price range by Ford Lincoln and Toyota Camry. GM has invested $46 billion in plant modernization (a sum equal to the amount needed to purchase Toyota Motors in 1990) and is still the high-cost producer. GM in the past three years cut

FIGURE 7.2

Value Chain: High-Speed Management Chain

Business Process Level

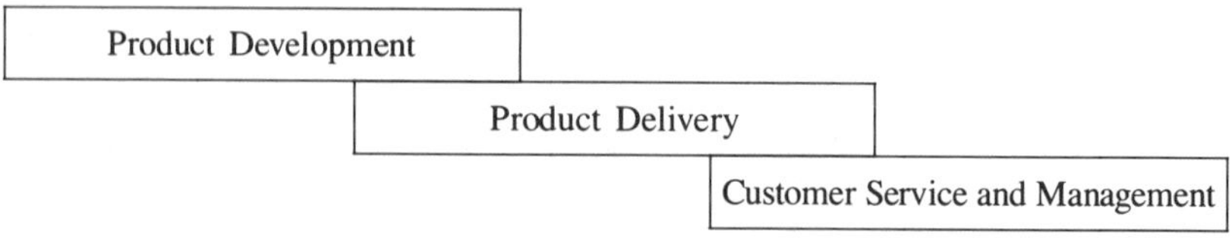

| Product Development |
| Product Delivery |
| Customer Service and Management |

Time for Business Processes

Example: Value chain to bring a new car to market

Company	Product Development	Product Delivery	Customer Service
GM	4 years	9 months	3 months
Ford	2 years 3 months	6 months	3 months
Toyota	14 months	4 months	4 months

TABLE 7.1

High-Speed Management Data for U.S. Auto Market 1992

	GM	Ford	Toyota
Market Shares 1980 (%)	45	20	6
Market Shares 1992 (%)	35	23	8
Productivity 1992 (worker hours per car)	20	12	12
Average Replacement Time 1992 (years per model)	5	3	2.5
Factory Utilization (% 1992 capacity)	60	72	80
Productivity Increase 1992 (%)	4.8	8.2	8.2
Recalls (25% of total sales)	60	78	3
Labor costs (on dollars per car)	$2,358	$1,563	$1,023

Source: Compiled from *Automotive News* 1980–1993.

$15 billion from its operating budget, closed several plants, laid off workers, and ran its remaining plant at 60 percent capacity compared to 72 and 80 percent for Ford and Toyota. As you can see from the high-speed management data, GM requires more worker hours per car, more model replacement time, and has a lower productivity increase than its two competitors. In addition GM's Buick cars ranked tenth in quality ratings, while Toyota's Lexus, Camry, Paseo, Corolla, and Tercel ranked in the Top Ten, with Ford's Crown Victoria appearing sixth in the top ten (Templen, 1993; p. B1).

The Ford Motor Corporation is one of America's most successful global competitors in the 1980s. Ford's market shares increased from 20 percent in 1980 to 23 percent by 1993. Ford produces vehicles at $795 less per unit than GM and $540 more per unit than Toyota. Over the past five years Ford has invested $21 billion in plant modernization and has significantly improved its production capabilities. It is evident from our high-speed management data that Ford outperforms GM in productivity, replacement time, factory utilization, and productivity increases in 1993. However, Ford still trails Toyota in most categories (Lohr, 1992; p. D2).

Toyota Motors has established itself as the high-quality and best value automobile producer among the top three. In addition Toyota leads Ford and GM in several high-speed management measures. It costs less, takes fewer worker hours per car, takes less time to replace a car, and on average, Toyota workers are more productive than those at Ford and GM. That may be why Toyota has gone from 6 percent of the U.S. market in 1980 to 8 percent in 1993. In 1989 alone, Toyota's market shares increased 3 percent in the United States, 3 percent in the European Economic Community, and 4 percent in Japan yielding a 10 percent increase worldwide, an increase in sales of over 1 million cars or $9 billion. Toyota's innovative, adaptive, efficient and rapid response systems, according to Taylor (1990), accounted for the firm's competitive advantage in product differentiation, scope, and timing and its increase in sales and profits.

Continuous Improvement Theory. Once environmental scanning and value chain theory have been applied to an organization and all the data is gathered to know what must be improved inhouse and out of house, the next step is to create the tension for and the ability to continuously improve the effectiveness in managing organizational interdependencies. This continuous improvement process can be enhanced by a self-managed, cross-functional, best practices benchmarking and a negotiated linking teamwork program.

A *self-managed teamwork* program is created within the organization to implement a worker continuous improvement program. The goal of this format is to improve an organizational unit's productivity, quality, flexibility, adaptability, and response time. Such formats take the form of meetings that may last from one to three days and may include workers, suppliers, or customers called together by the division head. The division head presents the key market issues, the organization's vision, the competitors' response to that vision, and specific organizational targets, then leaves. Teamwork facilitators generate lists of bad work to be eliminated and good to be instituted in meeting these targets. The group is divided into teams that debate these issues and provide a cost/ benefit analysis and action plan for the solutions recommended. The division head then returns and acts on all high-yield ideas by selecting a team champion, training the team champion in project management, empowering a team to implement the change, setting performance targets, measurement criteria, a time frame, and feedback procedures. The worker improvement team then implements the action plan.

A *cross-functional teamwork* program is created to set up teams whose goals are to map and then improve cross-functional organizational processes. Many of the most significant improvements in organizational performance have come from mapping an important cross-functional organizational process and asking those involved in the process to simplify or improve its functioning. These teams are assigned the task of mapping the process, improving it, implementing it, and evaluating it. This is achieved by developing a clear understanding of the process goals; identifying the necessary and critical factors for success; mapping and improving the essential sub-processes to meet these critical factors; ranking each sub-process and changing the lowest rank one (its productivity, quality, flexibility, and adaptability); outlining a program for improvement; and implementing the change and fine tuning its subprocesses.

A *best practice benchmarking program* is instituted in continuous improvement programs to set world class performance standards in regard to productivity, quality, flexibility, adaptability, and response time. Those who do not know how to do it study those who can. This program usually locates such organizations and arranges a site visit, develops a case study of the processes involved, and trains personnel at its own organization in ways to adapt these innovations. Monitoring and feedback procedures are established for implementing the change.

The primary focus of a *negotiated linking program* is to continuously scan the globe to locate resources in the form of customers, partners, technologies, or consultants capable of enhancing an organization's competitiveness. This program is especially important when, in the time allotted, an organization cannot achieve its objectives within its own organization. The result may be a joint venture, a buy-out, or the formation of an alliance. The purpose is to fit one organization with another to get a product to market ahead of the first company's competitors.

The process a negotiated linking program follows is to interact with units holding the potential resources to locate interests, concerns, and contributions to coalign; to develop the form of coalignment preferred by both units, such as acquisition, joint venture, alliance, partnership coalition, collaboration, licensing technology leasing, transfer, or training; and to set the world class benchmarking targets in market shares, productivity, quality, flexibility, or rapid response time to be met before coalignment can take place.

Continuous improvement programs make the changes required for sustainable competitive advantage by improving communication, learning skills, and performance to fit within the prescribed time frame. Focus is on the customers, the process to be improved, international benchmarks, and the competition. Continuous improvement programs aim at improving organizational coalignment through self-managed, cross-functional, best practices benchmark, and negotiated linking teamwork programs, as necessary elements in establishing a world class organizational information and communication capability.

Let us illustrate these uses of teamwork to effect change in the Danville, Illinois, bumper works. In 1978 Shahid Khan, a naturalized U.S. citizen from Pakistan, borrowed $50,000 from the Small Business Loan Corporation and took $16,000 of his own savings to establish the 100 person Bumper Works to design and manufacture truck bumpers. Between 1980 and 1985, Khan approached the Toyota Motors Corporation on several occasions attempting to become a supplier of bumpers for their trucks, but without much luck.

In 1987, the Toyota Motors Company called together a group of 100 potential suppliers and released their design, quality, quantity, and price range specifications for the product. The officials at Toyota Motors also indicated that they expected increased quality and a reduction in price each year from the supplier. By late 1988, only Khan's Bumper Works company could produce a product that met Toyota Motors exacting requirements. In 1989, Toyota Motors sent a manufacturing team to Danville, Illinois, *to negotiate the contract and coalignment agreement* between the two firms. The negotiations failed because the Bumper Works could not produce twenty different-sized bumpers and ship them in a single day. Not doing this would slow down the production of all Toyota trucks and increase their price dramatically (White, 1991; p. A7).

Khan called a "town meeting" of workers from his own and Toyota Motors Japanese factories to explore how this problem might be solved within Toyota's design, quality, quantity, and price requirements. It was decided that the Bumper Works would have to switch the factory from a mass production to a batch production line and that a massive stamping machine which took 90 minutes to change each cutting die would have to be modified so as to make such changes in 20 minutes (White, 1991; p. A7).

Next, the workers at both the Bumper Works and Toyota Motors set up cross-functional teams to make a process map of current production procedures. They studied, simplified, and restructured the process to allow for batch production. The large stamping machine was studied for modifications that would speed up die changes. All this was done with considerable help from Toyota Motors, who had solved these same problems, but in a different way, back in Japan (White, 1991; p. A7).

Then, the Bumper Works remodeled assembly line was ready to begin production. For six months employees with stop watches and cost sheets observed the restructured process and set *benchmarks of its operations against the world class standards of the Toyota Plant in Japan*—but still, could not meet Toyota's quality, quantity, and speed of delivery specifications. The workers videotaped the process, studied it, modified it, and sent it to Japan for review. In July 1990 Toyota Motors sent a team to help retrain the workers. They returned in December 1990 to fine tune the process, meeting Toyota Motors contract requirements.

The new production line increased productivity 60 percent over the previous year, decreased defects 80 percent, cut delivery time by 850 percent, and cut waste materials cost by 50 percent. A manual and videotape of the manufacturing process were prepared for training, the first of their kind at Bumper Works, and continuous improvement teams were formed to meet contract requirements for Toyota Motors of increased quality and decreased costs for each subsequent year.

Representatives of each unit involved in the value chain linking the Bumper Works and Toyota Motors communicated their interests, concerns, and contributions to the coalignment process. Each firm's management was able to forge a linking process satisfactory to the units involved and optimizing to the value added activities of each organization to create a sustainable competitive advantage. Khan the owner of Bumper Works has profited from this experience and is building a new plant that will employ 200 workers in Indiana and supply truck bumpers for a new Isuzu Motors plant located there (White, 1991; p. A7).

High-speed management responds to a volatile and rapidly changing environment by scanning a firm's environment and locating a pent-up demand, the customers' competitive dynamic for the product, its competition's response to this pent-up demand, and establishing a timeline for beating the firm's competitors to market. Next the firm examines its own value chain order to locate what continuous and discontinuous changes must be made to beat its competitors to market with a higher quality product. Then the firm decides which types of continuous improvement teams—self-managed, cross-functional, benchmarking, or outside linking—will be used to meet the timeline for making the change.

Having done this, a firm must now explore how to practically accomplish the desired change by utilizing its three communication systems—integration, coordination, and control. In the final analysis, continuous and discontinuous change can take place only through the appropriate use of these three practical communication processes.

Three Practical Communication Processes Within an Organization

Here the question is, *How must a firm's primary communication processes—integration, coordination, and control—be transformed to achieve its high-speed management goals?* High-speed management has as its goals the development of a steady flow of low-cost, high-quality, easily serviced, high-value, and innovative products that meet the needs of the customers and quickly getting these products to market before one's competitors to achieve market penetration and large profits. Success in achieving these goals will rest in great part on developing a world class information and communication system by transforming its integration, coordination, and control processes to a high-speed management system. Let us explain each in turn and provide a case study of its use.

Organizational Integration Systems. An organization's integration system has as its goal tying together, energizing, and creating a focused collective effort by all of a firm's various stakeholders. Three organizational communication processes serve in achieving this goal. *Organizational leadership* creates a vision, sets performance targets, empowers employees, and motivates action. The *corporate climate* outlines the values, activities, socializations, and reward and punishment processes involved in goal attainment. *Teamwork* delineates the skills, tools, and sequences to be employed by workers in implementing change.

When incremental change is required to adapt to the market, the power, trait, behavioral, and situational theories of leadership indicate the practical skills and techniques involved in motivating performance. However, when volatile change takes place, a new type of leadership—high-speed leadership—is required. In a turbulent global environment, organizations must develop the capacity to respond rapidly to changes in their environment by dramatically revamping a firm's vision, mission, product mix, value structure, knowledge, alliances, and technological base. Three research areas have converged that allow a clear characterization of this new high-speed management leadership pattern. This characterization emerges from the literature on transformational leadership; the management of the network organizations; and the management of organizational discontinuities.

Transformational leadership, required to implement volatile change, involves five unique skills (Byrd, 1987): anticipation of what the change must be, articulation of a vision of the new way to do business, development of value congruence between the old and new organizational practices, empowerment, and self-understanding skills. Those organizations that have been most successful have been those that responded rapidly to successive transformational visions by effectively altering and elevating organizational performance. Such responses normally included organizing primarily around process not tasks; flattening the hierarchy by minimizing subdivision of processes; setting middle-level managers in charge of processes and process performance; making teams not individuals the focus of organizational performance and design; helping to develop employee competencies; combining management and nonmanagement activities; focusing on teams; maximizing supplier and customer contact; rewarding team as well as individual performance (Jacobs, 1992).

The research and practice on the network manager adds to our understanding of a high-speed management leader. The emphasis for the network manager is on the identification, development, and expansion of a firm's core competencies that are difficult to imitate through outside linkages and thus they become a source of sustainable competitive advantage. These include improving knowledge-based competencies, alliance based competencies, and technology-based competencies. A high-speed management leader thus assumes a new leadership role, that of a coalignment broker between a firm and its outside links with other firms. Such a leader, who functions both within and between firms, must have three skills: that of architect, lead operator, and caretaker of interorganizational coalignment (Snow, Miles, and Colman, 1993).

Managing organizational discontinuities adds a third set of skills to high-speed management leadership and involves the motivational transformation of a firm's stakeholders from one vision and set of core competencies to another. Two skills are paramount: (1) the skill to create a tension for change that is commensurate with the degree of difficulty involved and blocks a return to the old way and (2) the skill to create a learning environment that motivates the successful completion of the change. These are normally accomplished by layoffs and plant closings and the opening of new facilities along with benchmarking, training, and outside linking teamwork.

The transformational leader focuses on anticipation of change, articulation of a clear vision, empowerment, value congruence, and self-understanding skills for directing and motivating worker involvement. The network leader adds to this the role of coalignment broker, who can enhance a firm's core competencies and function through one's skills as an architect, lead operator in the change, and caretaker of the new linkages. The manager of organizational discontinuity requires skill in creating tension to motivate choice and imparting knowledge of how to change successfully.

Effective human communication in an organizational climate permits a firm's stakeholders to share a common set of values, socialization, monitoring, and operating system capable of motivating, guiding, and providing the successful coalignment of significant collective performance. The goal is improved corporate performance. The corporate climate reflects the degree of fit between an organization's culture and values and the interests, concerns, and contributions of the individual stakeholders upon whom the organization depends for its effective functioning. These include the government that regulates an organization, the investors who provide financing, the employees who do the work, and the consumers who buy the products.

In incremental change, old conceptions of corporate culture are satisfactory. In discontinuous change, a new high-speed management conception of values, rituals, myths, and social dramas is sought to effect rapid adjustment to discontinuous environmental change. Such corporate values attempt to create an organization that is lean, agile, creative, learning, and responds quickly to rapid change. Individual values demand that stakeholders must be reality oriented and that there be candidness in their communication and simplicity in their solutions, which are carried out with dignity and integrity. A firm must have clear rituals that guide an organization in meeting its performance targets and strategic goals. These include precise targets on time to markets, quality and productivity levels and customer focus, and a clear and decisive reward and punishment system for those who do and do not comply.

Rapid change requires commitment and adaptation of change to the skills of workers involved. This is accomplished through teamwork. Successful teamwork is characterized by a mutually constructed, publically agreed to goal that integrates the interests, concerns, and contributions of all of those who contribute to the goal. The four types of teamwork patterns utilized to contribute to the achievement of goals are self-managed teams, cross-functional teams, benchmark teams, and outside linking teams.

As you may recall from our earlier discussion of high-speed management, the self-managed team functions within the New England town meeting format to eliminate the nonessential, nonproductive, or "bad work" and replace it with "good work." The cross-functional team is created to map and then improve organizational process performance. The benchmark teams bring world class performance within a firm's control. Outside linking teams improve a firm's core competencies and make them nonimitatable by linking up with other firms. An organizational integration system relies upon leadership to motivate focus, corporate climate to motivate group performance, and teamwork to motivate improvements in worker skills aimed at achieving organizational targets and goals.

Organizational Coordination. Organizational coordination is dependent upon each organizational unit or business process rapidly and successfully sharing information through communication and information technology. In any combination—R&D and marketing; R&D, marketing, and manufacturing; R&D, marketing, manufacturing, and MIS—the interface between units requires new information technologies and communication tools, a coalignment strategy, communication topics for coordination, and ways of institutionalizing high-communication performances. High-speed management provides the corporate strategy topics to be discussed by each unit for coalignment and the case studies for illustrating the most appropriate adaptation of topic in different situations.

The R&D and marketing interface can best be coordinated by employing several specific coalignment tools: environmental assessment, product portfolio modeling, and structured innovation. The interface is most appropriately controlled by a balance strategy focusing on the concerns, interests, and contributions of each unit. The topics to be discussed are customer pent-up demand and a firm's technological capabilities. This balance can be institutionalized through cross-functional teams and unique funding distributions.

The R&D, marketing, and manufacturing interface utilizes several tools in coaligning its functions: robots, integrated flexible systems, computer-assisted design, computer-aided manufacturing, and computer-integrated manufacturing systems. Economies of sourcing, scale, focus, scope, and time are primary for coalignment, and high-speed management provides a unique method of developing an integrated manufacturing system.

The R&D, marketing, manufacturing, and MIS interface tools for coalignment are data base management, network management, applications programming, design management, systems support management, and executive information systems, such as the telephone, the pager, electronic mail, voice messaging, mobile communication, fax, videotext, and teleconferencing. The advent of the wireless telecommunication networking capabilities adds a new dimension to the workings of this interface. Strategies for coalignment for this complex interface include business systems planning, critical success factors, applications portfolio, stages approach, value chain approach, and high-speed management approach.

Organizational Control. Successful organizations not only focus their energies and resources through organization integration processes and coalign necessary value chain function through organization coordination processes, they also plan, monitor, set benchmarks, and correct coalignment functions through organization control processes. Organizational control takes place at two points in a firm's activities: in the mapping and evaluation of organizational processes and in the outside linking process.

In process mapping and evaluation, two new tools of organizational analysis are utilized in high-speed management to exercise organizational control: environmental scanning to set time and performance targets designed to be first to market and organizational process maps to see where continuous improvement processes can be employed to meet the targets. The reengineering of organizational processes is executed through continuous improvement teamwork programs focused on increasing speed to market of new and old products.

Two tools are employed in an organizational linking program: a determination of a firm's core competencies and the implementation of a plan on how to expand them by outside and inside linking programs with other firms. The strategy employed is based on customer needs and competitor capabilities.

To summarize, the critical communication processes involved in organizational coalignment are in an organization's integration, coordination, and control processes. *Organizational integration* is achieved by three overlapping subprocesses: leadership, corporate climate, and teamwork. Organizational leadership creates a focused set of goals for an organization. An appropriate corporate climate is achieved when an organization's various stakeholders—workers, investors, customers, suppliers, and government—work together in such a manner to make these goals achievable. Teamwork functions effectively when separate units, individuals within units, and systems across tasks, are coaligned for goal attainment (Barrett, 1987). *Organizational coordination* is achieved through the rapid sharing of information in a manner to optimize the value added activities of each of an organization's subunits and environment. This normally involves linking customers, workers, and regulators, R&D, marketing, manufacturing, distribution, sales, and service in such a manner that the issues, concerns, and contributions of each link in the value chain can be optimized (Bowers and Hout, 1988). *Organizational control* involves setting of targets for time to market, sales, productivity, and quality; monitoring progress toward those targets in real time; and implementating improvements that can be made in performance. These planning, monitoring, and assessment functions involve coalignment processes between environmental demands and a firm's value chain performance.

GE as a Case Study in the Transformation of a Firm's Integration, Coordination, and Control Systems

Let us illustrate our analysis by examining Jack Welch, the CEO of the General Electric Company, and his attempt to transform his firm's integration, coordination, and control systems three times within a thirteen year period.

Transformation 1. To Make GE the Most Competitive
and Valuable Firm in the World

In 1981, Jack Welch became CEO of the General Electric Corporation and anticipated his first need for a transformational change. Welch (1988, 12) recalls his thoughts: "At the beginning of the decade...we...faced a world economy that would be characterized by slower growth with stronger global competition going after a smaller pie. In the context of that environment we had one clear-cut major competitor: Japan, Inc....powerful...innovative... and moving aggressively into many of our markets."

In an attempt to create and operationalize his transformational vision, Welch set two clear and simple goals for his firm and outlined the operational targets for reaching these goals.

1. To become the most competitive corporation in the world. This principle was operationalized to mean that each of GE's businesses should (a) invest only in businesses with high growth potential, where GE can become number 1 or 2 in market shares in the world; (b) increase productivity percent per year; (c) decentralize power and responsibility downward to make each business unit as fast and flexible as possible in responding to global competition; (d) develop low-cost, high-quality, easily serviced products that are customer oriented to yield increased market shares to fund the R&D and acquisitions necessary to remain number 1 or 2; (e) monitor carefully the ability of each business to meet productivity and financial targets; and (f) intervene when necessary to make each business become a "winaholic."

2. To become the nation's most valuable corporation. This principle is currently operationalized to mean the "most valuable" in terms of market capitalization. This principle manifests itself in a number of specific ways at GE: (a) keep earnings rising at 5 to 10 percent per year; (b) keep stock appreciation and yield at about 15 to 20 percent per year; (c) shift earning mix so 50 percent can come from a high-growth area; (d) keep supplier productivity rising at about 5 to 10 percent per year; (e) maintain exports as percent of sales at about 50 percent; and (f) maintain management's reputation as an entrepreneurial, agile, knowledgeable, aggressive, and effective competitor.

Jack Welch created an organizational tension by redefining his firm's goals and targets. He then released the tension in a series of dramatic and now famous moves. First, he cut GE's 150 independent business units down to 14, each positioned in a high-growth industry in which GE ranked number 1 or 2 in market shares in the world. These businesses were aircraft engines, broadcasting, circuit breakers, defense electronics, electric motors, engineering, plastics, factory automation, industrial power systems, lighting, locomotives, major appliances, medical diagnostics, financial service and communications (Sherman 1989, p. 40). Second, between 1981 and 1993, Welch sold over 200 of GE's business units worth $10 billion while acquiring and combining over 300 business units worth $20 billion into 14. He closed 78 production facilities, invested $25 billion in automating the remaining 200 U.S. units, and the 130 abroad in 24 countries, making them world class manufacturing facilities. Third, Welch shed over 200,000 workers, one out of every four workers. He reduced nine layers of management to five, releasing one out of every four managers. Fourth, he decentralized power, expanded his managers' span of control, built an all new executive team, and restructured every business, replacing thirteen of fourteen business leaders. "In 1988, Welch stood back and reflected on this effort: Now, how we went at this can be described from two different perspectives. One perspective would use words like 'downsizing,' 'reducing,' or, 'cutting.' We think that view misses the point. We see our task as a totally different one aimed at liberating, facilitating, and unleashing the human energy and initiative of our people." At the heart of this change and institutionalization process was Welch's (1988, p. 3) use of empowerment.

> Sure we saved. Simply by eliminating the company's top operating level, the sectors, we saved $40 million. But that was just a bonus that pales in importance to the sudden release of talent and energy that poured out after all the dampers, valves and baffles of the sectors had been removed. We can say without hesitation that almost every single good thing that has happened within this company over the past few years can be traced to the liberation of some individual, some team, some business.
>
> So we reduced the number of management layers in the company to get closer to the individual—the source of that creative energy we needed. In reducing these layers, we are trying to get the people in the organization to understand that they can't do everything they used to do. They have to set priorities. The less important tasks have to be left undone. Trying to do the same number of tasks with fewer people would be the antithesis of what we set out to achieve: a faster, more focused, more purposeful company.
>
> As we became leaner, we found ourselves communicating better, with fewer interpreters and fewer filters. We found that with fewer layers we had wider spans of management. We weren' t managing better. We were managing less, and that was better.

Finally, Welch and his new GE management team demonstrated self-understanding in what the institutionalization of change had done for the organization. Welch (1988, p. 3) continues:

> We found that the leaders—people with a vision and a passion—soon began to stand out. And when they did, we found our own self-confidence growing to the point that we began to delegate authority further and further down into the company. Businesses were allowed to develop their own pay plans and incentives that made sense for *their* marketplaces. They were given the freedom to spend significant sums on plant and equipment on their own, based on *their* needs, *their* judgment, *their* view of their marketplace. Freeing people to move rapidly and without hesitation makes all the difference in the world. . .we have found what we believe is the distilled essence of competitiveness—the reservoir of talent and creativity and energy that can be found in each of our people. That essence is liberated when we make people believe that what they think and do is important. . .and then get out of their way while they do it.

Transformation 1 employed discontinuous change to overhaul GE's integration and control processes. GE's businesses and their leaders, its goals, targets and structure were all revamped. Its control processes were reengineered through delayering and a change in its monitoring and reward systems.

Transformation 2. To a Firm Based upon Speed, Simplicity, Self-Confidence, and Boundarylessness

By April 1988 (1988, p. 4) Welch's first massive reengineering was all but complete and he began to anticipate the need for a second transformation in GE. Welch reflects

> today the world is even tougher and more crowded. Korea and Taiwan have become world-class competitors, as hungry and aggressive as Japan was in 1981. Europe is on fire with a new entrepreneurial spirit and leadership that is among the world's best. Many of its most aggressive companies, like Electrolux and ASEA of Sweden, Philips of Holland, and Siemens and Bayer of Germany, are after our markets through acquisitions and joint ventures—just as we are going after theirs.
>
> At the same time, the Japanese are more sophisticated and aggressive than eve—building servicing plants outside Japan, including dozens just over the Mexican border.

By 1988, GE's challenges were internal and even larger than in 1981. Welch (1988, pp. 1–2) reflects: "We had to find a way to combine the power, resources, and reach of a *big* company with the hunger, the agility, the spirit, and fire of a small company." The rationale for this change was simple, that only the most productive, high-quality, and rapid response firms were going to win in the 1990s. Any firm that could not produce a top quality product at the world's lowest price and get it to market in less time than its competitors, would be out of the game. In such an environment, 5 percent annual increase in productivity and quality would not be enough, more would be needed.

Welch argued that now a firm must (1) define its vision in broad, simple, and strategic terms; (2) maximize its productivity, quality, and speed to market; and (3) be organizationally and culturally innovative, flexible and rapid in responding to shifting customer demand for lows-price, high-value products; (4) think and act outside the firm's normal boundaries to increase performance; (5) go anywhere, listen to anyone, form an alliance with any firm that can make it more productive. He then called for GE to reorient its internal vision to "speed, simplicity and self-confidence, and boundarylessness. To meet this internal vision, two new goals and sets of targets were put in place.

3. To develop a skilled, self-actualizing, productive, and aggressive work
    force, capable of generating and employing practical and technical
    knowledge. This principle is operationalized currently to mean GE wants
    to create an environment in which GE will be viewed as a challenging
    place to work and that will significantly enhance management and worker
    skills so that they can find another job if the company no longer needs
    them—a place where employees are ready to go but eager to stay. To
    actualize this goal GE needs to develop employee awareness that the only
    road to job security is increasing market shares; develop employees who
    are more action oriented, more risk oriented, and more people oriented;
    develop employees who relentlessly pursue individual and group goals;
    develop employee skills and performance through timely and high-quality
    education programs; hold employees responsible for meeting productivity
    and financial targets; and reward high performance and deal effectively
    with low performance.

4. To develop open communication based on candor and trust. This principle
    is operationalized to mean sharing with all employees the corporation's
    vision, goals, and values, and opening up each employee to discussion
    regarding his or her strengths, weaknesses, and the possibility for change.
    This is accomplished by (a) speaking openly and listening carefully to
    discussions aimed at preparing, articulating, refining, and gaining accep-
    tance for unit visions; (b) showing candor and trust in sharing and evalu-
    ating personal and business plans; (c) motivating employees to become
    more open, more self-confident, more energized individuals in generating
    and employing practical and technical knowledge (Cushman and King, 1994b).

    Two new mechanisms were put forward to create a tension capable of
meeting these new goals: reengineering GE's corporate culture and creating
a continuous improvement program. A new corporate culture was devised and
put in place by GE to aid in the development of speed, simplicity, self-
confidence, and boundarylessness. This new culture focused on improving
organizational productivity, quality, and response time; and these goals became
the basis for all individual and business semiannual reviews. GE's new
management values were (1) creating a clear, simple, reality-based customer-
focused vision and communicating it to all constituencies; (2) setting aggressive
targets and understanding accountability and commitment; (3) having a passion
for excellence; (4) empowering others and behaving in a boundaryless fashion;
(5) growing globally; (6) seeing change as opportunity; (7) focusing on speed
as a competitive advantage.

    Next GE put in place a continuous improvement program aimed at
reengineering GE's organizational processes by increasing the firm's productivity
and quality while decreasing its response time. The program included a self-

managed team program called *workout*, a cross-functional team program called *process mapping*, a benchmarking *"best practices" program*, and an aggressive *outside linking program*.

The practical objective of *workout* according to Welch, was to "get rid of thousands of bad habits accumulated since the creation of GE 112 years ago. The intellectual goal was to put the leaders of each business in front of 100 or so employees, eight to ten times a year to let them know what their people think about how the company can be improved and then make the leaders respond to those changes. Ultimately we are restructuring the leader-subordinate relationship to challenge both to make GE a better place to work. It will force leaders and workers to combine in creating a vision, articulating the vision, passionately owning the vision, and relentlessly driving it to completion" (Tichy and Charon, 1989, p. 113).

By the end of 1993, over 70,000 employees had participated in three-day workout town meetings with remarkable results. In GE's plastic division alone, over thirty workout teams have been empowered to make changes. One team saved GE plastics $2 million by modifying one production process, another enhanced productivity fourfold, and a third reduced product delivery time 400 percent ("Workout," 1991; p. 1–2). Another business, NBC, used workout to halt the use of report forms that totaled more than 2 million pieces of paper a year (Stewart and Fierman, 1991; p. 44). GE Credit Services used workout to tie its cash registers directly to the mainframe, cutting the time for opening a new account from thirty minutes to ninety seconds. Similar results have been reported from workout projects in GE's other businesses demonstrating a remarkable companywide reorientation of coalignment processes between worker capabilities and organizational needs.

While this internal transformation of GE's value chain was taking place, Jack Welch also realized that some other global organizations were achieving greater productivity, quality control, flexibility, adaptability, and rapid response time than GE, even with the workout program in place. In the summer of 1988, GE began its "best practices program" aimed at locating those organizations that had outperformed GE in a given area, developing a case study of how they did it, and then employing these case studies as world class benchmarks for improving GE's performance.

GE scanned the globe and located twenty-four corporations that had in some area outperformed GE. They then screened out direct competitors and companies that would not be credible to GE employees. Welch then invited each corporation to come to GE to learn about its best practices and in return to allow GE to come to their companies and study their best practices. About one half of the companies agreed. They included AMP, Chapparral Steel, Ford, Hewlett Packard, Xerox, and three Japanese companies. GE sent observers to develop case studies and ask questions. These best practices case studies have been turned into a course at Crotonville, GE's leadership training center, and is offered to a new class of managers from each of GE's businesses each month (Stewart, 1992, p. 44–45).

Finally, as GE's top management team reviewed the projects that had been successful from both their workout and best practices programs they noticed a difference in the types of product that saved up to a million dollars and those that saved 100 million. The latter always involved changes in organizational processes spanning the entire value chain. They cut across departments and involved linking with suppliers and customers. All emphasized managing processes, not functions. This led GE to establish its cross-functional teamwork program aimed at mapping and then improving key organizational processes. Such process maps frequently allowed employees for the first time to see and understand organizational processes from beginning to end. They demonstrated also the need for a new type of manager, a process manager who could coalign an organization's total assets. It allowed employees to spot bottlenecks, time binds and inventory shortages, and overflows.

Since implementing such a cross-functional teamwork program, GE appliances has cut its sixteen week manufacturing cycle in half, while increasing product availability 6 percent and decreasing inventory costs 20 percent. The program has cost less than $3 million to implement and has already returned profits 100 times that (Stewart and Fierman, 1991 p. 48). Product mapping programs have provided also an empirical basis for changing how GE measures its management and workers' performance. GE now employs world class cross-functional process benchmarking standards to evaluate its various business performances and to award its bonuses and merit awards for process improvement practical knowledge (Cushman and King, 1994a).

The 1990's according to Jack Welch (1988, p.4) will be a "white-knuckle decade for global business...fast...exhilarating" with many winners and losers. But GE according to Welch is ready. His transformational vision, mobilization, and institutionalization in the 1980s has put GE in position to meet these new threats head on with minimal stress, and with the communication, speed, flexibility, and efficiency of a creative firm. Welch forsaw this development in 1988 (p. 4).

We approach the '90s with a business system, a method of operating, that allows us to routinely position each business for the short- and long-term so that while one or more are weathering difficult markets, the totality is always growing faster than the world economy. No one in the world has a set of powerful businesses like ours. They've never been stronger and big, bold moves are enhancing their global competitiveness: GE Plastics by expansion in the U.S., Europe and the Far East...GE Finance's numerous domestic acquisitions...Aircraft Engine with its

European partnership. . . Factory Automation's world-wide venture with Fanue of Japan. . . Medical Systems' French and Japanese acquisitions. . . NBC's new station and programming initiatives. . . joint ventures by Lighting in the Far East and, most recently, Roper's acquisition by Major Appliance.

The list of moves goes on and on and will continue at an even faster pace. Our business strategy, grounded in reality, has become real. Our businesses are number one or number two in each of their marketplaces.

To go with our business strategy, we've got a management system now in place and functioning that supports that strategy—one that is lean, liberating, fast-moving—an organization that facilitates and frees and, above all, understands that the fountainhead of success is the individual, not the system.

Transformation 2 employed discontinuous change to reengineer its integration and coordination processes. GE's corporate culture was totally transformed. Its coordination system focused on speed, simplicity, self-confidence, and boundarylessness. A continuous improvement system was put in place to reengineer each of the firm's value chain interfaces and improve its monitoring and control processes.

Transformation 3. The Push to Become a Major Player in the Pacific Rim Markets

In 1992 Jack Welch began to reflect on the need for a third transformation in GE. He believed that the slow 3 percent projected growth rate for European, U.S., and Japanese core markets over the next several years would limit GE's growth. He believed that, if GE were to remain a global leader, it must take steps to position itself in the major emerging markets of the Pacific Rim, China, India, Mexico, and Southeast Asia. These markets are growing and will continue to grow at 8 to 12 percent per year for the next ten to twenty years. In addition, GE's growth in revenue from these areas had gone from $10 to $20 billion in the last three years. Welch believed that to remain a global leader, GE had to shift its center of gravity from the U.S.–Europe relationship to the U.S.–Pacific Rim markets. This was to be accomplished through a two-pronged strategy with specific performance targets for each.

5.   GE must become a highly profitable multipolar, multicultural firm. This principle is operationalized currently to mean that although GE's fourteen businesses are currently number 1 or 2 in Europe and the United States and should defend this status, they must now become number 1 or 2 in the major markets of the Pacific Rim: China, India, Mexico, and Southeast Asia. To actualize this goal, GE must (a) develop profit centers in each of these markets; (b) develop a multicultural pool of business leaders and

employees; (c) integrate Pacific Rim nations into its R&D, manufacturing, sales, and service systems; (d) extend GE's management system into these major markets; (e) increase investment in GE from the region; (f) establish 30 percent profit margins as business targets; and (g) turn over inventories at least ten times per year.

6. To employ GE's strong infrastructure in technology transfer, management training and financial services to broadly and deeply penetrate these markets. To do this GE is (a) developing joint ventures in technology transfer with firms in the region; (b) training foreign nationals in the United States and then sending them back to Asia to head GE units; (c) exporting GE's training programs to the region; (d) using GE financial services to fund projects in the region that use GE products; and (e) making small $10 million investments throughout the region to hedge against foreign currency fluctuations and other forms of economic instability.

Thus far, the results of these strategies have been promising. GE's reality-based action training programs have taken managers from Asian cultures and trained them in management skills in the United States. Next these managers were shipped to the Pacific Rim's major markets to interview old, new, and potential GE customers, competitors, and business managers. Finally, GE asked these managers to develop market penetration plans and a value chain, reengineering plans to better position the firm's business in the region. Similarly GE's middle management training programs are rotating promising multicultural leaders through different businesses and markets in Asia to create a truly global multipolar, multicultural leader.

GE has invested over $100 million in factories to produce medical imaging equipment, plastics, appliances, and lamps in India. GE sales in India will go from $400 million to $1 billion by the year 2000. GE has moved boldly into China where the government plans to add $100 billion in power generators, 100 jet engines, 1,000 medical imagers, and over 200 locomotives in the next four years. GE Capital has been creative in helping the Chinese government set up a new development bank to fund these activities. In Indonesia GE is part of a $2 billion power plant project and offered an array of technology transfer projects to help upgrade Indonesia's industrial capacities.

In Malaysia, GE now owns a 49 percent interest in UMW Corporation. In Mexico, GE has over twenty factories with 21,000 employees who have upheld GE appliances as a household name. GE will have over $1.5 billion in sales this year, up from $900 million last year. GE broadcasting has joined with Rupert Murdoch's Star TV system to launch a new business and news channel throughout the Asian region. Finally GE Capital, a $155 billion per year financial arm, has made $200 million in funds available for loans to small business in Asia. In short, GE is on the move again, transforming its firm, people, and resources to fit the needs of customers in the Pacific Rim (Stewart, 1991, pp. 118–122). In so doing, it brings GE's unique brand of management to Asia. GE's blend of entrepreneurial spirit with a hard driving, intensely competitive focus transfers into an obsession with performance, an ability to shift strategy rapidly to take advantage of change, an appetite for risk taking and deal making, and an engineer's yen to run productive, highs-quality, and rapid response operations. In addition GE's CEO Jack Welch, may be one of the world's best transformational, network, and discontinuities leaders. He is looking to position GE as a dominant player in the Pacific Rim region while maintaining a dominant position in Europe and the Americas.

Transformation 3, again, invokes a discontinuous change to reorient GE's focus from Europe to Asia. Its integration, coordination, and control systems are expanded into this rapid growth region with a new strategic focus, new performance targets, and a shift in headquarters for various businesses.

What have been the effects of these three transformations on the General Electric corporation over the past 13 years? First, GE's sales rose from $27.9 billion to $62.2 billion. Profits rose from $2.9 billion to $4.7 billion. Stock appreciation went from $31 per share to $93 per share with stockholder equity reaching $73.9 billion. GE thus became the fifth largest industrial corporation in America, the third largest in profits, and the largest in stockholder equity. Second, GE is one of only eight U.S. multinational firms to make a profit in each of the last twenty years (*Fortune*, 1993, p. 185). In addition each of GE's businesses is number 1 or 2 in world market share in its area of specialization. Each has a thirteen year increase in productivity of over 110 percent and an average increase in quality and response time of over 70 percent. Third, Jack Welch has won *Foreign World* magazine's Outstanding Leader in the World award, *Fortune* magazine's Leadership Hall of Fame award, and numerous other leadership awards. Fourth, over twenty of GE's former top executives have become successful CEOs. This includes the heads of such global firms as GTE, Allied Signal, Goodyear Tire, Owens-Corning, Ryland Group, General Dynamics, Wang Laboratories, Sund Strand, Rubbermaid, MIA Communications, USF&G, Zurn Industries, and Systems Computer Technology. When IBM and General Motors faced the major challenge of turning their businesses around, both firms' board of directors turned first to Jack Welch to see if he would consider leaving GE and taking the CEO's job at their firms. In both cases he chose not to but recommended several of his former executives as candidates.

Three Internal Critiques
of Cushman and King's High-Speed Management Theory

First, it is argued that high-speed management theory is ungeneralizable because (1) factors other than time are more central to organizational success in a volatile and rapidly changing environment—the inflation rate, political stability and governmental restrictions—and (2) the generalizations provided from case study data are unique to the firm studied.

In response, Cushman and King argue that it is of course possible that in some environments, some factors other than speed to market may become determinants of market success. However, empirical studies of sample after sample of organizations operating in different cultures and different industries demonstrate a strong correlation between speed to market and increases in market shares, sales profits, productivity, and product quality (Cvar, 1986; Clark, 1989; Smith, Grim, Clen, and Ganion, 1989; Gupta and Wilemon, 1990; Vesey 1991; McDonough and Barczak, 1991). In addition case studies of firm after firm in different cultures and markets reveal the same results (Dumanine, 1989, p. 54; Pepper, 1989, p. 30; Hillkirk, 1989, p. 4B).

Second, it is argued that high-speed management firms place greater emphasis on organizational time, quality, and productivity, or performance measures than stakeholder satisfaction measures. This leads to the alienation of stakeholders and a decline in a firm's performance.

In response, Cushman and King argue that, although some stockholders, workers, managers, and supplies are alienated by an emphasis on high organizational performance measures such as time, quality, and productivity and the layoffs, plant closings, and retraining required by a firm's adjustment to discontinuous change, alienation would be greater if the firm failed. In addition, most high-performance, high-speed management firms have the opposite problem. For example, GE has more stockholders investing in the firm than any other company. They have sixty applicants for each position that is open and one of the lowest worker turnover ratios in the United States. Their managers are highly sought after and head more U.S. firms than any other company. Their suppliers are often trained and assisted by GE, and there is a long list of suppliers hoping to do business with the firm. A similar pattern of organizational stakeholder interest exists at Motorola, Toyota, Intel, and numerous other high-speed management firms.

Third, high-speed management makes a logical and empirical error by developing a highly rational theory for responding to volatile, discontinuous, and chaotic change when a chaos theoretic perspective is more appropriate and will provide higher explanatory power.

In response, Cushman and King argue that such a claim may or may not be true, but that the burden of proof in this case rests with the chaos theorists who have not as yet provided such an alternative theory.

Extensions of the original high-speed management theory have been made in three major volumes. The first by Yanan Ju and Donald Cushman, *Teamwork and High-Speed Management* (1994), provides an in-depth treatment of the functioning of various types of teamwork within the original perspective. The second by Kris Obloj, Donald Cushman, and Andrezj Kozminski, *Continuous Improvement: Theory and Practice* (1995), provides a detailed examination of self-managed, cross-functional, benchmarking, and outside linking teamwork within the original perspective. The third, edited by Sarah S. King and Donald Cushman, *High-Speed Management and Organizational Communication in the 1990s: A Reader* (1994), extends every aspect of the theory to over twenty firms around the world.

Summary and Conclusions

High-speed management is a new approach to organizational communication theory, one in which firms place a primary emphasis on improving the communication involved in getting a product to market rapidly. Improvements in a firm's rapid response system generate several competitive advantages. Getting to market first allows the firm to set prices so as to get high-end pricing. Getting to market first allows a firm to dominate the market, and when competition emerges market shares erode more slowly. In addition, high-speed management tends to generate affordable high quality and marketable productivity, and it creates a customer focus. Organizational communication, knowledge or organizational functioning, and organizational performance are all enhanced by the three subtheories of high-speed management—a theory of environmental scanning, a theory of value chain, a theory of continuous improvement. These three theories put communication at the forefront of all organizational functioning. Finally, improving an organization's communication, its integration, coordination, and control processes, allows the reinterpretation of the traditional topics of leadership, corporate climate, teamwork, auditing, and so forth and various organizational interfaces in way that transforms our understanding and use of these topics by placing communication and rapid response systems at the center of such activities.

Although there is a substantial body of research on this new theory, the future will bring new ways of extending it. Despite limitations of the high-speed management theory such as social problems that may limit performance, the lag between theory and practice, and the perceived quality of life limitations for employees, this is an exciting development for organizational communication theory at a time when few complete theories of organizational functioning are based on human communication processes.

References

Barrett, F. D. (1987). "Teamwork—How to expand its power and punch." *Business Quarterly* (Winter): 24–31.

Bowers, J. L., and Hout, T. M. (1988). "Fast cycle capability for competitive power." *Harvard Business Review* (November–December): 110–118.

Byrd, R. (1987). "Corporate leadership skills: A new synthesis." *Organizational Business*: 34–43.

Carnevale, A. (1992). *America and the economy*. Washington, D.C.: U.S. Department of Labor.

Clark, E. (1989). "What strategy can do for technology." *Harvard Business Review* (November–December): 94–98.

Cushman, D. P., and King, S. S. (1988). "High-technology and the role of communication in high-speed management." *Informatologia Yugoslavia*, special issue no. 7: 279–284.

———— (1989). "High technology, high-speed communication and its implications for international management." In G. Osborne and M. Midryal (Eds.), *International communication: In whose interest?* pp. 288–301. Canberra, Australia: Center for Communication and Information Research, University of Canberra.

———— (1992). "High-speed management: A revolution in organizational communizational communication in the 1990s." In M. Cross and W. Cummings (Eds.), *The proceedings of the fifth conference on corporate communication*, pp. 99–123. Reprinted in S. Deetz (Ed.), *Communication Yearbook* 16 (1993): 209–237; M. Goodman (Ed.), *Corporate communication: Theory and pratice*, Albany: State University of New York Press, 1994; and S. S. King and D. P. Cushman (Eds.), *High-speed management and organizational communication in the 1990s: A reader*, Albany: State University of New York Press, 1994.

———— (1993a). "Visions of order: High-speed management in the private sector of the global marketplace." In A. Kozminski and D. P. Cushman (eds.), *Organizational communication and management: A global perspective*, pp. 69–87. Albany: State University of New York Press.

———— (1994a). "An Eastern and Western European model of corporate communication." In R. Wiseman and R. Shuter (Eds.), *Communication in multicultural organizations: Annual of international and intercultural communication*, pp. 94–117. Beverly Hills, Calif.: Sage.

———— (1994b). "Old myths and new realities regarding development communication." In A. Moemeka (Ed.), *Communication for development: A multi-media perspective*, pp. 23–33. Albany: State University of New York Press.

———— (1995). *High-speed management: organizational communication in the twenty-first century*. Albany: State University of New York Press.

Cushman, D. P., and Kozminski, A. (1993). "The rise of global communication and global management: An overview." In A Kozminski and D. Cushman (Eds.), *Organizational communication and management: A global perspective*. pp. 3–9. Albany: State University of New York Press.

Cvar, M. (1986). "Case studies in global competition: Patterns of success and failure." In M. Porter (Ed.), *Competition in global industry*, pp. 483–517. Boston: Harvard Business School Press.

Dumaine, B. (1989). "How managers can succeed through speed." *Fortune* (February 13), pp. 54–59.

Ernest and Young, Inc. (1992). "Corporate study included in O. Port, J. Cary, K. Kelley, F. Forest, Quality," *Business Week* pp. 66–72.

Feder, B. (1992). "Companies find rewards in hiring GE executives." *The New York Times* (March 9), p. D1.

Fortune (1960). "The Information 500," (August), pp. 70, 80, 88.

Fortune (1993). "The Fortune 500," (April 9), p. 185.

Fraker, S. (1984). "High-speed management for the high-tech age." *Fortune* (February): 34–60.

Gupta, A., and Wilemon, D. (1990). "Accelerating the development of technology-based new products." *California Management Review*, 32 (Winter): 24–45.

Hillkirk, J. (1989). "It could be trade boom or bust." *USA Today*, p. 4B.

Jacobs, R. (1992). "The search for the organization of tomorrow." *Fortune* (May 18) pp. 91–98.

Ju, Y., and Cushman, D. P. (1994). *Teamwork in high-speed management*. Albany: State University of New York Press.

King, S.S., and Cushman, D. P. (1989a). "The role of communication in high technology organizations: The emergence of high-speed management." In S. S. King (Ed.), *Human communication as a field of study*, pp. 158–163. Albany: State University of New York Press.

———— (1989b). "Technology and market forces and their application in the international marketplace." In G. Osborne and M. Midryal (Eds.), *Internatioinal communication: In whose interest?* pp. 229–299. Canberra, Australia: Center for Communication and Information Research, University of Canberra.

———— (1994a). "High-speed management as a theoretic principle for yielding significant organizational behaviors." In B. Kovacic (Ed.), *Organizational communication: New perspectives*. Albany: State University of New York Press.

———— (Eds.), (1994b). *High-speed management and organizational communication: A reader*. Albany: State University of New York Press.

Lohr, S. (1992). "Ford and Chrysler outpace Japanese in reducing costs." *New York Times* (June 18), p. D1.

McDonough, E., III, and Barczak, G. (1991). "Speeding up new product development: The effects of leadership style and sources of technology." *Journal of Product Innovation Management* 8: 203–228.

Obloj, K., Cushman, D. P., and Kozminski, A. (1995). *Winning: Continuous improvement theory in high performance organizations*. Albany: State University of New York Press.

Pepper, C. (1989). "Fast forward." *Business Month* (February 25): 30.

Poling, H. (1989). "Interview." *Automobile News* (November 20), p. E7.

Porter, M. E. (1986). "Changing patterns of international competition." *California Management Review* 27, no. 2 (Winter): 9–39.

Rockart, J., and Short, J. (1989). "IT in the 1990's: Managing organizational interdependence." *Sloan Management Review* 30: 7–17.

Sherman, S. (1989). "The mind of Jack Welch." *Fortune* (March 27), pp. 39–50.

Smith, K., Grimm, C. Clen, M., and Garron, M. (1989). "Predictors of response time to competitive strategic action: Preliminary theory and evidence." *Journal of Business Research* 18: 245–258.

Smith, T., Engardio, P., and Smith, G. (1992). "GE's brave new world." *Business Week* (November 8), pp. 64–70.

Snow, C. Miles, R., and Colman, H. (1993). "Managing twenty-first century network organizations." *Organizational Dynamics*: 5–19.

Stalk, G., Jr. (1988). "Time—The next source of competitive advantage." *Harvard Business Review* (July–August): 41–51.

Stewart, T. (1992). "The firm of tomorrow." *Fortune* (May 18), pp. 93–98.

Stewart, T. (1991). "GE Keeps those ideas coming." *Fortune* (August 12), pp. 118–122.

——— and Fierman, J. (1991). "How Jack Welch keeps the ideas coming at GE." *Fortune* special issue (August 12).

Taylor, A., III. (1990). "Can American cars come back?" *Fortune* pp. 66–79.

Templen, N. (1993). "Toyota is stand out once again in J. D. Powers, quality survey." *Wall Street Journal* (May 28), p. B1.

Tichy, H., and Charron, R. (1989). "Speed, simplicity, and self-confidence: An interview with Jack Welch." *Harvard Business Review* (September–October): 112–120.

Venkatraman, N., and Prescot, J. (1990). "Environment strategy coalignment: An empirical test of its performance implications." *Strategic Management Journal* 11: 1023.

Vesey, J. (1991). "The new competitors: They think in terms of speed-to-market." *Academy of Management Executive* 5: 22–33.

Welch, J. (1988). "Managing for the nineties." GE speech reprint (April 27).

White, J. (1991). "Japanese auto makers help U.S. suppliers become more efficient." *The Wall Street Journal* (September 9), pp. A1 and A7.

"Workout." (1991). *GE Silicones News*, (sepcial edition) (September), pp. 1–2.

8

THE DEMOCRACY AND ORGANIZATIONAL COMMUNICATION THEORIES OF DEETZ, MUMBY, AND ASSOCIATES

BRANISLAV KOVAČIĆ

The work of Stanley Deetz, despite its complexity, belongs to the family of the intellectual Left. Of course, such a label indicates very flexible boundaries and intentions rather than the content of Deetz's ideas. Nevertheless, it is fruitful to locate his theory within the tradition of the "nonviolent" Left that currently faces serious dilemmas and challenges in the light of the exhaustion of its revolutionary ideal, the demise of socialism in Europe, and the laissez-faire philosophy and practice taking root all over the world (see Shumway, 1993).

This chapter on democracy and organizational communication from a critical theory's vantage point has four parts. In the first section I outline the philosophical assumptions of S. Deetz's intellectual project. The second part discusses the way Deetz constructed his theory of organizational communication. Elaborations and extensions of Deetz's critical theory of democracy and organizational communication in the work of D.K. Mumby, Deetz's associate, is presented in the third part. Finally in the fourth section I critically evaluate philosophical assumptions, theoretical specifications, methodological dilemmas, and practical implications of the critical approach to organizational communication in the work of Deetz and Mumby.

Philosophical Assumptions

This section discusses the philosophical assumptions Deetz makes regarding democracy and organizational communication. It examines Deetz's views on (1) communication as practice, (2) communication as a mode of analysis, and (3) implications of communication as practice and as a mode of analysis for research on and practical struggles for democracy.

Deetz defines communication both as practice and a mode of analysis (1992a, p. 66; see also Brown, 1992, p. 2). Communication as practice unfolds in the world, in real human communities or "natural interaction systems"— what Deetz calls the *life world*—and takes either face-to-face forms such as "self-expression, interpersonal interaction, or mediated forms." Communication as practice consists of the interplay of processes of *meaning production*—a politics of everyday life regarding meaning, experience, and sensuality—and *meaning transmission or reproduction* (Deetz, 1992a, pp. 7, 61, 68, 70). Communication as a mode of analysis takes place in the social science community. Although communication as a mode of analysis consists of theories as "interesting and useful ways of conceptualizing, thinking, and talking about life events," Deetz argues that "[t]he social science community and the life community differ primarily in what they take to be interesting and useful, based on their differences in community standards and in what events they take to be significant" (1992a, p. 68). Consequently, theorizing is articulation and examination of "the relations between theories and the world, relations of power and knowledge, and the relation of theories to real human communities" (Deetz, 1992a, p. 68). This is the position of the so-called linguistic turn in philosophy that claims that "the community of natural language-users" is "more central than consciousness as the site of knowledge and understanding" (Deetz, 1992a, p. 80). It is also a radical constructivist position which argues that (1) all crucial aspects of reality are socially constructed, (2) the social world studied is also constructed by theoretical traditions or "paradigms," (3) research methodology is also determined by the theoretical tradition or paradigm, and (4) because observations depend upon specific theories, observations alone cannot distinguish between "false" and "true" statements (for a discussion of philosophical constructivism see Boyd, 1991a, 1991b, 1991c).

Communication as Practice

Deetz (1994a) posits a model of reality consisting of three elements and four types of communicative relationship between the elements. The model of reality posits that (1) (*social*) world, (2) persons or actors, and (3) language are *produced* and *reproduced* and thereby interlinked through *communication, which is impregnated with different types and degrees of power inequality.* Reality is, then, a communicatively constructed and maintained map of power inequality relationships of (1) person to (social) world, (2) person to person, (3) language to people, and (4) language to (social) world. Let us examine this seemingly simple model of reality.

Conceptions of persons or actors. Human beings are "interpretive creatures" and "social ecologists rather than maximizers" in that they in principle take into account the interests of others (Deetz, 1992b, p. 27). In this view, actors' particular identities as conflicting selves arise from "cross-group membership" rather than coherent bundles of "traditional role categories and role expectations" (Deetz, 1994b). Persons or actors and their self-interests are always ideologically produced. Put differently, social actors are not simple, preexisting, independent, subjects with knowable interests. Deetz goes even so far as to say that the self is "the *spectacle* of the person," the self-referential system of symbolic representations (1992a, p. 295). Individuals or actors are communicatively produced and reproduced by systematically privileging one pole of the following opposites: (1) private-public person, (2) male-female, (3) career-family (4) friend-competitor, (5) self-group interest, and (6) in the long-short term (Deetz, 1992a, p. 296). Such individuals or actors are frequently unaware that their experience is always political, always anchored in power inequalities (Deetz, 1994b).

Language. Actors are not fools, however. Rather, they are unaware of power disadvantages because individual and collective experience is "imprisoned" within perceptions. In interactions guided by institutionalized practices common sense disguises the "political" fact "that certain social groups or practices are arbitrarily privileged over the others" (Deetz, 1992a, pp. 115–116). The political nature of institutional practices (routines) that "produce thoughts, perceptions, and beliefs" and embody "certain value preferences" is crucial (Deetz, 1992a, pp. 123, 125, 127). Because language is a social institution that produces and reproduces "both an order and a disguise for that order," the political nature of experience is hidden (Deetz, 1992a, p. 129). Consequently, the fact that social groups, their interests, and types of rationality are socially produced and reproduced can be brought to light only if we understand language as "a system of distinctions" that "contains the possibility of conflicting meanings" that are political. "The preference for one set of distinctions over other distinctions" and "the embedded values can be reproduced in expression [i.e., communication] without awareness" (Deetz, 1992a, pp. 130, 133). Even technologies are linguistic (as textual webs of signifiers) and political institutions in that they "are extensions of subjectivity" that "privilege one sense over another, that enable only some people to have access to some data, and that make only certain types of data available" (Deetz, 1992a, pp. 141–142).

(Social) World. Rather than assuming the naked, extralinguistic reality, Deetz rejects "a directly experienced, in-itself, version of the world" and the concomitant "subject-object [interior-exterior] split" (1994b; 1994c). Rather, we are presented with "various accounts of reality" by "different groups [who] are trying (often unwittingly) to create a world in their own image" and make "socially arbitrary distinctions between things reside in nature itself" (Deetz, 1994a). The linguistic production of the world rests on "the production of linguistic distinction and thus the development of categories of individuals and

events" (Deetz, 1992a, p. 300). The social world is a partial social totality consisting of simultaneous opposites, at once centralized and dispersed. The social world, therefore, can be described by *irony* as a metaphor of opposites.[1] More generally, society as a domain of reality made of contradictory and competing "institutions, practices, concepts, and bodies of knowledge" (Deetz, 1992a, p. 262) can be described by the metaphor of society as narrative text— as one of the nonlinguistic sign systems or as a code (for conceptualization see Brown, 1992, p. 118–143, 208).

Communication as Relationships of Power Inequality Between People, People and World, People and Language, and Language and the World. According to Deetz, communication is "a series of social interactions and social decisional processes," "social practices," that produce and reproduce psychological states and conceptions of personal identity, perceptions, feelings, experienced needs, social structure, social knowledge, work outcomes, and the nature of interaction itself (1992b, p. 8; 1994a). In this view, social life itself is a collaborative collective communication process that produces "objects" for "a social community" and entails representation of "different potential interests" in that process.

The *productive or constitutive mode* of communication engenders social reality. A moral-political dimension of the productive mode of communication is indicated by an answer to the question of who had or has how much say or power in the creation of social reality (Deetz, 1994a). At the most abstract level, Deetz (1994a) conceptualizes relationships of power inequality as deviations from communication in the form of (1) "genuine conversation," when actors ignore power differences and are guided solely by the subject matter (Gadamer, 1975); (2) an "ideal speech situation," in which actors try to reach understanding rather than preserve or enlarge their power advantage (Habermas, 1984); and (3) the poststructuralist views of actors responding to "otherness."[2]

Communication approximating the ideal speech situation would be characterized by (1) "a symmetrical distribution of the chances to choose and apply speech acts," (2) the absence of "privileging particular epistemologies or forms of data," (3) "the opportunity to establish legitimate social relations and norms for conduct and interaction," and (4) actors "able to express their own authentic interests, needs, and feelings" (Deetz, 1992a, pp. 169-170). In daily practices of communication, however, "conditions of mutuality are unproblematically suspended in authority relations such as parent/child, doctor/patient, or teacher/student where we can at least imagine an equable discussion in which the asymmetry could be freely affirmed" (Deetz, 1992a, p. 171). "Asymmetry and subordination are not themselves the problem" if they are the result of "an open interactional formation of relations freed from the appeal to other authorities" (Deetz, 1992a, pp. 170-171). The fact that "[s]ymmetry conditions are partially violated, because at each moment there is a primary speaker, and every expression is inevitably one-sided and imaginary" does not amount to *systematic* distortions that are latent strategic actions based on self-deception (Deetz, 1992a, pp. 173, 175).

Reproductive communicative processes or maintenance of social reality, according to Deetz, can take an unobtrusive or obtrusive form. The *obtrusive form* of communication as reproduction is the visible, overt transmission of information. It takes the form of self-presentation, self-disclosure, argumentation, explicit conflict and its resolution, integrative problem solving, explicitly strategic interaction (manipulation, persuasion, control, influence, and propaganda), politics, power, legitimacy of authority, and domination (Deetz, 1992b, 1994c). Actors accomplish the obtrusive maintenance of social reality by concentrating on the denotative, explicit content, and by taking for granted the basic rules of interaction that define the terms of the relationship as hierarchical or asymmetrical.

The *unobtrusive form* of communication, however, results in an "invisible" and "a relatively stable set of practices and linguistic forms" that are taken for granted (Deetz, 1994a). By taking for granted both the explicit content and the terms of the systematic interactional asymmetries, actors unobtrusively maintain social reality. Unobtrusive communication practices thus maintain the (self-)illusion that power inequalities and thus injustices in social life either do not exist or, if they do, that they are necessary and "natural" rather than contingent, arbitrary, and manufactured communicatively This (self-)illusion Deetz calls a *manufactured consent/hegemony* or *dominant constitution*.

Such a manufactured consent/hegemony is defined as hidden and taken-for-granted rules justifying power asymmetries. It is created and maintained through systematically distorted communication. Communication and decision making are systematically distorted under the conditions of the lack of "appropriately distributed information, openness to alternative perspectives, and reasoning based on personal insights and data rather than on authority relations" (Deetz, 1992a, p. 178). Put differently, decision making is systematically distorted when even "openly derived asymmetries are [not] reassessed and reaffirmed", that is, when the ideal speech situation is systematically violated (Deetz, 1992a, p. 178). Deetz's main contribution to the philosophical position of a radical constructivism is the conception of systematically distorted social reality produced and maintained through *discursive closure* that unfolds through "quiet, repetitive, micropractices" (Deetz, 1992a, p. 189). Such micropractices are (1) *disqualification* (only some participants have a right to a genuine say), (2) *naturalization* (the socially produced reality is understood as given in nature), (3) *neutralization* (value positions of communicators or stakeholders become hidden), (4) *topical avoidance* (the power of omission, of exclusion of certain topics from a conversation), (5) *subjectification of experience* (when and if interpretative processes are understood as private rather than social), (6) *meaning denial and plausible deniability* (similar to strategic ambiguity: said and not said), (7) *legitimation* (the rationalization of decisions and practices), and (8) *pacification* (the significance and the solvability of the issue, or the ability of the participant to act upon the issue is discounted).

Because of a very tenuous interlinkage between signs, concepts, and referents or "reality," such relationships are established or destroyed by symbolic "negotiation" of social order (Deetz, 1994a see also Baudrillard, 1983). Ultimately, then, "agreement on 'real,' 'truth,' and 'knowledge' rests in the power of one representational practice over another" (Deetz, 1994a, p. 219). Deetz then suggests that there are three types of symbolic "negotiation" of social order, each based on its own symbolic code or simulacra. First is *the symbolic or power code.* The political struggle over the preferred version of reality is tentatively and temporarily won when the most powerful social actors' political interests and cultural values are taken for granted by the subordinate groups. Second is *the money code.* If they use the money code, asserts Deetz, the most privileged actors can justify their power advantages in terms of rational or instrumental criteria such as equivalencies in the market exchange. The "universal," "neutral," "fair," and "objective" laws of the market rather than "arbitrary" cultural-political values are invoked to separate the "losers" from the "winners." Third is *the pure simulation code.* The most powerful actors define the world as *fragmented hyperreality* or *fiction* based on signs that, disconnected from any stable referent and concepts, refer only to themselves (see also, Baudrillard, 1983). These symbolic-political, instrumental-rational, and simulative faces of power form through communication ever shifting constellations and thus maintain social world as a partial, "dispersed" totality.

Although the social distribution of power and influence takes place through economic distributions, speaking opportunities within the existing mode of representation, the monopoly of the "code" itself, and the formation (production) of knowledge, experience, and identity as well as their expression (reproduction), "[t]he site of hegemony is the myriad of everyday institutional activities and experiences that culminate in 'common sense,' thus hiding the choices made and 'mystifying' the interests of dominant groups" (Deetz, 1992a, pp. 47, 62). This is why Deetz insists on "a micro-politics," "the politics in the moment-by-moment" and "a microanalysis of power and control" as a way to unveil that "control and influence are dispersed into norms and standard practices as products of moral, medical, sexual, and psychological regulation" (1992a, pp. 250, 252). In this view, democratic politics as micropolitics and micro-practices requires "the possibility of mutual decision making. . . in the moment-to-moment," and grounds "[t]he moral foundation for democracy. . . in the daily practices of communication" (Deetz, 1992a, pp. 290, 350).

To unmask systematically distorted social reality, Deetz distinguishes the power *in* knowledge from the power *of* knowledge (see Foucault, 1972, 1980).

The latter he calls *politics* (the orgainzation of sovereign power) or "influence in the explicit, direct sense of persuasion and control," and the former he defines as *Politics* (the organization of consent) or hidden and dispersed principles of normalcy and self-evidence, and "normalizing" routines and subject identities. In a more conventional vocabulary these are different mechanisms of social control. Thus *politics* refers to obedience to authority or submission to coercion (i.e., obtrusive reproduction), and *Politics* amounts to conformity or accepting without question prevailing rules of behavior (i.e., unobtrusive reproduction) (for conceptualization of social control, see Smelser, 1992, p. 47). Such *Politics*, conceived as "social formations, institutional forms, the distinctions made by language, and the particular technologies available," accounts for the fact that "power [as an advantaging practice] is invisibly exercised in the 'free' decisions of those influenced" (Deetz, 1992a, pp. 48-49). *Politics* as the "invisible" organization of consent operates through the strategic power apparatus or a combination of discursive and nondiscursive elements that show "how [disciplinary] power is deployed in various strategic moves" (Deetz, 1992a, p. 265). Discursive elements are material and materializable images and text (the explicit content); and nondiscursive elements include (social) structure as an abstraction from a set of practices, routines as standardized practices, and scripts as shared taken-for-granted recipes for behavior (the basic rules of interaction that define the terms of the relationship as hierarchical or asymmetrical). *Disciplinary power*, argues Deetz, "exists largely in the new "social technologies of control" " dominated by "experts and specialists of various sorts who operate to create *'normalized'* knowledge, operating procedures, and methods of inquiry and to suppress competitive practices" (1992a, pp. 255–256). Through disciplinary power "the body itself, rather than simply the thought processes is subject to. . .self-surveillance" and "an ever expanding technology of body and mind control" (Deetz, 1992a, p. 256–257). What matters, however, is that "[p]ower relations are always met by resistance" whose acts "are as dispersed and innumerable as sites of power" (Deetz, 1992a, p. 54).

Such dispersed acts of resistance, argues Deetz, keep alive "a democracy ideal that no social group or practice should be arbitrarily privileged in organizations or any social product." To the extent the three simulacra or codes of power overlap, share elements, enable spheres of co-action without consensus, have areas of reoccurring conflict, and at times simply coexist, there is a hope for the restoration and radicalization of democracy. This also means that "within the constraint of interests and values competing claims can be compared" (Deetz, 1992a, p. 7).

If oppression-domination is a subordination or systematic interactional asymmetry imposed on one against one's will (regardless of whether one is aware of domination or not), and if neither "power nor resistance is centered," but rather dispersed, then theory must capture "the microplay of domination, resistance, and mutual formation"; that is, it must understand domination "within shifting configurations" (Deetz, 1992a, pp. 266–267). Resistance is a poststructuralist (decentered) sabotage that provides for spheres of autonomy based on the determination to "choose the 'game' rather than choose a 'move' from the set prescribed by the game" (Deetz, 1992a, p. 336). In other words, resistance does not substitute one "truth" ("game") with another one; rather, resistance attempts to keep alive as many "truths" ("games") as possible (see Smirchich and Calas, 1987, p. 248).

Communication as a Mode of Analysis

Changes in communication as practice are linked to changes in communication as a mode of analysis; that is, "as fundamental social problems change, we expect fundamental shifts in the concept of communication" (Deetz, 1992a, p. 93). At this juncture Deetz makes a series of fundamental assertions.

Social problems are created by the disintegration of social order of modern Western society based on (1) psychological conceptions of the unitary, autonomous, stable, coherent and reflective person or actor; (2) sociological conceptions of legitimate and stable social structure and social groups; (3) analytic philosophy with a scientific method; and (4) economic conceptions of a progress-driven, cybernetic market rationality in the form of the "invisible hand" (Deetz, 1992b, 1994c). Because modernity as a social order cannot simply be taken for granted, processes of obtrusive and unobtrusive maintenance of social reality—social control—lose their legitimacy and thus become accessible to critical reflection and examination. Bases of social order have continuously to be renegotiated in social interaction as (1) "a responsive self" with the many forms of me in a dynamic and fluid relation with others; (2) only temporarily legitimate organizations and governments; (3) codetermined knowledge; and (4) the explicitly built, tentative, and temporary policy consensus. In this new era of social negotiation, which Deetz calls *postmodernity*, processes of social construction of reality become again crucial.

Communication as a Scholarly Discipline. Deetz then links his understanding of fundamental social changes and problems to his view of communication as a scholarly discipline—communication studies—based on a mode of a communication-textual-interactive-semiotic explanation of "how things come to be the way they are" (1994).[3]

Communication studies attempts to provide radically democratic alternatives to the pillars of modernity and, thus, "provides our best conception and chance for a meaningful response" to current social problems (Deetz, 1994c).[4] By using deconstruction and participatory research, it goes beyond critical studies that use ideological critique to unveil forms of domination and asymmetry, as well as beyond ethnographic cultural studies that use field work to demonstrate production and maintenance of particular social realities through norms, rituals, and so on. In other words, "[c]ommunication explanations cast adrift the social order with its assumed natural basis for asymmetrical identities and social structure" (Deetz, 1994c).

At this point Deetz introduces his main arguments regarding communication as an intellectual enterprise. By saying that "to specify a communication mode of explanation doesn't suggest a particular theory," he implies that a communication mode of explanation-analysis has a status of a new paradigm or theoretical tradition encompassing a multiplicity of theoretical positions (Deetz, 1994c). In this view, then, *communication explanations account for political practice* in the form of decisions "in the polis regarding morality, social propriety, laws, public projects"; that is, they account for issues of both macro and micro cultural politics (Deetz, 1992b, p. 8, 14).

Communication Theories. Deetz argues that a relevant standard for evaluating theories is the question of "which is the better frame to use to view the world, rather than the issue of accuracy and truth" (1992a, p. 72). Theories "differ more in the sizes of their domains and the realistic nature of their parameters than in correctness" (Deetz, 1992a, p. 69). Thus "[p]rediction and control should properly be seen as one human motive that is at times privileged over competing motives and organizing schemes that differ greatly from prediction and control" (Deetz, 1992a p. 74). Deetz emphasizes that, if "looked at from the perspective of society," *useful* must "be considered in terms of some conception of social good," rather than efficiency and effectiveness as measures of instrumental rationality.

Participation and effectiveness are two fundamental communication goals. *"Participation* deals with who in a society or group has a right to contribute to the formation of meaning and the decisions of the group—which individuals have access to the various systems and structures of communication and can they articulate their own needs and desires within them. *Effectiveness* concerns the value of communicative acts as a means to accomplish ends—how meaning is transferred and how control through communication is accomplished" (Deetz, 1992a, p. 94). Deetz, then, contends that "we must ask about both the nature of participation as well as who is allowed to participate," and that "participation for social good and truth" is "the central legitimizing force" (1992a, pp. 95, 97).

Ultimately, then, " [t]heories must be assessed in light of the kind of society we wish to produce" (Deetz, 1992a, p. 76). Deetz's intellectual-theoretical project, therefore, intends to contribute to "finding interesting and useful ways of thinking and talking about our current situations and helping us build the future we want" (1992a, p. 77). What are these interesting and useful ways of thinking and talking? And what is the future we want?

Interesting and useful ways of thinking and talking are about "a reconstruction of everyday life" and thus cannot be expected from "an elitist view of theory," the representational view of theory that blocks perception of otherness and difference" and "describes a particular relation of the theorist to the world, one of domination. . . fostered by fear of nature, fear of the lack of certainty and control" (Deetz, 1992a, p. 69, 70).

Communication studies as a new paradigm promotes theory and research anchored in radical participatory democracy as a social good and stresses "the role of the intellectual in using participative theory to guide ongoing practices of understanding, critique, and education" and in promoting "a conception of participation as a pretheoretical normative foundation for acting in and evaluating communication systems" (Deetz, 1992a, p. 6). Essentially, then, Deetz views participation as a social good and a means to that good in communication both as practice and as a mode of analysis (1992a, pp. 106–107).

In this view an intellectual is "anyone who systematically reflects on life experiences" and favors "tension between tentativeness and commitment" (Deetz, 1992a, pp. 83–84). However, the intellectual must take seriously that "[t]he political choice of what gets voiced and how it is represented are central to research" (Deetz, 1992a, p. 348). The intellectual plays the role of critical consultant when he or she does not "favor a particular segment of society based on money and power" and, moreover, recovers "alternative practices and marginalized alternative meanings" and through "a participative communicative act" reopens "effective communication to productive conversation" (Deetz, 1992a, pp. 87, 346). The intellectual plays the role of researcher by producing insight in "a type of practical knowing" necessary to comprehend the production of meaning and, thus, preserving "the possibility of competing discourses through the recovery of conflict and choice" (Deetz, 1992, p. 85). Finally, the intellectual plays the role of teacher by forming constructs to educate people about competing discourses, conflict and participation in decision making (interaction skills), and about "technologies for participation and skills in using technologies and communication media" (Deetz, 1992a, p. 89). In using "the case study-style research", the intellectual must go beyond ethnography in which "[o]ften either the research community or site community's conceptions were accepted a priori, hence the research oscillated between two privileges rather than retaining distanciation necessary for productive (rather than reproductive) understanding" (Deetz, 1992b, p. 22; 1994c). Through such distanciation facts should be socially negotiated because the research community and the site community have "different ways of articulating the same complex moment of interconnectedness that gains constancy as an event" (Deetz, 1992a, pp. 68, 79). A radical, participatory constructivism requires that facts be socially negotiated by researchers and the researched (the "other") in the ideal speech situation.[5]

Let me summarize. Deetz argues that interesting and useful ways of thinking and talking about our current situations have to do with a critique of "domination and the advancement of participation" (1992a, pp. 171–172). He formulates a new "utopian" vision of a more participatory future in the form of the ideal speech situation that provides "the hope of recovering conflicts that have been suppressed through latent strategic normalization and routinization," through "discursive closure and systematically distorted communication" (Deetz, 1992a, p. 351). Deetz is careful, however, to stress that he proposes only a procedural requirement that "norms based in communication and democracy do not define *a priori* how we should develop, but promote conflict and discussion where various power configurations have closed them down" (1992a, p. 4). He views the "ideal speech situation as a moral process but to the end of recovering and sustaining difference and conflict rather than to produce a new more legitimate consensus" (Deetz, 1992a, p. 8). Ideally, claims Deetz, actors not only anticipate equal participation as a structural condition, but also prefer "participation over effectiveness as an initial normative ground" (1992a, p. 164). This ideal is approximated to the extent that "the interaction includes all relevant positions and interests. Interaction cannot be effective in terms of social efficacy without representing the various interests, whether intentionally represented by the participants or not" (Deetz, 1992a, p. 165).

Implications of the Philosophical Assumptions

Deetz stresses that "a theory is ultimately answerable to real communities of actors rather than universal standards of truth" (1992a, p. 79). In this view, theorists simply cannot avoid "the issue of community-based social good . . . in the context of a communication perspective" (Deetz, 1992a, p. 82). Such a perspective, then, requires that scholars rethink "[f]act/fiction/value distinctions, objectivity, and the representational view of language" (Deetz, 1992a, p. 102). This requirement is crucial if, as Deetz asserts, meanings produced in the systematically asymmetrical form of "negotiation" congeal in hegemonic consensus (concealed systematic inequalities) that is, then, taken for granted and reproduced. Facts, then, come to represent mainly the interests of powerful and privileged social groups and suppress "perpetual critique and constant reclaiming of openness to the future" (Deetz, 1992a, p. 10). Deetz's theory of organizational communication is one of the means to reclaiming openness to the future. It is to the analysis of this theory that I turn next.

Theory of Organizational Communication

All morally and politically affirmative definitions of freedom become obsolete, and participation in society is restricted either to rituals of co-option masked as dissent, or to those public roles deemed functionally necessary by political elites and social engineers . . .

(Brown, 1992)

In this section I outline and discuss five issues: (1) Deetz's views on corporate colonization of the life world, (2) Deetz's definitions of constructs relevant to the theory of organizational communication, (3) communicative relationships between constructs, (4) the ways Deetz does empirical research on organizational communication, and (5) the practical implications of Deetz's theory and research on organizational communication and democracy.

Corporate Colonization of the Life World

Both personal advancement and corporate expansion are ever more dependent on communication systems and skills (Deetz, 1992a, pp. 99–100). Yet, at the same time "[t]he development of industrialization and the rapid growth in the size of corporations can be seen as reducing most individuals' communicative participation and power in decision making" in the workplace (Deetz, 1992a, p. 102). Consequently, most individuals have less and less control over the modern corporation, which is the dominant institution in society shaping personal identity, the structure of time and experience, education and knowledge, and entertainment and news.

Deetz invokes the image of "a new feudalism" to emphasize the centrality of the corporate institution to modern social processes such as the quality of life, intellectual ideas, state democracy, and deinstitutionalization and colonization of the life world.[6] Workplace values and practices not only shape the structure of our daily time, educational content, economic distributions, product development, and creation of needs, which in turn, structure our nonwork life, but corporations also distort "the expression of competing needs located in other institutions." Deetz also asserts that the corporate-led "growth of economic well-being has not led to an equivalent growth in mental and physical health" (1992a, p. 37). Similarly, "[t]he authoritative/submissive response style appears to be built into the modern corporation and reproduced in other institutional settings," and "[v]oting and public participation in societies with authoritarian work structures tend to be diminished in a number of ways" (Deetz, 1992a, p. 39).

A corporate colonization of the life world is the name for significant shifts in institutional relations in modern society such as the eclipse of the state by corporations, the corporate structuring of community and family, corporate education in and out of the workplace, and corporate control of media entertainment and news. It spells the demise of civil society—an array of freely formed social associations based on approximations of the ideal speech situation—as an institution that separates and yet links politics and economy (for conceptualizations of civil society, see Lipset, 1993; Angus, 1989). Colonization of the life world takes place when "the corporation becomes ever more central in the process of coordinating individual activity" (Deetz, 1992a, p. 41). More important, Deetz articulates colonization of the life world in terms of the systematic inequality between corporate stakeholders ("owners") such as "owners of labor, expertise, resources, and public good as well as investors" (1992a, p. 43). Money and power are "the primary steering mechanisms in the colonization process" through which "[t]he life world emphasis on practical reasoning is translated into instrumental-systems terms" (Deetz, 1992a, p. 233).

"The reduction of democracy to capitalism" means that of all modern "public" forums such as legislature, public bureaucracy, modern mass media, the shop floor, and corporate conference rooms, the corporation rather than the marketplace is "the more critical site of public decision making" (Deetz, 1992a, pp. 46, 53). In such conditions " [f]airness' of the means of domination, not domination, has been posed as the moral issue" (Deetz, 1992a, p. 64). Because corporations seriously erode democracy, the ideal speech situation (systematically symmetrical participation) without systematically distorted communication "should be central to corporate design and human interaction within them" (Deetz, 1992a, p. 69). To clarify his position, Deetz asserts that "distortions are produced by the structural configurations in the organization" that constitute "the monopoly of the opportunities to define the organization and its goals as well as the strategic processes of reaching them" (1992a, pp. 179, 180).

If "[t]he modern problem is not monopoly capital but a monopoly of information and dialogue chances...the 'monopoly of the code'," then the following questions become crucial: "Are the structures of discourse such that competing experiential structures can be understood and articulated? Do decision-making processes include competitive experiences?...If conditions of inequality exist, how are they justified?" (Deetz, 1992a, p. 19). Deetz then stresses that " [c]oncerns with economic growth, organizational survival, profit, and productivity have become the central criteria. Meaningful work, participation in decision making, and the enhancement of the autonomy of the personnel have rarely been treated as goods in themselves" (1992a, p. 231). Deetz thus takes the position that "[t]he reclaiming of the tension among multiple logics and human interests in corporations is of central importance to democracy" because "[t]here are multiple human needs that are currently being suppressed or distorted...and they need to be recovered with equal legitimacy in a democratic society" (1992a, p. 238).

Deetz is thus interested in whether and how corporations "represent their various stakeholders and contribute to the general welfare" (1992a, p. 2). Because of "the reduction of political questions to economic ones, the public becomes fragmented, recollected only by temporary images, and the possibility of meaningful decision making appears progressively less likely" (Deetz, 1992a, p. 2). However, in a radical participatory democracy only "the full representation of differing people and their interests would seem to be fundamental to ethical choices regarding development" (Deetz, 1992a, p. 3).

This is especially important when and if corporate members forge their identity only from (1) the product produced, (2) the position held, and (3) the corporate membership. In such a case symbolic identity becomes institutionally reduced to "monetary concepts of worth, legal responsibilities, mobile relations, and isolation from community" (Deetz, 1992a, p. 297).

The goal of communication analysis of and resistance in organizations is, then, "to reclaim the voices silenced...to recover the silenced conflict" (Deetz, 1992a, p. 312). Without resistance, of "three possibilities in corporate opposition—*exit, loyalty,* and *voice*—the worker can only conceptualize the first two" (Deetz, 1992a, p. 315).

Definitions of Theoretical Constructs

Deetz then states his theoretical position by "translating" philosophical constructs into theoretical ones. Thus, actors are defined as corporate stakeholders, language as managerialism, and the (social) world as the corporation. Communication as practice produces and reproduces corporate reality as a map of power inequality relationships between (1) stakeholders, (2) stakeholders and the corporation, (3) stakeholders and managerialism, and (4) managerialism and the corporation.

Stakeholders. Organizations embody and represent competing needs, interests, and "stakes" of multiple social groups and actors such as stockholders, managers, workers, consumers, suppliers, and the wider society. Of these, managerial groups through domination of "economic-based structures *and* systems of discursive monopoly" and by stressing "[o]rder, efficiency, and effectiveness as values" secure "advantages already vested in an organizational form" (Deetz, 1992a, p. 55). "Different stakeholders are not always in positions to analyze their own interests, owing to the lack of adequate undistorted information or insight into fundamental processes. Both stockholders and workers can be disadvantaged by particular accounting practices and the withholding of information" (Deetz, 1992a, p. 56). The modern organization rests on distinct interest differences between capital owners and management because the separation of ownership and management has shifted corporate control "from profit-centered owners to career-centered managers" (Deetz, 1992a, p. 210). Deetz argues that "often managers actually function as an independent group actualizing particular interests of their own," and, "[i]n takeover battles, shareholders nearly always lose...as do lower level managers, workers, and the community" (1992a, p. 212). More important, "even if stock ownership were equitably distributed in the society, domination and exploitation would still prevail through administration. Worker buyouts have rarely affected basic management practice or means of control...Owner interests are as difficult to represent as those of workers" (Deetz, 1992a, p. 213). As far as capital owners are concerned, "[b]oards are frequently prohibited from being involved in 'relations at the point of production,' which are central to everyday-life democracy" unfolding through "the actual micropractices of power" (Deetz, 1992a, p. 214).

Deetz claims that long-term stability and growth are more important to managers than profit maximization. In such conditions "[t]he produced corporate image and self-marketing become central activities of work itself and extend into nonwork areas of life. Corporate and personal identities merge. While the worker seeks freedom—from necessity and for self-fulfillment—and the owner seeks profit, the manager seeks control" (Deetz, 1992a, p. 216). However, "the owner/manager/worker division is never totally clear" (Deetz, 1992a, p. 218).

"The manager is produced as a special actor in the potential battle of the stakeholders—one with a different kind of structural stake, a stake in the process rather than the outcome, not unlike a lawyer in the modern judiciary system" (Deetz, 1992a, p. 226). In addition, "[g]iven management's actual ability to make decisions of allocation of resources, it is significant that they give themselves money and symbols of power rather than free time, autonomy, and flexibility" (Deetz, 1992a, p. 234). The reason is that *"[m]oney, power, and control operate as an invisible steering mechanism encroaching further into each stakeholder's conception of self and world"* (Deetz, 1992a, p. 37).

Corporation. By defining organizations as autopoietic, self-referential systems, Deetz eliminates "a simple distinction between the system [the insides] and environment [the outsides]" (1992a, p. 182). He argues that "corporations attempt to recreate and maintain their imaginary identity by projecting themselves outward, producing a boundary between themselves and an environment, and monitoring that environment for things that reflect their interests and concerns" (1992a, p. 182). Consequently, "corporations today operate more and more as systems of *simulations. . .*as images reflected upon each other" (Deetz, 1992a, p. 186). Deetz warns that "[o]rganizational research often treats the modern corporation and the managerial control of them as a naturally occurring, rather than a politically created, form" (1992a, p. 200). In such modern corporations, viewed as systems of simulations, "[c]onsent rather than coercion appears to better represent the modern worker's relation to the production apparatus" (Deetz, 1992a, p. 203).

The formal organization as narrative text, a particular type of fiction, is a kind of moral order because "the formal qualifies and disqualifies and gives an expressive privilege to a managerial voice. The "formal" supports control and exclusion rather than expression and open consensus" (Deetz, 1992a, p. 243). This is related to *disciplinary power* as "a way of thinking, acting, and instituting" that produces or reproduces "[t]he disciplined member of the organization [who] wants on his or her own what the corporation wants" (Deetz,

1992a, p. 259). It is important to understand, Deetz argues, that " [r]ather than being the 'real' world, the corporation is frequently one of many images playing upon images, artifacts upon artifacts...a closed and often systematically distorted system...[of] *simulations*" (1992a, p. 298). In other words, "The corporation is a special type of fiction held in place by a set of discourses, including legal statutes, contracts, and linguistic production of roles, authority and meaning" (Deetz, 1992a, p. 307).

Managerialism. Managerialism as the language of the modern corporation arbitrarily privileges certain interests, distorts the process of reaching decisions, and suppresses meaningful conflict (Deetz, 1992a, p. 5). Only radically participative communication can resist the career manager who uses "a new kind of discourse, one based on reason and consensual rules," managerialism, as a new form of domination (Deetz, 1992a, p. 210). Deetz defines *managerial capitalism* as "a new logic and daily practice of corporations," as "a kind of systemic logic, a set of routine practices, and an ideology, rather than the emergence of control by a particular group" (1992a, pp. 221, 222). Managerialism itself is a " "discursive genre," a way of conceptualizing, reasoning through, and discussing events." Deetz then warns that "[w]orker ownership changes little in actual corporate thinking and decision making, as long as managerialism as an ideology and practice continues to be reproduced" (1992a, p. 222). This is due to the following five elements of managerialism as a "discursive genre": (1) reduction of the corporation to management, (2) equating the corporation with control, (3) upholding the corporation through cognitive-instrumental reasoning, (4) anchoring the corporation in money, and (5) treating the corporation as the formal or moral entity (Deetz, 1992a, p. 222).

In addition, through the central organizing themes of "making a deal" and "everything went smooth" managerialism legitimizes only conflicts that are (1) disagreements within the corporate capitalist system but not about the system, (2) individual centered and situational rather than group based and structural disagreements, (3) episodic rather than perpetual disagreements, and (4) disagreements regarding technical difficulties such as lack of information and training (Deetz, 1992a, pp. 225, 226–227).

Communication. Through discursive closure "managerial groups and technical reasoning become privileged" (Deetz, 1992a, p. 187). We are witnessing "the move from an economically driven capitalism to a communication-driven one" (Deetz, 1992a, p. 208). In such a capitalism, the coordination capacity of "high-speed management" is far more important than the market to the corporate expansion. Deetz then argues, however, that managers "spend the majority of their time praising each other, discussing the difficulties of their jobs, making endless agenda lists, inventing elaborate strategies, and trying to decide what to do, and yet they communicate in ways that inhibit resolution of key problems and they rarely say what they mean" (1992a; p. 229).

Communicative Relationships Between Concepts

To link theoretical constructs of organizational stakeholders, organization, managerialism, and communication, Deetz relies on the notions of *strategic apparatus* and *disciplinary power*. These two constructs allow Deetz to demonstrate how arbitrary power asymmetries in organizations are produced and maintained through communication.

Managerial knowledge and expertise, argues Deetz, take the form of commonsense knowledge expressed in the "transparent" language of accounting and other organizational data that are circulated through and stored in information technologies and data bases. The strategic power apparatus deploys power in corporations through the social technologies of control such as managerial conceptions or categories, accounting, data collection, and information technologies. Through strategic apparatus "the accountant's report and data collection, [and] personal images are normalized along specific lines configuring. . . [t]he normalized individual [who] is predictable and, hence, instrumentally trustworthy" (Deetz, 1992a, pp. 298, 299). In corporations power rests on "rules limiting access to expression outlets, control of messages in reports and newsletters, determination of who may speak about what, deference in meeting and other forums, control of the expression of criticism, establishment of agendas, [and] control of information distribution" (Deetz, 1992a, pp. 302–303). In other words, power in corporations rests on a systematic violation of the ideal speech situation by managers who justify their monopolistic position by the logic of managerialism.

Managerial knowledge and expertise are commonsense, taken-for-granted knowledge impervious to critical reflection, insofar as "[t]he rational and scientific are privileged" (Deetz, 1992a, p. 272). Managerial expertise requires "the transparency of language" to accomplish "[t]he 'communication as transfer of meaning'. . .central to hierarchical systems" (Deetz, 1992a, p. 273). Deetz then warns of "the practical and arbitrary nature of [every] classification" suggesting that "[t]he accountant report is one of the most basic produced 'facts' of the corporation" responsible for "the privileging of certain interactants and particular distinctions and values" (1992a, pp. 276, 277, 278). However, "[s]tandard accounting practices, like scientific methods, remain outside of corporate discussion" (Deetz, 1992a, p. 279).

"Even more basic than accounting practices are the forms used to collect and construct both financial and nonfinancial data" (Deetz, 1992a, p. 280). Treating forms as a major mode of discourse in corporations, Deetz claims that "[t]he manners in which they constitute the data become invisible; data become an objective reality. Forms-as-medium become simply one more element in a linear communication sequence," that is, "a type of *administrative sedimentation*, an intentional practice that became routinized and institutionalized" (1992a, p. 281). The result is that "[t]he production of the facts, the records, deploy a system at a microlevel that webs out across discourses" (Deetz, 1992a, p. 283). Finally, the fact that "[c]odified, classified 'knowledge' is easily stored and retrieved in such [information] systems; [and that] intuitive, conceptual insights are not" accounts for "the domination of commercial decision making over political ones" (Deetz, 1992a, pp. 284, 286).

Over time, as the result of "the politics of the discursive production," corporations create their reality in the form of social memory (Deetz, 1992a, p. 307). The "text" of social memories in corporations is repressive because it "hides its own conditions of production and silences the voices of dialogic opposition" (Deetz, 1992a, p. 308). Social memory, if critically analyzed, reveals that "managerial power comes in directing the symbols rather than the events," because corporate *social memory* is always a moral and legitimizing force—one that helps achieve and maintain "rational" organizational consensus. Often enough, corporate social memory and its "routines are reconsidered in organizations but, in the managerial logic, only for the sake of greater efficiency or control" (Deetz, 1992a, p. 318). Because "[s]elf-surveillance is obviously a preferable solution for most managerial groups," it is often achieved through the new systems of control such as cultural studies and cultural management, and participation programs in the form of job enrichment and teamwork programs or policies, stresses Deetz.

Structural advantages of management do not go unchallenged, however. Hence, corporate members do fight over (1) the collection and production of data, (2) the meaning of data, (3) access to the data, and (4) use of the data. Construction of corporate forms for data gathering is also the result of conflicts between (1) the officers responsible for interpreting legislation and setting policies, (2) system developers, computer programmers and system analysts, (3) those who administer the filling out of forms, and (4) data processors. Such conflicts and forms of resistance, however, do not deprive managers of many advantages in storytelling, such as (1) privileged speaking forums, (2) access to relatively closed information sources making it difficult to check their stories and develop alternative ones, and (3) positions of authority (Deetz, 1992a, pp. 311–312).

Let me summarize. With help of discursive closure achieved through "quiet, repetive micropractices," systematically distorted social reality of corporations is produced and maintained. Discursive closure is a process of systematic violation of the ideal speech situation. *How is discursive closure achieved in corporations?* Deetz suggests that it is accomplished by a series of micro practices such as

1. *Disqualification* (managers systematically exclude all other organizational stakeholders from having a genuine say);
2. *Naturalization* (corporate social memory or reality as defined by managers is viewed by other organizational stakeholders as given in nature);

3. *Neutralization* (value positions of managers such as order, efficiency, effectiveness, and long-term organizational growth and stability rather than profit become "hidden" or taken for granted);

4. *Subjectification of experience* (organizational stakeholders interpret managerialism in terms of personal rather than social and communicative issues);

5. *Topic avoidance* (managers systematically exclude from corporate discussion topics that question managerialism in the name of a radically participatory democracy as social good);

6. *Meaning denial and plausible deniability* (managers use strategic ambiguity to ward off blame for failures and take credit for success);

7. *Legitimation* (managerialism rationalizes systematic exclusion from organizational decision making of all stakeholders but managers in the name of corporate growth and stability);

8. *Pacification* (managers rely on managerialism to discount the demands for a radical participatory democracy in corporations as being unfeasible and incompatible with corporate economic growth and stability).

As more of these micro practices take place simultaneously or sequentially, organizational communication becomes more distorted. Similarly, as organizational communication becomes more distorted, all organizational stakeholders, including managers, come to take for granted both the explicit content and the background rules of interaction that define the terms of communicative relationship as hierarchical-asymmetrical.

Deetz (1992c), then, argues that lack of public control of corporate decisions not only erodes democracy, but also enfeebles economic development and well-being. Public control of corporate decisions cannot be achieved either by "more government" or by "market pricing and accounting practices". This amounts to saying that public control of corporate decisions "must be a part of the internal corporate decision process" rather than come "from the outside" (Deetz, 1992c).

Radically Participatory Research

I turn next to the analysis of Deetz's empirical research. I will briefly outline one of his most recent studies that tries to live up to is radical, participatory, philosophical constructivism and his theory of organizational communication and democracy. The study reports how members of a "knowledge intensive firm" experience and talk about their identity in the workplace (1994b).

Deetz subscribes to the research process that approximates the ideal speech situation. His brand of ethnography—a case study approach that combines field observations and interviews—is a type of critical phenomenology in which "neither the subjects' nor researcher's conceptions can be privileged" (Deetz, 1994b). Rather, facts are to be coconstructed in symmetrical interactions. In a knowledge intensive firm, says Deetz, work groups enjoy high levels of autonomy and self-management but are also dependent on complex communication processes (1994b). The site "organization survives on the basis of environment enactment rather than adaptation" (Deetz, 1994b). It produces new, customer-tailored computer services. "Since products are new, there is no clear past standard to which to compare them. Since skill in the 'game' [of providing a particular service] often determines the time and other resources given to a product and the emergent standards of quality, neither the professional quality of the product nor the professional talent of the individual can be separated from the 'game' " (Deetz, 1994b, p. 40).

In some respects, then, the site organization resembles the ideal speech situation. It was lacking in "any fixed social structure, agreed upon product standards, or stable external environment to serve as a reference" (Deetz, 1994b). *However, employees described themselves to Deetz only in terms of their work and workplace payoffs.*

The employees claimed not only that they had not been trapped by the corporate "game," but also that by mastering the strategic "moves" they would succeed at work and, thus, subvert the game itself. The game "for both the customer and provider was to sound confident, to sound like the situation wasn't confused, complex, or out of control" (Deetz, 1994b). In such conditions, it was impossible to tell "lies" from "truth" because standards of truth were interaction specific: they always had to be renegotiated anew. Deetz calls the site organization the "simulated world order" that "has colonized the self" of organizational members. Organizational members fell prey to the corporate game, strategic self-deception and self-manipulation, and created and then uncritically accepted a false organizational consensus. They were not able to put up resistance.[7]

Alternative to Corporate Colonization: Workplace Democracy as a Responsive Micro Practice

As I stated at the beginning of this chapter, Deetz's intellectual project is an attempt to revitalize a radical participatory democracy in the face of the corporate erosion of a more moderate version of democracy—liberal democracy. Because government and the market are under the corporate thumb, the only "window of opportunity" is transformation of the internal corporate decision processes. Such internal corporate decision processes can become a vehicle for public control of corporate decisions through "programs for greater participation by workers, owners, and the general public" (Deetz, 1992c). To not be simply coopted by management, such participation programs require a public policy fostering (1) democratic corporate decision making; (2) new accounting and costing systems that balance production for both social and economic good; (3) willingness of all stakeholders to balance efficiency and participatory democracy; (4) communication skills in facilitation, negotiation, and collective creation of ideas; (5) personal control over work time and work processes; (6) new communication technologies that aid public (i.e., all stakeholders) participation; and (7) individual control of everyday lives at work and at home (Deetz, 1992c).

Deetz then outlines his approach to change as an ideal vision of the future based on the possibilities in entryism, resistance, and the concept of balanced responsiveness. A new "utopian" vision is of a more participatory future in the form of the ideal speech situation. Such a future is possible only *if all eight micro practices that bring about discursive closure are resisted and transformed.* For example, entryism could transform corporations only if an open access to corporations by women and minority groups results in a genuinely more diverse workplace rather than "simple cooptation" that ignores specific interests of women and minority groups (Deetz, 1992a, p. 336). The responsive agent, according to Deetz, must be conceptualized as the person who questions and resists disciplinary power—micro practices of unobtrusive control of a way of thinking and acting, of body and mind. This means "recovering the subject not as unitary and rational but as responsive" to "communicative processes that perpetually recover a space for exceeding personal and systemic restraints and distortions" (Deetz, 1992a, p. 340). Because "communication is not for self-expression but for self-destruction," "to overcome one's fixed subjectivity, one's conceptions, one's strategies," and because "[c]ommunication in its democratic form is productive rather than reproductive," it is necessary to develop "a sense of *care*, as an appreciation of *otherness*" to reclaim "a form of democracy appropriate for the modern age" (Deetz, 1992a, pp. 341, 343).

Thus, organizational stakeholders can "begin to work on behalf of the corporation (in its fuller sense) through enacting processes that subvert managerialism." Such subversion "requires responsiveness by the various types of 'owners of the corporations'" as well as by "the modern intellectual as a representative of the public, whether in the guise of the teacher, consultant, or researcher" (Deetz, 1992a, p. 343).

Because "[c]orporations are the new public sphere," then "greater shareholder involvement in corporate design, practices, and production decisions creates a value base more closely aligned with the general public and the goals that governmental bureaucracies only weakly represent" (Deetz, 1992a, pp. 348, 349). Because "[t]he moral foundation for democracy is in the daily practices of communication," the goal is not "to create forums for the expression and resolution of conflicts among stakeholders over and against domination but to understand the domination present in these interests and conflicts, with the hope of recovering conflicts that have been suppressed through latent strategic normalization and routinization" (Deetz, 1992a, p. 351).[8]

Extensions and Elaborations of the Critical Theory of and Research on Organizational Communication and Democracy: Deetz and Associates

In a series of publications Deetz and his associates have extended and elaborated the critical theory approach to organizational communication and democracy (Deetz and Mumby, 1985, 1990; Mumby, 1987, 1988; Mumby and Putnam, 1990). I will briefly outline and discuss D. Mumby's contributions.

Mumby's main contribution to the tradition of critical theory of organizational communication and democracy was to demonstrate how organizational stories function as mechanisms of the invisible power in the so-called deep structure (i.e., the rule structures of communication).[9] A careful study of organizational stories can reveal how repetitive organizational practices draw a fuzzy line between fiction and reality, between metaphysical unobservables and facts. Organizational stories reveal how *"events"* become *"facts"* which in a *"neutral"* fashion describe *"the way things are."*

Thus, narratives in organizations play the major political function. They both accomplish and hide the processes of meaning domination. Mumby also demonstrated how the so-called *dead metaphors* contain the "secret" of the production of organizational commonsense interpretations. Through such taken-for-granted interpretive frameworks managers get the willful consent of the managed in the relentless pursuit of control and economic goals. By accepting that organizational outcomes are inevitable technical or economic progress to be shared by all, organizational stakeholders "shut their eyes to" the option that organizational narratives systematically favor some stakeholders over others.

Mumby demonstrated an even more important process: the way some organizational stories become privileged and others marginalized. Without a critical analysis of organizational narratives, marginalized accounts would be forgotten and privileged ones would become "neutral" facts. More specifically, Mumby showed how stories of organizationai uniqueness are deeply concealed domination. Only a critical analysis could unveil how (1) interests of some stakeholders are represented as interests of all stakeholders, (2) categories of narrative characters become taken-for-granted archetypes that favor some stakeholders over others, and (3) how narratives hide systematically asymetrical-hierarchical organizational structures.

Critique

Just as persons need psychic and public space to examine their experience critically, so whole cultures must have such perspectives if they are to transvalue their traditions and let their choices shape their actions...

(Brown, 1992)

In this last section of the essay I offer the following critical remarks. *First,* Deetz, following Forester (1989), distinguishes *inevitable* from *socially unnecessary distortions of communication.* The former consists of cognitive limits to communication such as idiosyncratic personal traits and random noise and the impact of legitimate division of labor on information inequalities and communication across organizational boundaries. The latter is made of interpersonal manipulation in the form of willful unresponsiveness, interpersonal deception and bluffing, and structural legitimation of inequalities such as monopolistic exchange, monopolistic creation of needs, and class or power structure (Deetz, 1992a, p. 179). *Deetz's theory of organizational communication focuses on the structural legitimation of inequalities and claims that only a radically participatory democracy could subvert and transform inequalities generated by "the structural configurations institutionalized in the organization"* (Deetz, 1992a, p. 179). However, making distinctions between information inequalities resulting from the legitimate division of labor and structurally illegitimate inequalities complicates everyday struggles for participatory democracy in corporations. Even in the ideal speech situation organizational stakeholders may fail to agree on what is illegitimate and, consequently, to resist such practices.

Second, Deetz, again following Forester (1989), argues that power in organizations is exercised through decision making, agenda setting, and shaping of felt needs. Each of the modes of power includes systematically distorted "management" of understanding, trust, consent or legitimacy, and knowledge (Deetz, 1992a, p. 181). Systematically distorted communication could be resisted, argues Deetz, only if the ideal speech situation allows all organizational stakeholders to jointly control organizations. However, the ideal speech situation as the procedure does not guarantee that organizational stakeholders will hammer out democratic and effective decisions. Decisions have both intended and unintended consequences. More important, the ideal speech situation cannot by itself prevent eruption of violent disagreements between organizational stakeholders. The ideal speech situation is an ideal shared by only tiny segments of stakeholder groups, and it is not clear that its legitimacy will spread fast and in a peaceful fashion. In other words, the procedural norms of the ideal speech situation could be vigorously resisted and not only by management.

Third, Deetz's conceptualization of society and organization as partial, dispersed, totalities of simultaneous opposites precludes radical and total transformation. At most, a radical participatory democracy is a constant realignment of opposites to reduce structural inequalities. However, Deetz leaves unanswered the *crucial* question of the relationship between effectiveness and participation. Do they reinforce each other? Or do they work at cross-purposes? Are they, maybe, independent of each other? Do their relationships constantly change? *I do not see that Deetz (and his associates) discusses what kind of organizational interactional asymmetries—and under what time constraints—*

produce what kind of organizational decisions and what intended and unintended consequences these decisions trigger (for similar formulations, see Murdock and Golding, 1977). *And without these linkages the critical theory of organizational communication has dim chances of making bridges with real everyday struggles for a radically participative democracy.*

Notes

1. Brown (1992), for example, suggests that we use "the rhetorical trope and the logical method of dialectical irony as a potential discourse for humanizing political practice" (pp.3–4). Brown asserts that sociological theory of organizations is highly ironic. Example are "Michels' law" by which democratic movements become oligarchic, Karl Weick's claim that the orderly organization is unlikely to survive, and Donald Roy's study of how workers systematically subvert the efforts of time-study engineers to control output (p. 183).

2. Why, according to Deetz, are power inequalities unjust? Arbitrary power inequalities are unjust, argues Deetz, because they violate norms of "the *ideal communication community.*" In such a community "all socially determined asymmetries of interpersonal dialogue" would be eliminated, and, consequently, "presumptions of reciprocity and symmetry [would] exist" (1992a, p. 163).

Arbitrary power inequalities are also unjust because they are not the consequence of "*conversation and mutual understanding.*" Here Deetz draws on Gadamer's (1975) conception of the "genuine conversation" as "a special interaction among two persons and the subject matter before them" (1992a, p. 165). The "genuine conversation" is "a productive rather than reproductive conception of communication [that] shows the fundamental process by which mutual understanding arises in regard to the subject matter rather than in the sharing of opinions" (Deetz, 1992a, p. 166). This type of communication as "the undistorted expression of human interest and the formation of consensus on the subject matter" by which "the disciplines, routines of life, and ordinary ways of seeing are spontaneously overcome"—needs a "means or forum for "otherness" to be expressed" (Deetz, 1992a, p. 167–168).

To formulate a notion of justice, Deetz intertwines Gadamer's and Habermas's positions. Gadamer (1966) distinguishes between a *dialogue/conversation between friends* and *a dialogue/conversation as politics/management/statecraft/negotiation.* Friends through a more or less egalitarian and reciprocal interactions refine and enrich their initial positions, engender and nourish solidarity, and reach understanding through "the fusion of horizons." Politicians, however, as communicators of unequal power can at best engage in a more or less civil or tolerant weighing of different interests rather than in creating and preserving political solidarity (see also Misgeld, 1990). Habermas (1986) emphasizes social and economic relations of power that constrain and pervert the process of dialogue between friends or the ideal speech situation understood as a set of universally symmetrical structures of communication. Consequently, his own conception of why and how systematically evaded and distorted communication comes to be realized in empirical situations overlaps with Gadamer's conception of statecraft/negotiation (see also Grondin, 1990; Warnke, 1990; Wright, 1990; and Misgeld, 1990).

Deetz appropriates Habermas's (1979) division of social action into a communicative one and strategic one. *Communicative action* unfolds in a life world and is oriented to reaching understanding. *Strategic action* is embedded in systems of power and money and is oriented or instrumental to success. This action can be either openly strategic (propaganda) with open intentions or latentiy strategic in the form of manipulation (the other deception) or systematically distorted communication (self-deception). Systematically distorted communication consists of in-formational reproduction rather than production; it excludes alternative interests and discourses.

3. According to Deetz, there are three ways to think of communication as a scholarly discipline. *Discipline 1* refers to an academic unit and the administration of grants and teaching personnel. *Discipline 2* (information studies) clusters topical interests into a field of study. *Discipline 3* (communication studies) refers to a mode of communica-tion-textual-interactive-semiotic explanation of "how things come to be the way they are" (1994c).

Deetz draws a sharp contrast between *Discipline 2 (a topical field of study)* and *Discipline 3 (a mode of explanation or analysis)*. Although information studies, which examines state decisions and election politics and corporate decisions and office politics (or obtrusive and unobtrusive mechanisms of social control through asymmetrical interaction), is suitable to modernity, communication studies, which analyzes macro cultural state politics and micro cultural corporate politics (or processes of production of social reality through communication), is appropriate for postmodernity. Whereas information studies focuses on *interaction as reproduction of meanings*, communication studies concentrates on *interaction as the production of meanings*. Information studies is characterized by social science research based in philosophies of social order and control and epistemologies of explanation, prediction, and control. *Discipline 2* promotes the interests of dominant groups by taking social order of modernity for granted and concentrating on either explicit or obtrusive strategic action aimed at control or on implicit or unobtrusive manufacturing of consent/hegemony. Examples are the administrative research in mass media studies, managerialism in organizational studies, assimilation conceptions in intercultural studies, or compliance gaining in interpersonal studies.

4. More just social arrangements can be achieved, argues Brown (1992), through "entirely new forms of collective practice" rather than through "either bureaucratic liberalism or revolutionary movements" (p. 193).

5. Such a claim takes seriously the fact that both "the expert involved in conservative technical reforms" and "the activist engaged in radical institutional change" always presuppose "some talent or knowledge superior to that of" their audiences (Brown, 1992, p. 6). Brown asserts that this problem of communication can be overcome only if both the expert and the activist participate "in the ongoing communication process" by representing their "truths as witnesses and not merely. . .as bureaucratic or radical technicians" (p. 27). The social thinkers, thus, must be aware of "the possible moral-political implications of their own rhetorical practice" if they are "to make academic

discourses better serve public needs, not in any technocratic or policy-analytic sense, but more broadly and deeply, by enriching rather than denuding the grounds of civic understanding and decision" (Brown, 1992, pp. 3–4, 113).

6. Brown (1992) also warns of " "friendly fascism," a totalism in which efficiency becomes the guiding principle for all domains of social praxis" (pp. 199, 36).

7. Brown implies that "institutional bad faith" could be accounted for by two types of irony. First, ritual-official or safety-valve irony takes place when those in power "ironize themselves." Second, radically free-mastered dialectical irony is either suppressed or coopted by those in power.

8. Since "[d]istortions of communication reduce the range of experiences taken by people as real and the scope of interests perceived as legitimate," it is necessary to make "visible and audible the microrealities of class structures" and "the methods by which class structure is reproduced in everyday interactions (Brown, 1992, pp. 20–21).

9. "Narratives are still being written, but today they catch fish that are already dead" (Brown, 1992, p. 154). This is so because a meaningful narrative must link "personal conduct with the possible impersonal good of the community" (p. 170). Such social good, however, is replaced by judgments of profit efficiency or political expediency.

References

Angus, I. H. (1989). "Media beyond representation." In I. A. Angus and S. Jhally (Eds.), *Cultural politics in contemporary America*, pp. 333–346. New York and London: Routledge.

Baudrillard, J. (1983). "The ecstasy of communication." In *The anti-aesthetic: Essays on postmodern culture*. Port Townshend: Bay Press.

Boyd, R. (1991a). "Confirmation, semantics, and the interpretation of scientific theories." In *R. Boyd, P. Gasper, and J. P. Trout, (Eds.), Philosophy of science*, pp. 3–35. Cambridge, Mass.: MIT Press.

——— (1991b)."On the current status of scientific realism." In R. Boyd, P. Gaster, and J. P. Trout (Eds.), *The philosophy of science*, pp. 195–222. Cambridge, Mass.: MIT Press.

——— (1991c). "Observations, explanatory power, and simplicity: Toward a non-Humean account." In R. Boyd, P. Gaster, and J. P. Trout (Eds.), *The philosophy of science*, pp. 349–377. Cambridge, Mass.: MIT Press.

Brown, R. B. (1992). *Society as text: Essays on rhetoric, reason, and reality*. Chicago: University of Chicago Press.

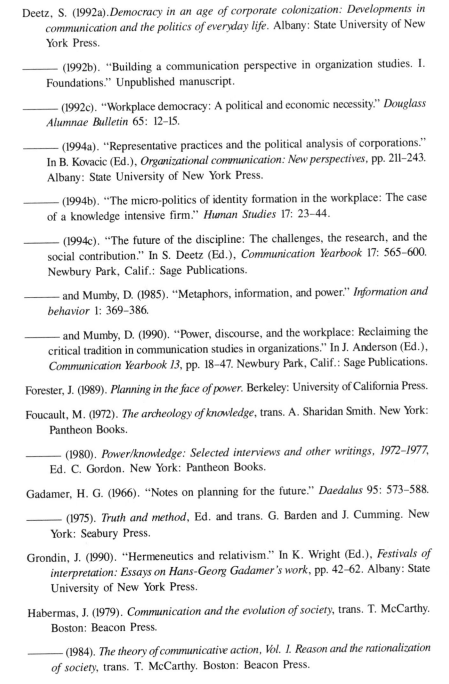

Deetz, S. (1992a).*Democracy in an age of corporate colonization: Developments in communication and the politics of everyday life.* Albany: State University of New York Press.

———— (1992b). "Building a communication perspective in organization studies. I. Foundations." Unpublished manuscript.

———— (1992c). "Workplace democracy: A political and economic necessity." *Douglass Alumnae Bulletin* 65: 12–15.

———— (1994a). "Representative practices and the political analysis of corporations." In B. Kovacic (Ed.), *Organizational communication: New perspectives,* pp. 211–243. Albany: State University of New York Press.

———— (1994b). "The micro-politics of identity formation in the workplace: The case of a knowledge intensive firm." *Human Studies* 17: 23–44.

———— (1994c). "The future of the discipline: The challenges, the research, and the social contribution." In S. Deetz (Ed.), *Communication Yearbook* 17: 565–600. Newbury Park, Calif.: Sage Publications.

———— and Mumby, D. (1985). "Metaphors, information, and power." *Information and behavior* 1: 369–386.

———— and Mumby, D. (1990). "Power, discourse, and the workplace: Reclaiming the critical tradition in communication studies in organizations." In J. Anderson (Ed.), *Communication Yearbook 13,* pp. 18–47. Newbury Park, Calif.: Sage Publications.

Forester, J. (1989). *Planning in the face of power.* Berkeley: University of California Press.

Foucault, M. (1972). *The archeology of knowledge,* trans. A. Sharidan Smith. New York: Pantheon Books.

———— (1980). *Power/knowledge: Selected interviews and other writings, 1972–1977,* Ed. C. Gordon. New York: Pantheon Books.

Gadamer, H. G. (1966). "Notes on planning for the future." *Daedalus* 95: 573–588.

———— (1975). *Truth and method,* Ed. and trans. G. Barden and J. Cumming. New York: Seabury Press.

Grondin, J. (1990). "Hermeneutics and relativism." In K. Wright (Ed.), *Festivals of interpretation: Essays on Hans-Georg Gadamer's work,* pp. 42–62. Albany: State University of New York Press.

Habermas, J. (1979). *Communication and the evolution of society,* trans. T. McCarthy. Boston: Beacon Press.

———— (1984). *The theory of communicative action, Vol. 1. Reason and the rationalization of society,* trans. T. McCarthy. Boston: Beacon Press.

———— (1986). *Philosophical discourse of modernity*, trans. F. Lawrence. Cambridge, Mass.: MIT Press.

Lipset, S. M. (1993). "The social requisites of democracy revisited." Presidential address given at the 88th Annual Meeting of American Sociological Association, Miami.

Misgeld, D. (1990). "Poetry, dialogue, and negotiation: Liberal culture and conservative politics in Hans-Georg Gadamer's thought." In K. Wright (Ed.), *Festivals of interpretation: Essays on Hans-georg Gadamer's work*. pp. 161–181. Albany: State University of New York Press.

Mumby, D. K. (1987). "The political function of narrative in organizations." *Communication Monographs* 54: 113–127.

———— (1988). *Communication and power in organizations: Discourse, ideology, and dominatin*. Norwood, N. J.: Ablex.

———— and Putnam, L. (1990). "Bounded rationality as an organizational construct: A feminist critique." Unpublished paper presented at the Academy of Management Association, San Francisco.

Murdock, G., and Golding, P. (1977). "Capitalism, communication and class relations." In J. Curran, M. Gurevitch, and J. Woolacott (Eds.), *Mass communication and society*, pp. 12–43. Beverly Hills, Calif., and London: Sage Publications.

Smelser, N. J. (1992). "External influences on sociology." In T. C. Halliday and M. Janowitz (Eds.), *Sociology and its publics: The forms and fates of disciplinary organizations*, pp. 43–59. Chicago: University of Chicago Press.

Smircich, L., and Calas, M. B. (1987). "Organizationsl culture: A critical assessment." In F. M. Jablin, L. L. Putnam, K. H. Roberts, and L. W. Porter (Eds.), *Handbook of organizational communication: An interdisciplinary perspective* pp. 228–263. Newbury Park, Calif.: Sage Publications.

Shumway, N. (1993). "What's left for the Latin American left?" *The New York Times Book Review* (September 26) p. 9.

Warnke, G. (1990). "Walzer, Rawls, and Gadamer: Hermeneutics and political theory." In K. Wright (Ed.), *Festivals of intepretation: Essays on Hans-Georg Gadamer's work*, pp. 136–160. Albany: State University of New York Press.

Wright, K. (1990). "Literature and philosophy at the crossroads." In K. Wright (Ed.), *Festivals of interpretation: Essays on Hans-Georg Gadamer's work*, pp. 229–248. Albany: State University of New York Press.

PART IV

ⱥⱥⱥ

MASS COMMUNICATION PARADIGMS

BRANISLAV KOVAČIĆ

Chapter 9: Illuminating the Black Box:
The Psychological Tradition in Media Studies

The fact that we have included only one mass communication paradigm—the psychological approach to media studies—does not necessarily mean that there are no other mass media watershed research traditions. It does, however, mean that the editors were looking for a position composed of the three interrelated levels: (1) the philosophical assumptions, (2) a web of the specified relationships (their direction and strength) between theoretical constructs, and (3) practical implications for communication strategies, techniques, and skills. The psychological approach is a kind of "uncoordinated" watershed research tradition. It is being formed by the convergence of a number of scholars working on related questions in different domains of mass media, but coming from the same philosophical tradition—cognitive psychology.

Desmond and Carveth argue at the philosophical level that the psychological approach to media studies focuses on the "behavior" of media consumers at the intrapersonal level, or the reception and assimilation of mediated messages. The psychological approach privileges a particular view of the individual by emphasizing a combination of cognitive-emotional (affective), private mental activity. Cognitive activities include memory, attention, problem solving, pattern recognition, and learning; emotional activities refer to arousal, fear, joy, anger, or entertainment. Although research programs in media studies generally emerge from social problems, contend Desmond and Carveth, the psychological approach is much more receiver driven than alternative positions. In other words, thinking and feeling are both outcomes of media use and predictors of media choice.

At the theoretical level, Desmond and Carveth discuss two groups of psychological theories of mass media: (1) a psychological approach to entertainment, and (2) a psychological approach to advertising.

Psychological theories of mass media and entertainment examine the decision to become a consumer of entertainment as well as decisions about what entertainment to consume. In general, there are two answers—people use mass media for entertainment experienced as either a stimulant or a depressant. In addition, such theories contend that processes of consumption of mass media entertainment may be effortful and mindful or effortless and mindless. For example, mindful and effortful entertainment consumption increases consumers' involvement in the process, which in turn enhances their comprehension of the content, which in turn prods arousal, which in turn is transferred to other contexts, which in turn may be responsible for selective exposure to a particular type of entertainment.

Psychological theories of mass media and advertising rely on two formal models: (1) the elaboration likelihood model (ELM), and (2) the dual mediation hypothesis (DMH). The ELM posits that individual consumers process ads as a type of persuasive message either through a central or a peripheral route. When processed through a central or "cognitive" route, ads are likely to bring about enduring attitude and behavioral change. However, when processed through a peripheral or "emotional" route, ads at best trigger temporary attitude and behavioral change. The DMH, on the other hand, postulates the following sequence: ads as a type of persuasive message shape attitudes (the affective dimension), which in turn shape brand cognitions, which in turn shape brand attitudes (the affective dimension), which ultimately shape purchase intentions. Thus, it is important to note that the two models differ in terms of (1) the emphasis placed on emotions and cognitions and (2) the time ordering of emotions and cognitions.

At the practical level, Desmond and Carveth discuss the relevance of psychological theories of mass media entertainment and advertising. For both individual consumers and mass media institutions, but for different reasons, it is crucial to understand what psychological mechanisms constrain choice of mass media entertainment programs. By understanding these mechanisms, mass media could, potentially, concentrate even more power in privileging certain kinds of entertainment and advertising. Individual consumers, on the other hand, could exercise a more rational self-control over their own mass media entertainment choices and over manipulative or harmful advertisement effects.

9

Illuminating the Black Box: The Psychological Tradition in Media Studies

Roger Desmond and Rod Carveth

It is possible that there simply are no theories of mass or mediated communication that are as identifiable as the other traditions discussed in this book. Pessimistically we might attribute the reason for this intellectual poverty to the pragmatic, bottom-line nature of problem generation—many of the questions we address are dictated not by intellectual curiosity, but rather are the product of social issues handed to us by those who praise or blame media for their role in the creation and resolution of problems such as child socialization, social and political change, efficiency of information exchange and numerous other concerns. Much of the history of American media research has been written by social engineers and their fellow travelers.

In a more optimistic vein, we might attribute the lack of a watershed tradition in media research to the sheer plurality of theories that have been developed in the field. The fact that some or all of the aforementioned social issues have been examined by theorists of persuasion, agenda setting, observational learning, functionalism, neo-Marxism, or whatever is the latest theoretical flavor simply attests to the magnificent plurality of contemporary thought about the role of media in society. Although we side more with the pessimists, there are many arguments for either position that all center on the history of the field. Rather than line up with other critics of the atheoretical quality of media studies, we will propose a research tradition in the field that has demonstrated great promise of becoming listed in our textbooks with the label *watershed.*

Our first difficulty is finding a name for this emerging tradition. The referent is easy enough: the body of research and theory that seeks to explain the behavior of media consumers at the *intrapersonal* level or the application of cognitive psychology to problems associated with the reception and assimilation of mediated messages. The nature of the concepts that build the tradition is what makes naming it so difficult. If we choose to label the tradition a *cognitive approach* to audience behavior, as have many of its incumbents, we would concern ourselves only with those concepts inherited from cognitive psychology, which include memory, attention, problem solving, pattern recognition, learning, and a few others. What we may not include is a family of concepts regarding emotion, including arousal, fear, joy anger, and the most global of all, entertainment. We might also exclude some important work with the concept *primary process*, or the relationships among daydreaming, fantasy and media reception. Out of a concern for inclusiveness, we will henceforth designate the tradition as simply the *psychological approach* to media studies.

The characterizing difference between the psychological approach and some of the other theoretical positions contained in this book represents the convergence of a number of scholars working on related questions in different domain areas of mass media. For example, a group of scholars are working on issues surrounding choices of entertainment and decisions around choices of entertainment. Later in this chaper we will review research by Zillmann and his colleagues, McIlwraith and his colleagues, and Kubey and Ruben. What they all have in common is that their ultimae dependent measure is choice of entertainment. Although each of these groups found it necessary to posit some type of mentalistic construct to predict choice and satisfaction, the nature of each construct is drawn from a different dimension of cognitive psychology (e.g., arousal theory, daydream and fantasy research, and ongoing monitoring of peaks and valleys of everyday life, i.e., "flow"). These approaches are more alike than different compared to sociological or interactionist perspectives. For example, Salomon's mental effort and Langer's mindful-mindless distinction both reify the notion of consciousness as adjustable and the driving force behind account taking from media. As psychological constructs, they are virtually synonymous, whereas work with reference groups compared to the uses and gratifications perspective portray wildly different concepts of reception processes. Because of the novelty of the psychological perspective numerous synonymous concepts are waiting to be refined, categorized, or discarded. Although researchers from the psychological perspective do not necessarily have contact with each other, their concepts have emerged from the same philosophical position: cognitive psychology. We could therefore characterize the psychological approach to media studies as an "uncoordinated" watershed tradition.

Philosophic Orientation

Philosophically, the psychological approach is rooted in three branches of cognitive science: Chomsky's grammatical paradigm, structuralism as developed in Piagetian developmental theory, and schema theory as applied to automaticity and thought sequencing and several refinements of precognitive psychology including neopsychoanalytic conceptualizations of the role of emotions in the creation and reduction of arousal and the philosophical assumptions that underpin operant conditioning. What view of the individual ultimately emerges from this amalgam of philosophical arguments? First, people organize mediated messages with the use of grammatical structures or schemas, and these schemas are invoked during reception. Second, people seek to alleviate stress and boredom through choice of enertainment. Third, thinking and feeling are mutually involved in reception and as concomitants that are both outcomes of media use or predictors of media choice. Early concepts in media research, such as agenda setting or information seeking or disinihibition all presupposed that people either think or feel and that these processes are most effectively investigated as discrete categories. The view of the individual as a receiver who employs schemata to understand and minimize aversive ideation emerges from the psychological tradition. In the following section, we will examine the philosophical assumptions of each of these subareas.

The sociological tradition in media research had run into a deadend, with its preoccupation with observable effects and probabilistic explanations using demographics and group variables to explain the role of media in campaigns, advertising, and social movements. Scholars confroned with electronic media increasingly began to see that so-called effects were probably not apparent within a sociological paradigm. One starting place was clearly the issue of television's function as an initiator of aggression. Social learning theorists had successfully demonstrated *how* children might learn through imitation, but not whether imitation ever takes place (McGuire, 1986). In a sense, media joined psychotherapy and education as processes supporting a "no effects" model. What was missing was a concern for meaning, long a welcome conceptual guest in other divisions of communication study.

Child development had long been concerned with issues of meaning, especially in the specification of the onset of semantics and syntax in achieving something akin to adult grammar. In the attempt to resolve questions about the nature of media effects in the socialization process, it became necessary to address questions like the following: How do children (of various ages) interpret stories? Under what conditions do they come to perceive the symbolic dimensions of heroism and villainy? How does attention develop, and what consequences does it have for the preceding? And, how do children differentiate fantasy from reality? These questions were necessary because the cognitive processes specified within them were seen to precede any process known as reception. As John Greene (1986) pointed out, a cognitive explanation is warranted only when it is impossible to specify the occurrence of a phenomenon without recourse to cognitive mechanisms. Initially, this level of rigor was not invoked—cognitive explanations of media effects were offered out of intellectual desperation, resulting from a failure of the sociological paradigm. More recently, a disparate group of media scholars have perceived psychological perspectives are necessary for the explanation of effects. Elements of television programming, such as commercials, were seen to consist of operations, or systems of logical problems, that a developing child must resolve and internalize before he or she could overthrow a literal interpretation of a program's meaning.

How Do Children Know? Lessons from Structuralism

A good deal of research directed at problems surrounding children and television from raw empiricism (surveys by Schramm, Himmelweit, and others) or the sociological tradition (nearly everything else) treated children as incompetent adults, who, when asked about the role of television in their lives, failed to produce adultlike answers. The same lack of competence is in evidence in early work on advertising directed to the child audience (Ward, Wackman, and Wartella, 1977). Under the psychological approach, it became necessary to provide methods for preschool children's responses that allowed them to, in Piaget's terms, either *recognize* (select from an array for possible responses) or *reconstruct* (order a sequence of events in alignment with the original order) the crucial elements of a commercial's message (Comstock and Paik, 1991). This strategy resulted in greater assessments of what children knew about commercials; given their difficulty with language, they knew more than they could verbally tell. Krippendorf (1994) points out that one of the most severe hindrances to progress in the media-oriented research on child development was the tendency of researchers to frame questions without taking into account children's know-tell distinctions. This resulted in vast underestimates of knowledge of a variety of media processes.

The significance of the cognitive perspective is that it facilitated a new way of thinking about how children perceived television, and in turn, new methodologies were created that led to a rapid accumulation of observations about how commercials were constructed in children's thoughts (VanDer Voort, 1991). Such commercial techniques as host selling, visual representation of products, separation of program and commercial content, and others were, as a result, incorporated into the federal legislation that has been referred to as The Children's Television Act of 1990.

The Role of Mental Effort

The two theorists most responsible for this domain are Gavriel Salomon and Ellen Langer. Initially, Salomon created the concept of amount of invested effort (A.I.M.E.) to account for differential learning of content from *Sesame Street*; Israeli children learned significantly more from the program than an American sample even when I.Q. was matched (Salomon, 1979). He argued that Israeli children were more experienced in educational television than

American children and thus allocated more mental effort when viewing. In later research with adult samples, he found that when expectations of difficulty are manipulated, "difficult" television content elicited more effortful viewing than "easy" reading (Salomon, 1983). In a more recent investigation, Raynolds (1991) found that forewarning samples of retarded adolescents and nonretarded fourth graders that they would be tested subsequent to viewing produced no effects, but for both populations, instructions to watch "for fun" resulted in fewer propositions learned from the program than from other instructions or controls. Although evidence for the potency of effortfulness continues, evidence is sufficient for (1) differential allocation of effort within and between individuals and (2) that effortfulness helps to predict what can be and is learned from television watching.

Mindfulness is a concept related to effortfulness in that Langer suggests that it is possible to think, behave, read, or watch television with varying degrees of awareness and that this awareness determines what can be learned, retained, or accomplished (Langer, 1988). When a sample of adults was instructed to watch television from a variety of perspectives (as a lawyer or a mother, say) they perceived more complexities in characters and plots than did subjects who simply "watched." Mindful subjects also learned more content than did the uninstructed sample.

These lines of work in mental effort and mindlessness alter the philosophical, theoretical, and practical dimensions of knowledge regarding television and child development. Philosophically, the dominant models of media use still center on the weak-moderate-strong effects debate with proponents switching models every decade or so (Katz, 1992). The psychological paradigm, in its concern with receiver motivation and patterns of learning, suggests a much more receiver-driven model than the effects tradition, with less consequence for sociological explanations based on reference groups or opinion leadership. Theoretically, the psychological paradigm suggests that the processing of mediated messages may be explainable from schema theory. Current work now in progress in media literacy projects represents attempt to improve schematic efficiency to maximize learning and attention (Kubey and Ruben, 1994). Practically, a number of emerging methodologies use secondary-task procedures or physiological measures to assess viewer interest and attention shifting during actual viewing (Reeves et al, 1989; Armstrong and Greenberg, 1990).

Emotions and Media: Contributions from the Psychoanalytic Paradigm

The most important researchers who address the concept of purposefulness in the selection of media fare are Dolf Zillmann and Jennings Bryant and their collaborators. They have proceeded to address issues such as the rise of media entertainment to alter aversive moods and perpetuate pleasant ones, the relative success of purposeful entertainment seeking, gender differences in choices of strategic entertainment, and numerous other subquestions (Zillmann, 1988a). They have also investigated the transfer of certain emotions from entertainment to specific behaviors such as aggression and erotic fulfillment (Bryant and Zillmann, 1984). In prolific research program, they have conducted a series of related experiments that have provided an impressive amount of support for their approach, with some major modifications of the general theory in the process.

In terms of support for purposive modification of moods through media entertainment, there is evidence that, given a choice, individuals in a state of unpleasant arousal will choose music, a TV program, or reading that will lessen their arousal (Zillmann, 1988b). Women in the premenstrual cycle or menstruating women offered an array of entertainment choices preferred comedy TV programs significantly more than did women midway through the cycle, presumably as a method of overcoming noxious mood states associated with menstruation (Meadowcroft and Zillmann, 1987).

Reasoning from arousal theory, Zillmann and colleagues argue that media use provides relief from hedonically negative arousal because it blocks the ability to rehearse negative affect (Zillmann, 1988b). The capacity of entertainment choices to achieve this relief is dependent upon their excitation potential as well as the extent to which they do not elicit the recall of hedonically negative states. Media choices can be used to regulate levels of arousal (boredom or stress) as well as mood, thereby acting as either a stimulant or a depressant. Given that audience members are often unaware of their levels of arousal and because it is nonspecific, sympathetic excitation can transfer to subsequent stimulus situations and combine with the previous excitation to elicit increasingly intense levels of stimulation often misattributed to the most salient stimulus. Labeled the *excitation transfer model*, the paradigm has been used to explain media effects as diverse as increased aggression resulting from exposure to pornography to the optimum combination of uncertainty and predictability for the appreciation of suspense and mystery (Bryant and Zillmann, 1984).

Research on Thought Content

Canadian psychologists McIlwraith and Schallow (1983) have employed Jerome Singer's imaginal process inventory (I.P.I.) to investigate the relationships among media use and daydreaming. They found that people who exhibited predominantly negative daydreams (guilty-dysphoric or anxious-distractable) were more likely to watch action-adventure TV programs and read pornographic and men's adventure magazines than were people with more positive patterns of ideation. They explained their results in terms of the "full-head" model, where media use by anxious individuals is not motivated by a scarcity of inner imagery, but rather by an overabundance of certain types of daydreams to which the individual would rather not attend. In later investigations, this tendency toward highly involving media was more pronounced for males than for females (Bhatia and Desmond, 1993; McIlwraith and Josephson, 1988). Although these results initially appear to contradict those of Zillmann et al., Zillmann (1988a) points out that surface characteristics of entertainment categories may be misleading; individuals may be responding to successful resolutions of conflicts rather than the anxiety-eliciting aspects of the plot element of fear. Personality characteristics (e.g., sensation seeking) may interact with certain forms of entertainment to modify simple conclusions made from the topic alone. It is clear that evidence is accumulating for complex, but comprehensible relationships among inner states and exposure to entertainment.

The philosophical argument of those who have used daydream-based explanations clearly has origins in Freud's concept of primary process, while Zillmann's emotion-based position that escape from aversive inner states or the perpetuation of positive affect is the goal of all entertainment seeking has roots in Aristotle's *Poetica*. The primary difference between the approaches lies in the construct *escape*: in the Freudian conceptualization, the individual seeks to alleviate aversive ideation by avoiding rehearsal of unpleasant imagery via involvement in externally produced imagery; in the Aristotelian conceptualization, individuals seek to escape from boredom through indentification with a fictional hero and his or her exploits. In a sense, the Freudian position posits entertainment as a depressant, in contrast to the Aristotelian notion of entertainment as a stimulant. In one case we are escaping *from* the inner world; in the latter mode, we escape *to* an exciting outer world.

Theoretical Orientation

A Psychological Approach to Entertainment

Theoretically, the entertainment theory of Zillmann and Bryant addresses one of the oldest observations in communication research: selective exposure. Traditionally, selectivity has always been addressed through attitudinal explanations where individuals avoid exposure to messages that threaten their attitudes or belief structures. Entertainment theory provides an explanation based on emotional patterns of avoidance, where constructs such as arousal or dissonance are avoided through strategic program choices. One advantage of entertainment theory explanations is that they have been used to link exposure with subsequent emotional and behavioral consequences. Through their program of research, its advocates have been able to demonstrate, for example, that messages that are less involving to audience members are more likely to facilitate subsequent behavioral aggression than messages that engage and involve the viewer (Bryant and Zillmann, 1984). Presumably, excitation can either be transferred to a high involvement message (then diffused) or to an arena of behavior. With respect to memory, emotional valence (positive or negative) can inhibit recall of broadcast news items if they precede or follow other emotionally evocative stories (Mundorf and Zillmann, 1991). Although many investigators have studied the psychology of media use, the entertainment theorists have been more thorough in their extension of conceptual linkages to a wide variety of media domains as well as to previously established theories. Practically, this group has invented ingenious techniques for invesigating these relationships, including varying the content of television programs and music lyrics to provide an array of potential outcomes for the investigation of drama and suspense, altering the structure and pacing of newscasts to control for emotional congruity, using original self-report scales for the assessment of mood, the use of I.P.I. to predict dominant thought patterns, and a variety of physiological techniques to measure responses to horror, drama, and erotica.

The foundation of the psychological approach to media studies rests on several theoretical propositions:

1.) The decision to become a consumer of entertainment as well as what entertainment to consume is motivated by mood, ideation, and other "inner processes" of which consumers are relatively unaware.
2.) Once chosen, processes of consumption may be effortful and mindful or effortless and mindless.
3.) Mindful and effortful entertainment consumption elicit involvement.
4.) Increased involvement elicits comprehension.
5.) Low-involvement entertainrnent consumption is characterized by reliance on schemata (scripts) for predictable entertainment consumption.
6.) Arousal from entertainment consumption may transfer to nonentertainment environments.
7.) Arousal from nonentertainment environments may initiate selective exposure to entertainment (see Proposition 1).

A Psychological Approach to Advertising

Not all the research involving processing of media content has been directed toward entertainment. The domain of advertising contains some concerns not shared by entertainment theorists, such as factors surrounding the decision to expose oneself to commercials, because the assumption is that commercial viewing will be a concomitant of program viewing. Another difference is that entertainment-based research establishes mood management as a major rationale for consumption; commercials have as their outcome such things as retention of key messages, brand identification, intention to purchase the products or services advertised, and so forth; nevertheless the similarities of research concerns outweigh the differences. Given the specific goals of advertising and the enormous economic implications of its effectiveness, numerous issues in the psychological approach are tested daily by both academic and industry researchers.

For example, several problems plague the study of the role of affect in persuasion. First, there is a great deal of conceptual ambiguity as to what constitutes the term *affect*. For example, as Cacioppo and Petty (1989) note, *affect* has been used to refer to "preferences, reported emotional state, evaluations, undifferentiated arousal tagged with an emotional label, any kind of positive and negative orientation toward a stimulus, and 'feeling states' " (p. 70). Moreover, Cacioppo and Petty observe that *affect* and *attitude* are often treated as interchangeable concepts: however, *attitude*, the authors note, can be composed of affective, cognitive, and behavioral elements.

In addition to conceptual difficulties, the operationalizing of affect is also problematic. Given that emotion is a social construction, then in assessing emotion, researchers must ask subjects and respondents to label their "feelings." The very act of labeling a "feeling" state requires a cognitive assessment of the situation to determine what the subject is "feeling." The cognitions associated with the labeling of the "feeling" may not be distinct from other cognitions (such as brand benefit information).

Thus, although conceptually and operationally it is difficult to isolate the roles of affect and cognition in persuasion, rather than focusing solely on cognition, researchers need to find ways to address properly the *independent* and *interactive* roles of affect in the persuasive process. This task is increasingly imperative in view of the striking trend in advertising toward more widespread and complex use of affective appeals (Carveth and Kretchmer, 1993).

Most of the literature that has examined the role of affect in persuasive advertising campaigns has been conducted to test either the elaboration likelihood model or the dual mediation hypothesis. The ELM, developed by Richard Petty and John Cacioppo (1986), proposes that individuals process information from persuasive messages with varying degrees of elaboration—the active, critical thinking about arguments and issues. The likelihood of elaboration in evaluating arguments ranges from very little to a great deal. Elaboration likelihood is a function of two crucial factors: ability and motivation. *Ability* refers to an individual's capacity to attend to and critically process a message. *Motivation* includes the variables that propel and guide purposeful information processing.

Petty and Cacioppo argue that a persuasive communication can be processed through either a *central* route or a *peripheral* route. When information is processed through the central route, previously acquired information is compared with the new arguments presented in the persuasive message. When information is processed through the peripheral route, factors other than the argument itself (such as affect) are influential. Petty and Cacioppo maintain that if attitude change results from arguments processed through the central route, the change will be enduring and lead to behavioral change. If attitude change occurs after information is processed through the peripheral route, the change will be temporary and less likely to result in any behavioral change.

Involvement is a significant component of motivation in the ELM. Petty and Cacioppo embrace the traditional definition of involvement, originally advanced by Krugman (1967), as the level of identification and personal relevance a product or persuasive message holds for the individual. As applied to ELM, the higher is the involvement, the greater is the possibility that the information in an argument will be processed through the central route. Hence, according to the model, involvement is a cognitive process.

However, the success of many advertising appeals calls the validity of the ELM into question. The first of these elements is the nature of the argument. For example, the appeal of the 1991–1994 TV advertising campign for Taster's Choice instant coffee rests on the argument that the taste of coffee is "sophisticated" (e.g., "Savor the Sophisticated Taste of Taster's Choice"). According to Petty and Cacioppo, in evaluating this argument a consumer would compare it to what they know about "sophisticated taste." But what is "sophisticated taste"? It is likely that the consumer has no conceptual reference point for "sophisticated taste" and, consequently, is unable to critically evaluate the concept. Therefore, if there is no critical evaluation, the information presented in the ad is processed through the peripheral rather than the central route. Based on the ELM, the ads should have little impact on purchase intention and behavior. Yet, as noted earlier, Taster's Choice has experienced a significant increase in sales. The point here is that the argument in the Taster's Choice ads is not cognitive, but affective, a situation for which the ELM is unable to account.

Similarly, the second problematic element is the definition of involvement. Petty and Cacioppo's standard cognitive interpretation of involvement fails to consider the possibility that the "conscious 'bridging experiences', connections or personal references. . .that the viewer makes between his own life and the stimulus" (Krugman, 1967, p. 355) can constitute an emotional-affective process. In contrast, effective emotional appeals nurture the primitive, instinctual, visceral, and arousing, rather than cognitive and rational, associations that exist between consumers and products; an emotional appeal in a persuasive message can increase *emotional* involvement. In fact, research has shown that skillful use of creative advertising can build brand involvement by linking the brand to a high emotional involvement situation. Unlike low-involvement strategies that emphasize the sheer number of *message repetitions* to increase the persuasive influence of a campaign, *message content* becomes key (Robertson, Zielinski, and Ward, 1984). In terms of Rossiter, Percy, and Donovan's creative strategy "grid" (1991), which links the involvement level of the product (low vs. high) with the type of message strategy (informational-negative appeals vs.

transformational-positive appeals), successful advertising campaigns differentiate themselves from the traditional low involvement-informational position by adopting a high involvement-transformational strategy. MacInnis, Moorman, and Jaworski (1991) outline several ways that creative executions can enhance consumers' motivation and opportunity to learn information about a product from advertising by increasing consumer emotional involvement.

The dual mediation hypothesis, which developed out of research on the construct attitude toward the ad (Lutz, 1985; MacKenzie and Lutz, 1989), examines the interrelationships among this concept and the other characterisics of ad exposure situations in the persuasion process. Attitude toward the ad (A_{ad}) is defined as the affecive (not cognitive or behavioral) response to a particular advertising stimulus during a particular exposure. The analysis of A_{ad} seeks to extend the elaboration likelihood model. The determinants of A_{ad} (ad cedibility, ad perceptions, attitude toward the advertiser, attitude toward advertising in general, and mood) are arrayed along a continuum based on the levels of central-peripheral processing. According to the DMH, A_{ad} has a direct effect on brand cognitions and direct and indirect (via brand cognitions) effects on brand attitude. The brand attitude then has a direct effect on purchase intention. Hence, as research has demonstrated, the effect of A_{ad} on purchase intention is moderately strong (Brown and Stayman, 1992).

The basic difficulty in the application of the dual mediation hypothesis to advertising campaigns is twofold. First, because involvement is defined cognitively, strong cognitive attitudinal reactions to the ad negate strong affective responses to the ad; ad credibility and other cognitive antecedents of A_{ad} are posited to lead to central processing, whereas mood and other affective antecedents have little or no impact on A_{ad} through peripheral processing. However, the emotional appeal of some advertisements is clearly the dominant influence in the explanation of A_{ad}, through not only its anticipated interaction with mood, but through ad credibility as well. For example, the ads for Taster's Choice instant coffee instruct viewers to "Savor the Sophisticated Taste of Taser's Choice." The ad credibility antecedent of A_{ad} should be high because ad claim discrepancy, the only second-order determinant controllable through the current Taster's Choice persuasive campaign, is probably low. Ad claim discrepancy is the "degree to which the message recipient perceives a discrepancy between what is being claimed about the brand in the ad and the actual characteristics or benefits of the brand" (Lutz, 1985, pp. 49–50). The only claim specifically made is that Taster's Choice has a "sophisticated taste"; richness, aroma, premium quality are all implied, but not specifically claimed. The consumer really cannot find any discrepancy between the claim and reality because (1) "sophistication" is a state of mind; (2) when Maxwell House claims, for example, that "Better Beans Make Better Coffee," people know what beans are, but *what is sophisticated taste?* Whereas a viewer-consumer can refute or argue about claims of dark color, good aroma, good taste, the best beans, and so on, it is very difficult to cognitively counterargue a nebulous, intangible, emotional imagery claim.

Second, given that cognitive reactions to the ad determine A_{ad}, the DMH proposes that A_{ad} must pass through the perceptual filters of attitude toward the brand and brand cognitions before exerting influence on purchase intention. But, what are the possible cognitive reactions to the ad? That Taster's Choice has "sophisticated taste," a rather undefinable notion? Or, that coffee represents gestatory foreplay? It is likely that the links between these concept and purchase intention after they have been processed through the perceptual filters of brand attitude and brand cognitions would lack sufficient strength to result in the high degree of purchase intention needed to account for the 10–12 percent increase in Taster's Choice sales. We would argue that the nature of the emotional appeal in the Taster's Choice campaign creates an attitude toward the ad that is directly linked to brand attitude and purchase intention, without being predetermined by ad cognitions or channeled through brand attitudes.

Based on the preceding discussion, the theoretical propositions of the psychological approach to the study of advertising are as follows:

1.) The decision to become a consumer of advertising is more often based on chance than choice.
2.) Once exposed to advertising, the processes of consumption may be effortful and mindful or effortless and mindless.
3.) Mindful and effortful advertising consumption elicit involvement.
4.) Increased involvement elicits comprehension.
5.) Low-involvement advertising consumption can be effective if the individual is exposed to the message frequently.
6.) Arousal from entertainment consumption may transfer to processing advertising messages.
7.) Learning from nonentertainment environments may initiate selective exposure to advertising (see Proposison 1).

The psychological tradition in media studies and the assumptions upon which the approach rests alter previously held notions about several areas of media theory. In the following pages, we will demonstrate how employing the psychological approach informs us about an important applied domain of media studies: advertising effeciveness.

Advertising Effectiveness

Few areas of the media, with the possible exception of media violence, have more been researched and written about than advertising. Yet, despite the plethora of studies conducted by both the advertising industry and academia, only a small amount of variance has been accounted for in determining what makes one advertising campaign work and another not. For example, one of the 1980s' most memorable TV advertising slogans was Wendy's "Where's the Beef?" Originally, the slogan was "Where's *All* the Beef?" However, Clara Peller, the actress who asks the question in the commercial, possessed poor hearing and thought the director wanted her to say "Where's the Beef?" Would the TV ad campaign have been as successful if Peller had better hearing and spoke the "correct" lines?

Involvement. The vast majority of studies done on advertising effectiveness support the first proposition of the psychological paradigm—that media effects are located in cognition. Research on the psychological components of consumer behavior has identified three concepts of importance: motivation, cognition, and learning. Traditionally, advertising research has been interested in cognitive elements to learn how consumers react to different stimuli, and research finds learning especially important in determining factors such as advertising frequency. In recent years, however, the major application of psychology to advertising has been the attempt to understand the underlying motives that initiate consumer behavior.

Research in consumer behavior reveals that three major factors influence a consumer's decision to purchase a product: psychological factors, such as motives and perceptions; sociocultural factors, such as demographics and psychographics; and situational factors, such as the physical and social surroundings a consumer is in. Most advertising researchers have focused on the first two sets of factors in explaining the effectiveness of advertising. Extensive research on sociocultural factors, ranging from CUBE to VALS 2, has identified targeted segments of the consumer market, thereby making the creative and media strategies of advertising campaigns more efficient.

The adoption of a psychological perspective that we have outlined provides a more in-depth understanding of the success of advertising campaigns. For example, the second assumption of the psychological paradigm proposes the involvement is critical for persuasion and that affect is a major component of involvement. Until recently, however, advertising research has largely overlooked the key element of affect in favor of cognition. Further, affect has been treated as a consequence rather than as a basic motivating force in the process of persuasion. Only recently have researchers begun to explore the possibilities of the role of emotion in persuading and informing. Such research has increasingly turned to trying to understand the effectiveness of emotional appeals in a way that allows affect to function independent of cognition while recognizing the interaction of these two elements in the persuasion process and the potential of either to be the motive force. This is especially true as advertising campaigns increasingly become a *component* of an integrated marketing communication strategy, combining advertising with sales promotion, direct marketing, public relations, and personal sales. Recent campaigns for Club Med, Smartfoods popcorn, Soloflex exercise equipment, Timberland boots, and Veryfine juices demonstrates the effectiveness and efficiencies created when all marketing communication disciplines are valued equally and practitioners from their distinct specialties support each other (Bencin, 1992; Everett, 1992; Warner, 1992).

Strong affecive stimuli, both positive and negative, have a greater impact than affectively neutral ads. However, when affective reactions to the ad alter the interpretations of the message content, there are differences between pleasant and unpleasant ads. Consequently, it is important to note that we are focusing on the effectiveness of positive emotional appeals. Negative emotional appeals are (in)famous in commodity advertising, as the history of "Always a bridesmaid, never a bride," "Ring around the collar," and "Morning breath" attest. Nevertheless, research has shown that positive emotional appeals are more effective than negative ones (Homer and Yoon, 1992; Isen, 1989). Very few advertisers, most prominently beer (e.g., Miller) and cigarettes (e.g., Marlboro), have realized and benefited from the effectiveness of positive emotional appeals.

Research has shown that emotional response is more important than cognitive response in explaining A_{ad} and brand attitude, yet negatively framed appeals make cognition more salient (Homer and Yoon, 1992). Thus, Folgers and Maxwell House attempted to appeal to emotion, but by choosing a negative-fear approach, they lost the value of the appeal and ended up with an undifferentiated, cognitive-based ("Mountain Grown—the richest kind") standard coffee ad.

It is not just that the affective stimuli in the ad are positive it is that they follow affective stimuli that are negative. Thorson et al. (1985) noted that ads that are poignant—that is, the resolution of the ad's drama is positive following some threat—are more effecive than ads that contain strong affect, even if that affect is exclusively positive. AT&T's "Reach Out and Touch Someone" campaign often featured close friends or loved ones separated by miles who could still connect with one another by a long distance telephone call.

Affect may work to produce independent effects in the persuasion process as well as interact with cognition to be a powerful motivating force in the implementation of persuasive appeals. Part of the explanation for why such creative executional techniques work is from research conducted on brain lateralization. It is thought that the left hemisphere of the brain processes linear information (such as reading or mathematics) and controls analytical thinking. The right hemisphere is viewed as the part of the brain that processes mental and spatial images and controls emotional response. Therefore, the print media relate to the left hemisphere of the brain, whereas television relates to the right brain. Krugman (1967) suggests that advertising strategies that appeal to the left brain induce consumer evaluation of product information. Alternatively, strategies that appeal to the right side of the brain tend to produce an emotional bond with the product message that can lead to left brain activity. Interactive imagery blending information with images and emotion, uses both hemispheres of the brain, and thus is more effective than appealing to either half of the brain alone; advertising effectiveness is increased with the use of interactive imagery (Lutz and Lutz, 1977). For example, Kretchmer and Carveth (1988) demonstrated that the use of music integrated with product information is effective.

Schemas. Theoretical Proposition 5 relates to the processing of media schemas. Most of the research conducted on consumer schemas has dealt with product-category schemas. The consumer's schema for a product category contains the cumulative knowledge about the product (such as typical product attributes). Research has shown that when new product information is presented to a consumer, the consumer evaluates the new knowledge based on his or her prior schema. The degree of congruity between the new information and the existing schemas can affect a number of processes related to consumer judgments (Alba and Hutchinson, 1987; Cohen and Basu, 1987; Loken and Ward, 1990). Meyers-Levy and Tybout (1989) examined the evaluative outcomes of a mismatch between schema-level representations and new product attributes. Their results indicated that more positive product evaluation may result when the schema representation and the new product information are moderately mismatched than when there is a match or extreme mismatch. Ozanne, Brucks, and Grewal (1992) examined how product-category schemas affect information search. Their result indicate that an inverted-U shape relationship exists between information search and the degree of mismatch between the product and the product-category schema, with the highest level of information search and processing effort associated with the moderate mismatch.

The implications for these findings are twofold and relate to schemata for media. First, these findings help explain why commercials "bum out" after a period of time. Because the content (the product information) is familiar with a preexisting schema, the processing is lower and appears more mindless. Thus, the more exposures to the commercial, the more familiar the consumer becomes with the ad, the more predictable its content becomes, and the more mindless the processing. Second, the findings provide support for the position many practitioners take in not trying to change the image of their product too radically. Stayman, Alden, and Smith (1992) found that when new product information contained content about product attributes that was very discrepant from a prior category schema, consumers may switch to another product category schema in forming pretrial expectations. Therefore, new commercials for a product are likely to be most effective when they contain some new content (to avoid the information becoming too familiar) but not so discrepant from previous product content as to force consumers to reconstruct their notions about the product.

Active Use of Content. As stated at the beginning of this section, although not immediately apparent, many of the concerns of entertainment theorists are shared by those in the advertising industry. In fact, it could be argued that commercials are merely shorter selections of media entertainment. Yet, there exists a relative paucity of research into the purposeful use of commercials when compared to that of media entertainment.

From the second set of theoretical propositions concerning advertising, we can better understand why viewers pay attention to some ads and not others. Specifically these propositions can be applied to both attention to the ad itself and attention to the program before the ad.

One way to heigten attention to an ad is to incorporate *appeals to intrinsic hedonic needs*. The Taster's Choice ads employ two clear appeals of this type. The first is the product-related appeal to the "sophisticated taste" of Taster's Choice. The implication is that consumers will be treated to a pleasurable taste experience not found in competitive brands. A second appeal is the image-related appeal of sexuality. The sexual tension between Tony and Sharon connotes to the viewer that Taster's Choice coffee is linked to romantic and sexual opportunities—a definite form of pleasure for consumers. Thus, Taster's Choice uses romance and sexuality as a high-involvement situation.

A second way to increase the processing of brand information is to *enhance the relevance of the brand to the self*. One method of doing this is to create dramas in which brand benefits are illustrated in the form of a story. The Taster's Choice campaign employs a continuing storyline that demonstrates a variety of contexts in which coffee is consumed. Such stories as well as personal interviews with the actors on television and in magazines, and the "Most Romantic First Date" essay contest, grand prize and survey all create empathic identification with the characters in the ads, thereby enhancing consumer involvement and attention to the product (Deighton, Romer, and McQueen, 1989).

Finally, executional cues that *enhance curiosity* are also effective. The use of a serial format to present the product helps to generate curiosity. As demonstrated by letters sent to Nestlé Beverage Co., viewers are highly involved in what will happen next in Tony and Sharon's relationship. The use of the serial format makes the ads distinctive from other campaigns, giving them wide attention and increasing emotional involvement.

Research on how program involvement affects viewer processing of commercials has provided some contradictory findings. Some research (Zillmann, et al., 1981) suggests that a high level of program involvement inhibits the recall of and learning from a commercial. However, Krugman (1983) found that as the level of interest in a program increases, so does the persuasive impact of only interesting commercials. In addition, Isen's "congruity" principle suggests that emotional cues that are congruent with the cognitive elements of a message will be remembered better than messages whose cognitive and emotional elements are incongruent. More recently, Murry, Lastovicka, and Singh (1992) revealed that the construct "program involvement" was composed of two elements, feelings and liking, and that liking a program influences attitudes toward the commercial, whereas feelings (either positive or negative) did not.

Practical Orientation

The practical difficulties of advertising research concern the most important dependent measure: advertising effectiveness. In the entertainment domain, the most difficult practical problem is in the nature of the independent measure, such as choice of program. For advertising, we do a good job of identifying the cognitive processes surrounding the consumption of advertising content. However, we lack an adequate understanding of the processes underlying advertising effectiveness. Advertising effeciveness is generally operationalized by two types of dependent measures.

1.) Immediate and delayed recall of advertising messages. One problem befalling this type of measure is the low correlation between immediate and delayed recall. We still have trouble answering such questions as, Why do we remember some ads over a long period of time? Does it have to do with personal salience? Does it have to do with message characteristics?

2.) Purchase decisions, such as bar code studies, that attempt to link ad exposure and purchase behavior, but that are quite flawed. These studies provide different ads or levels of ad exposure in different test markets, then have subjects in the study record their purchase behavior utilizing a wand to read the bar codes of product purchases. The researchers then see whether or not the different ad or exposure levels lead to increased sales. Unfortunately, a number of other variables can contaminate this type of research. For example, how accurate are the consumers in recording their purchases? How identical are the shopping outlets in terms of providing shelf space for the products in question? How close are the media consumption patterns of the consumers in the study, especially in cable environments where it is difficult, if not impossible, to control advertising exposure?

In one way, this problem may be resolved by the advent of truly interacive media, where message exposure and product adoption is relatively simultaneous.

At the time of this writing, several organizations are market testing instantaneous purchases by on-line payment from bank account or credit cards. In addition, the QVC and Home Shopping networks have demonstrated the efficacy of interactive media in the consumer markets. What remains to be seen is whether these immediate exposure-purchase behaviors will correlate with the purchase behavior of people who do not yet have access to this technology or who choose not to use it.

Criticisms of the Psychological Approach

A major criticism of the psychological approach is that it is individualistic, to the exclusion of social inputs such as peer and reference groups, and a concept central to communication in general, the influence of culture. As O'Keefe (1993, p. 74) suggests, "A view of communication as private mental activity is unlikely to attract the allegiance of a large community of scholars." Individuals are not constituted prior to culture nor are rational explanations likely to be literal descriptions of mental processes. A traditional emphasis on the social construction of meaning has received intensity from scholars who view standard models of intersubjectivity as problematic (Taylor, 1992 in O'Keefe, 1993). The strongest response to these criticisms is that advocates of the psychological approach have never intended to provide a comprehensive explanation of sense making. In light of the similar shortfall of self-reports of media effects from a sociological perspective and the embrace of impressionistic or ethnomethodological techniques by devotees of cultural studies, the psychological perspective offers another viewpoint from which to integrate media studies (Geiger and Newhagen, 1994).

Another, related, critique centers on the lack of integration of affect and cognition. As we have noted earlier, most progress toward integration has been made in the study of advertising. Specifically, future research should be conducted to better understand what strategies individuals adopt in integrating affect and cognition. For example, Pavelchek, Antil, and Munch (1988) conducted a study of the impact of the outcome of the 1986 Super Bowl on ad recall. Subjects were selected from Boston, Chicago, and Philadelphia. Results indicated that subjects from Boston and Chicago (the cities with teams competing in the Super Bowl) recalled fewer commercials than subjects from Philadelphia. The authors explain these results in terms of outcome—subjects from "participating" cities were more aroused, and this arousal inhibited learning from the ads.

However, upon further inspection of the results, self-reported arousal was negatively related to ad recall. In the winning city (Chicago), the level of arousal was high. In both the losing city (Boston) and the neutral city (Philadelphia), however, the levels of self-reported arousal dropped significantly. Thus, the relationship of arousal to ad recall was not a function of whether subjects were from a winning or losing city, but of some other untested variable. A third variable that could be tested is affect intensity. Larsen, Diener, and Cropanzano (1987) found that individuals who rank high on affect intensity adopt different cognitive strategies (such as personalizing, overgeneralizing, and selective abstraction) to deal with highly affect-provoking stimuli than do subjects who rank low on affect intensity. Thus, subjects in the Pavelchek et al. study, especially those in Boston, may have had their ability to recall ads diminished because they were taking the loss personally (personalizing) or seeing the loss as representative of the general state of affairs (overgeneralizing). Therefore, an individual predisposition such as affect intensity could be seen to mediate the influence of advertising. Similarly research by Zillmann suggests that personality traits such as sensation seeking mediate the relationship between highly arousing media fare and its effects.

Another variable that requires further investigation is whether there is a threshold effect regarding the level and intensity of affect, and how that mediates effects. For example, subjects exposed to arousing visual and auditory cues recall fewer news items than subjects who are exposed to less arousing cues. Yet, research in advertising (e.g., Thorson) suggests that level of affect promotes greater involvement and cognitive processing of commercials. These contradictory findings raise questions as to whether there is an upper bound of affect beyond which there are cognitively inhibiting effects or whether media content and level of arousal interact with one another, so that different types of content and arousal produce differential effects.

The Future of the Psychological Perspective

As we have noted earlier, research programs in media studies generally emerge from social problems and the psychological approach is no exception. As we write this chapter, a professional association representing the cable television industry has agreed to a monitoring body that will judge programs for violent language and behavior to facilitate parental censorship of objectionable content. It is a safe bet to assume that representatives of the psychological approach will continue to examine such issues as TV violence, the influence of popular music lyrics on children and adolescents, the role of pornography in sexual offenses, and numerous related issues. Emerging media technologies, such as virtual reality, are a likely target for the next wave of effects research. Although this is an inevitable course for further research, the instability in the approach might be remedied by a greater reliance on theory testing.

Just as there have emerged distinct domains of theory and research in communication (interpersonal, organizational, mass media), even within these domains are distinct subdomains for which the respective researchers can learn a great deal from one another. In mass communication, the two areas of research in which schemas have been investigated are children's processing of television content and consumers' processing of advertising messages. Yet, current research on relational and item-specific processing in the advertising literature on product schemas (cf., Meyers-Levy, 1991) could have important implications for such media theories as cultivation theory. For example, research has shown that television viewers who consume television content for habitual reasons are more affected by the incidental message patterns of that content (e.g., perceiving more violence in the world) than viewers who seek instrumental (goal-oriented) gratifications from television (Carveth and Alexander, 1985; Perse, 1986; Rubin and Perse, 1987). Drawing from the advertising literature, such cultivation findings may be explained by the supposition that instrumental TV viewers process item-specific information, while habitual viewers process TV content in a relational processing manner. Future research should seek to explore such explanatory mechanisms.

Specifically, a greater emphasis on the development of integrated cognitive-emotion theories would do for communication what Sylvan Tompkins's theory of emotion has done for several branches of psychology—create a heuristic model that generates research that serves as central themes from which variations can logically be made. Although none are on the horizon, the coherent program of research by Byron Reeves and his associates is one example of a possible future. Reeves and his colleagues have demonstrated the relevance of such cognitive-affective concepts as the orienting response, the prehistoric generalized arousal in the presence of threat, that may govern many of our responses to entertainment. If this sort of integration leads to similar well-crafted experiments to support critical stages of theory construction, then great advances may be forthcoming.

References

Alba, J., and Hutchinson, W. (1987). "Dimensions of consumer expertise." *Journal of Consumer Research* 13 (March): 411–454.

Anderson, D. (1985). "Online cognitive processing of television." In L. Alwitt and A. Mitchell (Eds.), *Psychological processes and advertising effects*, pp. 177–200. Hillsdale, N.J.: Lawrence Erlbaum Associates.

Armstrong, G., and Greenberg, B. (1990). "Background television as an inhibitor of cognitive processing." *Human Communication Research* 16, no. 3: 355–386.

Batra, R., and Ray, M. (1985). "How advertising works at contact." In L. Alwitt and A. Mitchell (Eds.), *Psychological processes and advertising effects*, pp. 13–43. Hillsdale, N.J.: Lawrence Erlbaum and Associates.

Bencin, R. (1992). "Telefocus: Telemarketing gets synergized." *Sales and Marketing Management* 144, no. 2: 49–53.

Bhatia, A., and Desmond, R. (1993). "Emotion, romantic involvement and loneliness: Gender differences among inner states and choice of entertainment." *Sex Roles* 28: 655–669.

Brown, S., and Stayman, D. (1992). "Antecedents and consequences of attitude toward the ad: A meta-analysis." *Journal of Consumer Research* 19: 34–51.

Bryant, J., and Zillmann, D. (1984). "Using television to alleviate boredom and stress: Selective exposure as a state of induced excitation." *Journal of Broadcasting and Electronic Media* 28: 120–131.

Bucklin, L. (1965). "The information role in advertising." *Journal of Advertising Research*: 11–15.

Cacioppo, J., and Petty, R. (1989). "The elaboration likelihood model: The role of affect-laden information-processing in persuasion." In P. Cafferata and A. Tybout (Eds.), *Cognitive and affective responses to advertising*, pp. 69–87. Lexington, Mass.: Lexington Books.

Carveth, R., and Alexander, A. (1985). "Soap opera viewing motivations and the cultivation process." *Journal of Broadcasting and Electronic Media* 29: 259–273.

———— and Kretchmer, S. (1993). "Stirring the emotion in with the beans: Examining the role of affect in advertising." Paper presented to the Speech Communication Association Conference, Miami.

Cohen, J., and Basu, K. (1987). "Alternative models of categorization: Toward a contingent processing framework." *Journal of Consumer Research* 13 (March): 455–472.

Collins, W. A. (1983). "Interpretation and influence in children's television viewing." In J. R. Anderson (Ed.), *Children's understanding of television*. New York: Academic Press.

———— and Wellman, H. (1982). "Social scripts and development in representing televised narratives." *Communication Research* 9: 133–147.

Comstock, G., and Paik, H. (1991). *Television and the American child*. Los Angeles: Academic Press.

Deighton, J., Romer, D., and McQueen, J. (1989). "Using drama to persuade." *Journal of Consumer Research* 16: 335–343.

Edell, J., and Burke, M. (1987). "The power of feelings in understanding advertising effects." *Journal of Consumer Research* 14: 404–420.

Everett, M. (1992). "Extra! Extra! Gannett helps Club Med mine its data base." *Sales and Marketing Management* 144, no. 12: 120, 122.

Geiger, S., and Newhagen, J. (1994). "Revealing the black box: Information processing ad media effects." *Journal of Communication* 43, no. 4: 42–51.

Goldberg, M., and Gorn, G. (1987). "Happy and sad TV programs: How they affect reactions to commercials." *Journal of Consumer Research* 14 (December): 387–403.

Grenne, J. (1986). "Evaluating cognitive explanations of communications phenomena." *Quarterly Journal of Speech* 70: 241–254.

Hawkins, D., Coney, C., and Best, R. (1980). *Consumer Behavior: Implications for marketing strategy.* Dallas: Business Publications.

Holbrook, M., and Batra, R. (1987). "Assessing the role of emotions as mediators of consumer responses to advertising." *Journal of Consumer Research* 14: 404–420.

Homer, P., and Yoon, G.-S. (1992). "Message framing and the interrelationships among ad-based feelings, affect, and cognition." *Journal of Advertising*, 21, no. 1: 19–33.

Isen, A. (1989). "Some ways in which affect influences cognitive processes: Implications for advertising and consumer behavior." In P. Cafferata and A. Tybout (Eds.), *Cognitive and affective responses to advertising.* Lexington, Mass.: Lexington Books.

Katz, E. (1992). Lecture to the Annenberg School of Communication, Philadelphia, October 19.

Kretchmer, S., and Carveth, R. (1988). "Music and contemporary advertising." Paper presented at the Annual Convention of the Popular Culture Association, New Orleans.

Krippendorf, K. (1994). "The past of communication's hoped-for future." *Journal of Communication* 43: 34–45.

Krugman, H. (1967). "The measurement of advertising involvement." *Public Opinion Quarterly* 30: 583–596.

———— (1983). "Television program interest and commercial interruption: Are commercials on interesting programs less effective?" *Journal of Advertising Research* 23, no 1: 21–25.

Kubey, R., and Ruben, B. (1994). *Literacy in the information age.* New Brunswick, N.J.: Transaction Books.

Langer, E., and Piper, A. (1988). "Television from a mindful/mindless perspective." In S. Oskamp (Ed.), *Applied social psychology annual*, Vol. 8. Beverly Hills, Calif.: Sage Publication.

Larsen, R., Diener, E., and Cropanzano, R. (1987). "Cognitive operations associated with individual differences in affect intensity." *Journal of Personality and Social Psychology* 53, no. 4: 767–774.

Loken, B., and Ward, J. (1990). "Alternative approaches to understanding the determinants of typicality." *Journal of Consumer Research* 17 (September): 111–129.

Lord, K., and Burnkrant, R. (1993). "Attention versus distraction: The interactive effect of program involvement and attentional devices on commercial processing." *Journal of Advertising* 22, no. 1: 47–60.

Lutz, R. (1985). "Affective and cognitive antecedents of attitude toward the ad: A conceptual framework." In L. Alwitt and A. Mitchell (Eds.), *Psychological processes and advertising effects*, pp. 45–61. Hillsdale, N.J.: Lawrence Erlbaum and Associates.

———— and Lutz, W. (1977). "The effects of interactive imagery on learning: Application to advertising." *Journal of Applied Psychology* 62, no. 4: 493–398.

McGuire, W. J. (1986). "The myth of massive media impact: Savagings and salvagings." In G. Comstock (Ed.) *Public communication and behavior* Vol. 1, pp. 173–257. New York: Academic Press.

Machleit, K., Allen, C., and Madden, T. (1993). "The mature brand and brand interest: An alternative consequence of ad-evoked affect." *Journal of Marketing* 57, no. 4: 72–82.

MacInnis, D., Moorman, C., and Jaworski, B. (1991) "Enhancing and measuring consumers' motivation, opportunity and ability to process brand information from ads." *Journal of Marketing*, 55, no. 4: 32–53.

———— and Stayman, D. (1993). "Focal and emotional integration: Constructs, measures, and preliminary evidence." *Journal of Advertising* 22, 4: 51–65.

MacKenzie, S., Lutz, R., and Belch, G. (1986). "The role of attitude toward the ad as a mediator of advertising effectiveness. A test of competing explanations." *Journal of Marketing Research* 23: 130–143.

McCall, S. (1977). "Meet the workwife." *Journal of Marketing* 41, no. 3: 55–71.

McIlwraith, S., and Schallow, R. (1983). "Adult fantasy life and patterns of media use." *Journal of Communication* 33, no. 1: 78–91.

———— and Josephson, D. (1988). "Fantasy styles, media choice and program preference." *Communication Research* 30: 26–47.

Meadowcroft, J., and Zillmann, D. (1987). "Women's comedy preferences during the menstrual cycle." *Communication Research* 14: 204–218.

Meyers-Levy, J. (1991). "Elaborating on elaboration: The distinction between relational and item-specific elaboration." *Journal of Consumer Research* 18: 358–367.

———— and Tybout, A. (1989). "Schema congruity as a basis for product evaluation." *Journal of Consumer Research* 16 (June): 39–54.

Mundorf, N., and Zillmann, D. (1991). "Effects of story sequencing on affecive reactions to broadcast news." *Journal of Broadcasting and Electronic Media* 35, no. 2: 197–211.

Murry, J., Lastovicka, J., and Singh, S. (1992). "Feeling and liking responses to television programs: An examination of two explanations for media-context effects." *Journal of Consumer Research* 18 (March): 441–451.

O'Keefe, B. (1993). "Against theory." *Journal of Communication* 43: 375–383.

Ozanne, J., Brucks, M., and Grewal, D. (1992). "A study of information search behavior during the categorization of new products." *Journal of Consumer Research* 18, no. 3: 452–474.

Pavelchak, M., Antil, J., and Munch, J. (1988). "The Super Bowl: An investigation into the relationship among program context, emotional experience and ad recall." *Journal of Consumer Research* 15, no. 3: 360–367.

Pearce, J. (1976). "Are Americans careful food shoppers?" *FDA Consumer* (September).

Perse, E. (1986). "Soap opera viewing patterns of college students and cultivation." *Journal of Broadcasting and Electronic Media* 30: 175–193.

Petty, R., and Cacioppo, J. (1986). *Communication and persuasion: Central and peripheral routes to attitude change.* New York: Springer Verlag.

Raynolds, T. (1991). "The acts of viewing instructions on the recall of a television story by mildly retarded individuals." E.D.D. dissertation, Columbia University.

Reeves, B., Lang, A., Thorson, E., and Rothschild, M. (1989). "Emotional TV scenes and hemispheric specialization." *Human Communication Research* 15, no. 4: 493–508.

Robertson, T., Zielinski, J., and Ward, S. (1984). *Consumer behavior.* New York: Scott Foresman and Co.

Rossiter, J., Percy, L., and Donovan, R. (1991). "A better advertising planning grid." *Journal of Advertising Research* 31, no. 6: 11–21.

Rubin, A., and Perse, E. (1987). "Audience activity and soap opera involvement." *Human Communication Reserach* 14: 246–268.

Saloman, G. (1979). *Interaction of media, cognition and learning.* San Francisco: Jossey-Bass.

——— (1981). "Introducing AIME: The assessment of children's involvement with television." In H. Gardner and H. Kelly (Eds.), *Children and the worlds of television*, pp. 223–246. San Francisco: Jossey-Bass.

——— (1983). "Television watching and mental effort: A social psychological view." In J. Bryant and D. R. Anderson (Eds.), *Children's understanding of television*, pp. 223–246.

Schank, R., and Abelson, R. (1977). *Scripts, plans, goals and understanding.* Hillsdale, N.J.: Lawrence Erlbaum and Associates.

Stayman, D., Alden, D., and Smith, K. (1992). "Some effects of schematic processing on consumer expectations and disconfirmation judgments." *Journal of Consumer Research* 19 (September): 240–255.

Thorson, E., Reeves, B., and Schlevder, J. (1985). "Message complexity and attention to television." *Communication Reserach* 12: 427–454.

VanDer Voort, T. H. (1991). "Children's written accounts of televised and written stories." *Educational Research and Development* 39, no. 3: 15–26.

Ward, S., Wackman, D., and Wartella, E. (1977). *How children learn to buy: The development of consumer information-processing skills.* Beverly Hills, Calif.: Sage Publications.

Warner, C. (1992). "Applying integrated marketing to brand positioning." *Public Relations Journal* 48: 10, 15–16.

Zielske, H. (1959). "The remembering and forgetting of advertising." *Journal of Marketing* 23, no. 3: 239–252.

Zillmann, D. (1988a). "Mood management: Using entertainment to full advantage." In L. Donohew, H. Sypher, and E. T. Higgins (Eds.), *Communication, social cognition and affect.* Hillsdale, N.J.: Lawrence Erlbaum and Associates.

——— (1988b). "Mood management through communication choices." *American Behavioral Scientist* 31: 327–340.

——— Bryant, J., Comisky, P., and Medoff (1981). "Excitation and hedonic valence in the effect of erotica on motivated aggression." *European Journal of Social Psychology* 11: 233–252.

PART V

⊘⌒⌄⌒⊙

CULTURAL COMMUNICATION THEORIES

BRANISLAV KOVAČIĆ

Chapter 10: The Ethnographic Communication Theory of
Philipsen and Associates

On the philosophical level, Philipsen and associates argue that communication
consists of competing messages about identity, proper social conduct, social
relations and others, and objects of emotion. Particular people, on particular
occasions, in their natural environments engage in local systems of practices
that always entail some general, cross-local principles. Philipsen and associates
state that communication as a socio-cultural performance, a prominent site for
the ordering of social life, is constitutive of part of socio-cultural life understood
as a combination of play and structure. Such assumptions provide the unique
insights into the central communication processes within cultures. Americans,
for example, employ the culture-specific communication rules to distinguish
two types of interaction: (1) communication as an episodic sequence deployed
to restore an individual's strained and challenged identity, and (2) mere
talk.

On the theoretical level, Philipsen and associates focus, at the "emic"
level, on a description of the communicative practices and an interpretation
of what the practices mean to participants. Such a grasp of the native's point
of view is possible only if the real structure of social interaction—"real-life"
sequences of conversation—is carefully researched. At the "etic" level,
Philipsen, and associates attempt to identify commonalities across these practices
through comparative studies of the ends and means of speaking that are both
culturally contingent. Philipsen and associates do not specify relationships
between concepts beforehand. Rather, they first collect evidence from a relatively
large number of case studies and the inductively look for common pattern of
communicative practices. However, such common patterns do inform the
subsequent ethnographic case studies. Such common cross-cultural patterns

of communication have been presented in the form of three interrelated arguments or theoretical models.

First, *a cultural communication theory* examines the ways culture influences communication. By focusing on speech codes and cultural forms, it unveils interpenetration of the forces of individualism and community. A community's consensus, its sense of shared identity, is created, tested, and restored through three cultural forms that organize and guide recurrent inter-action patterns: (1) ritual, (2) myth, and (3) social drama. Through the non-rational consensus ensconced in ritual, a community members sequence communicative interactions to coordinate and align diverse lines of action. Individuals appropriate myths or communal narratives to give meaning to their own lives by expressing in a narrative form their own relationship to society. Social drama provides rules or standards for the ways cultural codes, if violated, are to be negotiated and revised, or reasserted. Social drama thus defines boundaries of a group and reintegrates those members whose acts have tested its boundaries. Second, *a communication theory of culture and society* articulates the ways communication helps constitute culture and society through patterned use and interpretation of symbols, symbolic forms, norms or rules for action, and definitions of social positions, relations, and institutional arrangements. Finally, *a cultural interpretive theory* focuses on models of personhood, society, and strategic action that are embedded in the speech code.

On the practical level, Philipsen and associates use case studies or ethnographies of communication to present communication patterns of action and meaning and rules for speaking that may be legislated, transgressed, remedied, and negotiated in a particular community. In a general sense, this watershed research tradition contributes to our understanding of culturally specific communcative practices. Also, through comparative research, it demon-strates cultural similarities and differences in such practices. Consequently, it makes us aware of the rules for culturally appropriate communication in different contexts. Examples are ethnographies of communication in Teamsterville, in Israel, and other contexts studied by the researchers in this tradition. More important, this watershed tradition makes us aware of the arbitrary nature of cultural recipes for appropriate and effective communication. It also increases our repertoire of cross-culturally relevant rules for communication. There is a direct link between such a knowledge and communicative competence that can be taught, improved, and then applied by different individuals, groups, organizations, and social movements.

10

THE ETHNOGRAPHIC COMMUNICATION THEORY OF PHILIPSEN AND ASSOCIATES

DONAL CARBAUGH

The ethnography of communication (EC) is an approach to human communication with its own philosophy, theory, and methodology. The earliest practitioner of EC in the field of communication was Gerry Philipsen, who wrote a series of ethnographic field reports (1975, 1976, 1986), a methodological statement (1977), and a theoretical stance (1989a) for doing such study. Philipsen formulated the approach as a way to analyze communication as a cultural resource, with others in the field using this approach, for example, to investigate communication among Vietnam veterans (Braithwaite, 1990b), among Chinese (Chen, 1990–1991; Garrett, 1993), among Appalachians (Ray, 1987), and among church members (Sequeira, 1993). Many studies in EC have been conducted in the United States, but also the approach has been applied widely in a variety of other countries, for example, in Colombia (Fitch, 1991), Israel (Katriel, 1986, 1991), and Finland (Carbaugh, 1993). Additionally, EC has also been used to conduct cross-cultural analyses of silence (Braithwaite, 1990a), conflict management (Shailor, 1990), and terms for talk (Carbaugh, 1989). EC has been productively used, therefore—within and across cultural communities—as a way to apply and develop communication theory.

EC, as Philipsen (1989a, 1992) sees it, involves a philosophical commitment to investigating communication as something radically cultural, as a patterning of practices among particular people in a particular place. Although this is not the only philosophical commitment of EC, it is a principal one, as EC seeks to know how people communicate in the course of their everyday lives. Philipsen argues that this kind of "situated" knowledge about communication can be developed in a theoretically rigorous way. Practitioners of EC, from this view, then, investigate particular communication practices, and do so in theoretically informed ways.

It is the purpose of this chapter to introduce the basic philosophy and theory of EC, as well as detail some of its developments into cultural communication (CC). It is impossible to treat all aspects of the approach, so I will focus here only on its basic philosophy and theory, as well as some of its recent developments and applications. Some of the recent topics raised in ethnography such as modes of ethnographic writing, the critical impulse, experimental narration, will not occupy a central place in this chapter, although such concerns are of keen interest to ethnographers of communication, a point I note in concluding. My main purpose here is (1) to characterize EC as an investigative mode of inquiry, (2) to sketch its philosophical commitments about communication, (3) to explicate its basic theory, and (4) to discuss some of its recent developments and applications. But first, following the commitment to particularity espoused by Philipsen (1989a), let us enter our discussion close to the ground, through an example of a routine communicative practice.

Particularity: Investigating Communication Practices

"My NAME is Debbie Miller. I kept my REAL name!" The young woman was reacting to an older man while at a wedding reception in New England, in the northeastern area of the United States. When the older man met her, she had been introduced to him simply as Debbie. In the course of their conversation, he discovered that she was married to Randy Smith. Immediately after this discovery, the older man, a retired schoolteacher, presumed Debbie and Randy shared a last name and thus had expressed his presumed realization to Debbie, "Oh, Debbie Smith." It was this expressed presumption—that the younger woman would share a last name with her husband and thus be a Smith, rather than keep her birth name and thus be a Miller—that precipitated her assertion to the older man that she kept her REAL NAME.

Brought to the surface in this exchange are alternate forms of naming, and through these alternate forms are expressed various competing messages about identity, proper social conduct, social relations with others, and objects of emotion. Two countervoices are audible here. With the shared last name, an identity of the female is constituted as perhaps a "wife" or "mother." With the other, the birth name, an identity of the female is constituted differently, as perhaps an "independent woman." The alternate uses of these forms of naming, and the meanings associated with each, provided the symbolic resources through which this brief yet potent social drama was created.

What means of communication are used when people, like this woman and this man, talk to each other? What are the meanings associated with these various means of communication? What do they enable and constrain? How do these means and meanings get played into particular encounters between particular people? These are the kinds of questions that ethnographers puzzle over. If we cast the questions more generally, thus moving beyond questions of particular naming devices, we might ask, Through what forms and means of communication is life meaningfully conducted, here? The *here* is important because there is a commitment in ethnography in general, and in particular, to discovering the distinctive communicative means that particular people use, on particular occasions, and thus to exploring those distinctive means in their natural environments, in those particular places. Philipsen (1989a, pp. 258–260) has called this commitment to the distinctive nature and particular quality of communication, an *axiom of particularity*. Reflecting the ethnographer's commitment, he argues that knowledge of communication, of its nature, functions, forms, situations, and meanings, be erected at least partly by attending to local systems of practices. The logic is this: each such communication system requires discovery, and this process of discovery provides access into the communicative life of a people in their place.

Debbie Miller and the retired schoolteacher are in this sense of a deeply particular place, of a distinctive system of communicative practices. All communication can be understood in this way, as from a people or of a place. Understanding the communicative life of people, what is significant and important to them as they communicate, like what New Englanders think they are "up to" or "up against" as they use names, this is a primary objective of ethnographic studies of communication.

Generality

People also use communicative forms that can be understood absractly. For example, ways people address each other personally might involve different forms of first names, last names, or titles, and different meanings for each from intimacy to power. What forms of address are associated with which general dimensions of meaning can thus be understood more generally (see Fitch 1991; Sequira 1993). This double allegiance, to the particular shape and meaning of communication in place (i.e., New England patterns of address) and to what this might suggest generally (i.e., about address forms and meanings abstractly), demonstrates dual objectives in EC research. Investigators in this vein want foremost to know in particular the nature of communication in its place, yet also they want to know what this local way, and other local ways, suggest generally about human communication. This dual attention to local practices and cross-local principles creates a kind of balanced view of communication, an exploration into its particulars of practice and abstractions of the general principles exhibited in those particular practices. "The axiom of particularity" thus suggests listening carefully to the local and particular sounds of communication, yet to do so in ways that enable general knowledge of communication to be built (see Philipsen, 1989a, pp. 261–262).

Basic Philosophy: Assumptions about Communication

The ethnography of communication has been built on a basic philosophy of communication. This philosophy is the result not just of abstract conjecture, but of careful fieldwork that has attended both to the variety of cultural resources of communication and the various forms of life these have constituted around the world. In particular, the ethnography of communication has built knowledge about communication by presuming the following: that everywhere there is communication, a system is at work; that everywhere there is a communication system, there is cultural meaning and social organizations and thus, that the communication system is at least partly constitutive of socio-cultural life (see Philipsen, 1992, pp. 7–16).[1]

Communication Exhibits Systemic Organization

Ethnographic studies of communication have amply demonstrated that, when there is a communication pattern, some systemic organization is at work. The concept pattern, used here, draws attention to a particular and recurrent means of communication that is intelligible to some participants when it is used. An example of a patterned use is the use in New England of one's birth name after marrying. Such use is not random, but orderly, with the order of social life being partly constituted by the choice of this form, such that when it is used, it constitutes a particular organization of social life. The concept system draws attention to the larger communicative situation at play during such use, with this larger situation being something that involves participants, who say some things (rather than other things) to an other(s) about something in a particular way (e.g., language(s), channel, instrument) for specific purposes in some sequence of action on a particular occasion (see Hymes, 1972; Philipsen, 1992, p. 9). Repeatedly, ethnographic studies of communication have demonstrated that the choice to speak or not, in a particular way, to whom, for how long, and so on is not random but patterned and patterned in systematic ways. Communicating generally thus involves patterns of communication, with those patterns exhibiting order as part of social life (see Cushman and Cahn 1985).

Philipsen's studies of Teamsterville (1975, 1976, 1986, 1992) have been exemplary in showing how male members of a Chicago community say that they prefer, among other things, being silent rather than speaking, hitting someone rather than talking with them, exercising influence through intermediaries rather than speaking for oneself. In communicating these ways, community members partake and contribute to a local scene, thereby acting and interpreting actions in a local and systematic way. Preferences as these, Philipsen argues, are more than simply personal matters, they are part of a community's system of communication, in this case, a part that demonstrates ways to "be a man."

Similarly, if we revisit Debbie's exclamation to the older man—that she kept her "real" name—we notice that she chose a verbal means of referring to herself and, in so doing, was heard to react to something the older man had said earlier. Her exclamation says something, it communicates, precisely because participants hear her preferring her birth name over her husband's last name. Each form, her birth name or her husband's name, has its own meanings and constraints, its own significance, with each being used to organize this particular encounter. This example illustrates systemic organization of communication in several ways: it shows how verbal means, or forms, carry meanings; how different verbal means carry different meanings; how the play between means and meanings organizes an encounter between present participants in particular ways; and, how the preference and use of one means over others, in a context, carries significant cultural and social weight.

Such preferences for communication are sometimes characterized by ethnographers and others as *rules* for speaking, with the concept rule being used here to identify ways people account for, justify, or explain their conduct. Communication rules, in this sense, are subject to all the whims of social life, including their legislation, transgression, remediation, and negotiation. This adds an important caveat to our first starting point: to claim that communication exhibits systemic organization is not to say that the system is necessarily rigid or unchanging. Quite the contrary. Parts of systems, as Debbie demonstrates, can be challenged, and modified, or reasserted and solidified. As Philipsen (1992, p. 10) puts it: "To say that speaking is structured is not to say that it is absolutely determined. It is patterned, but in ways that its creators can circumvent, challenge, and revise. Its rules are violated, new rules and meanings are created, and there in play is brought into structure just as structure is brought into play."

Processes like these, and the various beliefs and preferences animating the performance, show a community in communication, the possibility of great diversity in dialogue. So, to claim there is systemic order in communication is not to require a bland uniformity of belief or morality (although that, indeed, is actualized on some occasions), nor does it require social struggle and difference (although on occasions, this also occurs). It does suggest that we be able to hear communication with all of its various forces, from commonality to difference, collusion to conflict, harmony to discord. Painful inequities and various moral, even personal, conflicts, if aggravating and perplexing, are nonetheless played together in communication, as are happier moments, in systemic ways.

Communication Is a Socio-Cultural Performance

A second assumption elaborates the first. It assumes that everywhere there is communication, there is to be found cultural meaning systems and social organizations (see Basso 1979; Carbaugh and Hastings, 1992; Goodwin, 1990; Schneider, 1976). As Philipsen (1992, 124) puts it, to "speak" is fundamentally, to speak culturally.

The logic in this belief can be put simply: if communication has something to do with meaning making, and meanings have something to do with participants' points-of-view, and participants' points-of-view have something to do with their particular cultural orientations, then communication creatively evokes *cultural meaning systems*.

This point is demonstrated forcefully in Philipsen's (1986) cultural interpretation of a passionate public speech made by the late Mayor Daley of Chicago. During his speech, the mayor explained one of his recent political appointments by referring to the appointee as "a son" of "a good mother" who contributed to "this [Daley's] society." He contrasted this act of appointment with the corrupt world of "the university," where a political antagonist of his, "a professor," worked. From one prominent view of Chicago journalists, his speech was heard as a "tirade." From another view closer to Daley's community, the speech was heard as an apt defense of his appointment. Philipsen's interpretation demonstrates the basic principle: ethnographers seek, at least partly, to interpret the culture that speakers (and hearers) like Daley use when they speak (and listen).

Distinctive philosophical commitments are operating here about the nature of communication and ways of inquiring about it. With regard to communication, EC presumes a pattern of action, or process of meaning making that is cultural (i.e., distinctive and meaningful). Further, it presumes that participants can (and do) use this pattern or process to constitute relations among themselves and others. With regard to a philosophy of inquiry, ethnographers are therefore committed to understanding the nature of participants' meanings in or about those processes. What do the participants consider significant and important? The role of the "native view" is thus a fundamental concern, but not the exclusive concern, in an ethnographic view of communication. This commitment distinguishes the interpretive stance of EC from other interpretive theories, such as those more Marxist or Freudian, because participants' meanings are less centrally foregrounded in these theories, if they are considered at all (see Carbaugh, 1991).

With regard to Debbie's assertion of her "real name," we might ask, then, how does this shift of name move participant meanings from one sort to another? Forms of a last name are on some occasions highly potent sources of meanings. These can be a site of communicative struggle. These ignite participants' meanings along dimensions of separateness-connectedness, independence-dependence, strength-vulnerability. These dimensions are associated with the institution of marriage. These meanings are at times greatly magnified with the introduction of the themes family and children. They can carry strong economic and political overtones. All of this and more exhibit the degree to which communication creatively evokes locally based, historically grounded, cultural meaning systems.

This becomes all the more apparent when contrasting cultural systems. Elsewhere, for example, in Finland, personal names are not so highly expressive and charged, nor are they prominent sites of struggle, nor meaningful in the same ways, and so on. A different if somewhat related system of participant meanings is invoked when names are used in Finland, as elsewhere, when persons marry.

The example between Debbie and the older man and the Finnish example help demonstrate two further principles regarding communication and cultural meaning systems: communication patterns and their meanings are distinctive to cultural people and place; and thus, although general principles of communication may be identified across systems, any practice of communication, its shape and meanings, also varies from cultural system to cultural system. The concepts culture and cultural meaning system help foreground this type of variability in communication patterns.

While creatively invoking cultural meaning systems, communication also socially positions persons (through roles or identities) and creates relations among them (e.g., from egalitarian to hierarchical). In this way, communication is a prominent site for ordering *social life*. With the term *social* knowledge about communication is grounded in these commitments: to the situating of communication in actual contexts; to the interactional dynamics (or social negotiation or conjoint activities) through which identities and relations are constituted; and to the local, moment-to-moment occasions that motivate them. The concept social thus helps ground cultural meaning systems in the specific scenes of social life, its specific interactions, occasions, and events.

As mentioned earlier, this philosophy of communication motivates a philosophy of inquiry that is "close to the social ground." It suggests these questions, How are identities and social relations interactionally accomplished? How are they organized into human institutions such as education, the arts, law, religion, or sciences? How are communication practices played out among participants on different occasions? What precipitates the performance? What are the social workings of institutional life? For example, when Debbie contested the form of last name used by the older man, the interactional dynamics displayed specific identities and relations among those in the exchange (i.e., saying something about those present, Debbie, the man, and how they were, in the moment, related). The exchange moreover carried significance beyond these participants. It said something also more general, to those who share some understanding of the system, about those who promote, or deny, each alternate form of naming. This further implicates models of those who promote or use each type and casts relations between these in particular ways. The drama of this occasion plays the present identities, relations, and institutions in a particular way for Debbie and the retired teacher, but what is communicated is also partly a cultural story, about men and women, young and elderly, and what it means to be married and to be a person in today's modern world. Identities and relations are thus socially grounded, for they are constantly subjected to an interactive and occasioned process, with repercussions of these being felt not only in, but beyond the present occasion. This demonstrates the social and cultural foundations of communication.

Communication Is Constitutive of Part of Socio-Cultural Life

There is a way of acting, interpreting, and reflecting that is communicational and this way constitutes part of social and cultural life. Particular case studies of communication from around the world demonstrate just how this is so, with the means and meanings of communication being forceful relationally (Carbaugh, 1988c; Katriel and Philipsen, 1981), politically (e.g., Brenneis and Myers, 1984; Huspek and Kendall, 1991; Philipsen, 1992), religiously (Bauman, 1970, 1983), environmentally (Carbaugh, 1992), racially (Kochman, 1981), ethnically (Katriel, 1986), sexually (Goodwin, 1990; Sherzer, 1987; Tannen, 1990), to sample just a few of the studies. Like the particular moment between Debbie and the older man, communication has been shown the world over to be forceful in giving fundamental form and meaning to socio-cultural life. Upon this role of communication, as constituting a basic part of social life, as structuring ways of living, ethnographers build their studies (Hymes, 1972; Sapir, 1931).

Yet, certainly there is more to life than we on occasion communicate. Species biologies, the workings of the physical environment, human psychologies, spiritual forces, such processes and others are, perhaps, on occasion, formative parts of social life. Yet, we cannot and do not say all that we know about all such processes on any particular occasion. But we do, on some occasion, say something of each. What we actually say on occasion, how it is put and what it means, this practice of communication and the system it implies—this is partly constitutive of social life, and it is this that we draw attention to when ethnographers study communication.

This is a potentially thorny issue, because it is obviously possible and sometimes productive to argue that all that is socially efficacious and commonly meaningful falls within the purview of communication, and thus communication is constitutive of all of social life. Yet, these two accents on "the constitutive" role of communication do not have to conflict or breed paradox. The one point, the first, is a point of actuality: simply, that persons indeed communicate, do so in particular ways on particular occasions, and by doing so can constitute a potent form of social life. Such patterns of actual use never exhaust the potential of any communication system nor do they say all there is to say about the various processes of social life. Neither do they construct, literally, the raw physical materials of living (although they do create a shared sense of such physical materials). Thus, communication is constitutive of part of social life.

The second point is a point of potentiality: simply, if something is to be socially efficacious, and commonly meaningful, it must be ably communicated. Such is arguably true, if not actualized on particular occasions. Further, there are parts of social life that are not fundamentally or typically communicative. Take for example some types of social organization that are demonstrated in some of the fascinating studies in ethnomethodology and conversation analysis. These kinds of studies, distinct from but complementing ethnographic studies, show that there are deep levels of social organization in human interaction that are not necessarily or routinely subjected to communication. For example, the ways we pause between utterances, take turns in conversation, or even hold our faces while walking alone in public are socially organized and culturally distinct, but they are not, typically, that is when social life proceeds as usual, sources of messages (Schegloff, 1972; Scollon and Scollon, 1981). Because parts of life as these are socially organized and culturally distinct and because these features are not necessarily communicative, it is a bit bold to declare that all social life falls within the realm of communication. Again, communication is constitutive of part of social life.

The basic philosophy guiding EC, then, holds that communication, when it occurs, exhibits some kind(s) of system or order; that in so doing it constitutes and creatively invokes, in the occasion, social organization and cultural meanings; that it does this in ways that vary from people to people and place to place; that its nature, functions, and structures vary from place to place, thus its patterns and systemic organization need to be discovered (described, interpreted) in each case. These provide the basic philosophical assumptions about communication that guide ethnographic inquiries into communication practices.

Ethnographic Claims About Communication

Philipsen's ethnographic field reports demonstrate how theoretical claims are made on two general levels: One kind of claim is about the way communication is organized in a place by a people. This claim is often of the form: X (the cultural practice of communication) is granted legitimacy (if X is a norm) or coherence (if X is a code) by participants in communication system Y (the speech situation or community). This is a claim about the qualities of a cultural *practice* of communication that actually occurs in a context. It is an "emic" kind of claim; that is, making the claim involves a description of the practice and an interpretation of what the practice means to those who participate with it, what it enables for them and what it constrains them from doing. This product of inquiry demonstrates how communication is being organized by a particular people and seeks to understand the meanings of that practice to those who produce it. For example, Teamster men enact the male role by speaking in symmetrical relations, but refrain from speaking in asymmetrical relations. This carries cultural meanings for Teamsters about maleness and organizes their social relations on a theme of solidarity (Philipsen, 1992). Such a claim is theoretical in that it identifies the general way, the patterned way, a people in a place constitute—conduct and interpret—their communicative lives.

A second kind of claim builds necessarily on the basic descriptive work about communication practices and identifies commonalities across these practices, often through comparative study. This enables more abstract claims or *principles* of communication to be formulated. This kind of claim is often of the following form: these cultural practices (CP$_1$, CP$_2$..., CP$_n$) suggest these general theoretical principles (P$_1$, P$_2$..., P$_n$) about this communication phenomenon (e.g., address terms, politeness, emotion expression). This kind of claim is more general than the previous ones, in that it identifies general principles, dimensions, or standards of communication that operate across cultural practices. For example, Braithwaite (1980, 1990a), drawing upon Basso's (1990a [1970]) earlier work and that of many others, has identified, across cultural uses and interpretations of silence, two universal warrants. Building upon her descriptive fieldwork in Colombia, Fitch (1991) explored the general dimensions operating in personal address. Another comparative work has identified across fifty cultural terms for *talk*, general ways in which communication is organized, when it is talked about, and the dimensions of cultural meanings implicated in such talk (Carbaugh, 1989). Claims such as these are theoretical and general, more "etic," or more abstract, in that they identify, across such communicative phenomena as silence, personal address, and terms for strategic action, general principles and parameters for organizing communication.

These provide examples of two general kinds of theoretical claims made by ethnographers, claims about cultural practices of communication and claims about general principles of communication. But how are these kinds of theoretical arguments generated? How do ethnographers create claims about cultural practices and more general principles of communication?

A Descriptive Theory Used to Generate Claims

These questions suggest that we think about the basic theoretical concept *perspective*, or *descriptive theory*, that is used by ethnographers to generate these claims. Ethnographers typically begin their studies by learning about and then subsequently using during fieldwork a theoretical framework or a conceptual system, a systematic way of asking about and thus analyzing communication practices. Among other uses, the framework provides, in principle, for adequate descriptions and interpretations or explanations of communication practices and is thus not surprisingly called a *descriptive framework*.

The descriptive theory informing most ethnography of communication research is based upon, or derives from Hymes's programmatic statement (1972). This formulation suggests that, to describe cultural practices and principles of communication, investigators organize their studies around one of various social units such as a speech community, a speech situation, communicative event, act, style, or general way of speaking. Chief among these concepts is the concept of *speech community*, an idea that grounds thinking about communication in a social group and the diverse resources being used by its members to constitute its patterns of social living.

EC studies use a schematic vocabulary of components for analyzing these social units. In other words, whether studying a speech community of Teamsters, a speech situation like the *Donahue Show*, a communicative event like a public conflict, acts of silence, or a style of directness, EC suggests a general strategy of analysis. The technical vocabulary guiding such analyses is nicely summarized with the SPEAKING mnemonic (*Situation* is the setting and scene; *Participants* are personalities, social positions, or statuses, relations; *Ends* are the goals and outcomes; *Acts* are the message content, form, sequences, dimensions, and types of illocutionary force; *Key* is the tone or mode; *Instrumentalities* are the channel, media; *Norms* are of interaction and interpretation; *Genre* are native and formal). Each italicized concept suggests a question about communication, such as, in what situation is it occurring? among what participants? toward what ends?

Over the life of an ethnographic study, the descriptive theory is used in different ways. It can be used as a way of describing communication in its contexts, thus serving as a theory for describing actual communication practices. It can be used also to interpret, where salient, the cultural status or participant view of each concept, thus serving as a theory for interpreting communication practices. For example, with regard to the *P* component, one might ask, how do participants characterize each other (and others) in the course of their social interactions? What do these acts of identification mean? Or, more generally, what is the norm for interpreting (*N*) this concept (e.g., *S, P, A*)? Further, the theory can be used to develop communicational explanations, as a theory for positing systematic relations among concepts. For example, in Philipsen's (1975) study of Teamsterville men, he found corelations between speaking (the *A*) and symmetrical relations (the *P*) and between not speaking (the *A*) and asymmetrical relations (the *P*). And finally, the theory can serve, as mentioned earlier, as a basis for comparative analyses (see Braithwaite, 1990a; Shailor, 1990). The theory thus has descriptive, interpretive, corelative, and comparative uses.

In addition to these specific uses, the schematic vocabulary of the theory suggests a holistic theoretical attitude with regard to the nature and functions of communication. For example, if one wanted to examine the force of "speech acts," one could do so by exploring the abstract dimensions and forces in speech that were formulated by John Searle (1969, 1990). If, however, one were designing such study from an ethno-communicative perspective, one would be led, by the descriptive theory, to explore and analyze the force of "speech acts" in communicative situations (e.g., the expression of gender inequality in an American speech community), thus focusing on the *A* part of the system within a social context (e.g., a particular social unit). Further, the vocabulary suggests that communicative acts occur as parts of scenes (*S*, *P*), within larger forms and sequences (*E*, *A*, *K*), through particular contents and domains of meaning (*A*, *N*), according to particular norms for conducting and interpreting conduct (*N*), with culturally targeted goals in mind (*E*). Each such component suggests something that is perhaps of relevance for understanding particular acts of speaking. Speech acts, from this theoretical view, may enact universal dimensions and types of expressive force, but they are conceptualized as something more. They are part of a socially negotiated, individually applied, culturally distinctive, and historically grounded expressive system. The schematic vocabulary, when used, invokes this theoretical attitude, with communication deemed not just generally, but particularly, as constitutive of socio-cultural life.

Consider similarly studies of the media and mass communication. One might want to study print media (e.g., newspapers, magazines) or electronic media (e.g., television). The descriptive theory in ethno-communication inquiry would suggest a conceptualization of these media (the *I* part of the framework) by exploring the various instruments (e.g., spoken words, visual images, singing, music, drumming) and channels being used (e.g., electronic, print). Further, an understanding of these would be grounded socially (e.g., within speech communities, events, situations) and further elaborated with attention to the role of particular media within configurations of participants, act sequences, particular genres, and so on. The media of communication would be conceptualized as part of social and cultural life. As a result, examinations of a particular mediated image out of its communicative context or beginning by generalizing across media productions without attention to particular mediated practices would violate a theoretical commitment of the ethnography of communication. The former, by abstracting images out of sequence, violates the communication of the image as a sequential and sociocultural force. The latter, by generalizing across media productions, fails to penetrate the particular sociocultural practice of each.

The two examples of a theoretical attitude help make the following points about the roles of descriptive theory within ethnography of communication research. (1) Ethnography of communication provides a basic philosophy and theory of communication, not merely a method for studying communication. (2) The theory generates particular claims about cultural practices of communication as well as general principles about communication. (3) The claims are generated through a perspective that focuses analysis upon particular social units and analyzes those units through particular components. (4) Particular studies of communication, descriptions and interpretations of unique config-urations of communicative practices, their affordances and limitations, are designed with the full conceptual framework in mind. Note, then, that the descriptive theory has of necessity many uses, including (1) suggested concep-tualizations of particular research problems (e.g., speech acts, personal address, media) (Philipsen, 1993; see also Carbaugh and Hastings, 1992), and (2) a sug-gested methodological design of research (Philipsen, 1977), (3) which yields local or domain theories of communication (Cushntan and Pearce, 1977; Philipsen, 1992) and (4) provides bases for more abstract theoretical claims, across cultural patterns, through comparative studies (Braithwaite, 1990a). Because of the nature and various uses of descriptive theory in ethnography of communication research, it assumes a prominent and indispensable part of this research program.

Some Recent Developments in the Research Program

Recent surveys of the ethnography of communication provide summaries of what it has accomplished since its inception. In various forms, these writings include programmatic statements (Philipsen, 1989a, 1993), schematic reviews (Bauman and Sherzer, 1975, 1990), critical reviews (Sherzer, 1977), and a bibliography of fieldwork (Philipsen and Carbaugh, 1986). Interested readers will want to survey this recent work if interested in the full range of activities involved in the research program. Here, I will focus on the developments of EC. I will give special attention to three recent developments: cultural com-munication theory, a communication theory of culture, and a cultural interpretive theory. These do not exhaust the contributions of this body of work and are thus selective, but they are nonetheless illustrative of some extensions of the program that some communication scholars have made.

Philipsen's Cultural Communication Theory

In 1987, Gerry Philipsen wrote an essay titled, "The Prospect for Cultural Communication." A longer version of the essay had been presented in 1980 at a conference in Yugoslavia on communication theory. Both versions stimulated considerable thinking and research about communication from a cultural perspective. Its main contributions were to advance a dialectical base for the study of communication systems, to foreground the communal function in some communication practices, to stipulate three cultural forms of communication, and later (Philipsen, 1992) to add the concept of speech codes.

Philipsen opens the 1987 essay with an assumption about a *basic dialectic* that grounds communication systems (1987, p. 245): "Every people manages somehow to deal with the inevitable tension between the impulse of individuals to be free and the constraints of communal life. . . . Locating a culture on this axis reveals a partial truth about it, a kind of cultural snapshot, but in order to perceive the culture fully, one must also know the culture's direction of movement along the axis and the relative strengths of the competing forces pushing it one way or another." Presumably, cultural communicative systems generally, and patterns for communicating particularly, elaborate some points on this dimension as the "dominant themes and warrants for human thought, speech, and action" (p. 245).

This formulation is highly suggestive. Suggested are a range of cultural communication systems from those that expressively elaborate "individual impulses" to those that elaborate "communal constraints." Note that the suggestion is of a dialectic not a dichotomy, so features of each are presumably parts of every system, even if elaborated differently. Suggested moreover are scenes or styles of communication within cultural systems that play more one way than the other, or play one way against another (see Philipsen, 1992, pp. 43–61). Suggested also is a kind of grand balancing between individual impulses and communal constraints, with hyperamplifications in one direction (e.g., of communal constraints) precipitating corrective actions in the other (e.g., of individual impulses). Recent events in Eastern Europe and the former Soviet Union provide fertile soil for applying this dynamic. The basic idea is this: a dialectical play is at the base of communication systems, with a "healthy balance [being sought] between the forces of individualism and community" (p. 249).

Some recent studies have been designed that are cognizant of and partly conceptualized on the basis of this basic dialectic (e.g., Carbaugh, 1988a, 1988b; Katriel, 1986, 1991). Another study was designed to investigate this dialectic, including its cross-cultural utility (Carbaugh, 1988–1989).

A second contribution has been to posit the existence, in speech communities, of a *communal function.* How do people constitute communal identities with their communication? The communal function draws attention to this process, to the creation and affirmation of "a sense of shared identity which nonetheless preserves individual dignity, freedom, and creativity" (Philipsen, 1987, p. 249). Or, put slightly differently, the communal function identifies "communication as a means for linking individuals into communities of shared identity" (Philipsen, 1989b, p. 79). This communicative accomplishment is enacted through various communicative forms, with each coordinating social actions and expressing common meanings. Such forms may treat individuality, or constraint thematically or both together, yet, in so doing, link people together as participants who share membership in a social group.[2]

Philipsen (1987) argued that there are three generic *cultural forms* that can serve as interpretive devices for analyzing the various ways in which the communal function is communicated: ritual, myth, and social drama. Ritual provides a structuring to communicative sequences such that the sequence, when conducted correctly, celebrates a sacred object (see also Philipsen, 1992, 1993). Several studies of communication rituals have been produced (Carbaugh, 1988a, 1988b, 1993; Katriel, 1990; Katriel and Philipsen, 1981), and the concept is the central organizing concern in Katriel's (1991) monograph. Myth provides communally potent narrative resources that an individual can use to "dignify and give coherence to" life (Philipsen, 1987, p. 252). As personal stories uniquely appropriate cultural narratives, as young children confess in the style of George Washington, such events can sometimes reach mythic proportions (see Philipsen, 1992, pp. 87–98). The third form, the social drama, drawn from the work of Victor Turner, is a processual form in four phases through which cultural codes are violated, negotiated and revised, or reasserted.

The theoretical importance of identifying a range of cultural communicative forms is significant. It suggests variability in the ways the cultural function is woven into communicative action, but also some generic cultural forms that hold considerable force in many communicative systems. As other forms are identified, further advances will be made in the ways culture animates communication. But further, the inclusion of multiple forms suggests a holistic, natural, and comparative theoretical attitude, as previously: to know a form is to know how it plays out in particular places and how it plays out differently than the other forms within that community (or differently from the same form as it is used in other contexts of a community). Thus, cultural forms of communication help provide heuristic tools from which to identify particular communicative practices and identify the diverse ways the communal function of communication is socially practiced (see especially Philipsen, 1993).

The concept *speech codes* helps elaborate the basic premises that communication is fundamentally a socio-cultural practice and partly constitutive of socio-cultural life. With regard to speaking, Philipsen (1992, p. 136) puts the basic idea this way: "Speaking is inextricably speaking culturally. . . . [It] is a radically cultural medium of human communication." Attending to speech codes helps ethnographers of communication identify a corelation between culture and speaking, such that (1) a distinctive culture carries with it (minimally) a distinctive speech code; (2) a distinctive speech code implicates models for personhood, society, and strategic action; (3) the cultural significance of communication depends partly upon interpretations of these spoken implications (of personhood, society, and strategic action); and (4) such "codes are inextricably woven into speaking" (1992, p. 136). These basic principles of speech codes are built upon careful fieldwork into the two codes of dignity and honor that carry cultural force among the Nacirema and Teamsters (Philipsen, 1992). Related work has described and interpreted similar speech codes as they are used in televised talk (Carbaugh, 1988c) and in intercultural encounters (Carbaugh, 1993, 1994).

The theoretical developments summarized here thus add to the ethnography of communication a basic critical dialectic, a communal function, three generic cultural forms of communication, and the concept of speech codes. Readers interested in these developments will want to consult the studies already cited for the more detailed field based demonstrations and explications of these developments.

Some Elements in a Communication Theory of Culture and Society

Two concepts of particular concern to ethnographers of communication are evident: the ways communication helps constitute *culture* and *society*. These two concepts are conceptualized uniquely and often implicitly by ethnographers. What, then, do ethnographers suggest as elements in a communication theory of culture or society? How can one integrate into communication theory models of culture and society? This of course is a very demanding and often neglected question, and one that requires more space than allotted here. What I can do, however, is briefly sketch ways the program already discussed is responsive to the question, referring the reader to other works that treat the topic at greater length, then hope such a brief discussion provides stimuli for subsequent inquiry.

With regard to the communication of *culture*, attention is drawn to certain basic elemental ingredients in the communication process: symbols, symbolic forms, their patterned use and interpretations. The concepts of *symbols* and *forms* draw attention to the basic materials, or vehicles, of expression in for example a speech situation. The intent is to include all of the possible linguistic and nonlinguistic material of messages that hold force somewhere, whether these are verbal, nonverbal, or visual and whether these are believed to be produced by humans, animals, or trees (see Crawford, 1992). Building upon earlier ethnographic work, these concepts help ground studies in the basic materials of expression (see e.g., Basso, 1990; Geertz, 1973; Schneider, 1976). *Patterned use* refers to the shape of symbols and symbolic forms and the ways these are employed on particular occasions by participants. *Interpretations* refer to the mutually intelligible beliefs or premises and values that are widely accessible to participants, deeply felt by them, and are thus associated with these expressions on the particular occasions (Philipsen, 1992). The communication of culture thus has something to do with the patterned use and interpretation of symbols and symbolic forms on particular social occasions (Carbaugh, 1988a, 1990b).

A communication theory of culture further sees that symbols and their meanings are not floating freely but are of course culturally accessible, historically grounded, socially occasioned, and individually applied (Carbaugh, 1991; Philipsen, 1992, pp. 7ff). This implies that some communicative dynamics, like some patterns distinctive to a particular dyad, are not cultural, in that they are not widely accessible, nor are they transmitted historically. For a pattern or practice to be culturally forceful, its expressive force would be felt deeply and accessible as part of a historically transmitted, communal conversation (Carbaugh, 1988a, 1988b).

Sometimes the concept of system is used to discuss cultural communication. The theoretical point made with this concept is that a patterned use and interpretation of a symbol is only one part of a larger "galaxy"—to use Schneider's (1976) term—of situations and expressions. To conceptualize culture, then, as a system of expression, is to emphasize that one explores how a symbol or form (like the choice of last name upon marriage) functions within a larger communicative situation; what the symbol or symbolic form is like and unlike in this system; on what various occasions it is used and to what ends; what are its limits of expression; and what ideas and ideologies go along with it or are refracted by it?

A communication theory of culture thus is erected upon the concepts of symbols, symbolic forms, social uses, and meanings, and the theory builds an idea of culture as a historically grounded, socially negotiated, and individually applied system of meaningful expression.

Some basic elements in a communication theory of *society* add to this, the concepts, norms or rules for action, social positions and relations, and institutions (Schneider, 1976). A communication or discursive theory of norms involves hearing norms more as symbolic expressions that actors' can use to evaluate, justify, or explain conduct (see Philipsen, 1989a, pp. 263–265; also Carbaugh, 1990a, pp. 7–9; Hall, 1988–1989). These are the communicative resources that are used to state the ways one should or should not act, to argue what is good in deed. How one can justifiably act, whether one can ably do so, and whether one can justify one's acts—all of this and more creates the basic social materials regarding one's rights and obligations as an actor. Processes as these exhibit the communication of norms.

Other elements in the communication of society are the creation, reaffirmation, or negotiation of social positions (e.g., male, female, boss, employee) and the resulting relations created among participants (e.g., egalitarian, hierarchical). As communication occurs, identities and relations among participants are being managed (Carbaugh, 1994). Furthermore, the concept institution suggests that certain symbols and their meanings, along with a particular system of rules, social positions, and relations, have become fairly robust. The communication of social institution thus implies a complex theoretical claim: that particular symbols, forms, and meanings are operative; that these are justifiable through a normative rule system; that this system of justification, or legitimation, solidifies certain positions for participants and certain relations among participants; and that this configuration is robust socially, relatively durable, and stable.

Taken together, then, these elements provide some elemental and basic concepts for constructing a communication theory of culture and society. Certainly, much further work is to be done, especially fieldwork, with these heuristic concepts at hand.

Interpretive Theory: Cultural Structures in Communication

A large body of ethnographic fieldwork has shown that three cultural structures are prominent in the conduct and interpretation of communication (see Carbaugh, 1989). These three are part of the speech code concept and are models of personhood, society, and strategic action. In other words, as people communicate, they employ symbols and meanings that explicate, or implicate, messages about persons, societal life, and strategic action. Let us examine each in turn.

In his studies of Teamsterville (1992), Philipsen discovered a system of symbolic expressions that constituted, in that community, a proper kind of person, a "man." Wieder and Pratt (1990) have described ways Osage communicate to be recognized as a "real Indian." Similarly, Fitch (1991) described how Colombian ways of addressing each other through terms that derive from *madre* (mother) create a cultural persona of mother and structure social relations in their use. Katriel (1986) described the communicative enactment of the Sabra Jew through a style of straight talk, or "dugri speech." Other studies have described how the person in middle America is symbolized as "an individual" who "has rights" and "makes choices" (Carbaugh, 1988c, 1994). These studies suggest that prominent among the symbols and symbolic forms used for communication are terms and meanings that identify persons, or kinds of persons, as social agents in society. The person one is, and what can and should be done by such, these provide basic materials for the conduct and interpretation of communication.

A second prominent structural feature is the way social relations, and perhaps human institutions, are culturally coded into the communication process. For example, as workers in one television station communicated with each other, they discussed themselves as "three completely different types." Part of the sense of this saying was that "the types" were arranged hierarchically and this hierarchical arrangement was the source of considerable tension (Carbaugh, 1988b). Similar communicative dynamics, although conducted in their own distinctive ways, are found to create solidarity among vets (Braithwaite, 1990b), gender relations among Colombians (Fitch, 1991), and egalitarian relations among Appalachians (Ray, 1987) or among others (see Brenneis and Myers, 1984). What the fieldwork suggests about communication is that the social position(s) one holds (or addresses), the ways it is related to others, the nature of these relations, and their possible solidification as an institutional form provide basic materials for the conduct and interpretation of communication.

A third prominent structure is the way conduct itself is culturally coded into the communication process. In other words, wherever people communicate, they can and do identify some of their cultural communicative actions with their own words. For example, Israelis identify one of their cultural forms of action with the term *griping* (Katriel, 1990). Americans identify certain communicative actions as "communication" and "chit-chat" (Katriel and Philipsen, 1981; Philipsen, 1992), and related others as "being honest" and "sharing" (Carbaugh, 1988c). Appalachians identify a form of action they call "huddling" (Ray, 1987). Such terms identify local forms of strategic action and are readily apparent in ethnographic studies of communication. A comparative study of fifty such terms identified in them messages about persons, society, and strategic action (Carbaugh, 1989). This fieldwork suggests that the kind of action that can and is being done, the actional force it holds for those present—these provide basic materials for the conduct and interpretation of communication.

Taken together, then, the following theoretical principles are operative in this recent ethnography of communication research and could thus be explicitly, if tentatively, formulated:

1. When there is a culture, three cultural structures are prominent in the communication.
2. The cultural structures are the symbols, symbolic forms, and meanings that identify ways of being a person, ways of being organized socially, and ways of conducting action.
3. These cultural structures provide material vehicles for the conduct of communication and general principles for the interpretation of communication.

The third principle needs further clarification. The fieldwork literature suggests two operations of the principle. First, that people on occasions will use symbols and forms that, for example, explicitly identify persons (e.g., personal names) and kinds of persons (e.g., "mother," "worker"). Second, that regardless of the explicit content of the communication, for example, whether it is about persons (social organization, strategic action) or not, it will still nonetheless convey something by way of a message about persons, social organization, or strategic action. This point suggests prominent interpretive domains that can be heard in cultural communication practices and that, when understood, create a kind of ongoing metacommunicative commentary in such practices—about persons, social relations, and strategic action. Such is amply demonstrated in recent fieldwork reports such as those just mentioned, among others (e.g., Baxter and Goldsmith, 1990; Harre, 1991; Scollon, 1992). Similar dimensions are evident in related theoretical work (Sigman, 1987). Being able to hear this ongoing commentary, amplifying its voice, and further refining this proposed theoretical model of cultural interpretation, this is a task for future ethnographic inquiries into communication (see Carbaugh, 1989, 1990b).

Particular Applications of EC to the Communication Field

The ethnographic approach to communication outlined here has addressed several concerns prominent in the field of communication. For example, explorations in interpersonal communication often ask questions about how identities and personal relationships are created and negotiated (e.g., Cushman and Cahn, 1985). Recent ethnographic work has addressed just these questions with special attention to the ways popular discourse creates models for identity and social relations (see Carbaugh, 1988c; Katriel, 1991; Katriel and Philipsen, 1981). A detailed ethnographic look at ways Osage Indians communicate their identity has also been produced (Wieder and Pratt, 1990). The relationship between the general ethnographic theory of interpersonal communication and others within the field of communication has been discussed (Carbaugh, 1988c, pp. 115–120; Carbaugh and Hastings, 1992), and a theory of identity and social relations that derives from this ethnographic approach has been proposed (Carbaugh, 1994).

Explorations into organizational communication often ask questions about how participants organize themselves to produce a product or service. Recent ethnographic work has examined these processes in a veterans organization (Braithwaite, 1990b) and in a television station (Carbaugh, 1988b). A descriptive framework for conducting such ethnographic work into organizational communication, deriving from Philipsen's 1980 essay, has also been proposed and used (Carbaugh, 1985).

Ethnographic work into political communication has been quite extensive. As Bauman and Sherzer (1990, p. xii) remark: "one of the most fully and richly developed lines of comparative inquiry generated by the ethnography of speaking concerns the nature, forms, functions, and situational contexts of use of political language." They go on to summarize much of that work. In the communication field, such work has also been conducted, drawing attention to the constitution of a "political voice" among blue collar workers (Huspek and Kendal, 1991), to different cultural orientations being used in the conduct of political dramas (Philipsen, 1992, pp. 43–61; Carbaugh, 1992), to the political implications of educational radio designed for children (Katriel, 1991), and to the political grounding of prominent features of an American cultural identity (Carbaugh, 1988c, pp. 21–59). Works as these explore how issues of empowerment and the wielding and distribution of material and symbolic resources are prominent in some cultural communication practices and rich sites for ethnographic study.

Several recent fieldwork studies of intercultural and cross-cultural communication have been collected into a recent volume (Carbaugh, 1990a).

Of particular concern in studies of intercultural communication are the sources of difficulty when one cultural communication system contacts another. With these concerns in mind, Griefat and Katriel (1989) have described how an Arab interactional style of "musayara," which focuses on harmonious relations, differs dramatically from an Israeli style of "dugri," consisting as it does of direct, contentious, even face-threatening utterances. Carbaugh (1993) investigated Russian and American interactional styles used on a single occasion and found Russians foregrounding issues of virtue and collective sentiment, with an American style foregrounding matters of fact and personal disclosure. Recent cross-cultural work has explored communicative silence and universal warrants for its use and interpretation (Braithwaite, 1990a). Leeds-Hurwitz (1990) has also given useful historical perspective to intercultural communication as a field of study.

Studies of mass communication often presume some connection between the media of communication and the culture or society in which the media are used. Foremost in this discussion is the force of television as a communicative channel and its relation to audiences. Some recent ethnographic work has been responsive to this concern, suggesting that some cultural terms, meanings, metaphors, and forms that are prevalent in the social life of a society are also prominent and exploited in some televised forms (Katriel and Philipsen, 1981). Later studies have shown similarly, how mass media can be studied in a way that integrates and perhaps amplifies certain cultural features (Carbaugh, 1988c, 1988–1989). On other occasions, a "spacebridge" television event staged a clash between dramatically different cultural styles of expression (Carbaugh, 1993). Ways media and channels of communication are parts of cultural systems, the different premises assigned to each such media and channel, ways single programs or media episodes get played differently into different cultural systems—these issues and more provide fertile grounds for future ethnographic work.

And finally, a most recent focus of some studies has been the relationship between language, a sense of place, and landscape. Earlier work by Basso (1990) has been followed by others who have examined stories that socially constitute a sense of place (Katriel, 1993; Katriel and Shenhar, 1990), and the different communication codes of economics and ecologics animating a land-use controversy (Carbaugh, 1992). The relationship among culture, communication, and nature is just beginning to be addressed (see, e.g., Cantrill and Oravec, 1992; Carbaugh, 1996).

Even though much ongoing work cannot be summarized or mentioned here, I hope this brief review gives some idea of the breadth of concerns addressed in some recent ethnographic work and the considerable promise it holds for future studies into human communication.

Critical Reflection, by Way of Concluding

As is evident in the variety of work mentioned here, the ethnography of communication is just now being incorporated into many corners of the communication field. Although there are only a few practitioners of the program in communication studies, their contributions evidence a concern for developing communication theory in a way that embraces local forms and the meanings that participants deem significant and important when using these forms. Theorized from this view then, by these practitioners, are the particulars of contexts and conduct of communication, as well as its general principles.

The ethnographic program however has of course not achieved everything. It has limitations and gaps that will require additional work. For example, the limitations in some existing work demonstrate the necessity of focusing rigorously upon social interaction itself, rather than relying only upon reports about it. In other words, we need studies that take observational data as seriously as interview data. This focus is especially crucial in studies of intercultural encounters, single communicative occasions in which multiple cultural orientations are being used. There is very little work in this area and much work to be done. The paucity of studies that examine actual intercultural encounters shows the considerable demands of such study. One needs a robust enough theoretical framework to embrace cultural particularity and variability. Such a framework must be nimble enough to be applied to naturally occurring social interaction, to come to grips with the unique configurations of one cultural system, then the other (and perhaps others) to unravel the interactional dynamic between these systems, to interpret the social relation created in the interaction between each, and to do so from the vantage point of each cultural orientation. Such study, or what quickly becomes a series of such studies, taxes the best theories available to us, especially if done in a culturally sensitive but theoretically rigorous way.

Related to the focus on intercultural encounters are the issues raised between the concepts of difference and dominance. Some presume that understanding a difference (cultural or otherwise) is a positive step toward harmonious relations. For example, by understanding Swedes better, Finns will like them more, or be more willing to cooperate with them, or at least better able to coordinate their actions with them (if not cooperatively). Or, by understanding Teamsters better, liberal Americans will somehow better deal with this difference (Philipsen, 1992). It is often presumed that a more harmonious world will result from this kind of knowledge. This might be the outcome sometimes, even most of the time, but it is not necessary as an outcome. It is at least possible that a better understanding of an Other leaves one predisposed to like that Other less, even better equipped to refute, refuse, or defeat that Other! So, knowledge about the difference of an Other does not *necessarily* create a better relation between Self and Other (as some divorce counseling has shown). How a better understanding of cultural difference influences subsequent interaction between those who are different is then a question to ask, rather than a panacea to presume. Questions of social relations thus become central as we explore what socio-cultural consequences—be they relations of dominance and subordination, or egalitarian, or some combination—are created by a better understanding of cultural difference. The various ways these dynamics are interactionally accomplished are not yet adequately addressed, nor understood, in an ethnographically informed way. Such work does not require an entirely different kind of study from that reviewed here, only a creative extension of some of the work already done.

Some work is being done to address these issues. Ethnographic field studies that investigate cultural differences in single encounters have been conducted (e.g., Philipsen, 1986; Carbaugh, 1993). Additionally, studies have been conducted that explore political differences in communication, including a working class political vocabulary (Huspek and Kendall, 1991) and the "dueling depictions" that occur between environmentalists and developers (Carbaugh, 1992). In the wake of these and other studies that explore similar dynamics (Carbaugh 1988c, 1988-1989), a theory of dueling structures has been proposed (Huspek, 1993). Emerging from such work is a useful extension of EC and CC into the dynamics of difference and dominance. Whether the most recent work is called *critical hermeneutics* or *cultural pragmatics* matters less than that it gets done, for we need to cultivate a critical reflection about these important concerns in our inquiries (see for example the forum on Ethnography and Critique in *Research on Language and Social Interaction*, 1989–1990).

Other future ethnographic work may want to explore the frequency or distribution of some of the cultural practices identified in some of the preceding studies. For example, perhaps the belief that open, supportive communication is good is held more by women than men, more by those of upper than lower classes. Or ideas of what such communication is might vary. This could be studied. Even though studies identified this communication pattern and value, they did not trace its frequency of use across sample populations. Similarly, other such patterns that have been ethnographically described, could be so studied. But such study of frequencies and distributions rely upon the basic qualitative work reported here and thus would not supplant this earlier work but nicely complement it in interesting ways.

A further dynamic not well integrated into ethnographic studies is a kind of dialectical play between various dimensions, such as novelty and conventionality, uniqueness and stability, change and permanence, as well as the temporal playing of past, present, and future. Some studies have made efforts to integrate such dialectical tensions, but many of the more prominent ethnographic studies play the forces of the latter over the former (see Carbaugh, 1990b).

Focusing on particular interactions, demonstrating how culture is in communicative action, there, as in the exchange between Debbie Miller and the retired teacher discussed earlier in this chapter, should help future ethnographers address some of these limitations and gaps in the existing literature. Although much has been done, theoretically, empirically, interpretively, and comparatively, there is still much work to be done, with many ethnographic threads yet to be woven into the fabric of communication theory.

Notes

1. These starting points reflect the assumptions explicated by Dell Hymes (1962) in his seminal essay on the ethnography of speaking. The program of study he evnisioned has produced a large body of work including the early anthologies of Gumperz and Hymes (1972) and Bauman and Sherzer (1990 [1974]) and more recent ones (Brenneis and Myers, 1984; Carbaudh, 1990a). The anthologies and a bibliography of published fieldwork in the ethnography of communication (Philipsen and Carbaugh, 1986) evidence the considerable work motivated by, and empirically demonstrate the assumptive bases formulated earlier by Hymes, and discussed here.

2. See Philipsen (1989b) for a review of "the communal function in four cultures."

References

Basso, K. (1979). *Portraits of "the whiteman"*: Linguistic play and cultural symbols among the western Apache.* Cambridge: Cambridge University Press.

——— (1990a). To give up on words: Silence in western Apache culture. In D. Carbaugh (Ed.), *Cultural communication and intercultural contact* (pp. 303–320). Hillsdale: Lawrence Eribaum. Originally published 1970.

——— (1990). Western Apache language and culture: Essays in linguistic anthropology. Tucson: University of Arizona Press.

Bauman, R. (1970). "Aspects of seventeenth century Quaker rhetoric." *Quarterly Journal of Speech* 56: 67–74.

——— (1983). *Let your words be few: Symbolism of speaking and silence among seventeenth century Quakers.* Cambridge: Cambridge University Press.

——— (1992). *Folklore, cultural performance, and popular entertainment: A communications centered handbook.* Oxford: Oxford University Press.

——— and Sherzer, J. (1975). "The ethnography of speaking." *Annual Review in Anthropology* 4: 95–119.

———— and Sherzer, J. (Eds.) (1990). *Explorations in the ethnography of speaking*, 2d ed. Cambridge: Cambridge University Press. Originally published 1974.

Baxter, L., and Goldsmith, D. (1990). "Cultural terms for communication events among some American high school adolescents." *Western Journal of Speech Communication* 54: 377–394.

Braithwaite, C. (1980). "Cultural uses and interpretations of silence." MA thesis, Department of Speech Communication, University of Washington.

———— (1990a). "Communicative silence: A cross-cultural study of Basso's hypothesis." In D. Carhaugh (Ed.), *Cultural communication and intercultural contact*, pp. 321–327. Hillsdale, N.J.: Lawrence Erlbaum and Associates.

———— (1990b). "Cultural communication among Vietnam veterans: Ritual, myth, and social drama." In R. Morris and P. Ehrenhaus (Eds.), *The cultural legacy of Vietnam*, pp. 145–170. Norwood, N.J.: Ablex.

Brenneis, D., and Myers, F. (Eds.) (1984). *Dangerous words: Language and politics in the Pacific*. New York: New York University Press.

Cantrill, J., and Oravec, C. (Eds.) (1992). *The conference on the discourse of environmental advocacy*. Salt Lake City: University of Utah Humanities Center.

Carbaugh, D. (1985). "Cultural communication and organizing." *International and Intercultural Communication Annual* 8: 30–47.

———— (1988a). "Comments on 'culture' in communication inquiry." *Communication Reports* 1: 38–41.

———— (1988b). "Cultural terms and tensions in the speech of a television station." *Western Journal of Speech Communication* 52: 216–237.

———— (1988c). *Talking American*. Norwood, N.J.: Ablex.

———— (1988–1989). "Deep agony: 'Self' vs. 'society' in Donahue discourse." *Research on Language and Social Interaction* 22: 179–212.

———— (1989). "Fifty terms for talk: A cross-cultural study." *International and Intercultural Communication Annual* 13: 93–120.

———— (Ed.) (1990a). *Cultural communication and intercultural contact*. Hillsdale, N.J.: Lawrence Erlbaum and Associates.

———— (1990b). "Toward a perspective on cultural communication and intercultural contact." *Semiotica* 80: 15–35.

———— (1991). "Communication and cultural interpretation." *Quarterly Journal of Speech* 77: 336–342.

———— (1992). " 'The mountain' and 'the project': Dueling depictions of a natural environment." In J. Cantrill and C. Oravec (Eds.), *Conference on the discourse of environmental advocacy*, pp. 360–376. Salt Lake City: University of Utah Humanities Center.

———— (1993). " 'Soul' and 'self': Soviet and American cultures in conversation." *Quarterly Journal of Speech* 79: 182–200.

———— (1994). "Personhood, positioning, and cultural pragmatics: American dignity in cross-cultural perspective." In S. Deetz (Ed.), *Communication Yearbook 17*, pp. 159–186. Newbury Park, Calif.: Sage Publications.

———— (1996). *Situating selves*. Albany: State University of New York Press.

———— and Hastings, S. O. (1992). "A role for communication theory in ethnography and cultural analysis." *Communication Theory* 2: 156–165.

Chen, V. (1990–1991). " 'Mien tze' at the Chinese dinner table: A study of the interactional accomplishment of face." *Research on Language and Social Interaction* 24: 109–140.

Conquergood, D. (1991). "Rethinking ethnography: Toward a critical cultural politics." *Communication Monographs* 58: 179–194.

Crawford, L. (1992). "Speaking with trees: A Taoist view of environmental discourse." In J. Cantrill and C. Oravec (Eds.), *Conference on the Discourse of Environmental Advocacy*. Salt Lake City: University of Utah Humanities Center.

Cushman, D., and Cahn, D. (1985). *Communication in interpersonal relationships*. Albany: State University of New York Press.

Cushman, D., and Pearce, W. B. (1977). "Generality and necessity in three types of communication theory with special attention to rules theory." *Human Communication Research* 3: 344–353.

———— (1989/90). "Ethnography and critique." Special Section in *Research on Language and Social Interaction* 23: 243–328.

Fitch, K. (1991). "The interplay of linguistic universals and cultural knowledge in personal address: Colombian *Madre* terms." *Communication Monographs* 58: 254–272.

Garrett, M. (1993). "Wit, power, and oppositional groups: A case study of 'pure talk'." *Quarterly Journal of Speech* 79: 303–318.

Geertz, C. (1973). *The interpretation of cultures*. New York: Basic Books.

Goodwin, M. H. (1990). *He-said-she-said: Talk as social organization among black children*. Bloomington: Indiana University Press.

Griefat, Y., and Katriel, T. (1989). "Life demands 'musayra': Communication and culture among Arabs in Israel." *International and Intercultural Communication Annual* 13: 121–138.

Gumperz, J., and Hymes, D. (Eds.). (1972). *Directions in sociolinguistics: The ethnography of communication*. New York: Holt, Rinehart and Winston.

Hall, B. J. (1988-1989). "Norms, action, and alignment: A discursive perspective." *Research on Language and Social Interaction* 22: 23-44.

Harre, R. (1991). "The discursive production of selves." *Theory and Psychology* 1: 51-63.

Huspek, M. (1993). "Dueling structures: The theory of resistance in discourse." *Communication Theory* 3: 1-25.

———— and Kendall, K. (1991). "On withholding political voice: An analysis of the political vocabulary of a non-political speech community." *Quarterly Journal of Speech* 77: 1-19.

Hymes, D. (1962). "The ethnography of speaking." In T. Gladwin and W. Sturtevant (Eds.), *Anthropology and human behavior*, pp. 13-53. Washington, D.C.: Anthropological Society of Washington.

———— (1972). "Models of the interaction of language and social life." In J. Gumperz and D. Hymes (Eds.), *Directions in sociolinguistics: The ethnography of communication*, pp. 35-71. New York: Holt, Rinehart and Winston.

Katriel, T. (1986). *Talking straight: "Dugri" speech in Israeli Sabra culture*. Cambridge: Cambridge University Press.

———— (1990). " 'Griping' as a verbal ritual in some Israeli discourse." In D. Carbaugh (Ed.), *Cultural communication and intercultural contact* pp. 99-113. Hillsdale, N.J.: Lawrence Erlbaum and Associates.

———— (1991). *Communal webs: Communication and culture in contemporary Israeli society*. Albany: State University of New York Press.

———— (1993). " 'Our future is where our past is': Studying heritage museums as ideological and performative arenas." *Communication Monographs* 60: 69-75.

———— and Philipsen, G. (1981). " 'What we need is communication': 'Communication' as a cultural category in some American speech." *Communication Monographs* 48: 301-317.

———— and Shenhar. (1990). " 'Tower and stockade': Dialogic narration in Israeli settlement ethos." *Quarterly Journal of Speech* 70: 359-380.

Kochman, T. (1981). *Black and white styles in conflict*. Chicago: University of Chicago Press.

Leeds-Hurwitz, W. (1990). "Culture and communication: A review essay." *Quarterly Journal of Speech* 76: 85-96.

Philipsen, G. (1975). "Speaking 'like a man' in Teamsterville: Culture patterns of role enactment in an urban neighborhood." *Quarterly Journal of Speech* 61: 13-22.

———— (1976). "Places for speaking in Teamsterville." *Quarterly Journal of Speech* 62: 15–25.

———— (1977). "Linearity of research design in ethnographic studies of speaking." *Communication Quarterly* 25: 52–50.

———— (1986). "Mayor Daley's council speech: A cultural analysis." *Quarterly Journal of Speech* 72: 247–260.

———— (1987). "The prospect for cultural communication." In L. Kincaid (Ed.), *Communication theory: Eastern and Western perspectives*, pp. 245–254. Orlando, Fla.: Academic Press.

———— (1989a). "An ethnographic approach to communication studies." In B. Dervin, L. Grossberg, B. O'Keefe, and E. Wartella (Eds.), *Rethinking communication*. Vol. 2. Paradigm dialogues, pp. 258–268. Newbury Park, Calif.: Sage Publications.

———— (1989b). "Speech and the communal function in four cultures." *International and Intercultural Communication Annual* 13: 79–92.

———— (1992). *Speaking culturally*. Albany: State University of New York Press.

———— (1993). "Ritual as heuristic device in studies of organizational discourse." In S. Deetz (Ed.), *Communication Yearbook 16*, pp. 104–111. Newbury Park, Calif.: Sage Publications.

———— and Carbaugh, D. (1986). "A bibliography of fieldwork in the ethnography of communication." *Language in Society* 15: 387–398.

Ray, G. (1987). "An ethnography of nonverbal communication in an Appalachian community." *Research on Language and Social Interaction* 21: 171–188.

Sapir, E. (1931). "Communication." *Encyclopedia of the Social Sciences*, vol. 4, pp. 78–81.

Schegloff, E. (1972). "Sequencing in conversational openings." In J. Gumperz and D. Hymes (Eds.), *Directions in sociolinguistics: The ethnography of communication*, pp. 346–380. New York: Holt, Rinehart and Winston.

Schneider, D. (1976). "Notes toward a theory of culture." In K. Basso and H. Selby (Eds.), *Meaning in anthropology*, pp. 197–220. Albuquerque: University of New Mexico Press.

Scollon, R. (1992). "The shifting discourse of American individualism from the authoritarian to the infochild." Unpublished manuscript.

———— and Scollon, S. (1981). *Narrative, literacy, and face in interethnic communication*. Norwood, N.J.: Ablex.

Searle, J. (1969). *Speech acts*. Cambridge: Cambridge University Press.

———— (1990). "A classification of illocutionary acts." In D. Carbaugh (Ed.), *Cultural communication and intercultural contact*, pp. 349–372. Hillsdale, N.J.: Lawrence Erlbaum and Associates. Originally published in 1976.

Sequiera, D. (1993). "Personal address as negotiated meaning in an American church community." *Research on Language and Social Interaction* 26: 259–285.

Shailor, J. (1990). "Cultural resources for conflict management: A comparative analysis." Paper presented at the Speech Communication Association, Chicago.

Sherzer, J. (1977). "The ethnography of speaking: A critical appraisal." In M. Saville-Troike (Ed.), *Linguistics and Anthropology* (GURT 1977), pp. 43–57. Washington, D.C.: Georgetown University Press.

———— (1987). "A diversity of voices: Men's and women's speech in ethnographic perspective." In S. U. Philips, S. Steele, and C. Tanz (Eds.), *Language, gender, and sex in comparative perspective*, pp. 95–120. Cambridge: Cambridge University Press.

Sigman, S. (1987). *A perspective on social communication.* Lexington, Mass.: Lexington Books.

Tannen, D. (1990). *You just don't understand.* New York: Morrow.

Wieder, D. L., and Pratt, S. (1990). "On being a recognizable indian among indians." In D. Carbaugh (Ed.), *Cultural communication and intercultural contact*, pp. 45–64. Hillsdale, N.J.: Lawrence Erlbaum and Associates.

11

THE MOVEMENT AND WATERSHED
RESEARCH TRADITIONS IN HUMAN COMMUNICATION

BRANISLAV KOVAČIĆ

At the end of this long journey, let us pause and ask three questions. First, do we have intellectual benchmarks to separate out what is central to our understanding of human communication processes from what is not? Second, do we have intellectual benchmarks to "rank" that which is central to our understanding of human communication processes? And finally, having separated out what is central from what is not and having ranked that which is central, do we have intellectual benchmarks to chart even more productive courses of theoretic inquiry into human communication processes? Let us discuss each of these questions in turn?

This book is an attempt to answer the first question. A conception of a watershed research tradition as consisting of the philosophic, theoretic, and practical arguments and evidence is one set of intellectual benchmarks that attempts to separate out what is central to our understanding of human communication processes from what is not. Such a benchmark is complex and multilayered. At the philosophical level, watershed research traditions presented in this book form a nested "hierarchy" of the preferred slices or domains of communicative reality: cultural coordination principles and mechanisms (Chapter 10) presuppose organizational activities and tasks (Chapters 7 and 8), which, in turn, assume dyadic interactions (Chapters 2, 5, and 6), which, in turn, require individual, private mental activity (Chapters 3, 4, and 9). In general, the narrower is the chosen slice of communicative reality, the more limited is the scope and function of possible theoretical insights and practical applications at a given level of precision.

At the theoretical level, each watershed tradition specifies a web of relationships between constructs—their type, direction, and strength. Even more important, watershed research traditions locate and specify significant stable generative mechanism of communication that are indispensable for constructing powerful communicative strategies and underlying skills. For example, the rules theory of interpersonal friend and mate relations (Chapter 6) isolates self-concept as a cross-cultural (universal) generative mechanism of interpersonal communication. In each culture friendships are distingushed from mate relationships by a set of crucial entry attributes and by a set of intensity attributes. Communication in the form of the mutual self-concept support for entry attributes must precede self-concept support for intensity attributes. Self-concept support for entry attributes establishes a particular type of relationship, whereas self-concept support for intensity attributes deepens the intimacy of that type of relationship.

Such specification of the generative mechanism allows for the selection of appropriate communicative strategies and skills. For example, effective communication in friendships requires the appropriate sequence and content of interaction. The rules theory of interpersonal relationships (Chapter 6) provides relevant insights for the appropriate communicative strategy and skills for communication in friendships. First, in every culture people must first communicate self-concept support for the entry attributes, and then for the intensity attributes (sequence). Second, content of self-concept support is generated by the culture-specific entry and intensity friendship attributes. Finally, people can be taught to recognize the relevant sequences and content of interactions between friends and then not only to engage in but also to improve their interactions.

In other words, watershed research traditions in human communication are themselves intellectual benchmarks for separating out what is central to our understanding of human communication processes from what is not. However, watershed research traditions develop differentially the philosophic, theoretical, and practical arguments, evidence and their interconnections. This allows for the comparison and evaluation of watershed research traditions themselves.

To answer the second question, it is necessary to demonstrate that the conception of watershed research traditions provides not only external but also internal intellectual benchmarks. Without such internal standards we would be unable to "rank" that which is central to our understanding of human communication processes.

I argued that, in general, the narrower is the chosen slice of communicative reality, the more limited is the scope and function of possible theoretical insights and practical applications at a given level of precision. Such a statement at the philosophical level must be qualified, however, by the relative sociocultural importance, stability, and urgency of the selected domain of communicative reality. However, it is not simply that in a given socio-cultural environment organizational activities and tasks may be "more important" than dyadic interactions in friendships and mateships. Rather, under certain conditions there may be significant differences even within the domain. For example, speed to market (Chapter 7) may be a "more important" organizational task than struggles for democracy (Chapter 8). Naturally, because such preferences are controversial, they are subject to discussion and debate. What is important is that debates may result not only in an irreconcilable discord, but also in a workable consensus or common ground of scholars across watershed research traditions. Such common ground reflects values, norms, and practices that are not only crucial to but also widely dispersed in a culture.

Let me provide an argument at the theoretical level. For instance, although the high-speed management theory (Chapter 7) argues that profitability is the ultimate criterion of organizational long-term viability, the critical theories (Chapter 8) privilege different forms of radical democracy as their highest goal. Obviously, in the United States profitability is more central and more widely dispersed value than radical democracy. (These two theories gloss over the possibility that complex tensions between profitability and radical democracy are the core of organizational activities.) High-speed management theory (Chapter 7) posits that, although strategies are organization specific, speed to market as the generative mechanism imposes necessary and stable constraints on all organizations. Though open to debate, success of such strategies is intersubjectively verifiable by different public measures of organizational performance in the marketplace. In contrast, critical theories (Chapter 8) argue that the strategy guiding different types of struggles and resistance is the generative mechanism for organizational communication needed to bring about radical forms of democracy. Different types of struggles and resistance are striving both to ensure symmetrical, equal participation in organizational interactions and to transform content-generating micro practices. Although most existing organizations are anchored in asymmetrical interactions, content-generating micro practices are organization specific. Consequently, different types of struggles and resistance must necessarily entail symmetrical interactions and unique mixes of alternative content-generating micro practices. More important, however, radical democracy is not easily verifiable by different public measures of organizational performance.

Such differences between high-speed management theory and the critical theories of organizational communication have serious consequences for the practical level of appropriate communicative strategies and skills. First, despite the many examples of the successful high-speed management organizations, in few models of organizations is sustained radical democracy the practice and the goal. Second, whereas communicative strategies and skills employed by the high-speed organizations are observable, measurable, and teachable, the same cannot be said for communicative strategies and skills needed to accomplish and sustain radical democracy. And finally, whereas the high-speed management theory is both descriptive and prescriptive in a skills-oriented manner, the critical theories are prescriptive only in an ideal sense. Consequently, it is relatively easier to specify communicative strategies and skills needed to accomplish the design, production, and delivery of products and services than to specify communicative strategies and skills required to realize moral and ideological programs. It can be argued that, ironically, high-speed management theory and practices contribute to democracy by improving and widely diffusing relevant organizational communication skills. Thus, it is incumbent upon the critical theorists to take practical constraints seriously and devise communicative strategies and skills with traction on the real, empirical actors.

To summarize, one watershed research tradition has a relative advantage over its counterparts to the extent that it develops more productively the philosophic, theoretical, and practical arguments and their interconnections. Consequently, a more productive tradition selects, at the philosophic level, a more significant domain in a culture. It also, at the theoretical level, specifies more accurately a web of relationships between constructs and provides a relatively significant and stable generative mechanism of communication. Finally, at the practical level, it uses the generative mechanism to operationalize communicative strategies and skills with traction on relevant empirical actors.

All said, do we really have intellectual benchmarks to chart even more productive courses of theoretic inquiry into human communication processes? Yes, we do. I would stress three crucial insights into theoretic inquiry. First, any significant new research tradition must choose a culturally relevant domain of inquiry. Second, any significant new theoretical endeavor must specify a web of relationships between constructs and a relatively stable, significant generative mechanism of communication. Without such a generative mechanism, communication theories cannot be used to explain, predict, and control culturally relevant communicative practices. Moreover, without such a generative mechanism, communication theories cannot operationalize communicative strategies and skills with traction on relevant empirical actors. Third, any significant new theory of communication must provide communication strategies and skills that actors need, want to learn, use, and improve, and when necessary discard.

Such insights will help us avoid a common but fatal trap—they will help us avoid developing elegant, elaborate, and awe-inspiring theoretic edifices that are socio-culturally irrelevant. Other mistakes are not worth mentioning.

CONTRIBUTORS

Donal Carbaugh has a Ph.D. from the University of Washington and is currently associate professor of communication at the University of Massachusetts. Carbaugh has written or cowritten over forty chapters in books and articles in journals, as well as four books, including *Situating Selves*, to be published by SUNY Press in 1996.

Rod Carveth received his B.A. in Sociology from Yale University and his M.A. and Ph.D. in Communication from the University of Massachusetts—Amherst. He is currently assistant professor and head of the communication program at the University of Bridgeport. He has conducted extensive research on the social impact of soap operas. His articles have been published in the *Journal of Communication*, the *Journal of Broadcasting and Electronic Media*, the *Journal of Applied Communication Research*, the *Journal of Business Communication*, and *Communication Research*. He is coeditor of *Media Economics: Theory and Practice*. Carveth has also been a scholar-in-residence at New York University.

Donald P. Cushman has a Ph.D. from the University of Wisconsin and is currently professor of communication at SUNY—Albany. Cushman is the author or coauthor of over 120 chpaters in books or articles in journals. He has written, cowritten, or edited ten books including *High-Speed Management: Organizational Communication in the Twenty-first Century* (with Sarah S. King, SUNY Press, 1995). In 1992 Cushman was awarded the Speech Communication Association of America's Donald H. Ecroyd Award as "the outstanding teacher in higher education." In 1972 he was awarded the Speech Communication Association of America's Charles Woolbert Award for "research of exceptional originality and influence which has stood the test of time." Cushman is coeditor of the SUNY Press book series on communication.

Roger Desmond (Ph.D. from the University of Iowa, 1977) is professor of communication at the University of Harford. He has written over twenty research articles for professional journals in communication and psychology and has contributed to four books. His early research addressed such topics as how children understand and respond to advertising, the development of thinking and language in children, and how adults process television programs. His most recent research has involved the creation and evaluation of print and video materials designed to teach young children about media and how they work, as well as the role of media in the emotional states and moods of university undergraduates. From 1984 to 1987 he was a visiting research fellow in psychology at Yale University. In 1992, he was awarded a fellowship in media leteracy at the Annenberg School of Communication at the University of Pennsylvania. He is also involved in professional media consulting.

William Gudykunst has a Ph.D. from the University of Minnesota (1977) and is currently professor of communication at the State University of California in Fullerton. Gudykunst is the author or coauthor of over seventy chapters in books or articles in journals and of twelve books including *Communication in Japan and the U.S.* (SUNY Press, 1993). Gudykunst has served on the editorial board of over thirty journals and edited the communication yearbook on several occasions.

Sarah Sanderson King has a Ph.D. from the University of Southern California (1965) and is currently professor of communication at Central Connecticut State University. King is author or coauthor of over sixty chapters in books or aritcles in journals and the author, coauthor, or editor of seven books including *High-Speed Management: Organizational Communication in the 1990s: A Reader* (with D. P. Cushman, SUNY Press, 1994). King has served as chair of departments of communication at the University of Hawaii and Central Connecticut State University and as director of the Division of Communication and the Arts at Marist College. She is coeditor of the SUNY Press book series in international management.

Branislav Kovačić is an assistant professor of communication at the University of Hartford. He received his Ph.D. in communication and sociology from SUNY–Albany. He was a former journalist and magazine editor in Yugoslavia. He has edited and contributed to a book on organizational communication published by SUNY Press in 1994. He has written journal articles and book chapters on organizational communication, mental health and communication, and rhetoric of social sciences. He is currently working on a book on communication and transformations in the public sector. He is also working on books on emerging theories of communication and benchmarking and organizational communication.

Andrew Moemeka has a Ph.D. from SUNY–Albany and is currently professor of communication at Central Connecticut State University in New Britain. Moemeka is the author or coauthor of over thiry chapters in books or articles in journals and the author or editor of five books including *Communication for Development* (SUNY Press, 1994). Moemeka has served as head of the Department of Communication at the University of Lagos in Nigeria and acting chair of the Department of Communication at Central Connecticut State University.

Anne Maydan Nicotera has a Ph.D. from Ohio University (1990) and is currently assistant professor of communication at Howard University. Nicotera is the author or coauthor of over fifteen chapters in books and/or articles in journals and has edited two books including *Interpersonal Communication in Friend and Romantic Relationships* (SUNY Press, 1993). Nicotera has won several outstanding teacher and scholarship awards.

Gerry Philipsen has a Ph.D. from Northwestern University (1971) and is currently professor of communication at the University of Washington. Philipson is the author or coauthor of over thirty chapters in books or articles in journals and the author or editor of two books including *Speaking Culturally: Explorations in Social Communication* (SUNY Press, 1992).

Robert Sanders has a Ph.D. from the University of Iowa (1971) and is currently professor of communication at the State University of New York at Albany. Sanders is the author or coauthor of over thirty chapters in books or articles in journals and the author of the book *Cognitive Foundations of Calculated Speech: Contrasting Understanding in Conversation and Persuasion* (SUNY Press, 1987). Sanders has served as the chair of the SUNY Communication Department and is currently editor of the *Journal of Research on Language and Social Interaction*.

INDEX